C0-CDM-250

Cambridge Studies in Medieval Life and Thought

FAMILY POWER IN SOUTHERN ITALY

This book explores how political power was exerted and family identity expressed in the context of a reconstruction of the noble families of the medieval duchies of Gaeta, Amalfi and Naples. Localised forms of power, and the impact of the Norman conquest on southern Italy, are assessed by means of a remarkable collection of charters preserved in the *Codex diplomaticus Cajetanus*.

The duchy of Gaeta, like its neighbours, was ruled as a private family business, with few formal offices visible. An integral part of its ruling family's power was its monopolisation of parts of the duchy's economy and the use of members of the clan to rule local centres. When the family broke up, the duchy followed suit. Gaeta, Amalfi and Naples reacted in different ways to the Normans. Gaeta flourished commercially in the twelfth century, and its unique political response to contacts with the cities of northern Italy (especially Genoa) forms the final part of this study. Dr Skinner demonstrates that the socio-economic basis for power is as important as its political exercise, and overturns many conventional views on the workings of early medieval power structures.

The series Cambridge Studies in Medieval Life and Thought was inaugurated by G. G. Coulton in 1921. Professor D. E. Luscombe now acts as General Editor of the Fourth Series, with Professor R. B. Dobson and Dr Rosamond McKitterick as Advisory Editors. The series brings together outstanding work by medieval scholars over a wide range of human endeavour extending from political economy to the history of ideas.

For a list of titles in the series, see end of book.

FAMILY POWER IN SOUTHERN ITALY

The duchy of Gaeta and its neighbours, 850–1139

PATRICIA SKINNER

University of Birmingham

Published by the Press Syndicate of the University of Cambridge
The Pitt Building, Trumpington Street, Cambridge CB2 1RP
40 West 20th Street, New York, NY 10011-4211, USA
10 Stamford Road, Oakleigh, Melbourne 3166, Australia

First published 1995

Printed in Great Britain at the University Press, Cambridge

A catalogue record for this book is available from the British Library

Library of Congress cataloguing in publication data

Skinner, Patricia, 1965–
Family power in southern Italy: the duchy of Gaeta and its neighbours, 850–1139 / Patricia Skinner.
p. cm. – (Cambridge studies in medieval life and thought: 4th ser., 29)
Includes bibliographical references and index.
ISBN 0 521 46479 X
1. Nobility–Italy–Gaeta–History. 2. Nobility–Italy–Amalfi–History. 3. Nobility–Italy–Naples–History. 4. Italy, Southern–Social conditions. 5. Italy, Southern–History–535–1268. 6. Land tenure–Italy, Southern–History. I. Title. II. Series.
HT653.I8S59 1995
305.5'223'0945623–dc20 94-9512 CIP

ISBN 0 521 46479 X hardback

CONTENTS

ILLUSTRATIONS

MAPS

FIGURES

PREFACE

This study began life as postgraduate research at the University of Birmingham, under the supervision of Chris Wickham. I am greatly indebted to him for his guidance, and continue to benefit from his advice. Graham Loud has been generous in his support, and his help and suggestions are much appreciated. It has been my good fortune to meet David Abulafia, whose encouragement led me to pursue the Gaetans further afield. I am indebted to Lucia Travaini, who has provided me with invaluable insights into the problems of southern Italian coinage.

I have been aided in revision work and further research financially by the British Academy and the British School at Rome. I owe a debt of thanks to the librarian at the latter, Valerie Scott; to don Faustino Avagliano, at the Archive of Montecassino, for his good-humoured assistance; and to the library staff at the University of Birmingham, whose persistance has unearthed many gems which I would not have expected to find in England. I also received much valuable assistance from the staff at the Archivio di Stato in Naples, especially from Elvira Pollastro; many of the placenames would not have come to light without the help of the staff at the Ufficio Catastale in Latina, particularly Messrs. Alfonzo Fiorito and Mario Gucciardo.

Rosamond McKitterick's editorial comments have been acute and stimulating, and I am grateful for her help in developing the final version of the study. At Cambridge University Press, Gillian Maude has provided invaluable guidance in the final production of the book. Any shortcomings remain my responsibility.

One problem that recurs in studies involving foreign languages is that of personal and placenames. No one convention suits all tastes. I have adopted Anglicised versions of common names (John, Gregory, Constantine) and titles (St). Lombard names present more difficulty, and I have followed the most commonly used version in most cases, for example Landolf and Atenolf, but Guaimarius, etc.

My acknowledgements would not be complete without recognising the enormous support given to me by my mum and my husband during the writing of this book; I dedicate the final version to them.

ABBREVIATIONS

Amatus	*Storia de'Normanni di Amato di Montecassino*, ed. V. de Bartholomeis (Rome, 1935)
ASPN	*Archivio Storico per le Province Napoletane*
ASRSP	*Archivio della Società Romana per la Storia Patria*
Barletta	*Codice Diplomatico Barese, VIII: Le Pergamene di Barletta*, ed. F. Nitti di Vito (Bari, 1914)
BISALM	*Bollettino dell'Istituto di Storia e di Arte del Lazio Meridionale*
BISI	*Bollettino dell'Istituto Storico Italiano per il Medio Evo e Archivio Muratoriano*
BN	*Codice Diplomatico Barese, X: Le Pergamene di Barletta del R. Archivio di Napoli*, ed. R. Filangieri di Candida (Bari, 1927)
CDA	*Codice Diplomatico Amalfitano*, ed. R. Filangieri di Candida, i (Naples, 1917), ii (Trani, 1951)
CDC	*Codex Diplomaticus Cajetanus*, Tabularium Casinensis, i–ii (Montecassino, 1887–92)
CMC	*Chronica Monasterii Casinensis*, ed. H. Hoffmann (*MGH, Scriptores* 34, Hanover, 1980)
CodCav	*Codex Diplomaticus Cavensis*, i–viii, ed. M. Morcaldi *et al.* (Milan, Naples, Pisa, 1873–93), ix–x, ed. S. Leone and G.Vitolo (Badia di Cava, 1984, 1991)
Corato	*Codice Diplomatico Barese, IX: I Documenti Storici di Corato*, ed. G. Beltrani (Bari, 1923)
CP	*Il Codice Perris: Cartulario Amalfitano*, ed. J. Mazzoleni and R. Orefice i (Amalfi, 1985)
CSB	*Chronica Sancti Benedicti Casinensis*, ed. G. Waitz (*MGH, Scriptores* series 3, i, Hanover, 1878)
Cusa	*Diplomi Greci ed Arabi di Sicilia*, ed. S. Cusa, 2 vols. (Palermo, 1868, 1882)
DCDN	Diplomata et Chartae Ducum Neapolis, in *Monumenta*, iiii

Epp	*Epistolae*
IP	*Italia Pontificia*, ed. P. F. Kehr, I (Berlin, 1906), II (Berlin, 1907), VIII (Berlin, 1935), IX (Gottingen, 1962)
LC	*Le Liber Censuum*, ed. P. Fabre and L. Duchesne, I (Paris 1905)
LP	*Le Liber Pontificalis*, ed. L. Duchesne, I (Paris, 1886)
MEFRM	*Mélanges de l'Ecole Française de Rome, Moyen Age, Temps Modernes*
MGH	*Monumenta Germaniae Historica*
Mon.Sopp.	Naples, Archivio di Stato: *Monasteri Soppressi* 3437
Monumenta	*Monumenta ad Neapolitani Ducatus Historiam Pertinentia*, ed. B. Capasso, I, II*i*, II*ii* (Naples, 1881, 1885, 1892)
NSK	*Die Urkunden der Normannische-Sizilienischen Könige*, ed. K. A. Kehr (Innsbruck, 1902)
PAVAR	*Le Pergamene degli Archivi Vescovili di Amalfi e Ravello*, I, ed. J. Mazzoleni (Naples, 1972); II, ed. C. Salvati (Naples, 1974); III, ed. B. Mazzoleni (Naples, 1975)
PBSR	*Papers of the British School at Rome*
PC	*Codice Diplomatico Pugliese, XX: Le Pergamene di Conversano*, ed. G. Coniglio (Bari, 1975)
PCT	*Codice Diplomatico Barese, III: Le Pergamene della Cattedrale di Terlizzi*, ed. F. Caraballese (Bari, 1899)
QFIAB	*Quellen und Forschungen aus italienischen Archiven und Bibliotheken*
RN	Regesta Neapolitana, in *Monumenta*, II*i*
RNAM	*Regii Neapolitani Archivii Monumenta*, ed. M. Baffi *et al.* II, III, IV (Naples, 1845–54)
Théristes	*S. Jean-Théristes*, ed. A. Guillou (Vatican City, 1980)
Trani	*Le Carte che si Conservano nello Archivio del Capitolo Metropolitano della Città di Trani*, ed. A. Prologo (Barletta, 1877)
Tremiti	*Codice Diplomatico del Monastero Benedettino di S. Maria di Tremiti*, ed. A. Petrucci (Rome, 1960)
Troia	*Codice Diplomatico Pugliese, XXI: Les Chartes de Troia*, ed. J.-M. Martin (Bari, 1976)

INTRODUCTION

The history of southern Italy is often ignored prior to the coming of the Normans in the late eleventh century, except for the moments when the peninsula impinged on the consciousness of the medieval rulers of northern Europe, particularly the German emperors. Recently, though, historians have attempted to treat the South less as an appendage of the rest of Europe than as a valuable area of study in its own right.[1] For varying reasons, however, no recent study has shed much light on the pre-Norman period, and pre-eminence in histories of the whole area is still held by works well over fifty years old.[2]

It is very hard to package pre-Norman southern Italy neatly into one study because it was a disparate area made up of several different political jurisdictions. The Lombards who had penetrated furthest South during the invasion of the peninsula in the latter half of the sixth century had coalesced into three Germanic principalities, Benevento, Salerno and Capua. In the territories remaining under Byzantine rule, Naples had become autonomous in the

[1] For example, *Storia d'Italia*, III: *Il Mezzogiorno dai Bizantini a Federico II*, ed. G. Galasso, (Turin, 1983); B. Kreutz, *Before the Normans: Southern Italy in the Ninth and Tenth Centuries* (Philadelphia, 1991); J. Decarreaux, *Normands, Papes et Moines* (Paris, 1974); the early part of D. Matthew, *The Norman Kingdom of Sicily* (Cambridge, 1992) and H. Takayama, *The Administration of the Norman Kingdom of Sicily* (Leiden, 1993). Recent local studies of quality include P. Toubert, *Les Structures du Latium Médiéval*, 2 vols. (Rome, 1973), G. Loud, *Church and Society in the Norman Principality of Capua* (Oxford, 1985). On Byzantine southern Italy, V. von Falkenhausen, *Untersuchungen über die byzantinische Herrschaft in Süditalien vom 9 bis ins 11 Jahrhundert* (Wiesbaden, 1967), and A. Guillou, *Studies on Byzantine Italy* (London, 1970). In general histories of Italy, the South perhaps tends to be treated as an appendix to discussions of the main developments in the North, for example, C. J. Wickham, *Early Medieval Italy*, (London, 1981), chapter on 'The South'; G. Tabacco, *The Struggle for Power in Medieval Italy* (Cambridge, 1989) integrates southern Italy, but fails to come to grips with the area on its own terms.

[2] J. Gay, *L'Italie Méridionale et l'Empire Byzantin* (New York, 1904) is still the standard work of reference; R. Poupardin, *Les Institutions Politiques et Administratives des Principautés Lombardes de l'Italie Méridionale* (Paris, 1909); F. Chalandon, *Histoire de la Domination Normande en Italie et en Sicile*, 2 vols. (Paris, 1907); C. Cahen, *Le Regime Féodal de l'Italie Normande* (Paris 1940).

eighth century, and Amalfi and Gaeta would do so in the ninth. In addition to these, Byzantium still ruled the far South of the peninsula throughout our period, but lost control of Sicily to the Arabs in the ninth century.

Loyalties did not divide along these political lines, however, and even in areas of political control by Byzantium, the culture of the Lombards might still persist strongly, and *vice versa*.[3] In the area I propose to study here, Campania[4] and southern Lazio,[5] the interaction between Lombard and Byzantine can be seen quite clearly; and there was the added complication in this area of a persistent Arab presence.

Early in the ninth century, neither Gaeta nor Amalfi were states in their own right, both being subject to the dukes of Naples. However, in the middle of the ninth century both Gaeta and Amalfi broke away from Neapolitan rule. The expansionist Lombard princes of Salerno may have been responsible for Amalfi's move to independence, having briefly captured the city in 838/9. After this, Amalfi never returned to the Neapolitan fold, maintaining instead its existence as an independent entity with continuing close ties to its Lombard neighbour.

Gaeta's detachment seems to have been precipitated by Arab incursions on the Tyrrhenian coast, as the people of Formia across the bay took refuge on the easily defensible rocky peninsula. From 839 onwards we have documented rulers of the castle, later city, of Gaeta, known as *hypatoi*. The first, Constantine, and his son Marinus, visible in documents of 839 and 866, seem to have had links with Naples, and still seem to have been under the sovereignty of the larger city. In 867, however, a change of regime occurred, with the previously unknown Docibilis I taking power. His relationship with the Arab raiders, who were causing chaos throughout the Tyrrhenian littoral, earned Docibilis the censure of the pope. It may have been in recognition of Docibilis' break with the Arabs that he and his son John I were made *rectores* of the papal patrimonies of Fondi and Traetto, estates whose exploitation allowed the Docibilans to grow in power. The Amalfitans, too,

[3] For example, the case of Byzantine Apulia, strongly Lombard in its customs despite its Roman rulers.

[4] Kreutz, *Before the Normans*, has looked at some of the areas I shall be exploring. Her book, however, was somewhat limited in its coverage, tending to focus on particular aspects of Amalfitan and Salernitan history rather than synthesising the whole.

[5] Toubert, *Structures*, concentrated largely on the documents from Farfa for his work on southern Lazio. Gaeta featured very little in his study.

frequently collaborated with the infidel, and this seems to have been a foundation for that city's rise to a great trading power.

The tenth century was one of Docibilan domination over Gaeta. Naples, too, enjoyed continuous government by one ducal family. Amalfi's rulers were somewhat less stable, perhaps reflecting the intensity of internal competition in a state that could not support the ambitions of all the noble families there.

Ducal power ultimately relied on landed resources and family unity. The gradual diminution of the former and the deterioration of the latter in Gaeta led to individual branches breaking away and setting up their own, smaller power blocs in outlying castles in the duchy. Militarily, the duchy had always been relatively weak; this development served only to weaken it still further. Amalfi experienced a similar instability of rule. Both smaller cities succumbed to the expanding power of the Capuan prince Pandolf in the 1030s, and then to prince Guaimarius of Salerno early in the 1040s. Naples was also briefly taken over by the aggressive Capuan, but his rule there did not last long, and the ducal dynasty was able to resume its rule, continuing in power until the city fell to the Norman king, Roger, in the mid-twelfth century.

Both Gaeta and Amalfi were eventually able to rid themselves of Lombard rule, but the vacuum left by the Capuans and Salernitans only opened the way to a more dangerous power. The dukes of Naples had used a group of Norman mercenaries to enable them to regain control of their city. These soldiers seem to have rapidly become aware that the rulers for whom they were fighting were weaker than themselves. It took only the rise of a talented leader, Robert Guiscard, to begin to fulfil the potential of the Normans to take over from their masters. It is important to realise, however, that different groups of Normans were trying to carve out their own spheres of influence. When Richard of Aversa and his son Jordan captured Capua, they swiftly extended their dominions to take in Gaeta as well. Thereafter the history of that duchy is one of Norman domination via a nominated duke; Gaeta's history as an independent duchy was at an end. Meanwhile Robert Guiscard captured Amalfi, and set about extending his Tyrrhenian territory. The process was by no means easy, and the late eleventh century can be characterised as the point when the Byzantine empire realised the danger to its territories in the South and began actively to campaign to resist the Normans as a whole. The campaign was based at Naples, which successfully resisted Norman siege action.

The actions of the papacy can be said to have been decisive in sealing the fate of the Tyrrhenian cities. The popes were at best ambivalent in their attitude to the Normans, but in the wider political context of their contests with the German empire and the Byzantine church, they appear to have regarded the army of occupation to the south of papal territories as simultaneously a danger and a potential ally. The creation of the kingdom of Sicily in 1130 legitimised the rule of the Normans and led to the fall of the now isolated city of Naples.

This brief history, based on existing historiography, suggests that each duchy underwent a series of tumultuous changes during the three centuries under review. The following study examines these changes, and investigates the extent to which the internal structures of the Tyrrhenian states were able to withstand much of the upheaval. How stable was the political life in each duchy? How strong were the ruling families and what was the basis of their relationship with their noble subjects? Did those subjects in turn rely on their wealth, their birth or their place at the rulers' courts for their position in society?

In attempting to answer these questions, the study will examine and compare the three duchies of Gaeta, Naples and Amalfi. This is a departure from the established local historiographical norm. Many monographs on the three cities have been inspired more by civic pride than by a desire to place them in their medieval south Italian context.[6] After an initial group of studies on Gaeta which appeared when the primary source material was first published at the end of the nineteenth century, including excellent work by Fedele[7] and Merores,[8] Gaetan history writing languished somewhat. Apart from a thesis written in 1941 by Fedele's pupil

[6] For example, for Gaeta: D. Monetti, *Cenni Storici dell'Antica Città di Gaeta* (Gaeta, 1872); O. Gaetani d'Aragona, *Memorie Storiche della Città di Gaeta* (Caserta, 1885); S. Ferraro, *Memorie Religiose e Civili della Città di Gaeta* (Naples, 1903); G. Fiengo, *Gaeta: Monumenti e Storia Urbanistica* (Naples, 1971). The latter work reminds us that not only nineteenth-century writers felt such pride. However, one should not now overlook the more recent work of local historical centres at Amalfi and Gaeta. For example, the Centro di Cultura e Storia Amalfitana's *Fonti* series has been responsible for the publication of much primary source material used in the present study, and its new *Biblioteca Amalfitana* series has recently commenced publication with Giuseppe Gargano's *La Città davanti al Mare* (Amalfi, 1992).

[7] In particular, 'Il ducato di Gaeta all'inizio della conquista normanna', *ASPN*, 29 (1904), 50–99. This and Fedele's other major articles on the duchy have recently been reprinted in P. Fedele, *Scritti Storici sul Ducato di Gaeta* (Gaeta, 1988).

[8] M. Merores, *Gaeta im frühen Mittelalter (8. bis 12. Jahrhundert)* (Gotha, 1911).

Leccese,[9] little significant work has been done on the duchy. This is largely due to the fact that Margarethe Merores' history of Gaeta, published in 1911, has remained unassailably the first point of reference for all subsequent studies, and is still heavily relied upon today. This is not necessarily a bad thing. Merores used the documentary material intelligently to produce a detailed history of Gaeta from its origins to around AD 1200, and most of her arguments remain valid to this day. What Merores did not do, however, was examine the socio-economic structures of the duchy; her work concentrated exclusively on the rulers of the Gaetan territory and the ways in which they exercised their power. So influential has her work been on later historians that no one has questioned its purely political nature, nor made any real attempt to expand its picture of Gaetan history. A recent article by Jean-François Guiraud,[10] examining the population patterns of the duchy, promised much in its title, but unfortunately limited itself to listing the appearance of new placenames in the documents. No real attempt was made to address the problem of who actually lived in the new settlements. Guiraud concentrated on the rise of newly fortified places within the duchy to illustrate the failure of centralised ducal power. He thus returned to one of Merores' main themes.

In the present study, I hope to widen the focus of Gaetan historiography and use it to illuminate other parts of the Tyrrhenian coast. I shall be examining Gaeta to see the extent to which it provides a model of a small state, and comparing it with neighbouring Naples and Amalfi in order to determine the degree to which they were culturally similar. Comparisons of the type I shall make may have been discouraged hitherto by the disparity of evidence available from different areas, a problem which is discussed below. However, if we approach the material using a point of contact between the three states – the existence of traceable landowning or mercantile families – rather than trying to

[9] A. Leccese, *Le Origini del Ducato di Gaeta e le sue Relazioni coi Ducati di Napoli e di Roma* (Gubbio, 1941), tried to unravel the early links with both Rome and Naples before the ninth century, when much of southern Italy was under Byzantine domination. However, her work succeeded only in illustrating the ambiguity of Gaeta's position, and it is not my intention here to reopen a question which, because of the lack of evidence, cannot be satisfactorily resolved.

[10] J.-F. Guiraud, 'Le reseau de peuplement dans le duché de Gaeta du Xe au XIIIe siècle', *MEFRM*, 94 (1982), 482–511.

concentrate only on the ruling dukes and prominent churchmen, comparison becomes not only possible, but valuable.

It may be possible to use the documents of a duchy less than 50km by 25km in area to generalise about the social structures of southern Italy as a whole. Its very smallness makes Gaeta the perfect testing ground, for it epitomises the fragmentation of southern Italy and lack of institutionalised forms of power here during the tenth and eleventh centuries, the feature which strikes historians when writing about the South. If, therefore, we can analyse how one of these fragments worked from day to day, we may be able to make more sense of the whole. It must be noted that the study focuses on the formerly Byzantine enclaves on the Tyrrhenian coast. However, some of the methods used may be applicable to the Lombard areas of southern Italy as well, and could be tested, for example, on the copious archive material relating to the abbey of Cava near Salerno and its hinterland.[11] Huguette Taviani has recently published a monumental work on the latter city.[12]

The three states on which I concentrate did not live in a vacuum. They came into daily contact with their Lombard neighbours, and were in some instances influenced by Lombard practice. Gaeta was taken over by the Lombards of Capua in 1032, and the city's ambivalent relationship with its Lombard neighbours, and the parallels between this and the relationship between Amalfi and Salerno will be examined.

After an introductory survey of the source material available, the study is arranged in three parts. The first investigates ducal power and how it was expressed. It goes on to look at what happened when dukes lost power, and what structures emerged to replace the single ruler. We have a great deal of material available from Gaeta to assess how dukes ruled, what property they held and what functions they performed in their daily dealings with their subjects. Indeed, the dukes of Gaeta loom so exceptionally large in the documentation that it would be folly to attempt any study which did not include some analysis of their rule. I intend, however, to approach the problem from a different perspective.

[11] *Codex Diplomaticus Cavensis*, I–VIII ed. M. Morcaldi *et al.* (Milan, Naples, Pisa, 1873–93); IX and X, ed. S. Leone and G. Vitolo (Badia di Cava, 1984, 1991) (= *CodCav*) represent a new campaign of editing, although its future is in some doubt. The published documents go up to 1080; the remainder are still kept in the abbey of the Holy Trinity, Cava. Preliminary work on Apulia in the tenth and eleventh centuries seems to support the applicability of the methods used in this study.

[12] H. Taviani-Carozzi, *La Principauté Lombarde de Salerne*, 2 vols. (Rome, 1991).

Firstly, the origins of ducal power at Gaeta have never been examined in any great detail. Who were the dukes of Gaeta, and what were their origins? Was there any clear basis for ducal rule in place in this area in the late ninth century? We have rather less evidence from Amalfi and Naples to test them against the Gaetan picture, though both cities have been the subject of detailed studies[13] and both seem to have followed the same pattern of dynastic rule.

How then do we delve further into ducal relations with each other and with their people? This is the subject of the second strand of the study, looking at the great men (and women) of each duchy who lived near, served and married into the ducal families. I shall be looking at ways in which we can examine the hitherto unexplored way of life of the nobility and aristocracy in this area, and how they reacted to the events around them. In doing so, many of the internal structures of these states will come to light.

The noble families in all three duchies are well documented, yet have not been systematically studied before. My research has revealed the existence of a large number of wealthy landowning and merchant clans who, despite being politically active, have never featured in the political histories of the duchies simply because they did not achieve the position of ruler. How they created and fitted into political patterns, and how their economic influence may have affected the political balance, forms one of the main themes of the present study. Their relationships with each other, their property and their power, both political and economic (much the same thing, in this context) are examined in detail. There is interest too in looking at how the noble families viewed themselves, and how their identity changed with the passage of time. Such investigations have been carried out as a result of a new prosopographical analysis of the documents: much can be achieved if we know to whom people were related, with whom they did business and where they owned land. The genealogical methods I have used to build up family profiles have been profitably used on northern European evidence, but rarely applied to material from the South.[14]

Establishing landowning patterns has necessitated a reappraisal

[13] G. Cassandro, 'Il ducato Bizantino', in *Storia di Napoli* II, i (Naples, 1967); U. Schwarz, *Amalfi im frühen Mittelalter (9–11 Jahrhundert)* (Tübingen, 1978) (pp. 1–68 trans. G. Vitolo as *Amalfi nel Medioevo*, Amalfi, 1985); M. del Treppo and A. Leone, *Amalfi Medioevale* (Naples, 1977).

[14] On the methods used, see below, chapter 4, section (a).

of the list of known place-names in the three areas. The third part of the study looks at the economic basis on which power was built up. Did monopolisation of land ownership affect the political make-up of any of the duchies? Figliuolo has argued convincingly that it did in part of Amalfi.[15] Was the political fragmentation of the area a cause or an effect of economic break-up? What part did the noble families play in the famed commercial activities[16] of the area in this period?

One issue which will be addressed is whether existing families, their property and their status were greatly affected by the coming of the Normans into the area in the eleventh century, or whether they remained undisturbed. Again, the experiences of the Tyrrhenian states could act as a microcosm of the whole of the South under Norman rule.

I hope to show from this examination of Gaeta and its neighbours that historians' attempts to package the South neatly into small, discrete states may be imposing an order on the area that never existed. Instead, the tendency of small states was to become even smaller, and even the Norman conquest may not have solved the 'problem' of this intense localisation. At the same time, even as political fission was occurring, the problems of daily life and property management faced by the documented population of each of these areas reveal notable parallels across political boundaries. This, I contend, is a far richer seam to mine if we are to understand southern Italy. We cling to dukes, counts and princes because there is little evidence of any other central power. Yet, if we juxtapose the histories of these leaders with the concerns of their leading subjects, we find more homogeneity and continuity of structures across political divides and beyond the Norman advance. By revealing these themes we could perhaps go some way

[15] B. Figliuolo, 'Gli Amalfitani a Cetara', *Annali, Istituto Italiano per gli Studi Storici*, 6 (1979–80), 31–82.

[16] Amalfi's commerce has formed the subject of work by A. Citarella: 'Patterns in medieval trade: the commerce of Amalfi before the crusades', *Journal of Economic History*, 28 (1968), 531–55; 'Scambi commerciali fra l'Egitto e Amalfi in un documento inedito della Geniza di Cairo', *ASPN*, 3rd ser. 9 (1971), 141–9; 'Il declino del commercio marittimo di Amalfi', *ASPN*, 3rd ser. 13 (1975), 9–54; see also del Treppo and Leone, *Amalfi Medioevale*. A new line of inquiry has recently been proposed by David Abulafia, 'Southern Italy, Sicily and Sardinia in the medieval Mediterranean economy', in *Commerce and Conquest in the Mediterranean, 1100–1500* (London, 1993), essay 1, p. 17. He stresses the need for further research into other cities of the South in order to more accurately assess Amalfi's importance as a trading city.

towards explaining the political events which have already received attention and have led to the characterisation of the South in the ninth, tenth and eleventh centuries as an area of anarchy.[17]

[17] Tabacco, *Struggle for Power*, deals with the period currently under review, including the South in the tenth century, in a chapter entitled 'Political anarchy'.

Chapter 1

SOURCES

The source material for this study is of two main types. Firstly, a large *corpus* of medieval charters, recording mostly land transactions, exists in published form, and has remained relatively unexploited as a source of information about life in this area between the ninth and the early twelfth centuries. This is despite the fact that it allows individual families to be examined in some detail. The landless and unfree, on the other hand, make only fleeting appearances in the documents. They never reached a level of wealth which allowed them a permanent presence in a written record that was concerned mainly with land transactions. And, as we shall see, even those who owned land sometimes seem not to have thought it necessary to write down all their transactions.[1] Nevertheless, the material at our disposal is copious, and offers a valuable opportunity to piece together the lives of many inhabitants of the Tyrrhenian coast. The charters will be discussed in detail presently.

The second body of written evidence consists of letters and narrative sources, and is useful in creating a wider framework in which to set the detailed information from the charters. Apart from specific material relating to individual cities, several sources are relevant for a history of the South as a whole. They include letters of the popes, especially John VIII,[2] and other material relating to the papacy's history and interest in its southern properties, including the *Liber Pontificalis* and the *Liber Censuum*.[3] In addition, there are several chronicles written in the South at this time. From the tenth century there is the anonymous *Chronicon Salernitanum* which, although its main focus is the history of the princes of Salerno, includes much information about Salerno's

[1] See below, this chapter, section (d).

[2] *MGH, Epistolae*, VII, eds E. Caspar *et al.* (Munich, 1978).

[3] *Liber Pontificalis*, ed. L. Duchesne, I (Paris, 1886) (= *LP*); *Liber Censuum*, ed. P. Fabre and L. Duchesne, I, (Paris, 1905) (= *LC*).

neighbours.[4] The eleventh-century source, the *Chronicle of Montecassino*[5] of Leo of Ostia, was described as the most balanced medieval history of its time by Ugo Balzani.[6] Such glowing praise should perhaps be treated with caution. Nevertheless, Leo's work and one of its main sources, the earlier *Chronicon Sancti Benedicti Casinensis*,[7] are valuable for the light they shed on the rise of the abbey of Montecassino, and on the abbey's self-image in the tenth and eleventh centuries. The views of a near contemporary from northern Italy, Liutprand, bishop of Cremona, offer us further glimpses of medieval southern life, and, being tangential to his main themes, may perhaps be relied upon as accurate.[8] Also relevant in this context are the occasional interventions by outside powers in the South, particularly the German emperors. All three Ottos have left some record of their presence here.[9] Later, the chroniclers of the Norman conquest, Amatus of Montecassino and Geoffrey Malaterra,[10] shed light on that tumultuous period in the history of the South. For the most part, however, I shall be examining the conquest from the documents of those conquered rather than the historians favourable to the conquerors.

Naples, Amalfi and Gaeta each furnish us with collections of charters and narrative sources to illuminate their past, and it is to these individual cities that the remainder of the chapter is devoted.

(a) NAPLES

Most of the Neapolitan charter material comes from the royal archives, and was published by the distinguished historian and archivist Bartolomeo Capasso in the nineteenth century. Capasso's

[4] *Chronicon Salernitanum*, ed. U. Westerbergh (Stockholm, 1956). Italian version: *Chronicon Salernitanum*, trans. A. Carucci (Salerno, 1988). Taviani-Carozzi, *Principauté*, I, p. 81ff. suggests an identification for the author of the chronicle.

[5] *Chronica Monasterii Casinensis*, ed. H. Hoffmann (*MGH, Scriptores* 34, Hanover, 1980) (= *CMC*).

[6] U. Balzani, *Le Cronache Italiane nel Medio Evo* (Milan, 1884), p. 156.

[7] *Chronica Sancti Benedicti Casinensis*, ed. G. Waitz (*MGH, Scriptores* series 3, I Hanover, 1878) (= *CSB*).

[8] Liutprand of Cremona, *Works*, trans. F. A. Wright (London, 1930); repr. with new introduction by J. J. Norwich (London, 1993).

[9] For example, in the document collections from individual cities themselves; also in isolated documents preserved in the *MGH* series. References will be given to these as they occur in the text.

[10] *Storia de'Normanni di Amato*, ed. V. de Bartholomeis (Rome, 1935) (= *Amatus*); Geoffrey Malaterra, *De Rebus Gestis Rogerii Calabriae et Siciliae Comitis*, ed. E. Pontieri (Bologna, 1927).

edition, under the umbrella title *Monumenta*, divides the charters into those issued by the dukes and all the remaining documents. These date up to 1139, and taken together number some 700. The edition also includes other evidence for Neapolitan history such as early evidence about the relationship between the dukes of Naples and their Lombard neighbours of Benevento, Salerno and Capua, and the chronicle of the bishops of Naples.[11] Some of the charter evidence, however, was published in an earlier edition of 1845.[12] Capasso drew on this for some of the documents in his edition. The earlier work also contains material which Capasso did not include in the *Monumenta*. Indeed, Capasso's selective method of editing sometimes leaves much to be desired. Although it is clear from surviving material that some of the documents he listed existed only in registers, in other cases he had access to complete documents and yet reproduces only what he considered the salient points: date clause, author, transaction and receiver. His frequent omission of formulae (though he signalled that he had done so) and signatures, is frustrating when one is trying to build up a picture both of how documents were used and who was using them. However, his edition remains the essential source of Neapolitan information, and preserves much valuable material.

Much of the documentation came from the great monasteries of Naples, whose documents were moved to the Naples State Archive.[13] It is certainly the case that Capasso had access to far more material than survives, and many of the documents that he published from the suppressed houses are now only listed in registers. One of the main collections was that of the monastery of St Sebastian, which preserved documents relating to its many subject houses as well as the monastery itself. The convent of St

11 B. Capasso, ed., *Monumenta ad Neapolitani Ducatus Historiam Pertinentia*, I: Chronicon ducum et principum Beneventi, Salerni et Capuae et ducum Neapolis, Chronicon Episcoporum Sancti Neapolitani Ecclesiae, Papal letters and documents, Acta Sanctorum, (Naples, 1881), II:i: Regesta Neapolitana, 912–1139 (=*RN*), (Naples, 1885), II:ii: Diplomata et Chartae Ducum Neapolis (=*DCDN*), Capitularia et pacta, Inscriptions and seals (Naples, 1892).

12 *Regii Neapolitani Archivii Monumenta*, ed. M. Baffi *et al.*, II, III, III, IV (Naples, 1845–1854) (=*RNAM*).

13 On the holdings of the Naples State Archive, based in the former monastery of SS Severinus and Sossus, J. Mazzoleni, *Le Fonti Documentarie e Bibliografiche dal Secolo X al Secolo XX conservate presso l'Archivio di Stato di Napoli* (Naples, 1978). The Introduction to this relates the destruction of much of the Archive during World War II; using inventories made by R. Filangieri di Candida in 1919, Mazzoleni also lists the destroyed material. See also Taviani-Carozzi, *Principauté*, I, xlvi and associated bibliography.

Gregory was also a rich source of information.[14] Thus the majority of the charter material from Naples is concerned with matters affecting the ecclesiastical institutions which preserved it. The number of ducal documents from the city makes up only a small part of the *corpus*.

Naples was by far the largest city in the area, and its documents record in detail the activities of an urban population. Both city life and written transactions evidently had a long history here. Whatever the ambiguities of the archaeological evidence concerning urban survival between the late Roman and early medieval periods,[15] the documents have an air of stability and unchanging practice,[16] which is also reflected in the political life of the duchy.

(b) AMALFI

By contrast, the documentary evidence from Amalfi has been published in a much less coherent form, though the editions are later and better. Until recently, the *Codice Diplomatico Amalfitano* of Filangieri di Candida was the only published material.[17] Since 1972, however, Jole Mazzoleni has doubled the amount of easily accessible evidence by producing editions of the diplomatic collections of the bishoprics of Amalfi and Ravello,[18] and more recently the archive of the church of St Laurence in Amalfi, known as the *Codice Perris*.[19] It is fortunate that Filangieri's first volume preserved the earliest charters from Amalfi, for the transfer of the Naples State Archive's most valuable material to a villa near Nola, for protection during World War II, proved disastrous when it was

[14] Some of the St Gregory documents were published by J. Mazzoleni, *Le Pergamene del Monastero di S. Gregorio Armeno di Napoli* (Naples, 1973). Filangieri's inventory of the St Gregory documents, taken from an earlier list, is held in the Archivio di Stato, Naples: Sezione Politico-diplomatica, *Inventari delle Pergamene*, 99. A copy of the earlier list is held in the same archive: *Monasteri Soppressi* 3437 (=*Mon.Sopp.*).

[15] On this, see P. Arthur, 'Naples: a case of urban survival in the early middle ages?', *MEFRM*, 103 (1991–2), 759–84; for a document-based view, P. Skinner, 'Urban communities in Naples, 900–1050', *PBSR*, 62 (1994, in press).

[16] A document of 1003 acknowledges this long history explicitly, stating that it is 'customary for a notary to record' documents, in this case a will: *RN* 319.

[17] *Codice Diplomatico Amalfitano*, ed. R. Filangieri di Candida, I (Naples, 1917), II (Trani, 1951) (=*CDA*).

[18] *Le Pergamene degli Archivi Vescovili di Amalfi e Ravello*, I, ed. J. Mazzoleni (Naples, 1972), II, ed. C. Salvati (Naples 1974), III, ed. B. Mazzoleni (Naples, 1975), IV, ed. L. Pescatore (Naples, 1979) (=*PAVAR*).

[19] *Il Codice Perris: Cartulario Amalfitano*, I, ed. J. Mazzoleni and R. Orefice (Amalfi, 1985) (=*CP*).

destroyed by fire in 1943.[20] Altogether, the Amalfitan charters number approximately 300 for the period under discussion.

The work of Schwarz has provided more material relating to the duchy, including his edition of the *Chronicon Amalfitanum*.[21] The work of the Centro di Cultura e Storia Amalfitana has also made more unpublished material available.[22] The Amalfitans have hitherto received more attention from historians for their pioneering, long-distance trading exploits than their domestic history.[23] Yet there is much that is comparable in the history of this small state and its territorially limited contemporary, Gaeta.

(c) GAETA

Despite an initially smaller number of documents, approximately 350 up to 1139, the charters of Gaeta have a homogeneity which allows us to look in more depth at the social structures of the duchy. Because topics are covered in these charters which are absent in the collections from Naples and Amalfi, they may enable us to fill in gaps in our understanding of the other duchies. It is worth pausing, therefore, to examine the Gaetan charter collection in some detail.

The city of Gaeta recently celebrated a notable anniversary: the centenary of the first systematic publication, by the monastery of St Benedict at Montecassino, of medieval documents relating to the city and its duchy. Certainly many of the documents had appeared in earlier publications, but the Cassinese edition was the first to add criticism of the material, as well as to publish a wealth of new Gaetan documents arranged systematically and dated where possible. This *Codex Diplomaticus Cajetanus*,[24] of which three volumes have so far appeared, has formed the basis for all studies of the city and duchy of Gaeta since its publication, and the recent Convegno held in the city to celebrate the centenary of the first volume recognised the fact.[25] Despite its availability, however, this charter collection has remained remarkably underexploited by historians of the South. Yet a closer examination of its contents

[20] Schwarz, *Amalfi nel Medioevo*, p. 28; see also note 13, above.

[21] Schwarz, *Amalfi im frühen Mittelalter*, pp. 193–224.

[22] *CP* was published as the first of the *Fonti* series; the latest volume (VI) of *PAVAR* has also appeared under this rubric.

[23] See above, Introduction, note 16, for bibliography.

[24] *Codex Diplomaticus Cajetanus* I, II (Montecassino, 1887, 1891) (= *CDC*).

[25] *Il Ducato di Gaeta Secoli IX–XII*, (V Convegno di Studi sul Medioevo Meridionale, Gaeta 23–8 October 1988, forthcoming).

reveals it to be unique among southern Italian document collections for several reasons.

It has become apparent that the *Codex Diplomaticus Cajetanus* is not entirely reliable as far as the authenticity and dating of all of the documents proposed by the editors is concerned. Nevertheless, its volumes remain an essential tool for Gaetan research. In the case of individual documents whose dates are in question, I have included discussions at relevant points in the chapters which follow. Here I propose only to discuss in general terms the origins of the collection and the reasons why these documents were preserved.

Over two-thirds of the documents published by the Cassinese monks came from their own archive, most in their original form, others surviving only in seventeenth- or eighteenth-century copies. It is not surprising that so much Gaetan material found its way to Montecassino, since in the course of the eleventh and twelfth centuries much of the duchy of Gaeta fell into the monastery's hands through gifts made by the Norman princes of Capua or the dukes and counts of Gaeta itself. It was common practice at this time to hand over documents relating to the pieces of land being donated, since production of such material alongside the document recording the donation itself was often a decisive factor in disputes over ownership.[26]

As the power of Montecassino grew in the late eleventh century, so did its ambitions, giving rise to a collection of documents known as the *Register* of Peter the Deacon. Their author sought to justify the Cassinese claim to as much territory as possible. Donations by princes and ex-dukes, not only of Gaeta, were forged to further these claims, and it was only relatively recently that some of these forgeries were brought to light and discussed.[27] Peter's documents rarely affect the present study's arguments; where they do, I have discussed them at relevant points in the text.

As well as the contents of their own archive, the monks used documents from the cathedral archive at Gaeta. Most of this material survived only in later copies, and many of these may have been destroyed in World War II.

[26] See below, section (d), for further discussion of this point.

[27] H. Bloch, 'The schism of Anacletus and the Glanfeuil forgeries of Peter the Deacon', *Traditio*, 8 (1952), 159–264; A. Mancone, 'Il Registrum Petri Diaconi', *Bullettino dell'Archivio Paleografico Italiano*, 2–3 (1956–7); H. Hoffmann, 'Chronik und Urkunde in Montecassino', *QFIAB*, 51 (1972), 93–206; Loud, *Church and Society*, pp. 78–9, 183–4; and 'A calendar of the diplomas of the Norman princes of Capua', *PBSR*, 49 (1981), 99–143.

The Cassinesi were also able to gather together material which had already been published, taking individual documents from Ughelli's *Italia Sacra*,[28] Contatore's history of Terracina,[29] and the mid-nineteenth-century edition of the royal archives at Naples.[30] The largest source of such material, however, was a two-part work by don Erasmo Gattola on the history of Montecassino, written in the eighteenth century.[31] The editors of the *Codex* themselves admitted that using Gattola's work was less than satisfactory,[32] since some of his transcriptions were incomplete. Given that the originals did not survive, however, they were forced to accept the limitations of his work, and unfortunately we are obliged to do so as well.

These were the sources upon which the editors of the *Codex* could draw, but what were the origins of the documents themselves, and why were they preserved?

The most striking feature about the *Codex* as it stands is the very high proportion – almost half – of documents authorised by, or relating to, the dukes of Gaeta, especially the family of Docibilis I, which ruled the city and its territory from the ninth to the middle of the eleventh century (see genealogy, Figure 1.1). No other contemporary collection from the states neighbouring Gaeta, nor further South, can match this proportion. Neither Naples nor Amalfi have many ducal documents. Their collections, like nearby Cava's, fall into the more usual pattern of being largely ecclesiastical in origin. If one adds to the Gaetan ducal documents those authorised by the bishops who belonged to the ducal family, and those of the churches known to have been founded by the Docibilan dynasty, the result looks very much like an archive kept by the family and augmented by their successors as dukes.

However, it is not quite as simple as this, for documents authorised by men and women with no apparent links to the ducal family survive in the collection as well. If these latter documents could be included in the ducal family archive on the basis that they mentioned lands which later fell into the hands of the dukes, we could continue to think of the Gaetan material as the ducal archive. This, though, does not appear to be the case. It is possible that what

[28] F. Ughelli, *Italia Sacra*, I–X, ed. N. Coleti (Venice, 1717–22).

[29] D. A. Contatore, *De Historia Terracinensi Libri Quinque* (Rome, 1706).

[30] See above, note 12.

[31] E. Gattola, *Historia Abbatiae Casinensis* (Venice, 1733); *Ad Historiam Abbatiae Casinensis Accessiones* (Venice, 1734).

[32] *CDC* I, p. 212.

DOCIBILIS I = Matrona

Sikelgaita · Leo prefect (906) · Anatolius duke of Terracina (906–24) · Megalu (906) = Rodipert · JOHN I (890–937) · Eufimia (906–24) = Stephen · Maria (906–18) = John · Bona (906)

John (944–6) · Docibilis (937–63) · Aligernus (955) · Theotista (937) · Bona (933) · DOCIBILIS II (914–54) = Orania · Matrona (949) = Kampulus · Maru · Sikelgaita (941–62) · Megalu abbess (958) · Constantine* (941–94) · Peter* (941–62) · Leo* (922–63) · Agnellus (924) · Angelarus (919–24)

KAMPULI

Megalu (954) · Drosu (954) · Gemma (954) · MARINUS duke of Fondi (945–84) · Anna (954) · Maria (954) · Leo prefect (954) = Maria · JOHN II (934–62) · GREGORY (939–64) = Drosu · Deusdedit (986) · Atenolf (937–78)

Gregory count of Castro Argento = Maria (992–1026) · Bernard bishop (997–1049) · Marinus (999) · Dauferius I count of Traetto (992) · JOHN III (978–1008) = Emilia (1002–1029) · Leo duke of Fondi (992) · Stephania = Docibilis (981–1010) · John · Gregory (992–1024) = Maria · Maria · Landolf (981–1013) = Polyssena · Docibilis (981–999) = Anna (1010) · Gregory (999–1002)

Dauferius II (1014) = Alzeiza (1029) · Girard (1071) · Leo (1071–95) · Littefrid (1072) · John (1053–69) · Marinus count of Castro Argento (1029) · JOHN IV (993–1011) · Leo (1014–24) · John (1014) · Crescentius (1049) · Leo = (1) Bona = (2) Amata · Laidulf (1024) · Gregory (1024) · John Papa (1002–12) · Docibilis (1002–25)

Dauferius III · Marinus John · Lando · Leo (1117) · Crescentius (1089–99) · Littefrid (1089) · John count (1045) · JOHN V (1002–32) · (1) Bernard (1069) = Offa · (2) Constantine (1039) · LEO II (1042) = Theodora · Hugh count of Suio (1023–40)

Dauferius V (1049) · Lando · Gregory (1045–48) · Docibilis (1054) · Raynerius (1054) = Mira · Leo bishop · Peter (1055) = Ageltruda · John (1056–79)

Leo (1062–4) = Aloara · Landolf (1062–8) = Domnella · Raynerius (1125) · Peter (1053–62) · John (1062–4)

*natural sons of John I

Figure 1.1 *The family of Docibilis I*

we are dealing with, in addition to the documents relating to the ducal family, are the contents of a public depository for private documents, used as insurance against future disputes.

As will become apparent as the study progresses, however, a public archive and a Docibilan family archive at Gaeta might have been much the same thing. The Docibilans seem to have claimed or gained control over much of Gaetan life, making little distinction between their public and private actions. Whether the documents record public actions of the dukes of Gaeta or the private ones as members of the clan may therefore be immaterial. Other inhabitants of the duchy may have seen the ducal archive as a secure place to deposit their own charters, and thereby turned it into a public one. Were it not for the unique situation whereby a large proportion of the lands of the duchy, which had been controlled by one family, fell into the hands of the most powerful of the southern Italian monasteries, which had a vested interest in keeping all the documents relating to its possessions, we would not have such a rich resource at our disposal. It is likely that, had Amalfi and Naples suffered much the same fate, we should find just as high a proportion of ducal documents in their collections as well. As it is, the Gaetan material offers a unique opportunity to study the workings of a medieval duchy from the point of view both of its rulers and of those they ruled. It thus has a significance beyond its immediately local context, providing comparative material from Italy for future research on the fragmented European states of this period.

The *Codex Cajetanus* is not the only evidence at our disposal. It is fortunate that many of the documentary collections of the area around Gaeta appeared in published form at the turn of the century, since the bombardments and wreckage of World War II destroyed much of the original material. Tragically, the archive at Terracina, a vital source of papal–Gaetan relations, was completely destroyed, leaving only documents published in 1706 by Contatore, fragmented copies of two others in the Vatican,[33] and an unpublished handful at Montecassino.[34] This means that we must rely heavily for information in this sphere on the letters of the popes, in particular those of John VIII, which to say the least

[33] Biblioteca Apostolica Vaticana, *Cod. Vat. Lat.* 12634.

[34] Montecassino, Archivio, *Aula* II, *Caps.* LIII, *fasc.* 1, nos.1–3; *Aula* III, *Caps.* VII, no.13; five other documents dated pre-1100 were published by I. Giorgi, 'Documenti terracinensi', *BISI*, 16 (1896), 55–92, but they add little to our knowledge of papal– Gaetan relations.

present a one-sided view of very specific events. One or two other published papal documents also have a bearing on the present study, and will be discussed in the main body of the text.

On a brighter note, the remarkable survival of much material at Montecassino means that we have the *Codex Diplomaticus Pontiscurvi*, an unpublished eighteenth-century copy of documents relating to the castle of Pontecorvo.[35] This castle was held by the duke of Gaeta, and its history is therefore relevant to a study of loyalties on the border between Gaetan and Cassinese lands. It yields information, too, on the relationship between the dukes and abbots. Also unpublished, but cited by several authors, is the notebook of C. Caietano,[36] a seventeenth-century list of documents held in the cathedral archive at Gaeta. This provides us with at least one piece of evidence not found elsewhere. Finally, the published documentary material of other neighbours of Gaeta, for example from Aquino and Capua,[37] may provide further comparative evidence and explain to some degree the attitudes and actions of the rulers who in turn took control of Gaeta.

(d) DOCUMENTS AS SOURCES

We are fortunate that so many documents survive from the ninth to the twelfth century to use as tools in recreating the patterns of life in the Tyrrhenian coastal cities during this period. Before examining their contents, however, it is necessary to address the question of why they survive, or exist, at all. What function did written charters perform in the three cities under scrutiny? And how far do they truly reflect the lives of those cities?

As I have already said, most documents recorded the movement of land between individuals or institutions, in the form of sales, gifts, leases, wills, or exchanges. A small number recorded the transfer of other, moveable, property. A significant proportion recorded the proceedings or final outcome of court-cases, when property was disputed between two parties. This gives the impression that documents were an essential adjunct to transfers of property, and formed a part of many people's lives in the three duchies.

[35] Montecassino, Biblioteca: *Codex Diplomaticus Pontiscurvi ab anno 953 ad anno 1612*.

[36] Biblioteca Apostolica Vaticana, *Cod. Vat. Barb. Lat.* 3216.

[37] Aquino: F. Scandone, 'Il gastaldato di Aquino dalla metà del secolo IX alla fine del X', *ASPN*, 33 (1908), 720–35, and 34 (1909), 49–77; Capua: J. Mazzoleni, *Le Pergamene di Capua*, I (Naples, 1957).

There are, however, important variations in distribution between one duchy and the next. For example, the number of lease documents from Gaeta is extremely small,[38] whereas in Naples and Amalfi they are relatively well represented. Does this mean that the leasing of land was virtually unknown at Gaeta? It is unlikely: the existence of evidence for leasing in the other two duchies, as well as further north,[39] suggests that it is the pattern of recording in writing that is exceptional here. Alternatively if, as I suggested above, Gaeta had a ducal or public archive, it may have preserved certain documents, made when ownership of land was transferred, rather than those which only recorded a change in tenure.[40]

The preservation of ducal documents in Gaeta indicates that the rulers thought written records were important, and it is, as I have stated, only an accident of survival that we do not have similar evidence from the other two cities. The rulers of Naples, in particular, might have been expected to place great emphasis on writing in their administration, since their city had been a key centre of Byzantine rule before drifting into autonomy in the eighth century.[41] Echoes of this can be detected in the numerous signatures in Greek script on Neapolitan documents of the tenth century,[42] their dating by imperial rule and in the coinage of the city.[43] The persistence of Byzantine culture, what Toubert has termed 'snobisme byzantinisant',[44] is explicable in terms of Naples' continued amicable, if distant, relationship with its erstwhile rulers. A persuasive case has also been put forward for an essential continuity of structures in the Byzantine enclaves, including Naples, which resisted the Lombard invasions of the sixth century.[45]

Gaeta originally formed part of the duchy of Naples, but became

[38] There are less than twenty surviving leases from a document total of over 300.

[39] Toubert, *Structures*, I, pp. 507–45 discusses leases from other parts of Lazio.

[40] For more discussion on this point, see below, chapter 7, section (b).

[41] On the importance of writing in Byzantine administration, see M. Mullett, 'Writing in early medieval Byzantium', in *The Uses of Literacy in Early Medieval Europe*, ed. R. McKitterick (Cambridge, 1990), especially pp. 162–3.

[42] Greek signatures of both clerics and laymen are ubiquitous in the tenth-century documents of the city. In the eleventh century most examples are found on the documents of the Greek monastery of SS Sergius and Bacchus. For a full list, see Appendix I; see also F. Luzzati Lagana, 'Le firme greche nei documenti del ducato di Napoli', *Studi Medievali*, 3rd series 23.2 (1982), 729–52.

[43] See below, chapter 3, section (h).

[44] *Structures*, I, p. 655, note I.

[45] T. S. Brown, *Gentlemen and Officers: Imperial Administration and Aristocratic Power in Byzantine Italy, 554–800* (Rome, 1984).

detached during the ninth century. It had not been a city during the Byzantine period; it was still only a small fortification when it became independent. However, its rulers imitated Naples in many areas of government,[46] and they valued written documents recording their actions. They also occasionally used inscriptions as part of this record, claiming credit for building work in the city of Gaeta.[47]

The latter use of writing by the rulers presupposes that there was a substantial number of people in Gaeta able to read and to take in the message that the inscriptions conveyed. Direct evidence of this ability is difficult to find.[48] The use of documents ostensibly indicates that even if people could not read they still valued written evidence of their actions. But was this use imposed from above or did the Gaetans, and for that matter the Neapolitans and Amalfitans, place as much importance on written records as their rulers?

We do have a great deal of evidence of use of documents, enabling us to recreate the histories of some of the noble families of the area,[49] but there is reason to believe that documents did not become a trusted record in these duchies until the eleventh century. I stated above that one of the main reasons a document was kept was to prove ownership in case of dispute. Yet the court-cases of the tenth century tell a rather different story.

For example, in 867 two men disputed with the bishop of Gaeta over a piece of land. Their case was heard by Docibilis I, and they won. A document was then drawn up recording their victory.[50] In 945 the case flared up again, this time between the bishop and the two men's sons. Again the duke heard their cases, and again the bishop lost.[51] What is important about this second case, however, is that the two sons swore oaths to the veracity of their claim. They did not use the 867 document, which is undoubtedly genuine, to prove their case. This suggests that either they did not have access to it or that they did have access to it (either in their possession or in a public archive) and chose not to use it. The latter seems more likely; the majority of court cases in both Gaeta and Naples were settled by oaths in the tenth century, sometimes in the face of

[46] See below, chapters 2 and 3. [47] See below, p. 62.

[48] I gathered together the circumstantial evidence in my paper, 'Women, literacy and invisibility in medieval southern Italy', read at the conference *Women and the Book*, St Hilda's College, Oxford, August 1993. [49] See below, chapter 4. [50] *CDC* 13.

[51] *CDC* 48.

documentary evidence which was rejected.[52] Thus the documents which we have may have been drawn up to record the actions of the Docibilans in hearing the case, rather than for the benefit of the disputants. It was important to the rulers that records of court-cases be kept, perhaps influenced by standard Byzantine practice,[53] but those in dispute did not place such trust in the written word at this time. This would change in the eleventh century, when there is far more evidence of charters being used to prove title.

The pattern of use has implications for the picture presented in this study, in that what we can now see happening represents only those actions thought worth writing down. In Gaeta's case, this in practice means that the prominence of the dukes may be a reflection of their early use of writing (in relation to their subjects) rather than their actual power. We are seeing their actions and those of their subjects through a 'ducal filter'. In other duchies one might detect an ecclesiastical slant, again reflecting the interests of powerful institutions which also thought charters to be an essential part of that power. Returning to an earlier theme, the documents are created by those in power, whether as rulers or as wealthy landowners, and for the most part exclude the powerless, the poor and the landless.

This picture must be modified to explain the presence of documents which do record the actions of those outside the apparent power structure of the duchies. I suggested above that in some cases these documents might include land now in the hands of the dukes or churches. Another factor to bear in mind, particularly as the tenth century gave way to the eleventh, is a perceptibly increasing use of written records by the inhabitants of these duchies, perhaps in imitation of their rulers or in response to some coercion on the part of the powerful to keep a tangible record of their actions. For, if rulers' endorsement of written evidence could successfully gain them land at the expense of their subjects, the latter would soon begin to employ the same weapon in defence of their property. The court-cases of the eleventh century are a prime example of such increased use, perhaps reflecting and being reflected in the growing awareness of the outward forms of public administration in the duchies.

[52] See, for example, *CDC* 16 (890), *CDC* 39 (936) and *CDC* 56 (958). In another case, in 945, a charter used as evidence is torn up, *CDC* 47; a compromise is reached in a case of 957 which oaths have failed to settle, *CDC* 54.

[53] See below, chapter 3, section (e), for further discussion of this point.

On the face of it, there was no need to write down transactions if oral agreements in the presence of witnesses were equally binding. The increasing use of documents may, therefore, reveal a greater complexity in transactions which could no longer rely on memory for their record. Alternatively, a conscious effort may have been made by those who needed to use documents to keep track of their widespread estates, that is, by rulers and the church, to encourage the acceptance of documents as valid proofs, and their adoption by their subjects and neighbours. Thus the pattern of surviving documents reveals how power was exerted, and that charters were part of that exercise. Use of the written word did not in itself convey power, but in the context of proving landownership it became a potent ally in preserving power. The documents can be used to explore this and reveal how networks of influence were created. The voice of the powerless is rarely heard; with this in mind, the remainder of this study examines the picture that the documentary sources present.

Part I

FROM THE BEGINNINGS TO THE ELEVENTH CENTURY

Chapter 2

THE ORIGINS OF DYNASTIC RULE

The histories of the three duchies examined in this study exhibit certain parallels, chief among which is the fact that all three came to be ruled by single, powerful clans for all or part of the period between 850 and 1050. We know something of the background of the ducal dynasties of Amalfi and Naples; these will be examined later in this chapter. Very little, however, has previously been written about the family who came to power at Gaeta in 867. This is partly due to the fact that they have no known history before their emergence in the Gaetan documentation. Who were they and how did they come to power? Was their rise similar to that of the ruling families of contemporary neighbours?

From the main source of documentary material for Gaeta in this period, the *Codex Cajetanus*, it emerges that a man named Docibilis appears to have taken control in 867. His family were to dominate the castle and its territory for some 150 years. In the following discussion, I shall examine the evidence from the *Codex* and other sources to build up a more detailed picture of the beginnings of Docibilan rule.

In 839 one Constantine son of Anatolius received from his sister Elizabeth and her son-in-law Theodosius, prefect of Naples, two landed estates at a rent in kind which had to be delivered to Naples. The document recording the transaction was witnessed by Constantine's son Marinus.[1] Both father and son were recipients of land from Elizabeth and Theodosius on similar terms in 866.[2] Constantine and Marinus, who are described as *hypatoi* of the castle, appear to have been the rulers of Gaeta at this time. The two lease documents have led historians to conclude that up until 866 Gaeta was a satellite of Naples, her rulers related to, and controlled by, the dukes of the latter city:[3] the use of Greek in the signatures of

[1] *CDC* 5. [2] *CDC* 12.

[3] P. Delogu, 'Il ducato di Gaeta dal IX all'XI secolo: istituzioni e società', in *Storia del Mezzogiorno*, eds. G. Galasso and R. Romeo, II, i (forthcoming), p. 193. I thank Professor Delogu for showing me his chapter in advance of publication.

the Gaetan rulers at this time is cited as an indication of their Neapolitan origins.[4]

The suggestion of a Neapolitan relationship will be examined in detail a little later in this chapter. By 867, however, a change had occurred. In that year we see our first document in the *Codex Cajetanus* written at Gaeta and dated by the rule of Docibilis the prefect. Furthermore, Docibilis himself appears in the document, holding court to settle a dispute between the bishop of Gaeta, Ramfus, and two inhabitants of the castle, Mauro the cleric and John.[5] He does not appear to have been a relative of either Constantine or Marinus, or of the Neapolitan dukes. Even his name is virtually unknown outside the Gaetan document collection. So who was Docibilis and how had he come to prominence?

This question has never been fully confronted in Gaetan historiography, nor has any attempt been made to explain the continuing domination of Docibilis' family in Gaetan affairs after his death. Merores was of the opinion that Docibilis owed his rise to the fact that he received large amounts of land from, and the patronage of, the papacy.[6] She based her argument on the documentary evidence of the gifts, discussed below, and the assertion of Leo of Ostia in the Chronicle of Montecassino that 'at that time [880–1] the Gaetans served the pope'.[7] Guiraud also used the papal link to explain the rise of the Docibilans to power.[8] Von Falkenhausen, however, questioned this assumption, pointing out that Docibilis and his son John may have received papal land because they were powerful, rather than to help them to power.[9]

Of what did the gifts consist, and how were they made? It seems that in the late 870s pope John VIII handed over control of the papal patrimonies of Traetto and Fondi to Docibilis in return for breaking off a pact with the Saracens.[10] This transaction was certainly not carried out in any atmosphere of goodwill; John's series of threatening letters to the rulers of all the Tyrrhenian states about their relationships with the Arabs are perhaps the most evocative and oft-quoted sources for the history of the area in the late ninth century.[11] And, if a fragment dated 873 of a letter to 'Degivili excommunicato' does refer to Docibilis, papal–Gaetan relations had clearly reached a low before the cession of the

[4] V. von Falkenhausen, 'Il ducato di Gaeta', in *Storia d'Italia*, III, ed. G. Galasso (Turin, 1983), p. 348. [5] *CDC* 13. [6] *Gaeta*, p. 15. [7] *CMC* I, 43.
[8] 'Reseau', p. 489. [9] 'Ducato', p. 349. [10] *CDC* 130. [11] *MGH, Epp.* VII.

patrimonies was made.[12] Of particular interest in this fragment is the way John addressed the Gaetan, who was 'redeemed with difficulty from the Saracens by the mercy of the Amalfitans'.[13] Before he became their ally, then, Docibilis seems to have been captured by the Saracens. That the Amalfitans had freed him illustrates their closeness to the infidel at this point, and Docibilis may have learnt much about such co-operation from them.[14]

The events of this period, particularly the cession itself, are shrouded in obscurity, not least because the documents recording the initial transaction between Docibilis and John VIII, and a later confirmation of the cession, by John X to Docibilis' son John in *c.*914, survive only in an eleventh-century charter recording a court-case about the boundaries of the two patrimonies, Fondi and Traetto.[15] The Chronicle of Montecassino records only that in 876 the Gaetans were among the Tyrrhenian states in league with the Saracens blockading Rome,[16] and that later Gaetans aided the Arabs against an expedition of Amalfitans and Neapolitans.[17] The cession itself may have taken place at a meeting held between pope John and the leaders of Gaeta, Amalfi, Naples, Capua and Salerno at Traetto in 877, at which the Amalfitans accepted a promise of papal cash for their renunciation of their links with the Arabs.[18] If the pope's concessions, including the handing-over of the patrimonies to Docibilis and John, were intended to detach the leaders from their infidel allies, they clearly only had sporadic success. A letter threatening excommunication against Docibilis, John and the Gaetan bishop, the prefect and bishop of Amalfi and Athanasius, bishop of Naples, survives from 879.[19] It is unclear whether the threat was carried out against the Gaetans.

The title that Docibilis took as controller of the patrimonies was *rector*, succeeding earlier holders of that post.[20] However, the essential point to note is that he only appears for the first time with this title in 890, over twenty years after he appears as ruler of Gaeta.[21] It could be argued that this is due to the extreme scarcity of ninth-century evidence in the *Codex Cajetanus*, and that the

[12] *Ibid.*, p. 275.

[13] 'vix a Saracenis Amalfitanorum miseratione . . . redemptus'.

[14] On Saracens at this time, N. Cilento, 'I Saraceni nell'Italia meridionale nei secoli IX e X', *ASPN*, 77 (1959), 110–22. [15] *CDC* 130. [16] *CMC* I, 40.

[17] *Ibid.* I, 50. [18] Schwarz, *Amalfi nel Medioevo*, p. 61.

[19] *MGH, Epp.* VII, p. 204.

[20] *Rectores*: Gregory, *CDC* 3 (830); Grossus, *CDC* 7 (841); Mercurius, *CDC* 9 (851), and *CDC* 11 (862). [21] *CDC* 15.

Gaetans did 'serve the pope', in the words of Leo of Ostia, before that date. However, it must be remembered that Leo's statement was written much later, and may have been affected by hindsight. That is, Docibilis' receipt of papal land may have been seen as the culmination of a period of obedience to the pope. Leo's own evidence illustrates that this obedience was at best sporadic. Whilst the cession of the patrimonies clearly enhanced Docibilis' position, it seems that other reasons must be sought to explain his initial rise. Although no evidence survives of Docibilis leasing land from the Neapolitans as Constantine had done, the title *hypatos* indicates persistent Neapolitan influence. Constantine had been *hypatos* of Gaeta, and the most notable parallels to his position are in the tenth- and eleventh-century references in the Neapolitan archive to the rulers of Sorrento, with the titles prefect[22] and *hypatos*.[23] Earlier rulers of Amalfi[24] and, as we have seen, Docibilis himself, also used the title prefect. Both Sorrento and Amalfi owed nominal allegiance to Naples, the former more than the latter, and Gaeta probably had a similar status under Constantine. Further investigation of Gaetan and Neapolitan archives, however, suggests that assuming the title of *hypatos* may not have automatically conferred on Docibilis the right to rule Gaeta, subject to Naples or not. For among the witnesses at Docibilis' first court in 867 was one Leo son of Tiberius *hypatos*, and alongside the *ipatos* of Sorrento documented *c.*1021 we can place six examples of men who, between 957 and 1038, bore the title, but were not subject rulers.[25] It would seem that the title *hypatos* had a vaguer honorific function and was borne by men to denote noble status. It is possible that Constantine and his son Marinus were *hypatoi* before they came to Gaeta. Certainly Constantine's brother John used the title in a witness list of 855 without, apparently, achieving the status of ruler.[26]

The difference between Docibilis and his predecessors and the Sorrentans, however, is that, whilst the latter two groups generally named their aristocratic fathers (the father of Constantine and John was count Anatolius), we have no information regarding Docibi-

[22] *RN* 220: Marinus son of Sergius prefect (979).

[23] *RN* 402: Sergius *ipatos* son of Marinus (1021?).

[24] *CDA* 584: Maurus prefect (860); *CDA* 1: Mastalus prefect (907). In 957 we have our first documented duke of Amalfi, at which point the title prefect was dropped: *CP* 31.

[25] Gaeta: *CDC* 13; Naples: *RN* 96 (957), heirs of John *kataypatiae*; *RN* 169 (968/9), John son of Stephen *kata domni ypatiae*; *RN* 287 (994), John son of Peter *ipati*; etc. At Naples the Ipati may even have been a family with that surname rather than a group of titled men. See below, chapter 4, section (b).

[26] *CDC* 10.

[27] *CDC* 19.

lis' birth or ancestry. This fact, coupled with Docibilis' will of 906[27] showing that he owned immense quantities of mobile wealth, but little land, suggests a man of non-noble birth who had perhaps enriched himself by trade and whose rise to power was, therefore, based on his wealth and opportunism. This picture must be modified by a later document of 924 showing that Docibilis had owned land and left it, undivided, to his children.[28] This may have been acquired while he was in power, however; the image of him as a wealthy newcomer persists. Docibilis is noticeably absent from the witness lists of pre-867 documents featuring members of noble families with whom he and his clan later associated. If he was not a nobleman, how did he gain acceptance as ruler of Gaeta? And if, as seems likely from the suddenness of the takeover, he came to power through some sort of *coup d'état* (a scenario favoured by Delogu[29]), why did Naples not take any action against the man who had deposed her own nominees?

The answer to these questions may lie in the will of Docibilis I and the eighteen Gaetan documents surviving from before 906. From these we can establish that Docibilis' father-in-law was a certain Bonus[30] and that the *hypatos* Constantine's brother was also called Bonus.[31] The latter certainly appears as a witness at Docibilis' first recorded court in 867.[32] Far from opposing the Docibilan takeover, we see Constantine's (presumably) younger brother in open assent with Docibilis' position, and it does not seem too far-fetched to suppose that he and Docibilis' father-in-law were one and the same.

If Bonus had a hand in the elevation of Docibilis to power, an opportune moment would have had to be sought. It is possible that Constantine died in 866, leaving his son Marinus vulnerable to attack. It does not appear that Bonus himself had a son; if he had, he would surely have tried to gain power for himself and his heir. Docibilis, wealthy enough to buy support, but with no ties with the existing nobility that could threaten Bonus' position, may have seemed the ideal candidate to marry Bonus' daughter and be promoted to power.

If we accept that what occurred at Gaeta in 866/7 was a shift in power within the ruling family, whom I have called the Anatolii, rather than its complete overthrow, we can explain why Naples did not intervene. Outwardly, there was little change in Gaeta's

[28] *CDC* 31. [29] 'Ducato', p. 198. [30] *CDC* 19. [31] *CDC* 10.
[32] *CDC* 13.

position *vis-à-vis* her nominally sovereign state. Perhaps, though, neither Naples nor Bonus was fully aware of what sort of man they had allowed to take over Gaeta.

That Bonus had underestimated Docibilis' ambitions or power, or both, is illustrated by the document of 867; Bonus did not appear alongside his supposed protégé as ruler of Gaeta. Instead, he was relegated to a secondary role as witness to the proceedings. One can only speculate that Docibilis was able to pay Bonus off, or force him to step down, whilst maintaining an honourable position beside his son-in-law.

Both of these options, and my entire hypothesis about Docibilis' rise, require that he had immense amounts of mobile wealth. He must have been noticeably wealthier than any of his contemporaries to attract Bonus' attention or, if we attribute to Docibilis the role of prime mover of the takeover, to persuade him to support the deposition of Constantine or Marinus. From where did this wealth originate?

The exotic mobile goods listed in Docibilis' will have suggested to Delogu[33] that he invested in trading ventures during his period in power. I would suggest that Docibilis' fortune was made before he came to power, as well as during his rule. The emphasis in his will on the moveables (each of his seven children is assigned a share of gold, silver, silk cloths, bronze and spices) and the rather careless clause stipulating that the children themselves should divide their landed inheritance, suggests that the former were held to be a more important part of the family's wealth.[34] We must also surmise that Docibilis' fortune was made outside Gaeta. Had it been possible to acquire such wealth within the city and its territory, we must ask why neither Constantine or Marinus were able to defend themselves against the takeover, and why the takeover bid did not come from those noblemen visible at Gaeta prior to 867.

The idea of Docibilis making a fortune from commerce gains added plausibility if we remember that Gaeta is recorded as having a fleet from at least the early ninth century. In 810 its ships joined those of Amalfi in an attack on the Saracens.[35] The latter were almost perennially present in the Tyrrhenian area throughout the ninth century. If Docibilis is to be considered as a spectacularly successful entrepreneur, he must have been able to come to some

[33] 'Ducato', p. 198.

[34] On the family's landed wealth, see below, chapter 3, section (a).

[35] Merores, *Gaeta*, p. 8.

arrangement with the Saracen pirates and raiders. We do not know under what terms such an agreement might have been made, but it may relate to the period he spent as a hostage of the infidels; that Docibilis was at least perceived to have a special relationship with the Arabs, particularly the group operating in the vicinity of Gaeta, is illustrated by the evidence of the Montecassino Chronicle. In 880/1, pope John VIII, presumably incensed at Docibilis' continued association with the infidels, took away from him control of the area around Traetto and gave it to Pandenolf of Capua. The latter began to attack Gaeta's territory, and in retaliation against the pope Docibilis unleashed a group of Arabs from Agropoli near Salerno on the area around Fondi. The pope was 'filled with shame' and restored Traetto to Docibilis. Their agreement seems to have sparked off a Saracen attack on Gaeta itself, in which many Gaetans were killed or captured.[36] Eventually peace was restored and the Saracens made a permanent settlement on the mouth of the Garigliano river.[37]

This account from Leo of Ostia is revealing in that it shows how unpredictable Docibilis' allies were.[38] It also seems to indicate that they were his main source of military power, for when they turned against Gaeta it was the Gaetans who came off worse. Nevertheless, he seems to have been able to call upon their aid when he needed it; possibly they were his trading partners as well as his military allies. Little wonder that Docibilis was accepted as the new ruler of Gaeta in 867.

Even with support of a member of the Anatolii clan, though, Docibilis may not have been able to take his new power for granted. From the register of pope John VIII we see Docibilis in power at Gaeta in 877,[39] and in the Montecassino Chronicle he is, as we have just seen, visible in the years 880–1. After his initial appearance in 867, however, we have only one document in the *Codex Cajetanus* from the following twenty-three years before Docibilis returns to view, as *hypatos* and papal rector, in 890.[40]

This apparent lack of documented activity from domestic sources may be an accident of survival, or may reflect Docibilis'

36 Evidence of such capture occurs in a document of 890, *CDC* 15.

37 *CMC* I, 43.

38 Leo's chronicle was written some two centuries after the events it relates. The earlier Cassinese chronicle, the *Chronica Sancti Benedicti*, does not include this episode, although it is clearly the source, sometimes *verbatim*, of other sections of Leo's work.

39 *MGH, Epp*. VII, p. 38.

40 *CDC* 15.

preoccupation with unruly Saracens and predatory Capuans in the late ninth century. Alternatively, he may have faced early opposition to his rise to power from the established noble families at Gaeta, or from the papal rectors whom he replaced, to the extent that his ability to establish a new regime and hold documented courts, and their ability to make land transactions, were both severely curtailed by the effort of a power struggle. The best indication of the insecurity of the takeover is that, whilst Docibilis' first document of 867 is dated 'in the time of lord Docibilis *magnificus* the prefect', the next occurring text issued by one John *comes* son of Ramfus in 887 reverts to the pre-Docibilan dating custom of referring to the rule of the Byzantine emperors Leo and Alexander.[41] This in itself is not conclusive; Docibilis' own will is dated by the emperor's rule, but this may be an acknowledgement on his part that some outward forms of power at Gaeta could not be quickly or easily changed. After a lengthy run of documents which have no date clause – itself indicative of uncertainty over who was in charge at Gaeta – imperial dating returned, followed by a system combining the date of the emperor's rule with that of the Docibilans at Gaeta. It was not until 936 that Docibilis I's grandson, Docibilis II, dropped the imperial dating altogether.

Docibilis' need to fit in with the established order at Gaeta extended further than marrying into the Anatolii clan and calling himself *hypatos*. In 890 he and his son John I confirmed a sale made by John son of count Anatolius, brother of the *hypatos* Constantine, to count Christopher, the founder of the dynasty whom I have termed the Christopherii.[42] This document is illuminating for two reasons. Not only does it illustrate Docibilis' desire to win the support of Christopher's grandchildren, but it also shows that Docibilis felt that it was his right to act as a member of the Anatolii family, confirming a land sale, which it was if he had married John's niece.

The frequent appearances of members of the Christopherii family as witnesses in the documents authorised by Docibilis and his family, as well as the transaction just cited, suggest that Docibilis needed, and actively sought, the co-operation and approval of men who had been associated with the rulers of Gaeta before his rise. His marriage into the Anatolii clan and other such associations gave his takeover a degree of respectability to compensate for the brutal fact

[41] *CDC* 14. [42] *CDC* 16; on the Christopherii, see below chapter 4, section (a) (i).

that he could afford to force the Gaetan lords into co-operation if he wished. Docibilis' observation of such political niceties was backed up by the threat of a Saracen attack against any who opposed him. At the same time he convinced the pope to hand over the patrimonies of Traetto and Fondi, on the understanding that he had broken off his relationship with the infidel. Docibilis was a talented and unscrupulous politician.

To become truly respectable in the eyes of others, Docibilis needed landed property of his own. His marriage to Bonus' daughter Matrona may have laid the foundations of that wealth and, as we shall see, Docibilis and his family were not slow to acquire land.[43] In his early years as ruler, however, Docibilis issued very few documents buying support by giving out land, indicating that he had not yet fully realised the potential value of the public lands he now controlled.

Docibilis' need for approval is particularly apparent in his relationship with another family associated with the old regime, the Kampuli. I have so named the clan after Kampulus the prefect (fl.890–949), and discuss their history below.[44] However, it is possible that the Kampuli clan should be regarded as continuing the line of the Anatolii. A series of clues suggests that Kampulus was the son of the *hypatos* Constantine's son Marinus. His father was one Marinus *comes*, possibly the title Marinus the *hypatos* assumed once deposed from power. If Kampulus was in fact the grandson of the *hypatos* Constantine he was, as far as heredity applied, an heir with a strong claim to the seat of power at Gaeta. Here we must be careful not to assume a right of inheritance which may not have existed. However, Constantine had associated his son Marinus, Kampulus' father, in power with himself by 866 and there is no reason to suppose that Marinus was not intended to take over as ruler when his father died.[45] Such attempts at establishing dynastic rule were common in the Tyrrhenian states throughout the period 900–1100, and we find sons being associated in power with varying degrees of success not only at Amalfi and Naples, but at Salerno and Capua too.

Kampulus, then, could claim some right to rule at Gaeta. His

[43] See below, chapter 3, section (a). [44] See below, chapter 4, section (a), (ii).

[45] Cassandro, 'Ducato', p. 85 is of the opinion that Marinus did rule for a short while, but bases his view on coinage which cannot now be safely attributed to either him or the later duke Marinus. For the latest analysis of the southern Italian coinage, see L. Travaini, *La Monetazione nell'Italia Normanna* (Rome, Istituto Storico per il Medioevo, forthcoming).

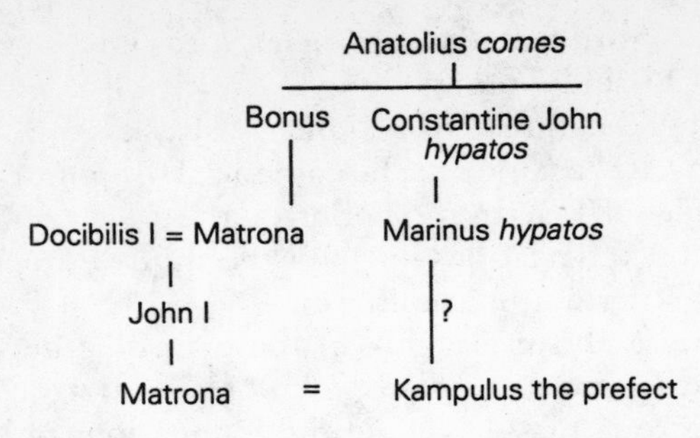

Figure 2.1 *Dynastic marriages of the early Docibilans*

father Marinus disappears from view after 866. We cannot be sure about the sequence of events due to lack of documentation, but, had Marinus acquiesced to, or survived, the takeover, we would surely have seen him in the witness list of Docibilis' first court alongside his uncle Bonus in 867. How was Kampulus persuaded to accept the new situation?

The first point to note is that he, like Docibilis in 867, used the title prefect. As we shall see in a later discussion, this title came to be associated at Gaeta with a very exclusive circle, consisting mostly of family members, surrounding the ruler. Given that Docibilis was apparently not from a noble background, he may perhaps have found the title already in use at Gaeta, and appropriated it for himself whilst allowing those who used it already to continue doing so.

The family of Docibilis was able to associate its fortunes more securely with the old ruling line when Kampulus accepted his granddaughter Matrona, daughter of John I, in marriage. We do not know when the wedding took place, but it had certainly occurred by 937, when John's other daughter Theotista referred to Kampulus as her relation[46]. It is significant that Matrona bore the name of her paternal grandmother, Docibilis' wife, and the parallel nature of these two unions between Anatolii and Docibilans cannot have been lost on contemporary observers (see Figure 2.1).

How did Kampulus benefit by his association with the Docibilans? The most important benefit was that he was one of the very few men seen to have received landed property from them, and the property itself was of a very special nature. The two

[46] *CDC* 40.

documents we have showing Kampulus as a property-owner feature him exchanging portions of mills with Docibilans, in 937 with his sister-in-law Theotista[47] and twelve years later with his brother-in-law Docibilis II.[48] Such property attracted high prices in the duchy, and rarely appears in documents other than those of the rulers.[49] In the latter transaction he states specifically that he received the shares from his father-in-law John I as a gift. Although not now visible in the documentation, it is likely that Kampulus received land as well as the mill shares which were, quite literally, status symbols.

The consequence of accepting the new regime at Gaeta, as Kampulus did by 890 when he witnessed a document authorised by Docibilis I and John,[50] was that he suffered no loss of his honourable position among Gaeta's elite. Although such calculations are always hazardous, the time between Docibilis I's and Kampulus' appearance suggests that in 867 Kampulus may have been too young to challenge the overthrow of his father and grandfather. In this situation his great uncle Bonus' candidate for power may have won acceptance over a child in the eyes of supporters of the Anatolii. This point gains added validity when we remember that this was the period of the greatest Saracen threat to the Tyrrhenian area, and that Docibilis earned the wrath of pope John VIII precisely because he had the resources either to bribe or to make an alliance with the invaders, and thereby protect Gaeta from the worst ravages of the later ninth century. It is worth noting that under Constantine in the middle of the same century the raiders had rampaged through the territory and sacked Formia,[51] the seat of the bishopric and the old centre of power across the bay from Gaeta. The Neapolitans were willing to lease the former *hypatos* land, but not, it seems, grant him armed protection. In accepting the new situation, Kampulus maintained for himself a position of prestige and wealth and, as we shall see, his family became some of the staunchest supporters of Docibilan rule.

What little documentary evidence we have indicates that, whatever the pope's attitude, local churchmen accepted, and may even have approved of, the takeover by a man who, ostensibly,

[47] *Ibid.* [48] *CDC* 50.

[49] This close control over milling, and some reasons for it, are discussed below, p. 72.

[50] *CDC* 15.

[51] For the Arabs' 846 campaign down the Via Appia, *CSB* 6. Formia is described as still *destructe* as late as 1058 (*CDC* 206).

could control the worst excesses of the Arab raiders. It would seem that as early as 831 the bishop of Formia had to take refuge in the castle at Gaeta. In that year bishop John had his will written there,[52] and after the sack of 846 the bishop used the formula 'bishop of the church of Formia and castle of Gaeta' as in an example of 855.[53] Did this reflect a desire on his part to maintain ties with the old seat and perhaps eventually to return there? If so, Docibilis must have seemed the ideal choice of protector, and in his very first documented appearance in 867 his court heard the plea of bishop Ramfus, a clear indication that the latter immediately submitted to the authority of the new ruler. The seat of the bishopric remained at Gaeta, where close ties were forged between the bishop and the Docibilans, as we shall see.

To conclude this discussion of the beginnings of Docibilan power, it is necessary to return to the question of the papal patrimonies of Fondi and Traetto, given to Docibilis I by pope John VIII, a transaction confirmed by John X to Docibilis' son John I in recognition of the latter's participation in the successful expedition to remove the Saracen settlement from the mouth of the Garigliano river in 915.[54]

Ostensibly, the original donation was intended to detach Docibilis from his Saracen alliance, but the alliance does not wholly explain the pope's action. The papacy had owned land in the Gaeta area for a long time. The *Liber Pontificalis* records the *massa Garigliana* as papal property as early as the fourth century,[55] and Fondi came into papal hands in the fifth.[56] Pope Zacharias (741–52) is recorded in an eleventh-century source as having acquired the *massa* called Formia.[57] Another source, the twelfth-century *Liber Censuum*, shows Zacharias leasing out the *fundus* Teianellum and the *fundus* Quadrantala, a field in Scauri and empty land outside the walls of the *castrum Caietani*, all property of the patrimony of Gaeta *iuris Romane ecclesiae*[58] (see Map 2.1). The overthrow in 866 of the *hypatos* Constantine may have represented a break with Neapolitan rule in papal eyes. For all that Docibilis' actions present a picture of

[52] *CDC* 4. [53] *CDC* 10.

[54] Further discussion in this study will focus on the lands rather than the 915 campaign itself, which has been the subject of several studies: Merores, *Gaeta* pp. 20ff; Cilento, 'Saraceni'; P. Fedele, 'La battaglia del Garigliano dell'anno 915 ed i monumenti che la ricordano', *ASRSP*, 22 (1899), 181–211; O. Vehse, 'Das Bundnis gegen die Sarazenen vom Jahre 915', *QFIAB*, 19 (1927), 181–204. [55] *LP*, 1, p. 173. [56] *Ibid.*, p. 221.

[57] Deusdedit, *Collectio Canonum*, ed. P. Martinucci, (Venice, 1869), p. 314.

[58] *LC*, 1, p. 353.

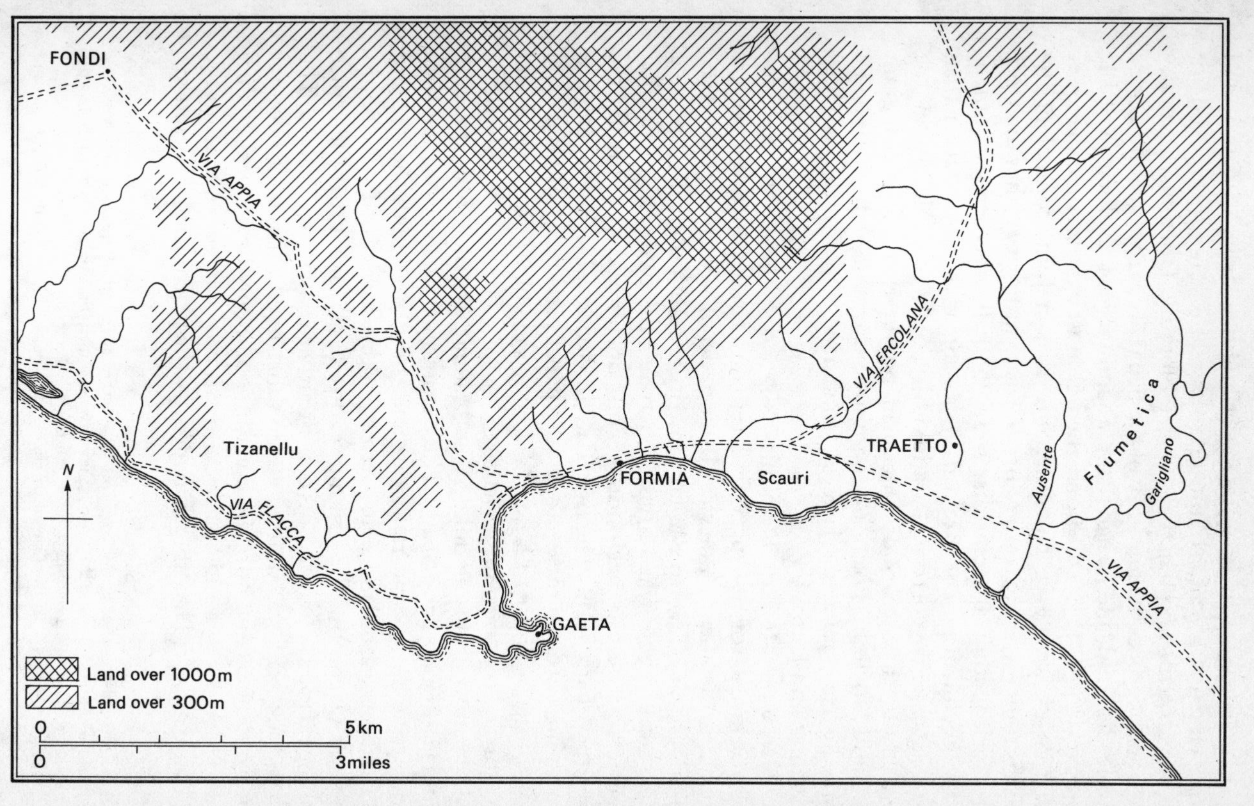

Map 2.1 *The papal patrimony in Gaeta*

a man trying to fit in with the established order at Gaeta, and marrying into a branch of the old ruling family, his position did not depend on Neapolitan patronage. Nor did Docibilis have any reason to respect the integrity of the papal properties around Gaeta; he needed land, and he had the Arab military force, albeit a volatile one, to acquire it. To the pope, then, it must have seemed the lesser of two evils to give Docibilis and his son John control of the patrimonies within a framework of papal authority rather than lose them altogether. It seems that Vera von Falkenhausen's argument that Docibilan power might have led to papal grants, rather than the reverse, is correct. Paradoxically, it was probably in the uncertain early years of Docibilan power that the papal grant secured Docibilis' position *vis-à-vis* the Gaetan nobility. He had a title, he had powerful relatives by marriage, and now he had papal backing and land.

The issue of why Docibilis chose to make his base in the promontory fortress of Gaeta remains to be discussed. If we examine the documentary evidence in detail, we can see that in the ninth century Traetto was far more important politically, and that historically there was a division between the two settlements that has not previously been noted. Four documents in particular are worthy of attention. The first, dated ?830, details the settlement of a dispute between the rector of the papal patrimony of Gaeta and John, the bishop of Gaeta.[59] The second shows the consul and rector leasing out some land in 841.[60] The other two show Mercurius, consul and duke of the Traettan patrimony also making land leases in 851 and 862.[61] The patrimonies of Traetto and Gaeta may have been territorially one and the same – both the 841 and 851 leases record land being let out in the district of Paniano, just outside Gaeta. But the striking feature of all four is that the centre of the rector's activity seems consistently to have been Traetto. The first document was written at the short-lived fortress of Leopolis nearby, the second bore the signatures of men who, since they then witnessed the 851 and 862 documents, might have come from the Traetto area.[62] The other two identify the patrimony as 'Traettan'.

[59] *CDC* 3; the text shows John as the bishop of Gaeta, but contemporary documents show that the episcopal see at this date was still centred at Formia. The document itself is a tenth-century copy, and the copyist may have amended 'Formia' to 'Gaeta' to reflect the state of affairs in his own day. [60] *CDC* 7. [61] *CDC* 9, *CDC* 11.

[62] *CDC* 7; the rector of the Gaetan patrimony's witnesses include counts Palumbus and Theophilact, both of whom appear in the documents issued by Marinus, rector of Traetto.

It would seem, then, that it was Traetto which was the original centre of what would become Gaetan territory, being the papacy's chosen centre.[63] Docibilis, however, owed his rise indirectly to Neapolitan backing, and made his base in the more easily defended Neapolitan fortress on the promontory. Subsequently, when he became rector of the papal patrimony, he brought it under the control of Gaeta rather than moving to Traetto. The memory of Traetto's formerly pre-eminent position would nevertheless cause problems to the Docibilan dynasty later on.

As we have already seen, one of the key factors in the successful establishment of Docibilan power at Gaeta was the fact that Naples did not intervene to prevent the overthrow of its nominees, Constantine and Marinus. This was probably due to Docibilis' care in maintaining an outwardly similar regime to that of his predecessors; no unilateral declaration of Gaetan independence was made and, as far as we can see, the documents of Docibilis' administration utilised the old form of dating by the reign of the Byzantine emperors, just as Neapolitan ones did. (This after a solitary attempt at dating 'in the time of lord Docibilis' in 867.[64]) The Gaetan nobility remained largely static, and Docibilis I seems to have made little attempt to raise his own men. This situation would change somewhat under his successors, as we shall see in chapter 4.

However, if the papal donations to Docibilis and his son John were made to counter the Neapolitan influence on the new rulers of Gaeta, they did not achieve their purpose, for the documentary evidence available to us suggests that intermittent contact continued with the Neapolitans (see Figure 2.2). John I's sister Eufimia seems to have married into the Neapolitan ducal family: her husband Stephen was a younger son of duke Gregory. John's son, Docibilis II certainly took a Neapolitan wife, Orania, daughter of duke Marinus I. She is mentioned as having given (or possibly bequeathed) to Docibilis land in Cimiterio and Liburia in the duchy of Naples in Docibilis' will of 954.[65] Coincidentally, Docibilis II was the first of his family to use the title *dux* alongside that of *hypatos*, which soon disappeared. He is first seen with the title in 933;[66] could this have coincided with his marriage to

[63] The choice of Traetto as the venue for the 'summit' meeting of 877 is indicative of its continued importance to the papacy. [64] *CDC* 13. [65] *CDC* 52.
[66] *CDC* 35.

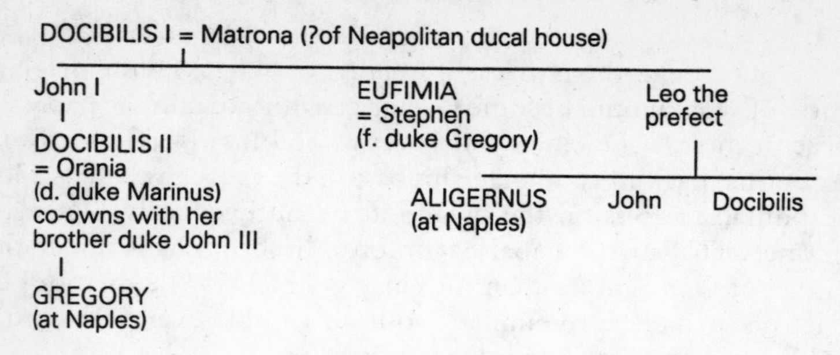

Figure 2.2 *Docibilans with Neapolitan links*

Orania? Docibilis may have used the opportunity of his marriage combined with the fact that he was the son of an imperial patrician to stake his claim to parity of status with his new father-in-law. The family of Docibilis I were now securely in control at Gaeta, and this may also have influenced Docibilis II to use the ducal title. The marriage links were accompanied by at least some exchange of property: Docibilis co-owned property with John III of Naples, Orania's brother, in the city of Naples itself, and one count Marinus of Naples is recorded as owning land at Mola in 954.[67]

Docibilis was not the only Gaetan property-owner in Naples. In 955, in a transaction recorded in both cities, Aligernus the Gaetan son of Leo the prefect leased an estate near the Garigliano to Angelus and Leo sons of Bonus for ten years.[68] It appears that Aligernus was resident in Naples, and the occurrence of the title prefect suggests he may have been a member of a cadet branch of the Docibilan house – John (fl.944–946) and Docibilis (fl.937–963) sons of Leo the prefect may have been his brothers – and may have been representing Gaetan interests at Naples. If this was the case and he was living there, he could also be the Aligernus son of Leo the monk who appears as a witness in seven Neapolitan documents between 952 and 964, many with links to the church of SS Sergius and Bacchus there.[69] Parallel name evidence suggests also that Gregory son of 'Decibilis' who appears as a witness to two Neapolitan transactions in 933 and 935[70] may have been the future duke of Gaeta and son of Docibilis II. His father's name occurs only on one other occasion in the entire Neapolitan document

[67] *CDC* 52. [68] *CDC* 53.
[69] *RN* 77, *RN* 80, *RN* 91, *RN* 124, *RN* 129, *RN* 130, *RN* 138. [70] *RN* 23, *RN* 285.

collection to 1050, suggesting that he was not Neapolitan. If Docibilis' family was linked more closely to Naples than has hitherto been thought, it would allow for younger members of that family, such as Gregory and Aligernus, to have spent a certain amount of time in the latter city.

The existence of parallel names in the Gaetan and Neapolitan document collections of the tenth century raises another question of relationships. I proposed above that Kampulus the prefect, who married Docibilis II's sister Matrona, was the son of the former ruler of Gaeta, Marinus. If Marinus and his father Constantine were of Neapolitan origin, it would be reasonable to suppose that (a) their family was of a relatively high status and (b) members of the same family might be visible in the documentation from that city. Although based on the most circumstantial evidence, it seems that this was in fact the case.

Particularly worthy of note are an early tenth century family headed by one John *miles* (see Figure 2.3). It seems that his children achieved a high degree of prominence as landowners. One son, Theofilact, may have been the count of Cuma; another, Sergius, used the honorific title *magnificus*; and a third, Anastasius, was a priest. It is the fourth son, Kampulus *miles*, who attracts our attention here, however. He appeared three times as a witness between 927 and 931,[71] and on a fourth occasion for his nephews and niece, the children of his brother Sergius, in 942.[72] He is also recorded as a landowner in the border area of Liburia between Naples and Capua, and defended his property successfully against his nephew John son of Theofilact in 937 and Peter, the abbot of SS Ianuarius and Agrippinus, in 942.[73] As we learn from a later document, the land was co-owned with a Lombard, Gari *exercitalis* son of Teudi, and Kampulus gave his portion to his son-in-law Stephen son of Leo.[74] The terms under which Liburian land was co-owned by Lombards and Neapolitans, the so-called *pars Langobardorum* and *pars militie*,[75] is the subject of controversy, and it is not my intention to reopen the debate here.[76] If we look a little more closely at the family, we can see on what their power was based.

[71] *RN* 14, *RN* 16, *RN* 18. [72] *RN* 42. [73] *RN* 36, *RN* 48.

[74] *RN* 102 (958).

[75] Translated: 'Lombard part', and 'military/soldiers' part'.

[76] Cassandro, 'Ducato', p. 129ff.; see also 'La Liburia e i suoi tertiatores', *ASPN*, n.s. 65 (1940).

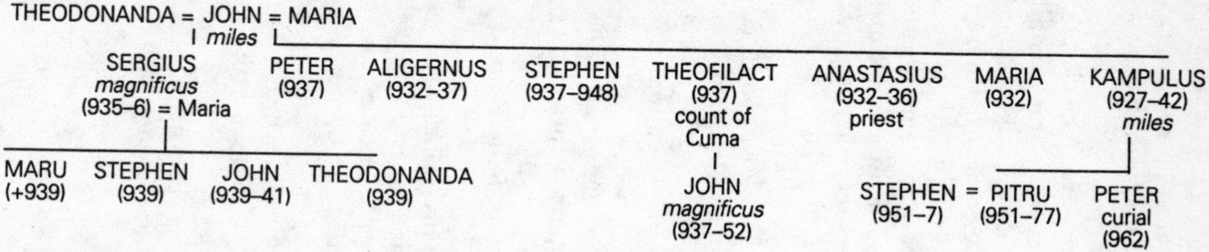

THEODONANDA = JOHN = MARIA
miles

SERGIUS *magnificus* (935–6) = Maria | PETER (937) | ALIGERNUS (932–37) | STEPHEN (937–948) | THEOFILACT (937) count of Cuma | ANASTASIUS (932–36) priest | MARIA (932) | KAMPULUS (927–42) *miles*

Children of Sergius: MARU (+939) | STEPHEN (939) | JOHN (939–41) | THEODONANDA (939)

Son of Theofilact: JOHN *magnificus* (937–52)

Children of Kampulus: STEPHEN (951–7) = PITRU (951–77) | PETER curial (962)

Maria and Anastasius the priest children of John *miles RN* 19. Theodonanda and Sergius wife and son of John *miles RN* 27.

Sergius *magnificus* f. John and Anastasius f. John and Maria, co-owners and landlords of land at St Ciprianum in 936, are probably stepbrothers, indicated by the stressing of Anastasius' mother's name *RN* 32.

The children of Sergius have an uncle named Theofilact *RN* 42.

Theofilact, Aligernus and Peter sons of John *miles RN* 35.

Dispute between John *magnificus* son of Theofilact count of Cuma and Kampulus *miles* son of John *miles*, Stephen son of John and Maria d. John may be a family dispute, *RN* 36. John owns house next door to Kampulus in *vico* Virginum, *RN* 45, and Kampulus' daughter Pitru buys another there, *RN* 99.

Figure 2.3 *The family of John miles*

The first point to note is that the family's history in the Neapolitan documents only seems to reach the late tenth century, with a concentration of family members and landowning towards the first half. This may be deceptive; in a group of people whose only identifying factor was that they were descendants of John *miles*, later generations may simply have dropped this titular identification and therefore 'blend' into the names recorded in our documentary sources. Members of the ducal family are remarkably anonymous in this way.

However, it is clear that this family wielded great power and influence economically. They owned land in the border area of Liburia, had a proprietary church of St Peter *ad Paternum* (S. Pietro a Paterno)[77] and also owned houses in the *vicus* Virginum in the city of Naples.[78] In 937 a group of family members allowed a certain Stephen to build a house on his garden next to theirs, suggesting that they had the power to prevent him if they so wished (not, in this case, that they owned the site; the document is clear that Stephen was building on **his** garden).[79] It is also quite striking that few other noble families can be identified alongside this one in the Neapolitan documentation, apart from the patchy evidence for the dukes of Naples themselves. We shall return to this point when considering the nobility.

Was the Neapolitan family of John *miles* another branch of that to which the *hypatoi* Constantine and Marinus and Kampulus the prefect of Gaeta belonged? Given their wealth, the fact that they had experience of dealing with non-Neapolitans through their Liburian property, and their obvious social standing from the point of view of titles, they seem likely candidates to provide a satellite ruler for Gaeta; the parallel occurrence of an unusual name, Kampulus, in the two lines certainly raises the possibility. Our most valuable clue though, is the fact that this family numbered a count of Cuma among its members; this links it inextricably with duke Sergius and his dynasty, of whom more presently, perhaps in a cadet branch. The possibility arises that the early Gaetan rulers were related to the Neapolitan ducal family in the same way.

What was the effect of this longstanding relationship? Although our evidence is again scarce, it appears that the friendly exchanges between Gaetan and Neapolitan rulers, particularly during the

[77] *RN* 113. On proprietary churches, see below, chapter 4, section (d).

[78] *RN* 99, *RN* 132, *RN* 141, *RN* 181.

[79] *RN* 35.

period of Docibilan ascendancy at Gaeta, led to a freedom of movement between their two states by their subjects. It is true that only one other Neapolitan, Theodore, appears in the Gaetan evidence in this early period, in 903,[80] but the main traffic is always likely to have been the other way. Several Gaetans were welcomed in the larger city in the eleventh century, and will be discussed later.[81]

Another consequence seems to have been the adoption by the Docibilans of Byzantine and Neapolitan honorific titles, adapted to suit the Gaetan political situation. The case of the titles of *hypatos* and prefect is illustrative of this, and, as we shall see, the latter title came to have a special role within the Gaetan ducal house.[82] Finally, if the Kampuli family at Gaeta were related to a powerful branch of the Neapolitan ducal dynasty it would help to explain their continued pre-eminence in Gaetan affairs long after other pre-Docibilan dynasties had failed. As we shall see, there is some fragmentary evidence that the Kampuli may have influenced the course of Gaetan politics even after the fall of the Docibilans, and we cannot rule out the possibility that they were acting with the support of their relatives in Naples. If we accept this hypothesis, then the image of Gaeta as a small but autonomous state in the tenth and early eleventh centuries must undergo serious revision.

Naples should perhaps, therefore, be seen as the source of many of the structures visible in Gaeta in our period. As early as the sixth century we see a duke in control there, though one who was still part of the wider Byzantine sphere in southern Italy at this time. The real founder of the duchy, however, in that he was able to establish himself and his successors on the ducal throne, was Sergius I (840–65), already count of the castle of Cuma and member of a well-established noble family. He came to power after a period of instability and ducal coups, being chosen by the Neapolitans to be their leader. Since there was by this time little of the Byzantine hierarchy left in which to operate, dukes were finding it difficult to legitimise their power. As at Gaeta, there were no formal means to set oneself apart from one's contemporaries, all of whom were equally fitted to rule. Docibilis had risen because he was able to use a mixture of diplomacy and outright threat – his relationship with the Arabs was a decisive factor. But the way Docibilis held onto power was to associate his son John in power with himself, thereby

[80] *CDC* 18. [81] See below, chapter 7. [82] See below, chapter 4, section (b).

ensuring that the latter grew up expecting, and being expected, to take over. Sergius, too, used this method, associating his son Gregory alongside him, and went a step further by installing members of his family in other prominent posts (see Figure 2.4). His son Athanasius became bishop of Naples in 849, his other son Stephen bishop of Sorrento.[83] We shall return to this issue of the ducal relationship with the church, but it is important to highlight that in Naples the closeness was such that at least two early dukes took on the episcopal role as well.

Like the Docibilans, Sergius' descendants were able to establish themselves as rulers over many generations, but we have very little documentation from which to piece together their activities. Of course, they did not need to overcome the feeling of illegitimacy that had surrounded the beginnings of Docibilan rule. I stated above that Naples may not have intervened in the changeover of power at Gaeta in 865/6 because little change was perceived. However, it may also be significant that Naples herself had a new duke, Sergius' son Gregory, at precisely this time. Since he was attempting to consolidate the notion that as successor to his father he had the right to rule, Gregory may not have had too much time to worry about Naples' former satellite.[84] Also, there is some evidence that the threat from the Saracens was growing at this time: in 868 the author of a document written in the city acted on behalf of his brother who had been captured by the infidel.[85]

Internal tension in the family in the ninth century partly caused by this threat is revealed by the coup of bishop Athanasius II, who blinded his brother Sergius II and took control of both the duchy and the episcopate in 878. He ruled for twenty years, but acted just as any other secular Tyrrhenian ruler at this time. It is possible that Athanasius was acting under papal instruction, or at least with John's tacit approval, when he blinded Sergius and sent him to Rome.[86] Sergius had already blinded their uncle, bishop Athanasius I, who had protested at his pro-Saracen actions.[87] The rule of a bishop at Naples, however, did nothing to lessen the duchy's involvement with the Saracens who were perennially present in the Tyrrhenian area. In 879 pope John, frustrated that Athanasius

[83] Cassandro, 'Ducato', p. 69.
[84] He may have been more concerned about Amalfi than Gaeta: see below, p. 50.
[85] Capasso, *Monumenta*, I, p. 266, document 4.
[86] Cassandro, 'Ducato', p. 96.
[87] Kreutz, *Before the Normans*, p. 84.

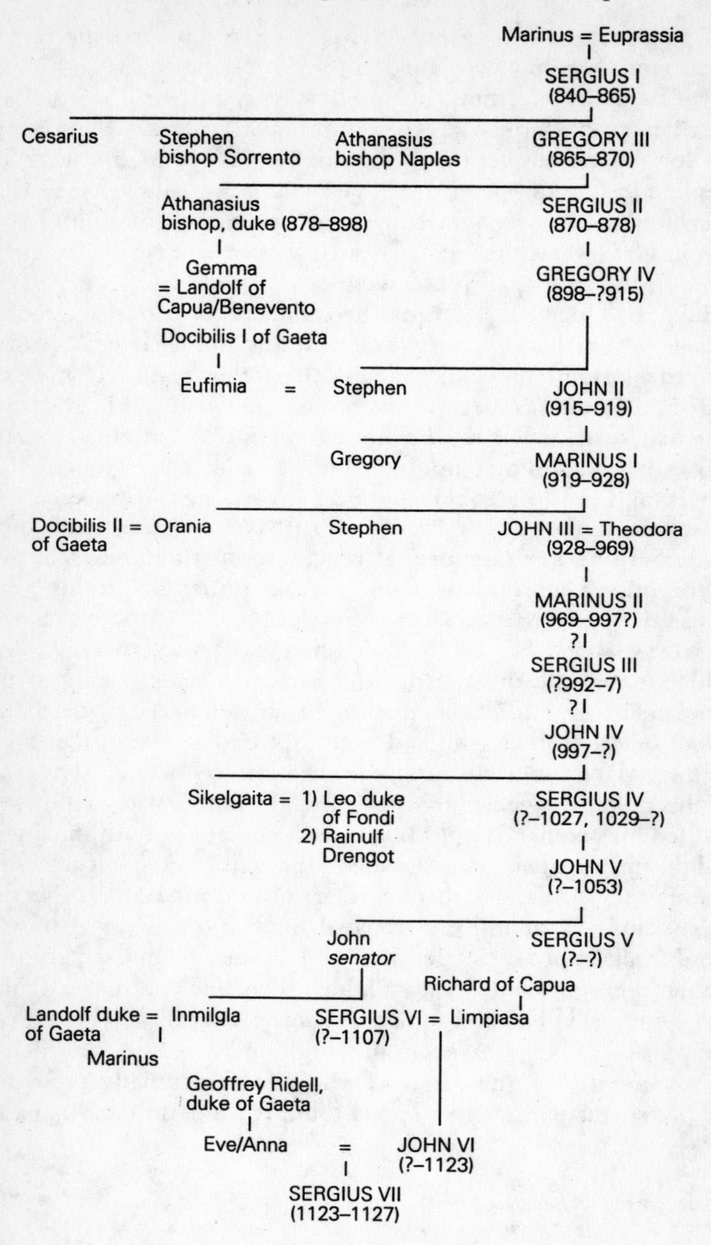

Figure 2.4 *The Neapolitan ducal family*

was unwilling to detach himself from the entanglement, excommunicated him.[88]

Although we can build up a fairly complete list of the dukes of Naples throughout the reigns of Sergius' descendants, there is very little evidence up to 1050 of land transactions within the family, such as those which occurred frequently at Gaeta. This perhaps points to a level of family unity among the various members which did not need constant reinforcement by means of small land exchanges, or may reflect a family who did not produce quite so many members per generation as the highly fertile Docibilans did. Whatever the case (and the ninth-century coup suggests that all was not harmonious within the family), all of the early Neapolitan ducal documents point to a concern to establish external contacts and support. The majority which survive chronicle the dukes' relationship with the church.[89]

The dukes of Naples seem to have been particularly keen to establish marital relationships with other dynasties in the area (although, conversely, other dynasties may have seen the Neapolitan ducal family as the most important in the area with whom to establish marital links). The marriages between Neapolitans and members of the Docibilan family at Gaeta have already been noted; the always uncertain relationship between the Neapolitans and their Lombard neighbours at Capua was occasionally strengthened with dynastic marriages. For example, bishop-duke Athanasius' daughter Gemma was married to Landolf, son of Atenolf of Capua-Benevento in 897.[90] In the middle of the tenth century, the *senatrix* of Rome, Theodora, cousin of Alberic II, became the wife of duke John III.[91] The issue of relations with Rome is an important one for all the Tyrrhenian duchies, and will be discussed separately, but the marriage is just one indication that the duchies were by no means insular in their outlook.

This statement is especially true of the third duchy under examination, Amalfi. The city is held to have detached itself from Neapolitan overlordship in 838, when it was briefly taken over by the Lombard prince of Benevento, Sicard. When Sicard was assassinated the following year, the Amalfitans drifted into self-

[88] *MGH, Epp.* VII, p. 246; the Campanian bishops were informed of Athanasius' excommunication.

[89] See below, chapter 3, section (c), for a discussion of church patronage.

[90] Cassandro, 'Ducato', p. 120.

[91] She is documented in a land transaction of the duke in 951, *RN* 75.

government.[92] This would not be surprising, given that the Neapolitans were at that time in the middle of a struggle to decide who their duke should be. The events of 839 are probably not as cataclysmic as they have been portrayed, nor was there a specific 'moment' when Amalfi became detached. The eastern border of Amalfi's territory was never really firmly defined, and exchange across it with the Salernitans, as we shall see from later evidence, was a permanent feature of life here. After a period of rule by a shadowy figure named Peter, one Marinus became prefect of the city, and handed on power to his son Sergius.[93] A prefect named Mauro is documented in 860,[94] but when he was assassinated in 866, Sergius son of duke Gregory III of Naples became prefect of Amalfi. His rule lasted just thirteen days,[95] perhaps reflecting his father's inability to devote resources to maintaining him in power here when Gregory himself was newly in power at home. The fact that Naples intervened at all, however, suggests how concerned its dukes were at Amalfi's apparent drift into the Lombard sphere of influence in the ninth century.

After a brief period of uncertainty in 866, in which several families were involved in the fight for power, the prefect Marinus returned to rule, and associated his son Pulcharus. Marinus is best known for his intervention in 870 in the political life of Naples, when he provided the ships to rescue bishop Athanasius I from the prison into which duke Sergius II had thrown him. He also seems to have been on good terms with his Lombard neighbour, prince Guaiferius I of Salerno, to whose daughter he married his son Pulcharus.[96] The latter features more prominently in the sources as the third in the trio of Tyrrhenian rulers who defied pope John VIII in 879. Like Gaeta and Naples, Amalfi was not inclined to war with the Saracen invaders of the Tyrrhenian in the 870s, and although it, like the other cities, signed the pact of Traetto arranged by the pope in 877, its observance of the treaty was at best half-hearted. When Naples and Amalfi did join in a concerted attack on the Arabs of the Garigliano in 903, they were beaten off by the invaders and the Gaetans. There is no mention of Amalfitan participation in the 915 campaign, and Kreutz links this with the fact that Amalfi's development as a trading power was partly influenced by the rise of the Fatimids in North Africa in 909.[97] The Amalfitans would,

[92] Kreutz, *Before the Normans*, p. 23. [93] Schwarz, *Amalfi nel Medioevo*, p. 48.
[94] *CDA* 584. [95] Schwarz, *Amalfi nel Medioevo*, p. 53.
[96] Taviani-Carozzi, *Principauté*, p. 807. [97] *Before the Normans*, p. 83.

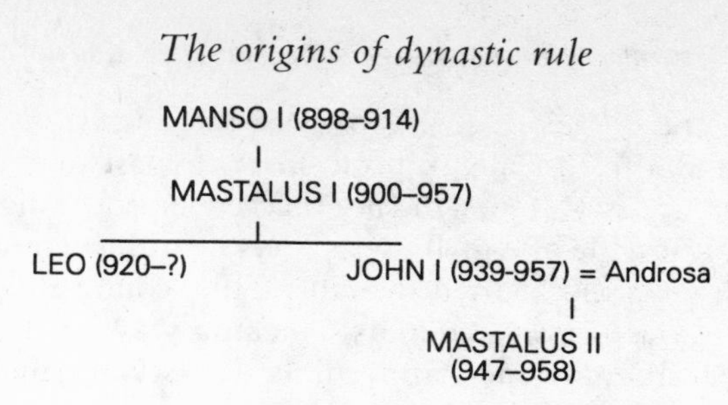

Figure 2.5 *The family of Manso the prefect of Amalfi*

therefore, be reluctant to upset relations with their Muslim partners.

Pulcharus was succeeded by a relative named Stephen, but the family of Marinus fell from power in 898. From the end of the ninth century for about sixty years control was exerted by the dynasty of prefect Manso (Figure 2.5). The family of Marinus had tried to make the position of leader at Amalfi hereditary; Manso's clan succeeded in doing so. They, just like Docibilis I at Gaeta, did not automatically assume a ducal title on coming to power. Up until 957, the rulers of Amalfi styled themselves prefects, and Manso associated his son Mastalus in 900.[98] Mastalus succeeded in his own right in 914 when his father retired to the monastery of St Benedict in Scala.[99] Mastalus associated two sons in turn with himself in power. In 920 he and his son Leo appear in a dating clause as *gloriosi iudicibus*, ('glorious judges'),[100] and two years later as imperial patrician and *protospatharius* respectively.[101] After a period of sole rule,[102] Mastalus associated his second son John as co-ruler, and the pair are documented until at least 947.[103] When John retired from power, his son Mastalus II became his grandfather's associate;[104] they appear together in a dating clause of 952.[105] Mastalus II was probably still a minor when he succeeded – the *Chronicon Amalfitanum* says he ruled with his mother Androsa.[106] One significant change occurred at this time: Mastalus II was the first of his family to be called 'glorious

[98] They are recorded as co-rulers in a document of 907, *CDA* 1.

[99] Schwarz, *Amalfi nel Medioevo*, p. 69. Manso is recorded in 922 as having donated a mill to the monastery; this may have coincided with his entry to the community, *CDA* 2.

[100] *CDA* 585; on this role, see below, chapter 3, section (e).

[101] *CDA* 2.

[102] Dating clause of 931 has just Mastalus in power, *CDA* 3.

[103] John first appears in 939, *CDA* 4 and a series of documents thereafter; his last appearance is in 947, *CDA* 6.

[104] Schwarz, *Amalfi nel Medioevo*, p. 72.

[105] *CDA* 587.

[106] Schwarz, *Amalfi nel Medioevo*, p. 72.

duke'.[107] The conscious changeover to the ducal title may have been prompted by the weak position of the last member of the early ruling dynasty. If so, it did not succeed in protecting him. The shifting political life of Amalfi, with several families competing for power, ensured the swift downfall of the young duke and his mother. He was assassinated in 958, making way for the accession of the third, and most successful, ruling dynasty of Amalfi (Figure 2.6).

The name of the head of this family, Sergius, hints at Neapolitan involvement in the takeover, even if we have no direct proof of the Neapolitans becoming entangled in the local politics of Amalfi at this time. The *Chronicon Amalfitanum* identifies the new ruler as a member of an Amalfitan comital family, but this does not necessarily rule out Neapolitan influence. The documented activity of a family descended from one John, 'comes Neapolitanus', in Amalfi during this period attests to close links.[108] Cassandro suggests that the ducal families of Amalfi and Naples had marital ties during this period as well,[109] but does not specify any examples. Although such ties are likely, I have been unable to find any conclusive proof of their existence.

Sergius and his descendants retained the ducal title, thereby establishing themselves on an equal footing with their Neapolitan and Gaetan neighbours. That the rulers of both the smaller states became dukes within twenty-five years of each other in the middle of the tenth century has not attracted much attention from historians,[110] but must have completed the process of detachment that each had undergone since the ninth century.

Sergius ruled with his son Manso II from the start of his reign, and the latter succeeded him as sole ruler in 966.[111] Manso's rule was perhaps the most eventful of the dynasty's so far, and can be characterised by its intervention in the affairs of Salerno. When prince Guaimarius II died, Amalfi opposed Naples and Capua-Benevento in its support of Gisolf as his successor.[112] But in 973, when it seemed that Gisolf was going to die without an heir,

[107] *CP* 31 (957). [108] See below, chapter 4, section (b), and Figure 4.6.

[109] 'Ducato', p. 223.

[110] Brown, *Gentlemen and Officers*, p. 56, sees the delay in claiming the ducal title as evidence that the rulers of Amalfi and Gaeta still respected the official *cursus honorum*, and did not wish to appropriate a title that rightfully belonged to the military governor in Naples.

[111] Dating clauses of that year show this succession; Sergius and Manso: *CP* 59, *CP* 60, Manso alone: *CP* 29. [112] Kreutz, *Before the Normans*, p. 100.

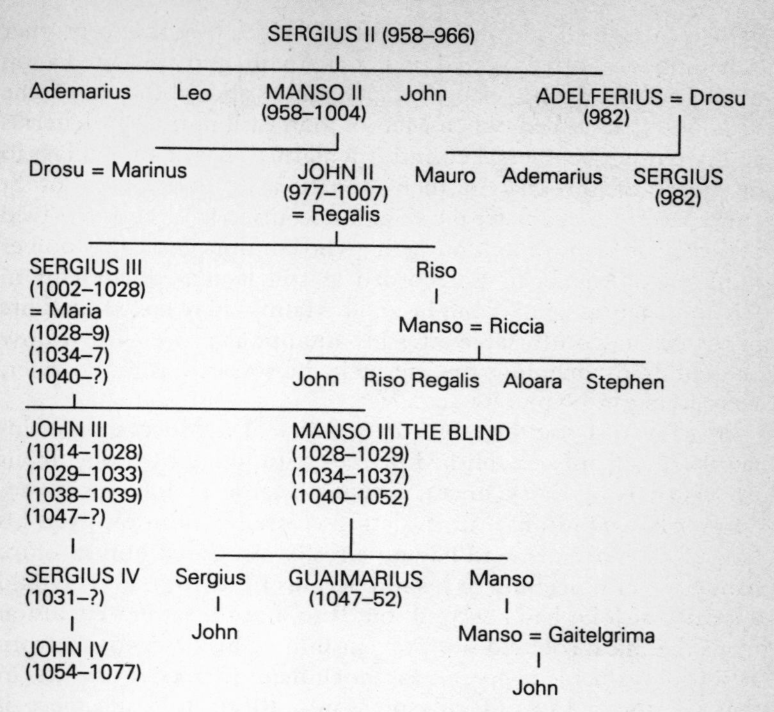

Figure 2.6 *The family of Duke Sergius of Amalfi*

Amalfi joined with Landolf of Conza and the Neapolitan duke in deposing him.

This episode was brief, and Gisolf was restored with the help of Pandolf of Capua, whose son he made his heir. Manso did not give up his aim to rule the principate, however. Having associated his son John in 977,[113] Manso did not have long to wait for his chance. When Pandolf died in 981, he was able to take and rule Salerno himself. His rule lasted two years,[114] and he was deposed in a coup in 983. Although his son John was taken hostage in this coup and not released until 990,[115] he continues to appear in Amalfitan dating clauses alongside his father.[116] His Lombard wife Regalis makes no reference to her husband's imprisonment in a document

[113] The two are documented as co-rulers in 979, *CP* 21.

[114] Recorded in contemporary Salernitan dating clauses, *CodCav* II/343 and *CodCav* II/344, *RNAM* 192 (all 982).

[115] Schwarz, *Amalfi nel Medioevo*, pp. 81–2.

[116] *CDA* 11 (984).

of 986, in which she made a gift of land.[117] Manso's brother Adelferius also briefly seized power at Amalfi and associated a son in 985.[118] A dating clause of 988 gives an indication of the weakness that ensued, when Manso, John (still unfree), Adelferius and two other brothers, Leo and Ademarius, all state themselves to be rulers of the city in their donation to the church of St Laurence.[119] A year later the situation seems to have been resolved in favour of Manso and John again, who continued to enjoy power until 1002. Adelferius is recorded as still issuing documents in Amalfi as late as 998,[120] but he and his family may have found life in the city uncomfortable after his attempt at power; his widow and children, including the son he had associated as his co-ruler, were living in Naples by 1012.[121]

In 1004/5 Manso died, but the security of the succession of his family was firmly established in 1002/3 to judge by a document preserved by Matteo Camera, showing 'Manso 44, John his son 27, Sergius his grandson 2' in its dating clause.[122] John outlived his father by two years, and having already associated him in office handed over peacefully to his son Sergius III in 1007.[123] It would appear that John had a second son, Riso, but the latter's exclusion from the ducal role did not prevent him or his descendants from acquiring valuable property, as a document of ?1006 illustrates. In that year the widow of Riso's son Manso, Riccia, sold off a piece of land in the *plano Amalfi* for an enormous sum, 450 *solidi*.[124] The buyer was her nephew John, grandson of a Salernitan count and judge. There must have been some intermarriage between the ducal house and the Salernitan nobility which is now not visible. Close ties with another Lombard state are suggested by the marriage of John's elder son and successor Sergius to a sister of Pandolf IV of Capua, Maria. Sergius nominated his son John as co-ruler in 1014.[125]

[117] *CodCav* II/386; however, since she seems to have been acting according to the customs of her homeland, her father substituted for John in giving her permission to make the transaction. [118] *CDA* 12. [119] *CDA* 588. [120] *CP* 80.

[121] *RN* 346; the memory of their previous position had not escaped Adelferius' widow or children, however. She appears as Drosu 'duchess' and her son as Sergius 'duke'.

[122] Cited in Schwarz, *Amalfi nel Medioevo*, p. 88 note 194. The document does not survive in any other publications.

[123] A document published from Cava, *CodCav* IV/586, is perhaps wrongly dated 1006 in this context, as it has 'Sergius and Manso' in its dating clause. Unless Sergius had by this time already produced the son he would later associate in power, it is difficult to see who Manso was. I would suggest that the document should be redated later or rejected as spurious. [124] *CP* 82. [125] Schwarz, *Amalfi nel Medioevo*, p. 89.

The next decades were traumatic ones for the ruling family. When Pandolf expanded his power as far as Naples, Sergius and John fled to Constantinople in 1028, leaving Maria and another son, Manso, in charge. John III returned in 1029 and captured his mother and brother, appearing in dating clauses as sole ruler in that year;[126] Sergius remained in exile.

John associated his son Sergius 1031, but was unable to maintain his position, and by 1034 Maria and Manso were back in power. By this time, however, the Capuans had been dislodged from Naples, and John and Sergius were able to find refuge there. In 1038 Guaimarius IV of Salerno became prince of Capua; without external support, Maria and Manso were once again ousted by John and Sergius. This time Manso was blinded, but Maria remained formally in power and in dating clauses of 1038 and 1039.[127] In the latter year the rapid spread of Guaimarius' power led to a third self-imposed exile for John, this time taking his son to Constantinople. At first Guaimarius ruled Amalfi directly, then he used the blind Manso as his puppet. The latter even named a son after his patron, whom he associated in power with himself in 1047. This may have been the final straw for some Amalfitans, although it was five years before a rebellion ousted Guaimarius and his protégé and finally reinstated John and his son Sergius.[128] These two would rule until the coming of the Normans in the 1070s.

Perhaps the most striking feature of the histories of the rulers of these three ducal families is the way they intersected each other repeatedly. None existed in isolation, whether their power was secure or less stable.

They all saw intermarriage as an important way of gaining mutual support, and it is likely that more unions of this type took place than are now visible from the surviving evidence. Without any other formal structures of power, the extension of the family and its influence was paramount. The success of the Docibilans, newcomers at Gaeta, was due as much to their establishment of advantageous marriages and numerous children as to any other factor. One might speculate that the failure of the early ruling families at Amalfi was caused by their lack of numbers, although this must remain speculation. Even duke Sergius I of Naples, who only had three known sons, used them efficiently to root his family in power.

[126] *CP* 40. [127] *CP* 37, 36.

[128] The last document dated by Manso and Guaimarius his son was dated 1052, *CDA* 62.

Also remarkable is the coincidence of the periods of instability for each duchy. When Naples was racked by in-fighting for its duchy in the 830s, Amalfi became detached; in 866 new dynasties rose in both Amalfi and Gaeta just as Naples' first duke, Sergius, died. The coincidence of the two smaller states becoming titular duchies in the middle years of the tenth century has already been noted, and the weakness of all three in the face of Lombard aggression, be it from Capua or Salerno, is graphically illustrated in their histories.

Another feature is their rulers' continued use of Byzantine titles. Byzantium repeatedly conferred honours on the Tyrrhenians as a tenuous hold on them, but these were probably more valuable to the dukes as an extra legitimisation of their power, implying Byzantine back-up for their rule over their compatriots, than as an obligation to loyalty. The Byzantine connection proved of limited use to the dukes of Amalfi in the mid-eleventh century, when Constantinople provided a refuge for Sergius and John, but could not actively participate in John's restoration.

We shall return to the issue of the states' relationships with their erstwhile sovereign, and the titles they used, in the next chapter, but one should perhaps see the latter as a purely honorific phenomenon, with little practical effect on the life of the Tyrrhenian cities. The more solid foundations of ducal power form the subject of the next chapter.

Chapter 3

THE FOUNDATIONS OF DUCAL POWER IN THE TENTH CENTURY

Once the families discussed in the previous chapter had established their hold on their respective seats of power, the exercise of authority became their goal. In this chapter, the bases on which ducal power was founded will be examined. There was a high degree of common ground between the three duchies, as might be expected from their common background of ruling traditions, but each modified these traditions in the tenth century to suit the needs of autonomous cities. Chief among the priorities of a family such as the Docibilans was the acquisition of control over the lands of Gaeta, as land formed the mainstay of any ruler's power. In all three duchies we see land termed public and private under the control of the rulers, and the origins of the distinction need clarification. At its most basic, land gave a ruler the resource with which to pay for military support. But other factors were present as well, even as early as the tenth century. Rulers associated their heirs in power with themselves, and thereby kept their dynasties in power. There was a notion of the duke as the ultimate source of justice; he derived this status, in part, from the authority that the support of the Church conferred upon him. Yet we need to determine how much support these petty rulers received, and how they cultivated the clergy. In raising, and responding to, these questions, we shall begin to see the development of political structures which were to mature in the eleventh century, and change still more in the twelfth.

(a) LAND: PUBLIC AND PRIVATE

The papal cession of the patrimonies of Fondi and Traetto may not have brought Docibilis I his initial rise to power at Gaeta, but it certainly elevated him to a position of prestige which the assumption of titles such as prefect and *hypatos* did not automatically guarantee. What limited evidence survives suggests that

Docibilis used his wealth to acquire some land of his own to control alongside the papal properties. His will of 906[1] reveals some of the property he acquired during his period of rule. We know from the 906 text that he built the church of St Michael at Planciano and owned land surrounding it on what is today Monte Orlando above the city of Gaeta. Docibilis also states that his family had bought land at St Laurence (near Mola) and near to St Theodore's church at Gaeta. Later in the will, among the clauses freeing slaves and endowing them with small plots of land, we learn that Docibilis 'both bought and inherited' land at Paniano (Pagnano) and owned more at Pertusillum. He also clearly owned a substantial amount of property in the city of Gaeta itself; each of his seven recorded children received at least one house, two daughters received the church of St Irene in the city, and his son Leo was to have the care of a further two churches, St Angelus and St Silvinian. A measure of Docibilis' liquid wealth can perhaps be gained from his statement that he had spent 120 gold *solidi* on the latter church; in comparison a house in the city with a small plot of land cost just 8 *solidi* eight years later.[2] Docibilis' will did not list all his property. In a specific clause, he stated that all lands and houses outside the city were to be divided equally among his children.

We are fortunate to have a document of 924 in which such a division took place.[3] It is clear that the original division envisaged by Docibilis had occurred earlier, for this version took the form of a settlement of a dispute between Docibilis' son, Leo the prefect, and the other six children or their heirs. Although not all of the place names are identifiable, the amounts of land and the extent over which they spread present a complete contrast to the limited holdings mentioned in the will. The specific assertion in the document that the lands belonged to Docibilis and Matrona his wife obviates any confusion with the lands he held from the pope.

A survey of these lands reveals that, as well as consolidating his holdings in the central region around Gaeta, Docibilis had broadened his horizons and owned property in the fertile eastern plains as well (see Map 3.1). In the central area we learn that he owned land at Saraquiano above Mola and in Azzano (Arzano). In the east his heirs divided among themselves over a hundred *modia*[4] of arable land in Cupano. At least 112 *modia* in unlocatable places

[1] *CDC* 19. [2] *CDC* 22. [3] *CDC* 31.

[4] A. Lizier, *L'Economia rurale dell'Età prenormanna nell'Italia meridionale* (Palermo, 1907), p. 180, equates one *modium* with about 360 square metres.

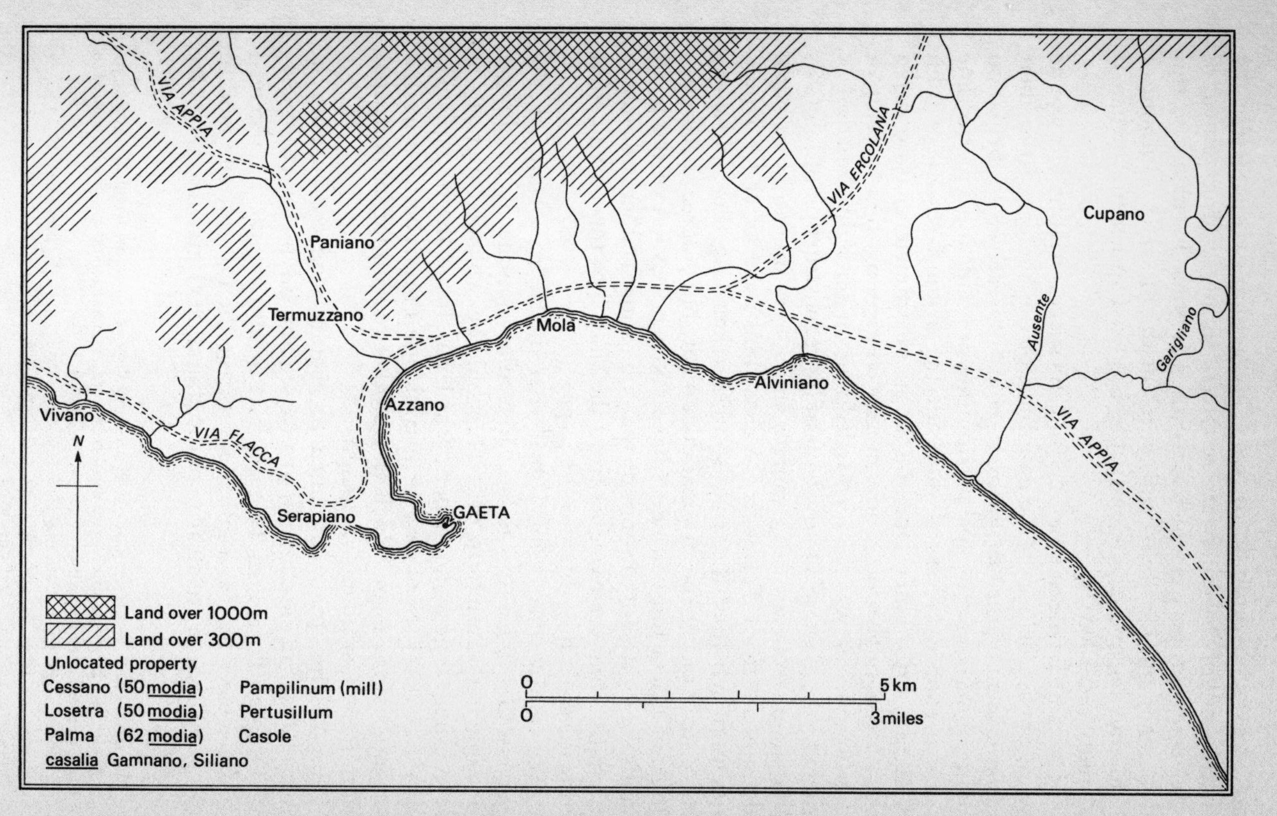

Map 3.1 *Property of Docibilis I*

are recorded in addition to this. The division may represent the sharing-out of Docibilis' entire estate, or simply an arrangement of a select few properties which had caused disputes. In either case, this document and Docibilis' will represent the minimum amount of land that he owned; he probably acquired much more than is actually recorded.[5]

The same is true of Docibilis' son and successor, John I. It was he who, having helped in the expulsion of the Saracens from their encampment on the Garigliano river in 915, received confirmation of his rights over the papal patrimonies of Fondi and Traetto. The confirmation is preserved alongside the original cession of John VIII to John's father Docibilis in an incomplete citation dated 1014.[6] Was pope John X now merely confirming the rectorship of papal lands, or was he acknowledging an outright donation of them to the Gaetan? On the basis of his reconstruction of John X's document from the 1014 sources and a 1347 inventory of papal documents from Terracina,[7] Vehse thinks the latter.[8] I would question whether the two sources taken together allow his reconstruction of the original document, but I agree that in 915 John of Gaeta must in effect have taken possession of the papal lands. Delogu[9] is of the opinion that John and his father had already been diverting the revenues from the lands into their own coffers instead of sending them to the pope.

We know that John I had shared the rectorship of the patrimonies with his father, but after 890 he is no longer documented as using the title. This could be explained after 915, at least if he was now the owner of the lands. It can also be explained by the fact that after that date he could use a much better title, that of imperial patrician, which was another reward for his participation in the Garigliano campaign.

For all this, John continued to acquire land by purchase in relatively small amounts. In 919 we see him buying up two pieces in Dragoncello (near Torre Argento) and in 921 he received another piece here as a gift.[10] John gave the Dragoncello land to Gregory his son, archdeacon of the church of Gaeta, in 923/4.[11] By

[5] We should note, however, that not all property showed up on medieval wills; the share of heirs who had to inherit by law would not need to be written down, being assumed to pass to them automatically.

[6] *CDC* 130.

[7] Biblioteca Apostolica Vaticana, *Cod. Vat. Lat.* 12634.

[8] 'Bundnis'.

[9] 'Ducato', p. 196.

[10] *CDC* 25, *CDC* 26, *CDC* 27.

[11] Biblioteca Apostolica Vaticana, *Cod. Vat. Barb. Lat.*, 3216, f.203v.

933 he owned (and may even have built) the mill called Minore; in that year he gave 4 months' and 20 days' use of it to his daughter Bona.[12]

In Gaeta, although a fortified stronghold did exist on the hilltop, the Docibilans at least seem to have preferred to live in purpose-built dwellings nearer the harbour. In his will of 906, Docibilis I is recorded as having built at least eleven houses;[13] by the tenth century a ducal palace had been constructed. It is described in the will of John's son Docibilis II, dated 954,[14] but had probably been built by John I. The remains of the palace are modest today, but from the will we learn that the complex stretched down to the sea, had baths, houses, separate kitchens, aviaries and courtyards, and must therefore have taken up quite a considerable area of the lower part of the city. John's awareness of his power is reflected in several structures in Gaeta incorporating inscriptions proclaiming the patrician's new building work in the city (see Figure 3.1). These suggest that John expected others to be able to read them and be impressed by his work, reinforcing the image of Gaeta as a state where literacy was the norm.[15]

As we shall see later, the Docibilans mirrored other Tyrrhenian rulers when they sited the palace on the seashore, for this seems to have been the most prestigious area to have the ruler's residence. The dukes of Amalfi certainly controlled the shore area of that city, and the Neapolitan evidence suggests that the same was true of the dukes there.

The richness of the ducal accommodation contrasts with that of their subjects. In 980, we learn, servants of dukes Marinus and John III lived in a wooden house measuring seven metres by six.[16]

Although we have very few documents authorised by John I himself, more evidence for his acquisitions can be found in later charters. For example, we know from a document of 944 that John owned at least 30 *modia* of corn-growing land at Paternum, near Suio,[17] and among the bequests of his son Docibilis II in 954 we find an estate called Aralectum (near Castellonorato) which John had owned, and land at Ventosa which he had bought.[18] A much later document, from 983, reveals him to have owned the estate

[12] *CDC* 34. [13] *CDC* 19. [14] *CDC* 52.

[15] On literacy in southern Italy generally, Skinner, 'Women, literacy and invisibility'; see also chapter 1, section (d).

[16] *CDC* 75; eleventh-century documents from Traetto also record similar-sized house plots: *CDC* 183, *CDC* 214. [17] *CDC* 44. [18] *CDC* 52.

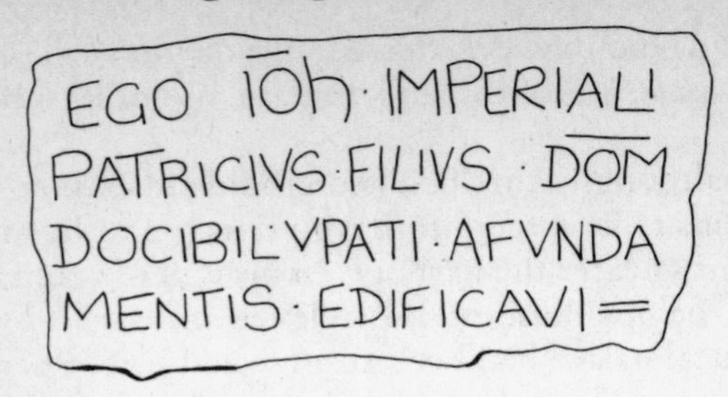

(a) *Piazza Comestibili, Gaeta*
inscription *circa* 1 metre by .7 metre, in fabric of tower; drawing: PES.

(b) *Via Docibile, Gaeta*
inscription *circa* .8 metre by .4 metre, in city wall

Figure 3.1 *Inscriptions of John I*

called Cucilli (near the Ausente river) and to have given it to his daughter Sikelgaita.[19]

These transactions and John's ownership of land at Alviniano (near Torre Argento) as a result of the division of 924 illustrate the statement above that the papal patrimonies, in this case that of Traetto, did not encompass the entire Traetto area, but were made

[19] *CDC* 83.

up of individual estates and pieces of land interspersed with privately owned properties (see Map 3.2 for the distribution of John's lands). Here perhaps we have the origin of the distinction, which is documented from the reign of Docibilis II, between public and private land.

In 1907 Auguste Lizier, working from the Gaetan document collection among others, defined the *publicum* or public land in southern Italy as that belonging to the state, regardless of who was ruling at any one time. It could be increased, he said, by confiscation or by the fisc inheriting from those who died without heirs, and was constantly being depleted due to grants to public officials, the relatives of rulers and the church.[20] It is difficult to improve on the acuteness of his definition, which could apply to Gaeta alone,[21] but some modification and comment is appropriate. Parts of Gaeta's *publicum*, for instance, may have been assembled as a result of its ninth-century history. In 890 Docibilis I and John I claimed land, whose original owners had been captured by the Arabs, and sold it off for cash.[22]

What public land existed in the area prior to 867 is unclear. The castle of Gaeta itself was under Neapolitan control and probably considered public. Similarly, the lands leased to the *hypatoi* Constantine and Marinus may have been public – its revenues were certainly delivered to Naples. But there must have been very little public land for the *hypatoi* to draw upon; this may in part explain their swift overthrow in 866/7.

It is arguable that most of what later Docibilans termed public land consisted of the patrimonial lands granted by the pope to Docibilis I and John I, and held initially by them only as rectors, whilst land without the description could have been obtained by way of private transactions. As we have already seen, both men were considerable landowners in their own right. It is difficult to prove this theory, since no descriptions of public land survive from the reigns of the first two Docibilans. However, a link can at least be established between papal and public land in a document of 950, in which Docibilis II gave public land in Marana, Maranula, Soriana and Quadrantula in Flumetica to his son Marinus.[23] The latter property, as we saw earlier, had been part of the papal

[20] *L'Economia*, p. 25.
[21] Lizier's statement was based also on evidence from Salerno and Naples.
[22] *CDC* 15. [23] *CDC* 50.

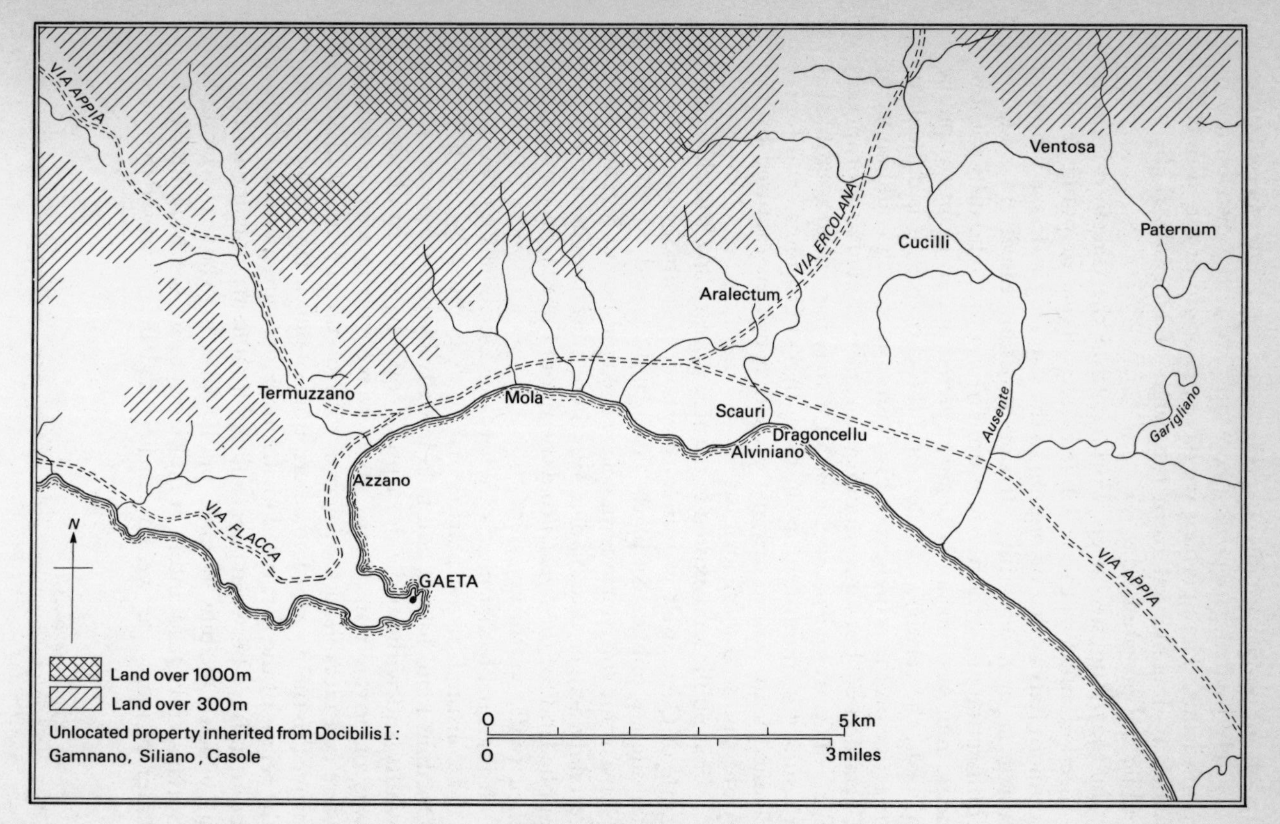
VIA APPIA
Ventosa
Paternum
Cucilli
VIA ERCOLANA
Aralectum
Garigliano
Ausente
Termuzzano
Mola
Scauri
Dragoncellu
Alviniano
Azzano
VIA FLACCA
GAETA
VIA APPIA
N
Land over 1000m
Land over 300m
Unlocated property inherited from Docibilis I :
Gamnano, Siliano, Casole
0
5km
0
3miles

Map 3.2 *Property of John I*

patrimony of Gaeta in the eighth century, making it more likely that other 'public' properties had papal origins.

It can be ascertained that Docibilis II felt at liberty to grant out the lands described as public. He gave some in Costranu (in Flumetica) to his son Gregory in 939,[24] 30 *modia* in Paternum near Suio to his cousins John and Docibilis in 944,[25] and more to Gregory in Timozano (near Piroli?) in the same year.[26] Unfortunately the Paternum land is described in the same document as both 'public' and 'the property of John I', and it is striking to notice that another piece of public property, at Timozano (also spelt Temuzzano or Termuzzano), lay in the same area as one of the bequests of Docibilis I shared out by his heirs in 924. How did the dual description of the Paternum land arise?

Two solutions present themselves. The first is that John had been the rector of papal or public land there, and had bought some of the land lying alongside. The second, and more likely, is that John had come to treat the papal land as his own, whether or not the 915 document of pope John X had given him title to it, and that not even his own son could establish the legal position (even assuming he would want to: he would not want to prove conclusively that the land was not his to dispose of).

The difficulty of stating the origins of the land that he was giving out is best summed up by a document issued by Docibilis to his son Marinus in 945.[27] This handed over land in Mola, Aqua Longa (Aqualunga), near the Ausente river, in Seriana, and land 'up the cartway to Corene' (Ausonia). The property, Docibilis said, was 'either inherited, public, bought, given or exchanged'. Such vagueness was dangerous, as a court-case of 946 illustrates. In that year Docibilis disputed two estates, Caput Piro and Iuniano, with his cousins John and Docibilis sons of Leo. They claimed part of the estates had been bought by their grandfather, Docibilis I, and came to them via inheritance from Leo (if this was so, the land did not appear in the division of 924). Docibilis II claimed the land on the basis that it was all public. Eventually the parties settled on a compromise and divided the spoils.[28]

The fact that Docibilis II gave out public land only to members of his own family may indicate that he was under some constraint not to dissipate it. However, if this was the case, those who received the land felt themselves under no such obligation. Docibilis' son

[24] *CDC* 41. [25] *CDC* 44. [26] *CDC* 45. [27] *CDC* 46. [28] *CDC* 49.

Gregory promptly exchanged the public land he had received in Costranu for land in Cupano nearby with Docibilis son of Leo Cacafurfure in 939.[29] There may be a reason for Docibilis II's limitation of his public gifts to his own family, however. If there were any doubt about the status of the land (which the examples cited above show there was), giving out the property to his family as the public act of the duke of Gaeta[30] was a far more secure way of leaving it in Docibilan hands than assuming that he owned it and leaving it to his heirs in his will. This theory is lent weight by the fact that we have Docibilis' will,[31] and that neither the pieces of land mentioned above, nor any other land described as public, appear in it.

The will does show another group of previously unrecorded properties in the hands of the Docibilans. Unlike his grandfather, Docibilis II specified each piece of land and who should inherit it. The responsibility for some of the new acquisitions lay with Docibilis himself; quite apart from the striking number of houses that he says he bought or built in the city of Gaeta, we learn that he had been given land in Vetera, had inherited Neapolitan territories from his wife Orania and had bought property at Alipi, Virga near Scauri and Serapiano (Serapo). Closer examination shows that at least some of these purchases had been made from Docibilis' sister Maru and her husband. It could be argued that the lands had therefore been part of the Docibilis' family property before Docibilis himself bought it. Alternatively, if Maru's husband Guaiferius was a Lombard, as his name suggests, Maru could have received the land from her husband after her wedding, for under Lombard law she had a right to a quarter of Guaiferius' property as a morning-gift (*morgengab*).[32] A final point to note about Docibilis' will is that alongside the landed bequests was a vast amount of moveable treasure – gold, silver, silks – Docibilis bequeathed 200 'bizants' or gold *solidi* for his soul alone, a vast amount by contemporary standards.

It is easy to be dazzled by the contents of Docibilis II's will, and his widespread control of Gaetan lands (see Map 3.3) might suggest

[29] *CDC* 42; but Docibilis son of Leo Cacafurfure may have been another member of the Docibilan clan, despite his rather bizarre nickname. He was probably the son of Leo the prefect, and therefore Gregory's cousin.

[30] He assumed the title, the first of his family to do so, in 934, associating his son John in power with himself: *CDC* 36.

[31] *CDC* 52.

[32] Laws of king Liutprand, no. 7, *The Lombard Laws*, ed. K. F. Drew (Philadelphia, 1973), p. 147.

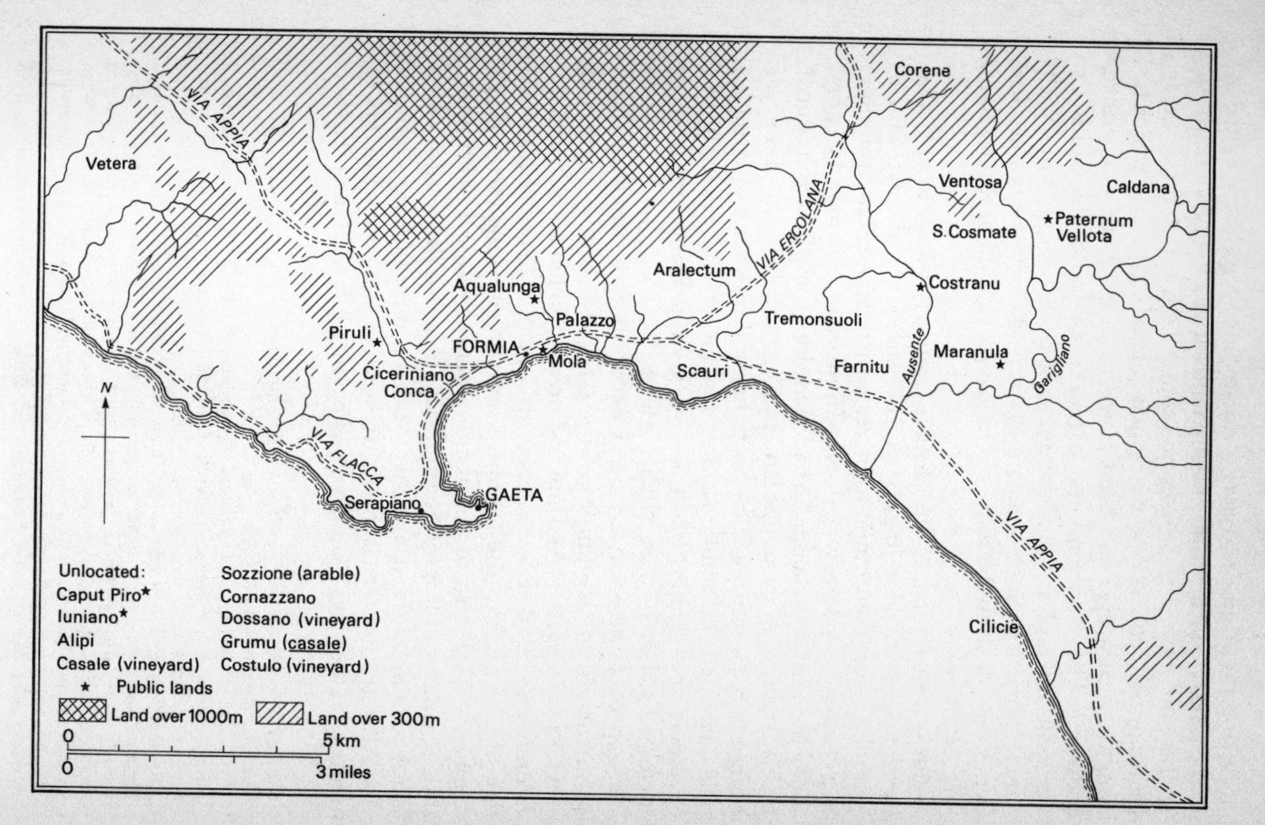

Map 3.3 *Lands under the control of Docibilis II*

that during his reign the dynasty reached its apogee of wealth. In fact the family continued to acquire lands after Docibilis' death. In 962 his son John II contested some land at Cilicie (near Mondragone), which lay in the principality of Capua and which he claimed (successfully) had been given to him by the late prince Landolf.[33] This case, and the earlier evidence of Docibilis I's possessions in Naples, reveal the dukes of Gaeta forging links with their neighbours. Such exchanges, and their implications for Gaeta's status within the southern Italian world will be discussed in more detail below.[34]

John was succeeded by his brother Gregory as duke in 963. The reign and extant documents of the latter reveal that, if the Docibilans were continuing to increase their private landholdings, the *publicum* of Gaeta was slowly diminishing. In 963 Gregory echoed the earlier exchange he had made by giving Docibilis son of Leo Cacafurfure more public land in Costranu.[35] In the same year he augmented a gift made by his father and brother by giving his uncle Leo[36] all the public land in Iuniano,[37] and finally in 964 continued the family tradition by giving Planciano land to Docibilis I's church of St Michael there.[38]

A gap of some fourteen years occurs before our next ducal documents. In 978 we find Marinus, Gregory's brother, in power with his son John III.[39] Marinus had previously held power as duke of Fondi, and this is reflected in his gift of an estate on the northern edge of that plain to the foremost monastery of the territory, St Magnus.[40] The rest of his many documents deal with more familiar lands, but it is interesting that almost all the territories are described as public land, and that the dukes were making a series of gifts. Also striking is that these gifts were no longer exclusively to members of the Docibilan family. The only gift to a Docibilan was

[33] *CDC* 61. [34] See below, chapter 5, sections (b,ii) and (c). [35] *CDC* 64.

[36] The natural son of John I. [37] *CDC* 65.

[38] *CDC* 66; Docibilis I himself had endowed the church, and the 964 document mentions a gift by John I as well as Gregory's offering. Further discussion of ducal gifts to the church follows later in this chapter.

[39] Although Gregory had succeeded John II, his elder brother, it seems to have been due to the latter having no sons. (Daughters, apparently, were not eligible to succeed.) Gregory, though, is known to have had at least three sons. It is possible that they were too young to succeed, although this did not prevent John V from coming to the throne as a minor in 1012. Alternatively, there may have been a power struggle at Gaeta. An internal conflict would explain the big gap in the documentation of a family who had no external threats to their power. Marinus won the struggle, but Gregory's sons do not disappear from view. [40] *CDC* 74.

made in 983. In this Marinus and John III gave to Marinus son of Constantine, 'our relative' one third of the estate Cucilli from the public land. The other two thirds had belonged to Sikelgaita, daughter of John I; again we see the blurring of the distinction between public and private land when it came to benefiting the clan.[41]

We must not make the assumption, however, that alienation of public land within the family ensured that the dukes retained control of it, nor that it guaranteed internal harmony. The duke's own family was perhaps the most potent threat to his power. In a family which produced many sons in each generation, it would have been all too easy for one brother to overthrow another. Land grants bought loyalty, and overall seemed to have worked well. Who then received land from outside the family circle? Two of Marinus and John's grants were to churches,[42] another two were to Leo son of Constantine,[43] (otherwise unknown, but perhaps related to the Marinus son of Constantine mentioned above) and Docibilis son of Mirus, (grandson of Kampulus the prefect and so perhaps to be included among the very distant branches of the Docibilan clan).[44] The remaining two transactions are particularly interesting. Both dated 980, the first was a grant of a plot of public land outside the city walls to the dukes' *fideles* Martin and Marinus, the other a similar grant to one Mauro and his wife Martha.[45] The two men in the first document had already built a wooden house on their plot, implying either that they had previously leased the land, or that the dukes were recognising a *fait accompli* in the medieval equivalent of squatter's rights. The former would seem more likely – the men would hardly have been termed faithful had they usurped the land.

What did these men do to earn the title *fideles*? Clearly they served the dukes in some way. They may have sworn an oath to do so, and are likely to have been soldiers, settled close to the city to protect their lord in times of trouble. We are very poorly informed about Gaetan military arrangements, but if, as stated earlier, Docibilis I relied on Arab mercenaries, some replacement for these allies must have had to be found after the Garigliano expedition of

[41] *CDC* 83: given his designation as a relative of the dukes, it is possible that Marinus was the son of John I's natural son Constantine, the latter being the only member of the Docibilan clan with that name. [42] *CDC* 74 (979), *CDC* 78 (980).

[43] *CDC* 76. [44] *CDC* 84.

[45] *CDC* 75, *CDC* 77; on Mauro and Martha's descendants, see below, p. 123.

915. The will of Docibilis' eponymous grandson reveals that large amounts of liquid wealth continued to be available to the Docibilans by the middle of the tenth century. The example of Martin and Marinus and another piece of evidence from the latter half of the century suggest, however, that the lords of Gaeta may have moved from cash payments to mercenaries (whether Arab or Christian), to grants of land from the *publicum*. In a boundary clause of a document dated 991 we have a reference to the *territorio de milite* just outside the city at Valle Helena.[46] The reference is isolated, but its designation is a striking parallel to that in Naples, discussed earlier, and it does give the impression that the dukes of Gaeta had a small standing army paid in land, perhaps augmented from time to time by mercenaries. This hint at land set aside for the military also serves as a reminder that there may have been far more demand on the public land the dukes had to give out than our documentary evidence now shows.

Slightly later evidence from Amalfi shows that granting public land in return for services was not merely a Gaetan phenomenon. In 1058 dukes John and Sergius confirmed to Mauro son of Peter de Mauro, and Urso, public land which they had bought from Berta daughter of Hademar. Hademar had received the land from duke Manso, and now John and Sergius confirmed Mauro and Urso's ownership in recognition of their services.[47] More important than the confirmation itself here, however, is the fact that the land is described as public in the past tense. When had it ceased to be so? Had duke Manso changed its character by giving it to Hademar, or was Hademar's bequest to Berta the point at which the property was deemed to have passed into private ownership? Or did Berta's subsequent alienation include a convenient neglect of the public nature of the land, which John and Sergius were now legally recognising? We shall never know, but the case highlights the fluidity and progressive diminution of the *publicum* which would soon cause real problems for rulers of territorially limited states such as Gaeta and Amalfi. An earlier document from the latter city may reveal one member of the ducal family attempting to reverse the decline. Leo son of duke Sergius is seen buying land which the vendor co-owned with the *publicum* and another individual;[48] it would have been all too easy for the vendor's family to ignore the public part of the property later and claim it as their own.

[46] *CDC* 89. [47] *CDA* 66. [48] *CP* 66 (992).

Only one document from tenth-century Naples refers specifically to public land, when duke Marinus in 975 confirmed to the monastery of SS Severinus and Sossus all rights over the servants of the monastery together with any *publicum* they might hold.[49] It is sometimes unclear whether the dukes are doing business as private individuals or in their public role as dukes, though the latter is always more likely in the case of donations to major churches or grants of water-related rights, discussed below. The overt and stated distinction in a high number of Gaetan and Amalfitan documents cannot but be related to the scarcity of land in these two duchies, making more important the careful recording of what belonged to whom and how it did so. We shall return to the land transactions of the Neapolitan and Amalfitan dukes shortly.

Perhaps it was the awareness that he was running short of land which led duke Marinus of Gaeta to attempt to take control of some property in the territory of Aquino. In 982 his seizure was challenged by the abbey of Montecassino, owner of the land, and at the court of the German emperor Otto II the monastery won its case.[50] Significantly, Marinus claimed the land on the basis that it had been granted to the *hypatoi* of Gaeta by pope John VIII. Clearly the memory of where the Docibilan dynasty's public wealth and power had originated remained strong in the family.

By the latter years of the tenth century, however, that power was beginning to wane. The only major addition to Docibilan landholdings was the castle of Pontecorvo, granted to John III by emperor Otto III in 999. Even this may have been only a nominal gift, however, for contemporary Pontecorvan documents up to 1032 are dated exclusively by the reign of the Capuan, not Gaetan, rulers.[51] That land was becoming too scarce even to support the ambitions of the Docibilan clan's various offshoots is signalled by the occurrence of disputes between different branches. Such a dispute took place in 992 between Dauferius count of Traetto and Leo the duke of Fondi over some public land in the county of Traetto. Leo won the case, claiming that it was his own private property.[52] Disputes such as this were ultimately very damaging to

[49] *RN* 208.

[50] *CDC* 81; the intervention by Otto illustrates the concern of the German emperors to gain some influence in southern Italy, using patronage of Montecassino as a starting point.

[51] *CDC* 102; dating clauses at Pontecorvo from 1030, 1030, 1034 and 1036: Montecassino Archive, *Codex Diplomaticus Pontiscurvi*, fos. 64, 69, 73, 75.

[52] *CDC* 90.

the Docibilans' hold on power, as they revealed divisions within the family and gave their enemies the opportunity to exploit the arguments.[53]

The Docibilans' problems by the end of the tenth century may have been caused by the fact that they gave away too much public land. Evidence from elsewhere in the Tyrrhenian region suggests that other dukes were more careful about keeping control of their valuable resources. In a document from Amalfi dated 1048, for example, we see duke Manso leasing out public land on Capri for an annual rent of 4½ *modia* of vegetables, 2½ pigs, 1 sheep, some quails and some willow boughs. By prohibiting the lessees, Peter and Anastasius sons of Sergius de Iordano, from alienating the land, Manso was clearly indicating that their tenure did not allow them to control the property.[54] However, duke Manso also apparently granted out public land permanently,[55] an illustration of how dukes could exploit public land in different ways. They could either grant it in return for loyalty from local lords, or they could lease it directly to cultivators and enjoy the revenues produced. The fact that we have no examples of the Docibilans doing the latter at Gaeta does not mean they did not lease public land; it is simply that the documents recording the leases have not survived, or that the leases were never recorded in writing.[56] In this context, the fact that the Docibilans used unfree cultivators on their own lands may be significant; these too would not usually be documented, and the Docibilans may have used them on public land as well.[57]

One type of public property which we do see the Docibilans jealously guarding throughout the tenth century was the right to construct water-mills and to control all inland water resources in the duchy. This part of the *publicum* was perhaps the most valuable to the dukes in terms of revenue.

Bread was a staple of the medieval diet, and, whatever type of grain used, the flour needed milling. For domestic purposes, small hand-mills could be used, and the will of Docibilis I in 906 mentions a horse-mill which he left to his son Anatolius.[58]

[53] As the Traettans seem to have been wooed away from the rest of the family: see below, chapter 5, sections (b,i and ii). [54] *CDA* 591. [55] See above, p. 70.
[56] On the production of documents, see above, chapter 1, section (d); on the leases specifically, see below, chapter 7.
[57] For further discussion of the Docibilans' use of unfree cultivators, see below, chapter 7.
[58] *CDC* 19.

However, under the Docibilans we have our first evidence of water-mills in Gaeta, and it seems likely that many were built in the early tenth century, possibly by the Docibilans themselves. Most of those mills recorded were water-mills, and their concentration around Formia can be explained by their need for fast-flowing water to drive them, in that the mountains behind the destroyed settlement gave rise to several fast streams. The largest of these flows down the same gorge as the Via Appia from Itri, and may have given the district through which it passes, Pontone ('ferry' or 'large bridge') its name. We know of one mill at Pontone,[59] but the majority of water-mills lay on the stream flowing into the sea at the place which took its name from them, Mola. Here we know of at least five mills, all of which were specifically named, for example St George,[60] de Tauro 'under the road',[61] Armenia,[62] Maiore,[63] and Minore.[64] The latter two, despite the adjectival nature of their names, do seem to have been particular mills, as we have references to their proximity to each other and to other mills.[65]

The striking feature to note about the mills of Gaeta is the fact that they were usually co-owned in the most complex way. From a very early date, mills there were divided down into days. Thus in 933 the imperial patrician John I gave his daughter Bona 4 months and 20 days of the mill called Minore.[66] In 937 another daughter, Theotista, exchanged her 15 days' use of the mill called Padula for Kampulus the prefect's similar stake in the mill Armenia.[67] Did these unusual units of division relate to a kind of time-share arrangement, with each owner controlling specific weeks and days in the calendar, or was this just a strange way of expressing portions of one twelfth (a 'month') and smaller? The Gaetan material gives us no clues; it contains no references to named months or specific dates. However, mills in Amalfi were also subdivided into 'months' or even smaller portions for the purpose of ownership, and an Amalfitan document of 1036 does reveal fluctuation in the price for two different portions of the same mill.[68] Another of 1079 seems to seal the matter. In that year, an Amalfitan widow, Maru, sold off the portion of a mill in Atrani bequeathed to her by her

[59] *CDC* 2. [60] *CDC* 52, *CDC* 200, *CDC* 284. [61] *CDC* 143.
[62] *CDC* 40, *CDC* 132, *CDC* 162, *CDC* 190, *CDC* 206, *CDC* 235.
[63] *CDC* 34, *CDC* 50, *CDC* 52, *CDC* 107, *CDC* 120, *CDC* 121, *CDC* 122, *CDC* 176, *CDC* 202, *CDC* 270, *CDC* 284. [64] *CDC* 34, *CDC* 50.
[65] Maiore upstream from Minore: *CDC* 34, *CDC* 50. Maiore downstream from St George: *CDC* 284. [66] *CDC* 34. [67] *CDC* 40. [68] *CDA* 46.

mother. The portion was 1 month and 5 days 'that is the month of May and five days of July'.[69] The complexity of mill divisions in Gaeta suggests that the portions, as in Amalfi, did relate to real days and months.

If this were the only method used in dividing mills for ownership in Gaeta, it would be relatively easy to compare one person's stake with another's. However, on the river Caput Aqua (Capo d'Acqua) we meet the term 'one foot of a mill' in 1060.[70] This may relate to a length of the channel leading into the mill, and says much for the high value of mills if such a small portion was thought worth owning. An alternative explanation may possibly be provided by a later English example, where use of the mill-stone was sold or rented at a fixed rate per inch of wear.[71]

Finally, in ?1058 one Docibilis son of Marinus Frunzo expressed his stake in the mill Armenia as 2 *modia* of grain per year – presumably the amount he had the right to mill there.[72] Unfortunately we cannot reconcile this measurement with the more common ownership of days in the mill, since it is impossible to calculate with any consistency the amount of grain which could be milled in a day. Nor do we know for how much of the year a mill was in operation. It is possible that here we have moved a step down from the 'time-share' owners, to those who actually used the mill and bought the right of use from those who controlled the time.

In Gaeta at least, the latter group appear to have been very exclusive. During the period of Docibilan rule, only members of that family are documented as mill-owners. After their fall from power in the city of Gaeta itself in 1032, others entered the mill ownership market, suggesting that up until that date the Docibilans had exercised some kind of monopoly. Certainly mills in Gaeta were very expensive throughout the tenth and eleventh centuries. Some idea of their price in comparison with land can be gained from a document of 1056, recording the sale by John, count of Suio, of an unspecified portion of the mill Maiore for 24 pounds of silver.[73] For that price, a year before, a purchaser could have bought 250 *modia* of prime grain land at Cozara in the eastern half of the duchy.[74] To put the price even further into perspective, in

[69] *CDA* 74. [70] *CDC* 211. [72] *CDC* 206.
[71] R. Holt, *The Mills of Medieval England* (Oxford, 1988), p. 99.
[73] *CDC* 202. [74] *CDC* 199: 1½ *modia* sold for just over 2oz silver.

1054 the main candidate had renounced his claim to the bishopric of Gaeta for just 20 pounds![75]

Evidence from other parts of Italy shows that expensive mills were not only a Gaetan phenomenon. In Amalfi in the early eleventh century, for example, $1\frac{1}{2}$ months of a mill were sold for 30 gold *solidi*.[76] In the same year, 1012, a piece of vineyard went for the equivalent of $1\frac{1}{4}$ *solidi*;[77] a piece of empty land in 1013 was sold for just half a *solidus*,[78] and even two pieces of land nearer the coast (and therefore both more accessible and fertile) in 1013 only raised 10 *solidi*.[79]

Further afield, Chiappa Mauri has noticed a similar difference between the prices of fields and mills and pieces of land around Milan in the eleventh century, citing the average price of the latter as being five times the price of the former.[80]

The inflated price of mills is a particularly notable feature of the southern Italian documentation under discussion. Lizier attributes the high prices to the large amount of capital needed to construct them, and del Treppo too sees them as investment opportunities for wealthy merchants with spare capital.[81] But if, as seems likely from the size of some of the streams on which they were built, the Gaetan and Amalfitan mills at least were small, horizontally wheeled constructions, Lizier's theory is not entirely convincing.

Why were prices so high? The elevation in the price of land which had a mill built on it as demonstrated by Chiappa Mauri is understandable, but in the South the disproportion seems to have reached an extreme level. A clue may lie in the degree of partition involved. Unfortunately, we have no idea of mill prices in Naples, but we can see that some mills were owned as whole entities.[82] In Milan the division of mills did occur, but those divided into tenths

[75] *CDC* 197: this event is discussed more fully below, chapter 5, section (a).
[76] *RN* 346. [77] *CP* 72. [78] *PAVAR* I/6. [79] *CodCav* V/664.
[80] L. Chiappa Mauri, 'I mulini ad acqua nel milanese (secoli X–XV)', *Nuova Rivista Storica*, 67 (1983), 14. There is as yet only a limited amount of literature on water-mills, particularly Italian ones. In addition to Chiappa Mauri and Holt, *Mills*, see the classic article by M. Bloch, 'The advent and triumph of the watermill', in *Land and Work in Medieval Europe*, trans. J. E. Anderson (London, 1967), pp. 136–68; also, J. Muendel, 'The distribution of mills in the Florentine countryside during the late middle ages', in *Pathways to Medieval Peasants*, ed. J. A. Raftis (Toronto, 1981), pp. 83–112; C. Dussaix, 'Les moulins à Reggio d'Emilie aux XIIe et XIIIe siècles', *MEFRM*, 91 (1979), 113–47; and B. Condorelli, 'La molitura ad acqua nella valle del torrente Farfa', in *Atti del 9° Congresso Internazionale di Studi sull'Alto Medioevo*, II (Spoleto, 1983), pp. 837–41.
[81] Lizier, *L'Economia*, p. 8; del Treppo and Leone, *Amalfi*, p. 50.
[82] E.g. *RN* 72, *RN* 268, *RN* 335, *RN* 367, *RN* 414, *RN* 443, dating from 951 to 1033.

were regarded as extremely fractionalised.[83] Mill division into even smaller parts in Amalfi and Gaeta may therefore be an indication of rarity, partly explaining their higher value.

The fact remains, though, that such mills were not difficult to build and so did not need to be rare. In northern Italy even peasants owned mills.[84] The paradox can be partly explained in the case of Amalfi and Gaeta by the geography of these two territories. Both were limited in extent, and both, being predominantly limestone areas, had only limited numbers of reliable streams for mill building. Nevertheless, mill ownership in Gaeta, Amalfi and Naples too seems to have been limited to very wealthy laymen (including two dukes of Naples) or ecclesiastical institutions.[85] It is difficult to provide an adequate reason for this phenomenon – it may be the case that mill ownership was seen as a sign of prestige in the South.[86] Could the apparent attempt at monopolisation of mill ownership by the Docibilans in the tenth and early eleventh centuries be a manifestation of this?

It is likely: there is some evidence to suggest that the rulers of Gaeta went to some lengths, even within their own family, to ensure that they maintained a strict control over their milling facilities. For example, Docibilis I's bequest to Anatolius in 906 stipulated that the latter was not to build anything on to his horse-mill, that is, increase its capacity. And in 933, John I's gift to his daughter Bona was made on condition that she did not use any other mill. There are also indications in our documents that the siting of several water-mills was planned deliberately to maximise their use. Quite apart from the necessary water-power, they also needed to be easily accessible. Thus the mills Maiore and Minore, we learn, were next to a bridge, possibly at the point where the Via Appia crossed the stream of Mola.[87] In 978 Marinus and John III gave two of Kampulus the prefect's sons a water-mill in the Ausente river 'next to the bridge where travellers cross'.[88] This type of care seems to show that the Docibilans were keen not only to restrict mill ownership to themselves, but also that the ruling

[83] Chiappa Mauri, 'Mulini', 22.

[84] Their ubiquity in the Casentino valley near Arezzo is commented on by C. J. Wickham, *The Mountains and the City* (Oxford, 1988), p. 165. Even in northern Lazio they are visible as co-owned by small allod-owners: Toubert, *Structures*, I, p. 460 note 3.

[85] *DCDN* 3, *DCDN* 8; see below, this chapter, for further discussion of the mill owners of Naples and Amalfi.

[86] I suggest another reason for their importance in Gaeta and Amalfi in chapter 7, below.

[87] *CDC* 120. [88] *CDC* 73.

members of the clan wanted to control the amounts of grain that could be processed. And, whilst the public land controlled by the Docibilans gradually diminished, they held on very tightly to their mills, suggesting that the revenues from milling far outweighed the value of selling mills (which in themselves were relatively modest structures) or granting them away.

With only two exceptions, Docibilan ducal gifts or sales of mills are all exclusively to other members of the Docibilan clan. The exceptions occurred under special circumstances. In 954 Docibilis II bequeathed two and a half months' use of the mill of St George to the slave Rosula, who perhaps should be identified with the slave of the same name listed among those manumitted earlier in the will.[89] But even as a freedwoman neither Rosula nor her stake in the mill need necessarily have passed out of Docibilan control. The will of Docibilis II's grandson Gregory, dated 1024, shows five personal slaves being manumitted on condition that they did not take servile wives or husbands and that they offered a gift of chickens to Gregory's heirs every year. Three female slaves were to serve Gregory's daughters until the latter married and the two males were freed to the 'protection' of Gregory's son Laidulf.[90] It is likely that Rosula enjoyed the same status as these five slaves, and the value of her manumission gift makes it probable that her freedom was hedged round with even more restrictions than theirs.

The other example we have of a Docibilan duke granting away milling rights is in a document issued by Leo II in 1042.[91] In that year he granted a portion of the mill Maiore to Marinus son of Kampulus and Gregory son of John 'in return for their services'. This grant must be viewed against the political background at Gaeta; since 1032 the city had been in Capuan hands, and Leo's brief appearance as duke may represent a last attempt by the Docibilans to wrest back their position of supremacy. In this case extreme measures, even granting away their most prized assets, may have been required to gain support. Such localised measures, however, were not sufficient to prevent Guaimarius of Salerno imposing his own candidate for the dukedom of Gaeta, Raynulf, on the city in the latter half of 1042.[92]

The situation at Gaeta is mirrored by evidence from the other Tyrrhenian states. In 1012, duchess Drosu of Amalfi sold off a

89 *CDC* 52. 90 *CDC* 143. 91 *CDC* 176.

92 On the history of Gaeta's rulers in the eleventh century, see below, chapter 5, section (a).

portion of a watermill to archbishop Leo.[93] We know that the rulers of Naples and Salerno also owned mills[94] in the tenth century and later, although in larger states such as these there does not seem to have been such a conscious effort at monopolisation as there was in Gaeta and, possibly, Amalfi. In 949 duke John of Naples exchanged mills in the Tertium district with Peter, the abbot of SS Severinus and Sossus in Naples. This transaction was followed shortly by another in which Peter exchanged some land for the mill he had given to the duke.[95] Unfortunately we have no indication as to whether mill prices in the larger state were lower as a result of the greater availability of mill-building sites.

Not only the mills themselves, but the water supply to them, was considered within the ruler's jurisdiction. In 1028 duchess Emilia of Gaeta was involved in a dispute about a channel or *clusa* built to feed a mill with water.[96] As Chiappa Mauri has put it, the right to build this channel was the right to use the water for any purpose. That is, by winning the right to block off part of the river, the ruler emphasised his or her public authority.[97] In the same way, duke Sergius of Amalfi in 1018 granted all the water running through an aqueduct to the church of St Peter to its abbess Blattu.[98] That control over aquatic resources continued to be a public prerogative into the twelfth century is illustrated by the list of public or regalian rights demanded of the Italian communes in the north by Frederick Barbarossa in 1158. They included mills, fisheries, bridges and all the use accruing from running water.[99]

Apart from those in the lake called Capratica Longa, granted out to the monastery of St Theodore in 957,[100] the Docibilans controlled fishing rights on the Ponzian islands as well. In 1019 Leo I granted fisheries and other public property there to Kampulus son of Docibilis.[101]

Elsewhere, in 997/8, duke Sergius of Naples gave the monastery of SS Severinus and Sossus permission to fish in half the lake called Patriensis.[102] In 986, princess Aloara of Capua had allowed the monastery of St Laurence to fish in the same lake, and it is possible that each ruler may have claimed rights over the lake, or possibly half each.[103]

93 *RN* 346. 94 Naples: *DCDN* 3 (949); Salerno: *CodCav* III/425 (990).
95 *DCDN* 3a and 3b. 96 *CDC* 155. 97 'Mulini', 11. 98 *CDA* 33.
99 Rahewin's continuation of Otto of Friesing's *Deeds of Frederick Barbarossa*, trans. C. C. Mierow, p. 238. 100 *CDC* 55. 101 *CDC* 135. 102 *RN* 306.
103 *RNAM* 206.

Whilst their public land was beginning to dwindle, we can see the Docibilans holding on very tightly to their private property. Their gifts and exchanges of their fortune took place almost entirely within the family circle. Thus duke Docibilis II gave property in various parts of the duchy to his son Marinus.[104] Another son, Gregory, bought Vetera land from his aunt Megalu, daughter of John I,[105] and passed on land to be divided between his sons.[106] No member of the family was excluded from this web of transactions, and it is interesting to see that the three natural sons of John I were substantial landowners. In 991 they divided up property in Bluzano outside Gaeta, Rubiano in Flumetica and Melogranu (Migliorano?).[107] Their inclusion in family affairs may have owed something to the influence of Lombard law, as observed by the Gaetans' southern neighbours, the Capuans. According to this, natural sons, that is those born out of wedlock, but not of illegal (for example, slave-free) unions, had a claim on their father's inheritance alongside their half-brothers and sisters born of his wife.[108]

The Docibilan family extended well beyond the direct ruling line, and the measure of the wealth of one of its more minor members is provided by a will of 1024.[109] Gregory 'the magnificent' was the son of Leo the prefect and grandson of Docibilis II. Quite apart from the collection of mobile goods which he left to his wife Maria (gold, silver, silks (*siricos*), linen (*lineos*), both *cositi* and *excositi* (cut and uncut), bronze and reeds), what is remarkable is the long list of landed properties that he owned, stretching from Sperlonga to the Garigliano river (see Map 3.4). Notable too is the fact that Gregory's two sons were to receive all of this land, and that his daughters received only 30 pounds of silver and three slaves. It appears that Gregory was avoiding the alienation of large chunks of family land in the form of dowries by providing liquid assets for that purpose, and his careful husbandry of his land contrasts with the bequests of, for example, Docibilis II, to his daughters, which reflect a greater confidence and wealth of land in the tenth century than in the eleventh.

Given that several different families appear to have provided Amalfi's rulers at different stages in its history, and that external intervention was also not unusual, the political struggle may have

[104] *CDC* 46. [105] *CDC* 58. [106] *CDC* 79. [107] *CDC* 43.
[108] Rothari 154 and 155, *Lombard Laws*, ed. Drew, pp. 77–8. [109] *CDC* 143.

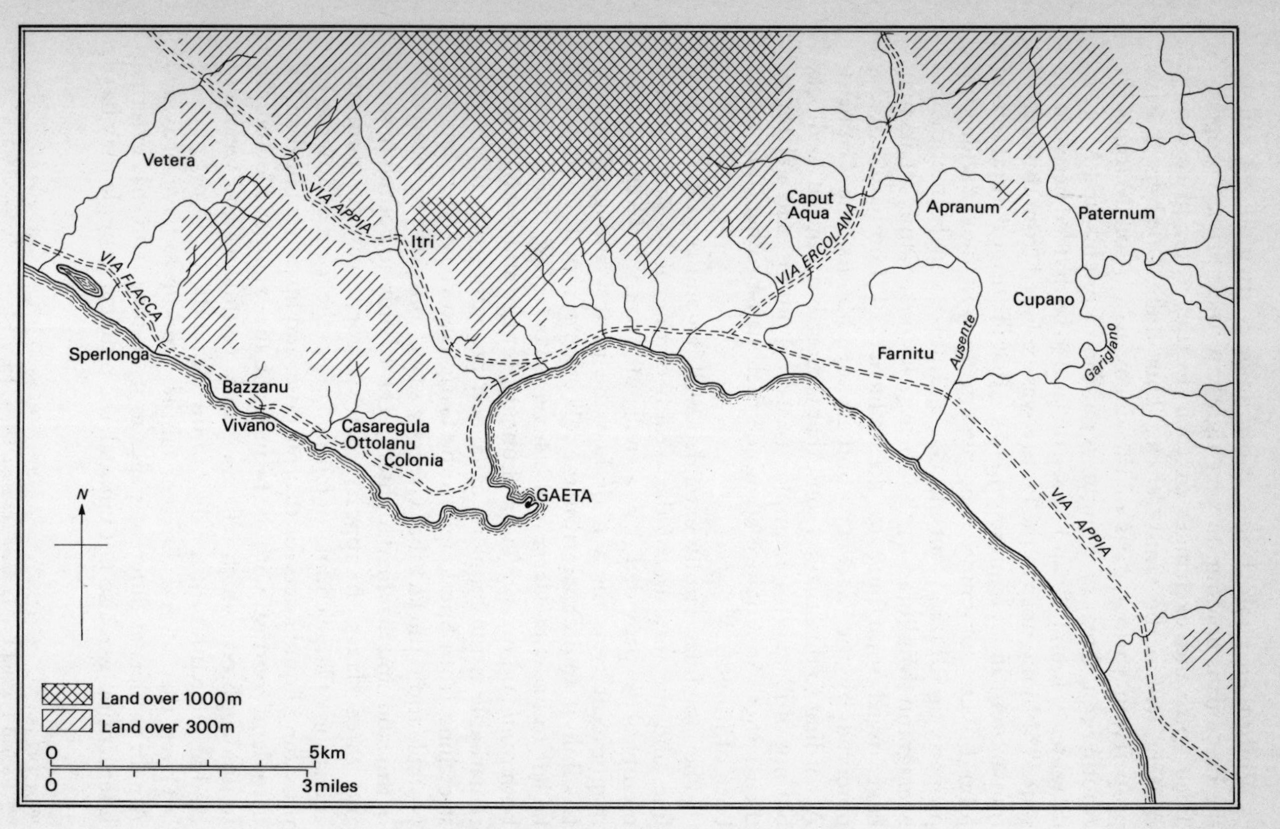

Map 3.4 *Properties of Gregory the Magnificent*

had economic repercussions. Although the ducal family clearly controlled valuable public[110] and private[111] property in the city of Amalfi itself, what evidence we have of rural ducal possessions in the tenth and eleventh centuries suggests that the dukes were forced to buy peripheral land (see Map 3.5). In 992 Leo the son of duke Sergius bought land on Capri which had been co-owned with the *publicum*,[112] and in 998 another son, Adelferius, leased out land on Capri to John son of Anastasius.[113] This does not appear to have been public, but Adelferius took great care in defining the boundaries of each piece that he handed over, suggesting that a potential for confusion existed. Capri continued to be the focus of ducal transactions in the eleventh century; in 1033 Capritan land, apparently with public obligations, was still owned by duke John's aunt Drosu.[114] In 1048 duke Manso assigned public land on the island to two brothers at a rent in kind.[115] After the Norman takeover of Amalfi we lose sight of the public land on Capri, but in 1090 and 1098 descendants of duke Manso are seen giving property on the island to the church of St Laurence.[116] In 1004 part of the public land under the duke's supervision was in Stabia.[117] All of this land still lay within the duchy of Amalfi, but in 986 we see that there were Amalfitan ducal possessions in Salerno as well. In that year Regalis, wife of duke John, gave to Niceta the imperial *spatharius* a piece of land in Vietri.[118] This land is likely to have been Regalis' own, probably her dowry, but John's motives for marrying her may have included the extension of landed property that she would bring. Certainly many of John's compatriots seem to have seen the benefits of owning Salernitan land, as we shall see.

From what limited evidence we have, it is clear that the dukes of Naples had widespread landholdings, perhaps privately owned. The dukes and their family are documented as owning land in Gualdo,[119] Quillaci,[120] Calvizzano and S. Iacobo,[121] Tertium and Arcora,[122] Faragnano,[123] Pozzuoli[124] and St Peter ad Cancellata.[125] In addition, duke Sergius leased land from the wealthy monastery of SS Sergius and Bacchus in 1016.[126] Frustratingly, we cannot get much sense of the extent or location of most of these

110 As discussed in this chapter: see above, pp. 70, 72.

111 John, grandson of duke Manso, made a gift of a house and four *apotheke* in the city to St Laurence in 1090, *CP* 85.

112 *CP* 66.

113 *CP* 80.

114 *CDA* 591.

115 *CDA* 60.

116 *CP* 85 (1090), *CP* 91 (1098).

117 *CDA* 18.

118 *CodCav* II/386.

119 The heirs of duke Sergius, *RN* 8, (921).

120 *RN* 55, (945): Maria widow of Anastasii, daughter of duke John.

121 *RN* 75, (951): duke John exchanges in one area for land in the other.

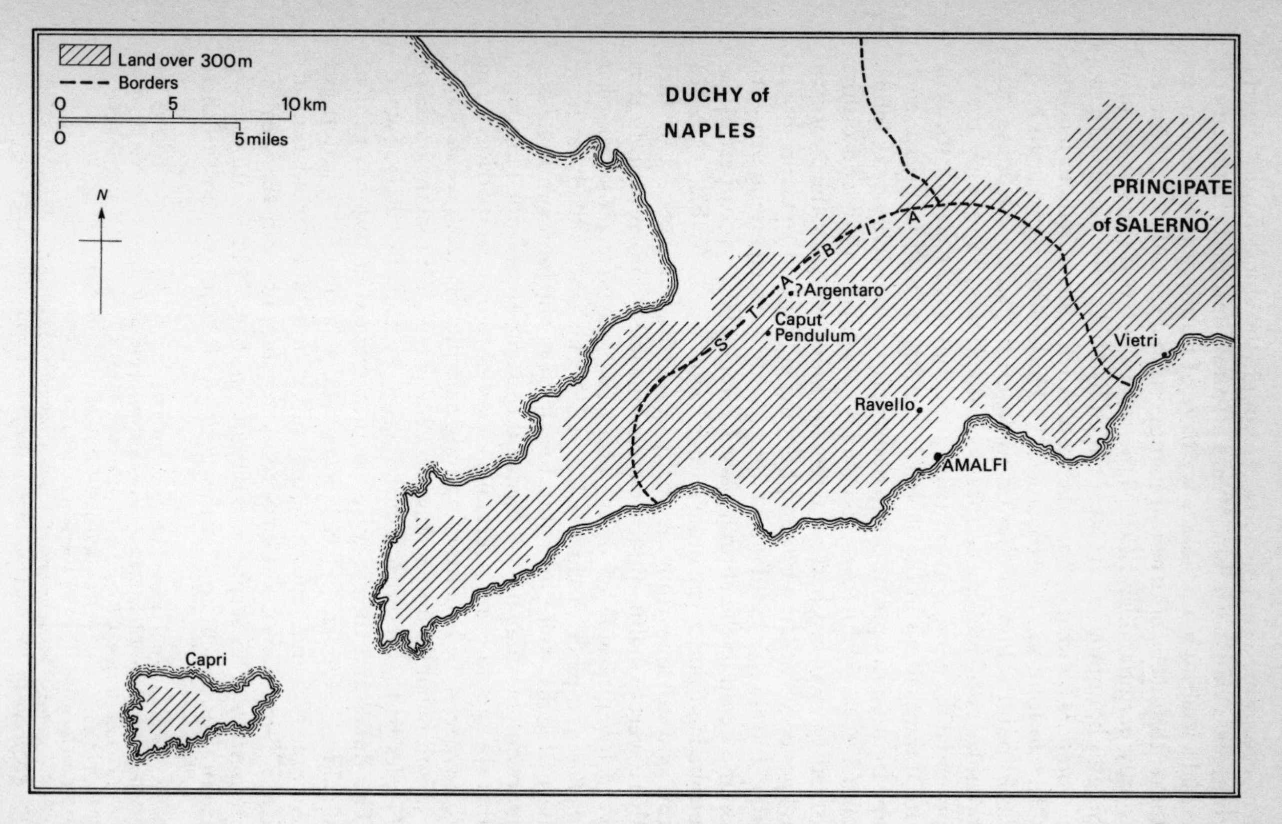

Map 3.5 *Amalfitan ducal Land*

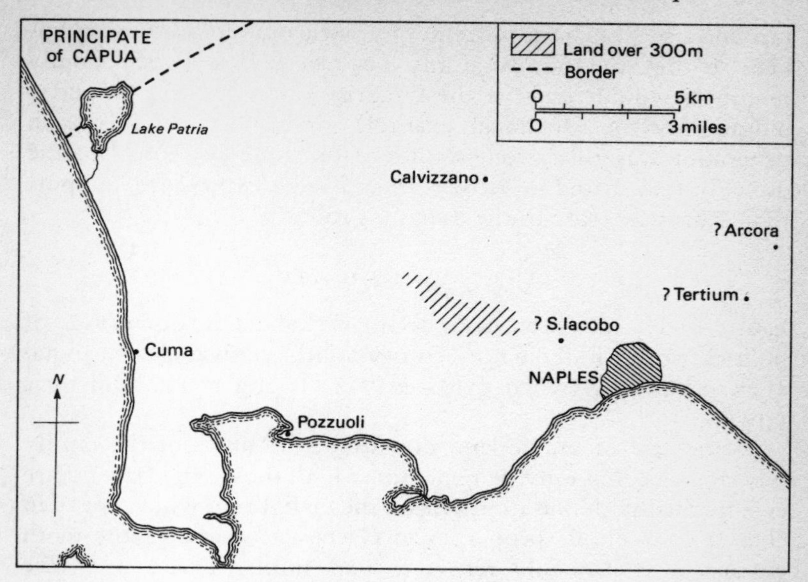

Map 3.6 *Neapolitan ducal Land*

possessions (but see Map 3.6 for those which are locatable). Perhaps the latter transaction illustrates a lack of land disguised only by the numerous locations where the family owned property. There is some indication that within the city of Naples the dukes may have defined their territory very precisely: the entire coastal sector of the city near the ports may have been part of the palace complex. This at least is the impression gained from the fact that no places recorded in urban transactions in this period lay in the palace sector. Either it was a very poor area, whose residents did not record their transactions in writing,[127] or very exclusive, so that no transactions occurred. A similar vacuum visible in contemporary Milan can be explained by the ducal compound lying there,[128] and Naples may have witnessed a similar phenomenon.

If we were better served with evidence for the ducal possessions in Naples and Amalfi, it is likely that a similar picture to that

[122] *DCDN* 3, (949): duke John exchanges land and mills.
[123] *RN* 212, (977): heirs of duke Stephen, predecessor of the Sergian dynasty.
[124] *RN* 381, (1019): Drosu daughter of duke John had exchanged land here with SS Sergius and Bacchus.
[125] *RN* 426, (1030): the heirs of duke John.
[126] *RN* 372.
[127] See above, chapter 1, section (d).
[128] Personal communication Ross Balzaretti: I thank him for pointing this out.

provided by Gaeta would emerge, with numerous transactions kept within the family. Only co-operation between family members would preserve the integrity of the family property: judging by the Docibilan example, division of land at each generation was still a strong tradition. Only one son could become duke, but all shared in his wealth and were expected to support him. This was a key to the dynasty's rule.

(b) FAMILY UNITY

Family unity seems to have been overlooked in discussions of political power in the tenth-century South, yet was clearly a vital asset, particularly when dynasties were trying to establish their power.

In the case of public land donations, the unity of the family inheritance could only be maintained if all those who had a share co-operated with one another, and the in-fighting which began in earnest over public properties in Gaeta at the end of the tenth century was probably reflected in a similar partition of the Docibilan patrimony. Throughout their period of rule, we see members dividing lands which they had inherited, rather than holding them in common, and this can only have accelerated the process of disintegration. As soon as their wealth waned, they were bound to begin losing their hold over the duchy. But was Docibilan power simply a matter of their position as the richest family in the territory? In the tenth century it had to be allied with another factor, that of co-operation, and for a while the Docibilans exhibited a very high level of this as they established themselves as the leading family. This may have been the key to enabling them to ride the storms of their early years in power, as we have no recorded disputes between members of the family until at least the mid-tenth century, and family coherence was consolidated by attaching themselves by marriage to the Neapolitans. In a way, their peaceful sharing-out of the important posts in the duchy of Gaeta is made more remarkable if we look at their genealogy; there were many brothers in most of the early generations of the family, yet no sign of tension between them until localised areas of power began to coalesce in the latter half of the tenth century.[129]

[129] Taviani-Carozzi, *Principauté*, p. 468, illustrates the instability which could occur in states which retained the idea of all male heirs sharing the sovereign power, as at Capua, and contrasts this with the relatively stable situation at Salerno, where single, patrilineal succession was adopted.

The family of Sergius of Naples was even more successful, in that it retained a high level of unity throughout its rule. Sergius recognised that one way of ensuring at least some hold on the position that the people of Naples had conferred upon him was to insert his family into both lay and ecclesiastical posts. This worked as long as each family member was content with his role and the support of the people lasted. Even when someone stepped out of line, as bishop Athanasius did in 878 when he blinded duke Sergius II and took over in both roles, the family were able to remain dominant, and Athanasius was succeeded by Sergius' son Gregory as duke in 898. The stability of the ducal family's hold on power was such that they remained the only clan to provide the rulers of Naples, with a brief hiatus in the mid-eleventh century, until 1137, when the last duke was killed in battle. Perhaps a reason for the family's dominance can be found in the history of Naples prior to 840, which is best characterised as bloody, with incessant coups and assassinations. The desire for peace and stability must have played a strong part in the people's choice and continued support of the count of Cuma and his family as their rulers.

In Amalfi, three dynasties ruled between the ninth and eleventh centuries, and the late tenth and early eleventh centuries were the apogee of such dynastic rule, as the family of Sergius II held onto power. Even the disastrous enterprise of Manso in trying to rule Salerno, which resulted in him losing power briefly to his brother at Amalfi, did not dislodge the family itself from power, and the strong tradition of dynastic rule created by the family was able, ultimately, to withstand the upheavals of the mid-eleventh century.

(c) CHURCH PATRONAGE

No medieval ruler could hope to gain any support without some kind of help from the church, and it is a fact that all of the rulers of the states on this part of the Tyrrhenian coast saw the foundation, endowment and protection of churches as part of their role. The rulers provided protection and landed wealth. In return they received spiritual approbation of their rule and heavenly rewards.

An early example of such a gift occurs at Amalfi, where the prefect Manso is recorded in 922 as having given a mill to the church of St Benedict in Scala.[130] In 979, the priests of St Felix in

[130] *CDA* 2.

Caput de Amalfi acted with ducal permission in a land transaction, suggesting that the dukes had control of the church or had founded it, or both.[131] The most frequent beneficiary of ducal generosity, however, was the church of St Laurence to which gifts were made in 988, 1004 and 1018.[132] In the first, made by the duke Manso and his brothers, they stated that they had built the church, and now gave to it another foundation of their family, St Peter's in Bostopla. The second gift comprised public land in Stabia, the third the right to use water running to St Peter's. Bearing in mind that part of the Amalfitan document collection is preserved in St Laurence's archive and so may exaggerate the favour in which the church was held, we should nevertheless suppose that it was the recipient of many more ducal gifts as a family foundation.

In Naples, as well as controlling the installation of abbesses to the convent of SS Gregory, Sebastian and Pantaleo,[133] the dukes made gifts to the churches of SS Severinus and Sossus and St Salvator. The former church seems to have been an early favourite of the dukes of Naples, although this may simply be a matter of chance documentary survival again. It features in several ducal documents, receiving a church dedicated to St Severinus in 907 from duke Gregory,[134] exchanging mills with duke John, receiving immunity from ducal control over its servants in 975 from duke Marinus,[135] and concessions of fishing rights in lake Patriensis from duke Sergius in 997 and 998.[136] Documents from 1036 and 1037 show patronage of St Salvator. In the first the church received one dedicated to SS Sergius and Bacchus,[137] and in the second the monastery sold off land to a son of its former abbot with duke Sergius' permission.[138] As well as founding[139] and patronising Neapolitan churches, the dukes also made gifts to the powerful monastery of St Vincent on the Volturno river.[140] Duke John gave

[131] *CP* 21.

[132] *CP* 79, *CDA* 18, *CDA* 33; a further gift is reported in 1090, *CP* 85.

[133] In 1009 (*RN* 335) and 1033 (*DCDN* 10).

[134] *DCDN* 1.

[135] *RN* 208.

[136] *RNAM* 246, *RN* 306; the earlier document included the right to cut wood there too.

[137] *DCDN* 11.

[138] *RN* 460.

[139] Dukes John and Marinus are recorded as having built the church of St Michael Portanoba in Naples in a document of 950, *RN* 70; an unidentified duke John is recorded as the founder of St Simeon's in a document of 1038, *RN* 468.

[140] The monastery has been the subject of a number of studies, including: M. del Treppo, 'La vita economica e sociale in una grande abbazia del Mezzogiorno: S. Vincenzo al Volturno nell'alto medioevo', *ASPN*, 74 (1955), 31–110; C. J. Wickham, *Il Problema dell'Incastellamento nell'Italia Centrale: l'Esempio di S. Vincenzo al Volturno* (Florence, 1985). Archeological work on the site of the monastery by the British School at Rome

it a cell in Naples and some land in 944.[141] This transaction was confirmed by his son Marinus four years later.[142]

How closely did Gaetan documents reflect patterns elsewhere? How did the Docibilans cultivate the support of the church? We have a gratifyingly large amount of material with which to attempt to answer these questions. In view of the aid they had received from the pope, it is perhaps not surprising to see that, from the very start of their rule over Gaeta, Docibilis I and his heirs were concerned to be seen to be patrons and benefactors of the church.[143] That they were aware of their need for continued ecclesiastical support is best illustrated by the level of expenditure on the churches he built recorded by Docibilis I in his will of 906. His major foundation seems to have been the church of St Michael at Planciano. With Docibilis' permission this church had already received the church of St Maria outside the city gates and all of its lands from Deusdedit the bishop of Gaeta in 899.[144] Now in the will Docibilis enriched it further with lands near to the city and a water-mill at Pampilinum, the latter having the potential to be a very rich gift indeed. Docibilis did not limit his spending to one church alone. Since he left the choice of the priest of St Silvinian's church in Gaeta to his son Leo, it is likely that the latter church was also a Docibilan foundation. The 120 gold *solidi* which Docibilis spent on the church seems designed to impress; St Silvinian's was adorned with a pavement, marble blackbirds, roofwork and beams, a store for sacred objects, a gold procession cross, jewels and pendants.[145]

After Docibilis' death, his son Leo also had control of St Michael's, and in 930 we see him appointing an abbot, Anastasius.[146] This fact is significant for our perception of Docibilan 'power', for, whilst Leo was a member of the ruling family, it was his older brother John I who was perceived as the ruler of Gaeta by contemporaries. One had the care of his family's churches, the other was indulging in rather more spectacular feats driving the Saracens from the Garigliano and winning papal favour. Both

has provided much new and important information about the significance of S. Vincenzo to Carolingian political aspirations in southern Italy in the ninth century. The results are to be published in a series of reports, of which one, *San Vincenzo al Volturno*, I, ed. R. Hodges (British School at Rome, 1993) has so far appeared.

[141] *RN* 52. [142] *RN* 64.

[143] Although external relations with the papacy, and internal ones with the local church, were not necessarily dependent on, or affected by, each other.

[144] *CDC* 17. [145] *CDC* 19. [146] *CDC* 33.

were ensuring continued ecclesiastical support for their family's position; their complementary actions underline the fact that early on the Docibilans acted as a mutually supportive group, not yet divided by the quarrels which are a feature of their documents later on in the tenth century.

St Michael's acquired more land in 935, with the permission of Docibilis II and John II.[147] In 958, the latter's concern to protect the family foundation's land is shown in a court-case. The natural sons of John I claimed a piece of land which lay within the territory of St Michael's, and at John II's court they lost their case.[148] John also gave land to the church, as a document of his brother and successor Gregory making a donation in 964 records.[149]

St Michael's may have remained the family's favourite church throughout the rule of the Docibilans, but from a relatively early date it seems to have been in competition for their grants of land with the monastery of St Theodore, also in Gaeta. In 914 John I and Docibilis II agreed to bishop Deusdedit's sale of a house and a piece of land to the church,[150] and in 923 they gave St Theodore's a piece of shoreline.[151] In 980 dukes Marinus and John III made a gift of public land to the same church[152] and in 993 we learn that St Theodore's had been given control of the Docibilans' own foundation at Planciano.[153] It seems that whilst St Michael's acted as a family chapel, endowed with private lands, St Theodore's was seen as the ecclesiastical establishment which, after the bishopric, could provide most support for the dukes in power, and was cultivated accordingly. The fact that two much later rulers of Gaeta, dukes Atenolf I and Atenolf II, also patronised the church suggests that this was the case.[154] Whether St Theodore's was a Docibilan foundation, or pre-dated their rise, is unclear, but, by the end of the tenth century, dukes John III and John IV were styling themselves as its *adiutores, protectores, defensores et pastores* ('helpers, protectors, defenders and caretakers').[155]

Whilst there were a few major churches patronised by the Docibilans, this did not prevent them from making isolated gifts to, and taking control of, other churches. In 906 Docibilis I left the church of St Irene in Gaeta to two of his daughters.[156] In 954 Docibilis II made a bequest to the church of St Maria outside the

[147] *CDC* 37. [148] *CDC* 56. [149] *CDC* 66. [150] *CDC* 22.
[151] *CDC* 30. [152] *CDC* 98. [153] *CDC* 91.
[154] *CDC* 203 (1057), *CDC* 218 (1063). [155] *CDC* 91. [156] *CDC* 19.

gates, which belonged to St Michael's.[157] Other recipients of the dukes' generosity included St Michael's at Altino in 978,[158] the church of St Innocent at Vetera which Leo of Fondi acquired in 995,[159] and St Magnus' at Fondi, in 995.[160] John III and his wife Emilia also founded the church of St John at Filline, endowed by their son Leo with the *casale* or estate Ercli in 1036.[161]

A survey of the documentation reveals that, as elsewhere, the Docibilian dukes at Gaeta claimed control over churches which they had not founded, as well as those which they had, and made gifts to them. These churches are to be seen as part of the *publicum* of Gaeta, to be exploited as the dukes wished, and in fact were dealt with little differently from the public lands under Docibilan control. Thus in 934 Docibilis II and his son John sold control of the ancient church of St Erasmus in Formia to Bona, widow of Leo, and her son Leo for their lives at a price of 25 pounds of silver.[162] Bona and Leo were still alive and in possession of the church in 959, when it was promised by John II to his brother Leo as soon as they should die.[163] That the Docibilans should claim control, and successfully, over this church is not surprising, since St Erasmus was seen as the protector of Formia, and would later be translated and adopted as the patron saint of Gaeta as well.[164] If Docibilis and John could be seen as the protectors of this saint's church, it could only fuel the idea that their rule had a spiritual legitimacy.

The point of making donations to the church was not usually to gain protection against external enemies. Land in this case was probably better directed towards buying military rather than ecclesiastical aid. Church support was needed to legitimise and maintain the power of the Docibilan family in the eyes of their own subjects, and in this respect the Docibilans succeeded in gaining it. They established major foundations and endowed them with lands which the monasteries themselves could not permanently alienate. They exerted control over the bishop too, and thereby gained not only spiritual, but also economic, aid.

[157] *CDC* 52. [158] *CDC* 72. [159] *CDC* 94. [160] *CDC* 74.
[161] *CDC* 165. [162] *CDC* 36. [163] *CDC* 59.
[164] It is unclear when the adoption took place, but it may have been the occasion for John of Gaeta to produce his version of the saint's life in the 1080s: O. Engels, 'Papst Gelasius II (Johannes von Gaeta) als Hagiograph', *QFIAB*, 5 (1955), 1–45, gives bibliography on this subject. This would fit well with the appearance of bronze coinage stamped with SE (Sanctus Erasmus), which Lucia Travaini dates to the late eleventh century. (See below, note 218).

(d) EPISCOPAL SUPPORT

One of the most potent allies of any ruler was the bishop of the city. Our documentary evidence shows that, moved from the old episcopal seat at Formia to Gaeta after the former was destroyed by Saracen attacks, the bishops very quickly acknowledged the power of the new lords of Gaeta. Deusdedit deferred to Docibilis I and John I in both his recorded transactions.[165] Bishop Bonus helped John I to increase Docibilan lands by selling him one piece of land in Dragoncello and approving the sale of another in 919.[166] The land, as we have already seen, seems to have been destined for Gregory, John's son, who was also archdeacon of Gaeta and thus Bonus' effective deputy. This series of transactions perhaps illustrates better than any other the mutually beneficial relationship between the Docibilans and the Gaetan church. The relationship was not without times of friction, however. In 936 Docibilis II and his son gave security to bishop Peter about an estate called Logrezzano, suggesting that there had been a dispute over its ownership.[167] Peter's successor, Marinus, also won a court-case against a Docibilan, this time one of John I's natural sons Peter, in 945. The case was judged by Peter's half-brother Docibilis II, indicating that in some cases political expediency could overcome family loyalty.[168] Peter received better treatment at the hands of bishop Stephen, who gave him land in Flumetica in 962.[169] We may see here the bishop taking advantage of the fact that there were many male members of the Docibilan line to choose from to endow with land, and hinting to those in power that the bishop's voice should not be ignored.

It may have been desire to eliminate this inherent threat to Docibilan power which led to the installation of Bernard, son of duke Marinus, as bishop of Gaeta at the end of the tenth century. In one move a compliant bishop was, in theory, obtained and the pretensions to the dukedom of a younger son contained. (Although men who held both posts were not unknown in southern Italy – the bishop/duke of Naples in the 880s, Athanasius, is a case in point.[170])

As part of two landowning networks, those of the church and the ruling dynasty, Bernard was uniquely powerful – he held onto his position as bishop until his death in 1047, twelve years after his

[165] *CDC* 17, *CDC* 22. [166] *CDC* 25, *CDC* 26. [167] *CDC* 39.
[168] *CDC* 47. [169] *CDC* 62. [170] See above, chapter 2.

family had been ousted as dukes of Gaeta. How did he achieve this?

Part of Bernard's success must be due to his longevity. He had fifty years in power to establish respect for himself and, more importantly, an economic base from which to meet his episcopal obligations. Many of his documents survive, revealing him to have been a careful collector and manager of land, but the two which interest us most are those in which he had dealings with his relatives. In 999 he was involved in a dispute with his nephew, count Dauferius II of Traetto, over the estate called Spinio (Spigno Vecchia), and settled on a division of the land.[171] In 1002 he gave his sister-in-law duchess Emilia a piece of land in return for the help she had given the bishopric.[172] The significance of these two cessions is that they occurred just as the Docibilan family faced a critical period in their rule, when those branches of the clan ruling the counties, especially Traetto, were acting more and more independently.[173] In the first document, we see the aggressiveness of a new power trying to establish a landed base. In the second we perhaps see the drawing together of allies at the centre in a defensive mood. After years of ducal gifts to the bishopric, the bishop was reciprocating with his support for the old regime. If land was the way to express this, then that was what he would give.

However, if Bernard saw himself as the defender of his family's position at Gaeta, Emilia and her successors did not. In 1009, she confirmed the decision of a court-case against him in favour of the monastery of St Benedict at Montecassino,[174] and signalled the beginning of a new era.[175]

At Naples, the closeness between rulers and bishops reached a high point with the holding of both offices by Athanasius between 878 and 898. Pope John VIII, so disappointed with Docibilis' attitude towards breaking off relations with the Arabs, had high hopes that a bishop in power at Naples would set a better example. If so, these hopes were dashed; Athanasius had just as acute a sense of needing to come to some arrangement with the raiders as his contemporary at Gaeta, and suffered the same excommunication. Subsequent bishops of Naples also seem to have come from the ducal family, although information is somewhat lacking as to their precise relationship, since only two documents refer to ducal–

[171] *CDC* 101. [172] *CDC* 105.

[173] For the relationship between Bernard and Emilia, and for the detachment of Traetto, see below, chapter 5, sections (a) and (b) respectively. [174] *CDC* 118.

[175] Relationship between Gaeta and Montecassino, see below, chapter 5, section (c,iii).

episcopal action. The first records bishop Acculsarius and duke Gregory's donation of the monastery of St Severinus at Lucullano to SS Severinus and Sossus in 907.[176] The second attests to the closeness between individual dukes and their bishops: after the death of archbishop Leo following a visit to Constantinople, dukes John and Marinus commemorated him by ordering books to be made. He had apparently been an avid reader, and so this was a fitting tribute to him.[177]

The remaining Neapolitan episcopal documents from the early period, however, are remarkably detached from ducal affairs. They mostly relate to the churches and property over which the bishops had control.[178] Another series of documents perhaps reveals why the bishops do not seem to have been as prominent in Neapolitan affairs as we might have expected. In a trio of disputes over land with the powerful Greek monastery of SS Sergius and Bacchus, the bishops lost twice and came to a compromise settlement in the other case.[179] This may reflect a contest for authority between the two main ecclesiastical institutions in the city which now can only be glimpsed, and our ducal documents can give us no further information as to which the dukes favoured.

At Amalfi again the fragmented survival of the documents makes establishing a relationship between the dukes and bishops difficult. In 1012 archbishop Leo bought a water-mill portion from members of the ducal family including duke Sergius.[180] But only one document, dated 1023, shows the dukes actively supporting the archbishop, when Sergius and John ordered the goldsmiths Sergius and Ursus to make a document of security to archbishop Leo.[181]

Otherwise, episcopal documents follow the familiar pattern of control over smaller churches in the duchy, and leasing out of pieces of landed property. For example, in 993 archbishop Leo

[176] *DCDN* 1. [177] *Monumenta*, 1, p. 339.

[178] E.g. *RN* 3, (915): Athanasius agrees to a lease by SS Festus and Desiderius; *RN* 8, (921): Athanasius signs a document of the abbess of SS Gregory, Sebastian and Pantaleo to the episcopal church; *RN* 153: Athanasius recorded as having sold land in Balusanu before 966; *RN* 266, (990): Sergius signs a sale by servants of the episcopal church of Mauganum land to St Severus; *RN* 273, (992): Sergius signs a settlement involving SS Marcellinus and Peter over land; *RN* 318: Athanasius recorded as having agreed to gift to St George *Maioris* before 1003.

[179] *RN* 125, (962): Niceta disputes land with St Sebastian and loses; *RN* 154 (966): Gregory disputes land with SS Sergius and Bacchus and divides it; *RN* 356, (1015): John disputes and loses land at Nonnaria to the same church. [180] *RN* 346.

[181] *CDA* II, 590.

appointed a priest to St Sebastian in Pigellula, and seems also to have supervised St Benedict in Scala.[182] In 1007 he lost a court-case over land in Stabia to one of the more prominent families of the duchy.[183] In 1008 a trio of documents show the son of a former archbishop, Constantine, buying up land, and the signature of the current archbishop Stephen suggests that he had initiated the action or at least approved of it.[184] In 1012 archbishop Leo received a piece of land near Radicosa from a tenant unable to continue working it because 'the Lombards came'.[185] Further evidence of the archbishop's economic activity comes in documents of 1024, when Leo bought land in Stabia, and 1035, when he leased out land in Carniano.[186] Several of the transactions reveal that the archbishops performed a dual role as incumbents of the episcopal seat and as abbots of SS Ciricus and Iulicta. The latter monastery, however, does not appear to have attracted ducal patronage.

(e) JUSTICE

Merores[187] discusses the role of the early *hypatoi* or dukes of Gaeta as judges of court-cases, and this is just as important a manifestation of Docibilan power as the other aspects. The fact that the first document[188] we have of Docibilis I in 867 shows him in the role of judge is significant, for the act of submitting a dispute to his judgement meant that the disputants, Ramfus bishop of Gaeta and Maurus and John of Gaeta, recognised his authority and that his decision would, it was hoped, be respected by any other interested parties. The presence of such illustrious witnesses as Bonus, son of count Anatolius, also implies recognition of Docibilis' position of superiority. A generation later the dispute flared up again between the bishopric and the sons of Maurus and John. Again the case was brought before, and settled by, the dukes of Gaeta.[189]

We see the Docibilan rulers sitting in judgement at court-cases throughout the tenth century. In 945, for example, bishop Marinus disputed with Peter, the natural son of John I, about land in Traetto's territory; Docibilis II and John II decided in favour of the bishop.[190] Peter did no better before John II in 958, when he and

182 *CDA* II, 589.
183 *CDA* 21; the case went to the Neapolitani, of whom more later: see below, chapter 4, section (b).
184 *CDA* 25, *CDA* 26, *CDA* 27.
185 *CDA* 31.
186 *CDA* 37, *CDA* 41.
187 *Gaeta*, chapter 2.
188 *CDC* 13.
189 *CDC* 48.
190 *CDC* 47.

his brothers Leo and Constantine clashed with the priest of St Michael's at Planciano.[191] Both decisions may have owed more to the dukes' desire to maintain good relations with the church than with the facts of each case; we cannot justifiably interpret them as a way of keeping potential challengers for power in their place. When the heirs of Kampulus the prefect and the three natural sons of John I were in dispute in 957, the decision of John II was to divide the contested territory, thereby attempting to appease both parties.[192]

What happened when the dukes themselves were in dispute? In 946, when Docibilis II fought over the estates called Caput Piro and Iuniano with his cousins John and Docibilis sons of Leo the prefect, no external help seems to have been available to appeal to, so a compromise and share-out of the estates was reached.[193] This reveals the weakness of a situation where the disputes of the great men of Gaeta could only be heard by the duke. However, our documentary evidence may be rather deceptive here; just thirty-five years later the two sons of duke Gregory quarrelled over some land, and referred their dispute not to the reigning dukes Marinus and John III (their uncle and cousin), but to the *nobiliores* of Gaeta.[194] To ask for the judgement of their peers must have been a normal practice for those outside the ducal circle throughout the tenth century. We have several references in our witness lists to men bearing the title *iudex* in the tenth century, even if we do not see them at work until the eleventh.[195]

It is possible, therefore, that the role of judge was one which the dukes would lose to men who specialised in the work during the eleventh century. (In a case heard at Pontecorvo in 1058, we even see duke Atenolf I, 'growing tired of' a particularly long-running dispute and handing it over to an appointed judge, ordering him to settle the matter.[196]) The important point to note, however, is that they had established their right to judge others very early on in their period of rule, and that this right does not appear to have been questioned.

The right to sit in judgement over court cases was one claimed by most medieval rulers, and it is not surprising to find the dukes of Naples fulfilling the same role. Their interest, however, suggested

[191] *CDC* 56. [192] *CDC* 54. [193] *CDC* 49. [194] *CDC* 79.

[195] Nicephorus *CDC* 43 (941); Paul *CDC* 62 (962), *CDC* 63 (963), *CDC* 66 (964); on eleventh-century judges, see below, chapter 5, sections (d,ii) and (e,ii).

[196] *CDC* 207.

by the two surviving tenth-century cases judged by the duke, lay in the affairs of the great men of their duchy. In 932 duke John was present at a dispute involving men titled *magnifici*; in 992 duke Sergius was called in to a dispute involving the powerful Neapolitan monastery of SS Sergius and Bacchus.[197] This reflects Gaetan evidence, where most cases coming before Docibilans were contested by the nobility, it seems. What is striking about the two Neapolitan examples is that although the disputes came before the dukes of the day, John in 932 and Sergius in 992, in neither case was a decision by the duke recorded. Instead, the mere bringing of the cases seems to have acted as a catalyst to a settlement; the earlier case was decided by an oath, the latter apparently by written evidence. It may well be that the duke was in no position to enforce a decision, even if he had made one. Alternatively, the function of bringing the case before him may have been to ensure that the correct procedures were seen to have been followed before a settlement was reached. In northern Italy, slightly earlier, the function of judges at court seems to have been precisely this; their primary aim was not to adjudicate, but to oversee the process of producing proofs and settlement.[198] The 932 case mirrors other Neapolitan evidence of disputes being settled by oaths,[199] although not, apparently, before the duke. The earliest recorded judge at Naples appears in 927, but this is in a document preserved at Cava outside Salerno, and his title may reflect local customs rather than Neapolitan ones.[200] Certainly men known by the title of *iudex* are extremely difficult to find in the Neapolitan documents, and it is only in the eleventh century that we have any further record of their activities.[201]

The importance of oaths in settling disputes is again illustrated in evidence from Amalfi, where the earliest evidence of ducal involvement occurs in 969. In that year, duke Manso ordered the two parties in a land dispute to swear to their cases, and a settlement was obtained.[202] In 1023, the dukes of Amalfi backed up the

[197] *RN* 21, *RN* 277.

[198] C. J. Wickham, 'Land disputes and their social framework in Lombard-Carolingian Italy, 700–900', in *The Settlement of Disputes in Early Medieval Europe*, ed. W. Davies and P. Fouracre (Cambridge, 1986), p. 110.

[199] Oaths: *RN* 36 (937), *RN* 48 (942), *RN* 73 (951), *RN* 114 (960), *RN* 127 (963), *RN* 136 (964), *RN* 143 (965), *RN* 180 (970), *RN* 193 (972), *RN* 201 (974), *RN* 210 (976), *RN* 217 (978), *RN* 259 (989), *RN* 276 (992).

[200] *CodCav* I/46; the public judge of Naples made a decision about a house. The parties in the case are not nobles, it seems.

[201] *RN* 466, (1039).

[202] *CodCav* II/261.

archbishop in a transaction with two goldsmiths.[203] In 1055 duke John took a more active role when a case was brought before him involving a piece of land disputed between one Gregory of the powerful Monteincollo family and two women. Since the women refused to attend the court, for unknown reasons, John decided in favour of Gregory.[204] The latter two examples are relatively late; it is likely that the dukes sat in judgement as elsewhere in the Tyrrhenian from an early date. In a document of 920, the dating clause refers to the rulers Mastalus and his son as 'glorious judges', which is fairly conclusive evidence of a role they were expected to play.[205] However, judges are fairly heavily documented from 977 onwards in the Amalfitan evidence, and they may have taken on most cases. If they did, we have no record of it. The relatively few Amalfitan disputes which survive reveal only that the parties in the disagreement sometimes had recourse to a 'court'.[206] The majority of judges' documents, on the other hand, shows them as witnesses, suggesting that their presence was becoming necessary to validate a transaction. It is striking, too, that a high proportion of surviving ducal documents include judges in their witness lists.[207] This closeness between ruler and judges would be significant later in the duchy's history, when the latter began to take on a more active governmental role.

It is worth pausing for a moment to consider what the evidence from the Tyrrhenian cities tells us about dispute settlement in this area in the early medieval period. Very few court-cases were held before judges during this period. Instead, dukes presided over courts; but their concern might only have been for the disagreements of their major subjects. This brings up the issue of how well the documentary evidence reflects the actuality of everyday disputes. Although 'the recording of cases and judgements was . . . of paramount importance' in the Byzantine world of which these three cities were the direct heirs,[208] the documents which we have

[203] *CDA* II, 590.

[204] *CP* 33; for more on the Monteincolli, see below, chapter 4, section (b).

[205] *CDA* II, 585; see also Schwarz, *Amalfi nel Medioevo*, p. 69.

[206] *CP* 30 (984), *CDA* 21 (1007), *CDA* 49 (1037).

[207] Judges witnessing ducal documents: John *CodCav* II/386 (986), *CDA* 588 (988); Manso *CDA* 590 (1023); Sergius *CDA* 591 (1033), *CDA* 60 (1048); John son of Niceta *CDA* 591 (1033); John *CDA* 60 (1048); Constantine *CDA* 66 (1058); John *CDA* 592 (1079); Leo and Pardus *CDA* 87 (1091); Sergius, John and Leo *CDA* 593 (1098).

[208] R. Morris, 'Dispute settlement in the Byzantine provinces in the tenth century', in *Settlement of Disputes*, p. 140. Morris uses evidence from southern Italy to support her findings.

reflect only the cases which were thought worth recording. Winners were likely to want documentary evidence of their victory in court; churches in particular kept records of this type, and feature in the majority of cases which survive.[209]

However, many surviving documents record cases which seem to have ended in compromises being reached, and it is likely that far more disputes were settled in this way without even reaching the court. In cities which do not, at this time, seem to have had professional judges, the arbitration of peers (as in the case of the *nobiliores* at Gaeta mentioned above) may have worked on a far less formal basis to end disagreements. Those cases which did come before the duke might, therefore, be seen as the ones which could not be settled in private, perhaps requiring a document to be made as proof of the winner's case.

Thus, although dukes claimed the right to judge disputes in the ninth and tenth centuries, the surviving evidence suggests that they may have overseen only a small minority of the processes of settlement between their subjects. Most disagreements may have been settled by verbal agreements in the presence of neighbours. It is important to bear this in mind when assessing the level of 'power' the role of judge conferred on a duke.

(f) PUBLIC FINANCE AND PUBLIC SERVICE

We have no evidence of how the Docibilans in the tenth century controlled the public finances of Gaeta. This is not really surprising in a document base which deals primarily in land transactions. However, given their apparently conscious monopolisation of such public assets as milling, we can perhaps postulate that any revenue to be had from such things as market or port dues was swiftly taken over. The evidence from the wills of men like Docibilis I, Docibilis II and Gregory son of Leo the prefect points to some interest in the luxury goods reaching Gaeta, but no firm documentary evidence points to their active participation in the importation of such merchandise.

Such problems dog the Neapolitan evidence as well. It is unlikely that the dukes of Naples monopolised commercial undertakings as perhaps the Gaetans did. However, a hint of the sources of public revenue which the dukes could call upon may be

[209] Wickham, 'Land disputes', p. 105, makes this point for northern Italy.

contained in a document of 999, in which John, consul and duke, gave the monastery of SS Sergius and Bacchus the right to sail its ships and boats wherever the abbot wanted, and permission to use *nauticis extraneis*, or foreign sailors.[210] There is clearly an issue of ducal control of shipping here, and we can only assume that those who wished to sail and land their ships in the duke's ports would be charged for the privilege. This image is strengthened if we remember that the area covered by the ducal palace complex in the city may well have comprised most of the shoreline. In a more direct reference, although later, duke Sergius gave the church of SS Sergius and Bacchus to that of St Salvator and exempted it from any public services or *angaria*.[211] Other public controls which seem to have been enforced at Naples included that over water, already mentioned, over walls and towers and over gates. Gate duty seems to have been 'privatised', from twelfth-century evidence;[212] giving out such sources of income to other families may have reinforced their ties to the dukes. One role in which the dukes of Naples are quite frequently seen is that of consenters to transactions, all but one involving alienation of land.[213] In one document the reason for the ducal intervention is specified – the party authorising the document is a minor[214] – and it is likely that the other examples are similarly motivated. Such protection of minors might have been highly profitable for the dukes, who in effect gained control over their property.

Again at Amalfi we can get only a glimpse of the kind of fiscal revenues that the dukes could call upon, and our one reference to them is late, from 1033. In that year duke John excused his aunt, Drosu the wife of Marinus son of duke Manso, from dues owed to the treasury on a piece of land she had bought on Capri. These consisted of 27 *congia* of wine, 3 *modia* of vegetables, 10 sheep and 20 quails.[215] Such a document hardly suggests a sophisticated fiscal administration in the duchy at this time, but Amalfi's neighbours do not seem to have been much more advanced.

210 *RN* 309. 211 *DCDN* 11 (1036).

212 Cassandro, 'Ducato', p. 206.

213 *RN* 195,(973): Marinus consents to a sale; *RN* 366, (1016): dukes Sergius and John give permission for a sale; *RN* 395, (1022): Sergius gives permission for a lease; *RN* 412, (1027): Sergius gives permission for a sale; *RN* 470, (1038): duke John gives permission for a sale; see also Cassandro, 'Ducato', p. 215. 214 *RN* 390 (1021).

215 *CDA* 591.

(g) CENTRAL AND LOCAL POWER

In all three of the Tyrrhenian duchies, we have a sense of the duke forming the focus of political power, but varying amounts of documentation as to the actual functions he performed. None of the three issued laws, adhering perhaps to the notion that they were still in effect subjects of the Byzantine emperor, and, therefore, to the laws issued by him.[216] There seems also, from the documentary evidence, to have been a distinct lack of fighting men in the three duchies, but this image may be illusory. The *milites* documented among Naples' citizens clearly performed some defensive function on that duchy's border with Capua. But it is apparent that these men were not directly answerable to the duke. They protected their own property, which lay on the border, and to some extent power to administer these areas must have devolved to them.

The devolution of power from the centre is an issue which I shall return to in a discussion of the duchies in the eleventh century, when the reasons for fragmentation in Gaeta are examined. The dukes of Gaeta too shared their power out to local counts, but in their case the exercise proved disastrous.

(h) RELATIONS WITH BYZANTIUM

It remains only to comment briefly on the relationship that the three duchies had with their former overlords, the emperors of Byzantium. Dating clauses can be revealing when looking at formal acknowledgements of power. The Docibilans flirted with dating by their own rule, reverted to imperial dating for a time, but then took the plunge when they began calling themselves dukes in the mid-tenth century and dispensed with the imperial regnal years in their documents. The Amalfitans seem not to have had such qualms, perhaps because they were ruled briefly by Salerno before becoming independent, and the earliest document we have, from 860, is dated by Manso the prefect's regnal year.[217] But Naples'

216 That the dukes' subjects certainly had a vague idea that they were part of a wider sphere is suggested by the continued citations of 'Roman law' in some documents. But the lack of legislation in the tenth century was mirrored in Lombard states as well, where royal laws of the seventh and eighth centuries continued to be cited.

217 *CDA* II, 584.

documents were dated by the imperial regnal year in the ninth and tenth centuries and would continue to be so in the eleventh. In this city, with a long curial tradition and a long memory, formalities were strictly observed even when they clearly had no basis in reality. The air of conservatism that surrounded the ducal dynasty permeated the documents written during their reign.

Another indicator of attachment, or lack thereof, to their erstwhile ruler can be seen in the coinage of the three duchies. Although the documents reveal a variety of gold and silver coins in use, the most frequent currency in use for accounting purposes was the Byzantine *solidus*. If we look at the everyday bronze coins used in the three cities, however, we see that they struck their own. Gaetan bronze or copper *follari* bore the name of the duke and a representation of the city's patron saint, Erasmus;[218] Naples' coins were similar, with saint Ianuarius depicted. But Naples also struck silver coinage, and this continued to show the current Byzantine emperor, *not* the duke.[219] Amalfi, perhaps not unexpectedly, was the least inclined to maintain an outward show of deference to the Byzantines, and her coinage followed the Arabic example in producing gold *tari* or quarter-dinars from the mid-eleventh century.[220]

A final link with the Byzantine empire was the continued use of Byzantine honorific titles in all three duchies, and here the different types of charter evidence, discussed above, may be responsible for producing a somewhat surprising picture. For, whilst both Amalfitan[221] and Gaetan[222] documents reveal a continued use of

[218] On Gaetan coinage, S. Ferraro, *Le Monete di Gaeta* (Naples, 1915), cannot now be relied upon. The coinage of Gaeta and the surrounding area is the subject of new work by Lucia Travaini, who is engaged in a critical reappraisal of how many surviving coins are genuine, and how many of these can be attributed to a Gaetan mint: Travaini, *Monetazione*. [219] Cassandro, 'Ducato', p. 257.

[220] Ferraro, *Monete*, p. 30; see also G. Sambon, *Il Tari Amalfitano* (Milan, 1891): again, the work of Travaini is providing a critical survey of both the Amalfitan *tari* and the surviving bronze coinage from the city. See L. Travaini, 'I tari di Salerno e Amalfi', *Rassegna del Centro di Cultura e Storia Amalfitana*, 19–20 (1990), 7–71, now to be modified by Travaini, *Monetazione*.

[221] Titles were conferred on several rulers of Amalfi, as dating clause evidence reveals: Manso imperial *spatharocandidatus* (907, *CDA* 1); Mastalus imperial patrician and Leo *protospatharius* (922, *CDA* 2); Mastalus again with his son John imperial patricians (947, *CDA* 6); Manso imperial patrician (966, *CP* 29); Sergius imperial patrician (1018, *CDA* 33); John imperial patrician (1033, *CDA* 39) and then patrician, *anthipatus et vestis* (1055, *CP* 33). A few of their subjects also had titles: John son of Niceta imperial *protospatharius* (1005, *CDA* 19, onwards); John son of Sergius imperial *protospatharius* (1006, *CDA* 20); Niceta son of John *protospatharius* son of Niceta archbishop (1007/22?, *CDA* 23); John son of Mauri son of Sergii *protospatharius* (1013, *PAVAR* 1/6); Ursus son of Niceta

Byzantine titles throughout the tenth century and into the eleventh, such titles are extremely rare in those from Naples.[223] Given the fact that Naples seems to have been the most 'Byzantine' of the three duchies, this lack is initially puzzling. However, if the titles were conferred to bring recalcitrant subjects back into the Byzantine fold, the reason for their frequency at Amalfi, particularly the high number awarded to the rulers of that city, and low number at Naples, becomes clear. For the Amalfitans, since 839, had maintained a relationship with both the Arabs attacking the Tyrrhenian and with their Lombard neighbours in Salerno. Neither was viewed with any amity by the Byzantines[224] or, after 915, by Naples. When duke John of Amalfi faced the Lombard challenge to his power in the mid-eleventh century, Byzantium reacted by conferring titles upon him, almost as a show of support. Similarly, the Garigliano campaign against the Arabs in 915 was accompanied by the conferring of imperial patriciates on all the main parties to reinforce their adherence to the alliance. Thus titles did have a function beyond honouring their bearers, but as the eleventh century progressed only Amalfi seems to have been seen as a duchy needing attention from the Byzantines (perhaps related not only to its proximity to Lombard Salerno, but also to its role as an important trading partner of the eastern emperors). Naples, as we have seen, had very few title-holders, and Gaeta seems to have experienced a sharp drop as memories of men honoured in the tenth century faded.

CONCLUSION

This chapter has attempted to illustrate the wealth which the early dukes had at their disposal, and the administrative functions they

protospatharius (1037, *CDA* 50). These were clearly not handed on, but were important enough to be remembered by the descendants of those who had held them.

[222] Apart from the imperial patriciate awarded to John I for his part in the Garigliano campaign, we see no other rulers of Gaeta with imperial titles. Several of their subjects did, however, have minor titles: Marinus *spatharius* (924, *CDC* 31); Leo son of John *spatharius* (936, *CDC* 39); Leo son of Leo *protospatharius* (983, *CDC* 83, 1002, *CDC* 108), and a significant number of John's children continued to cite their father's title, for example Leo in 922, *CDC* 29, Theotista in 937, *CDC* 40, Mirus, Leo and Constantine in 941, *CDC* 43, Megalu in 958, *CDC* 58, and duke Docibilis in 946, *CDC* 49.

[223] In Naples, only the title *spatharius* occurs, and this is rare: two men named Gregory bore the title in 941, *RN* 44, and in 1015, *Mon.Sopp.* 532.

[224] Even the conferring of titles upon individual Lombard rulers can be interpreted as a means to encourage cooperation.

performed. At Gaeta land was used to secure the position of the Docibilans *vis-à-vis* the nobles who came to their courts and the church.

There is one intangible aspect of power which cannot be proven from the documentary evidence, however, and that is the energy, industry and charisma of men like Docibilis I and his son John I. It was these which allowed them to overcome their lack of family background, and possibly some opposition, and to lay the foundations of dynastic rule. For the dukes of Amalfi and Naples there was perhaps less of an air of illegitimacy about their rise, despite the rather traumatic circumstances of the former's break from the latter.

The tenth-century duchies can be characterised as lacking strong administrative structures. Central power revolved around the dukes and their families, all of whom had a relatively loose notion of their public function. Public and private land were intermingled; their rule was based purely on dynastic inheritance and received no outside legitimisation from either the Byzantine empire (although the conferring of imperial titles on all three rulers at least suggests approbation of their position) or the church. The latter's co-operation was useful, but not essential.

The distinct lack of bureaucratic or fiscal offices visible in the documents may owe something to the fact that the latter largely recorded property transactions, but an argument from lack of evidence probably is safe in this period. Later on, as chapter 5 will illustrate, such offices did exist, and they show up in the documents of the rulers. In the tenth and early eleventh centuries, however, these small states really do look like extended family businesses. However, none of the ruling families could exercise power without the co-operation of their leading subjects. Taking Gaeta as its main example, the next chapter will explore how different families could influence the fortunes of the ruling house, and how they built up power bases of their own.

Chapter 4

NOBLE FAMILIES IN THE TENTH CENTURY

(a) GAETA

The economic and political power of the Docibilan rulers of Gaeta can only be appreciated fully if it is treated within the context of a comparison with the fortunes of other contemporary families in Gaeta. This subject has only been patchily dealt with in the Gaetan historiography so far. Both Merores and Fedele have discussed certain eleventh-century clans, but neither really addressed those of the tenth century.[1] And Delogu, whilst recognising the importance of the early Docibilans' relationships with the sons of count Anatolius and with Kampulus the prefect, did not examine the family histories of either man or cast his net wider to discuss other noble families.[2]

One reason for this oversight may be that during the tenth and early eleventh centuries, the use of surnames to identify blood ties was still extremely rare at Gaeta,[3] which renders the tracing of tenth-century lines of descent less obviously simple. Only one of the families to be discussed in this chapter, the Caracci, consistently used that surname after their first appearance in 1020,[4] relatively late. It is likely that they derived it from the genitive form of the name of an ancestor, Caraccius, losing the final -i.[5] In a similar way, for ease of identification, I have created genitive-form

[1] Merores, *Gaeta*, p. 118; P. Fedele, 'La famiglia di Gelasio II', in *Scritti Storici*, pp. 434–440.
[2] 'Ducato', p. 200.
[3] It would become common from the middle of the eleventh century: see below, chapter 6. [4] *CDC* 138.
[5] Merores, *Gaeta*, p. 118, thinks that the family were descended from one Stephen of Tremonsuoli. His sons, John and Ferruccius, are visible in 981 (*CDC* 80), and we have one Carruccius son of John Firruccius authorising a document of 1012 (*CDC* 125). The name Carruccius is unusual enough to make some kind of family link likely, but perhaps not via direct descent, for the three Caracci brothers who appear in 1020 (*CDC* 138) are the sons of John Caracci, and thus may be too close to Carruccius in date to be his grandsons.

surnames based on their earliest or most prominent member for the families discussed in this chapter. Thus the family of count Christopher are called the Christopherii, that of Kampulus the prefect the Kampuli, and the descendants of count Anatolius, whose son Constantine ruled Gaeta from *c.*839 to 866, the Anatolii and so on.

In the absence of surnames in the documentation itself, other methods were used to establish relationships by blood or marriage. Whilst none guarantees absolutely that family ties exist, they could be used effectively in conjunction with each other to build up a substantial case in favour of a relationship.

The first method which yielded promising results when applied to the Gaetan documentation was the use of lead-names, that is isolating names which recur within a family from one generation to the next. Karl Schmid demonstrated the use of this method in building up a history of the Carolingian Udalriching clan,[6] that is a family in which the name Ulrich or Odalrich recurred. The lead-name came from the founder of the family's fortunes, who was a brother of the wife of Charlemagne, Hildegard. However, as he pointed out, could we really assign to this same family all occurrences of the name throughout the Carolingian empire? Clearly not, but, if one limited the investigation to a restricted region within the empire (Schmid used the district around Lake Constance), more localised groups could be built up who, because of their proximity to each other, were more likely to be related.

This method seemed to be ideal for Gaeta, a territorially limited area. Using names of men who could be said to have founded or greatly enhanced their family fortunes, such as those of count Anatolius, his possible great-grandson Kampulus the prefect, count Christopher and Docibilis I himself, it soon became apparent that the lead-name method worked very well on Gaetan material. An emergent pattern was that of the lead-name occurring in alternate generations, which can be illustrated if we look at a truncated genealogy of the Docibilan clan (see Figure 4.1).

Even within such a limited area as Gaeta, however, it is clear that not all occurrences of a particular name, such as Docibilis, automatically represent a relationship with the dynasty whose lead-name it is. Other traceable families also named the occasional

[6] K. Schmid, 'The structure of the nobility in the earlier middle ages', in *The Medieval Nobility*, ed. T. Reuter (Oxford, 1979), pp. 37–59.

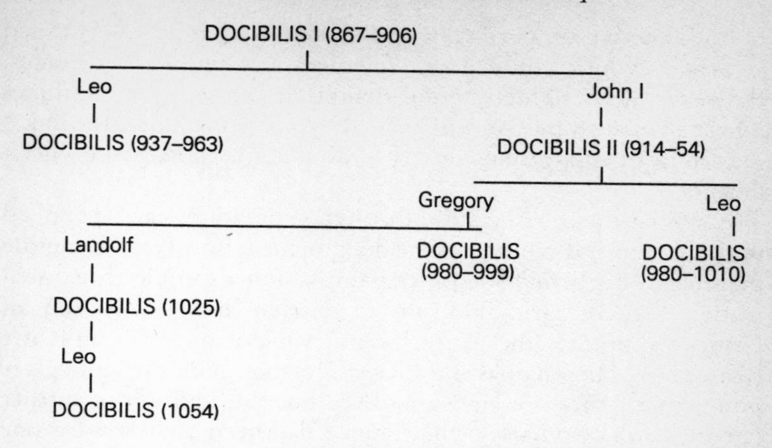

Figure 4.1 *Recurrence of the Docibilis lead-name*

son Docibilis. But it is a sign of their eagerness to associate themselves in a literally nominal way with the ruling line, and it is noticeable that the Docibilan genealogical table in full does not feature one blood-relation by the name of Kampulus or Christopher, the lead-names of other dynasties. Particularly significant, though, is the fact that Docibilis I used the lead-name of the former ruling family of Gaeta, the Anatolii, for one of his own sons, Anatolius the duke of Terracina. This fits very well with the discussion above of Docibilis' aspirations to links with the Anatolii, almost giving the impression of blood ties, as well as the marital ones which occurred.

Similar lead-name patterns to the one in the Docibilan genealogy can be built up for the three other families mentioned, and are included in the discussions of each in the main body of the chapter. What should be noted also, in this context, is a less strong, but nevertheless identifiable, tendency to use female lead-names within the clan as well. The parallel Matronas mentioned earlier are one example of this.[7]

The second method of family identification which yielded results was to examine cases where possible members of the same family, but perhaps of different generations, could be associated with the same piece of land. This clearly has limitations; it would be hazardous to assume a relationship between two people on the basis

[7] See above, chapter 2 and Figure 2.1.

of both owning unspecified pieces of land in a named district such as Scauri, which could have contained any number of estates. However, if we tighten up our definition and use only examples where an estate (*casale* or *curtis*) called by a certain name is the link,[8] we can justifiably propose a relationship between its two owners/tenants.

A similar use of association through generations can be applied to those men and women in the documents who appear alongside members of a firmly identified family. For example three men named Franco, Grimaldo son of Franco and Guitto son of Grimaldo appear in the eleventh century in documents from Fratte (Ausonia).[9] Their names and their association with the same place points to a father, son and grandson, but the addition of further circumstantial evidence – that Franco had been a witness for one Peter Giczi in 1030 and that Grimaldo and Guitto were both co-witnesses with Peter's son in 1048 and 1079 respectively – tipped the balance. For, if two men were friends or regularly acted together in business transactions, in all likelihood their sons would follow suit. (Men with less obviously linkable and unusual names have also been successfully related using this method.)

Such methodology is not without its risks, and so the genealogies which follow are footnoted to provide additional information. It is also true to say that one can fall into the trap of isolating one family too much from another, when in fact marriage ties not readily visible in our documents could have existed. A consequence might be that two families acted far more as one clan. Conversely, in neatly packaging sets of relatives, it is easy to overlook the fact that they may not have co-operated with each other all the time; the Docibilans are a prime example of this. Why then attempt to associate them with each other at all and write their family histories? Because these noble families owned land outside Docibilan control, in some cases had lived in Gaeta prior to Docibilan rule, and yet are visible in Docibilan documents and never seemed to have questioned their subordinate position. Such a situation requires explanation. This can only be attempted if the families are examined in more detail.

[8] See, for example, the case of the casale Faonia, discussed later in this chapter, section (a,ii).

[9] *CDC* 159, *CDC* 185, *CDC* 252 (from Suio): for more on this family, see below, chapter 5, sections (b,iii) and (c,iii).

(i) *The Christopherii*

The landowning history of the first major family in the documents, the Christopherii, begins long before Docibilis I came to power in 867. In a document dating from between 800 and 814[10] count Christopher, the family's chief ancestor bought a piece of land near to the church of St Sabae outside Sperlonga from John, a son of count Anatolius. Christopher himself was thus linked with the Anatolii, the previous rulers of Gaeta, and his successors soon won their way into the good graces of the new rulers from 867 onwards. This seems to be indicated by the appearance of one Christopher son of Sergius as witness to the court held by Docibilis I in 867,[11] and from then on the Christopherii benefited from Docibilan patronage. In 890 count Christopher's son Peter leased some land in Paniano from Docibilis I and John I in perpetuity, for a cash payment of 6 *solidi*.[12] In the same year Peter's three children were confirmed as owners of the land near St Sabae, which the count their grandfather had bought,[13] by Docibilis I and John I. Whether Docibilis did this because he felt himself to be the heir, however tenuously, of the vendor, John son of Anatolius, or whether it was because he was asserting himself as the new lord of the lands which his predecessors in power had controlled, is unclear. There may have been some dispute over the ownership of the land, particularly since the record of the sale contains errors in the date clause.[14] But the effect of the confirmation itself must have been to draw attention to the fact that however rich and influential the Christopherii had been before, they now had to depend on the goodwill of the new regime.

From then on, records of the Christopherii family's landowning exhibit both a gradual spread of their lands from the early centre around Sperlonga eastwards towards the Garigliano river, and continuing links with the Docibilans (see Map 4.1). In 909 Christopher son of John agreed to his presumably now quite aged grandmother Anna's gift of St Laurence land (near Mola) to the

[10] *CDC* 1; the dating clause of this document, by the reign of the emperor Charles, means that the date assigned to it by the editors of the *Codex Cajetanus*, 787, cannot possibly be correct. I disagree with Brown, *Gentlemen and Officers*, p. 60, note 39, who redates the document to the late ninth century. The names recorded in the charter undoubtedly place it earlier. [11] *CDC* 13. [12] *CDC* 15. [13] *CDC* 16.

[14] That the original sale document may be forged remains a possibility, but one which is difficult to prove.

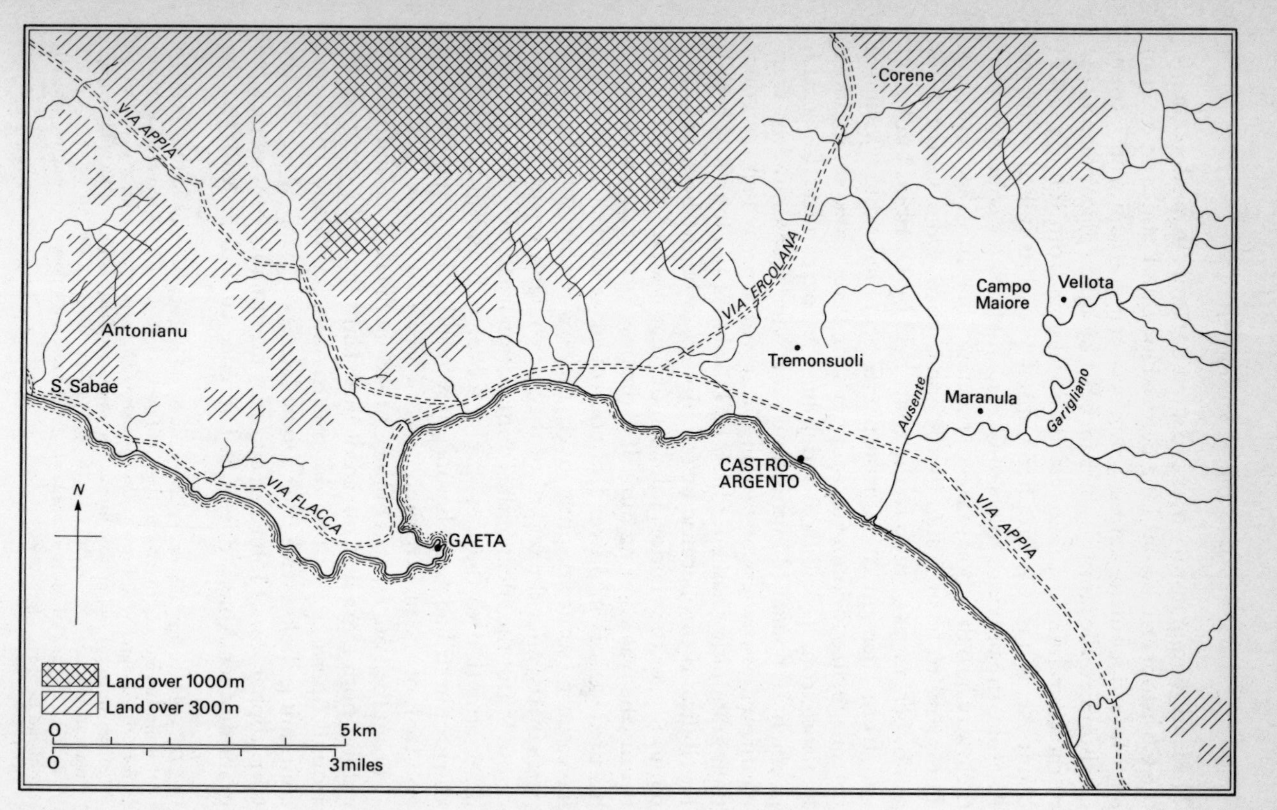

Map 4.1 *Lands of the Christopherii family*

Docibilan foundation of St Michael at Planciano.[15] He appeared as a witness for members of Docibilis' family in 918 and 919,[16] as did his cousin Christopher son of Leo in 939.[17]

Acting as their witnesses over several generations is one indication that the Christopherii were quite close to the ruling Docibilan dynasty. The family genealogy is an illustration of their continuous activity in this area (see Figure 4.2).

Meanwhile their property-owning spread. In 991 we learn that they had land at Marana in Flumetica.[18] In 1006 Gaetanus son of Christopher bought some land in Castro Argento,[19] and Leo son of Christopher *magnificus* is mentioned as owning land near Corene, Simproniano (in Gaeta) and Passignano near Traetto.[20] In 1032 the daughters of his brother Docibilis divided lands owned at Vellota and Campo Maiore, again in Flumetica.[21] As well as all their land in the eastern half of the duchy, there is evidence that members of the family did not forget the original centre of their wealth in the Sperlonga area. In 1021 we see John and Marinus sons of Christopher dividing the estate Antonianu in Calvi.[22]

Had the Christopherii obtained these lands from their patrons, the Docibilans? There is no direct evidence that they did, but the fact that five out of the named locations where they owned land were also the sites of Docibilan-controlled public land suggests that they may have owed their wealth to this source. After the family of Docibilis was ousted from power, the Christopherii soon disappeared from view. Their last appearance is in 1041, when Ramfus son of Christopher *magnificus* witnessed a document.[23]

Ramfus himself is worth investigating in more detail. A frequent witness to Gaetan documents, he co-owned land with his brothers Leo and Docibilis at Passignano and Vellota. In 1012, however, we see him in quite a different role. In that year he gave a guarantee via Marinus son of Constantine that he would pay Ubertus *magister Romanus* 7½ pounds of silver, silk, pepper and cotton for a house and a piece of land eight days before Ubertus' ship was to sail for Rome.[24]

This document, which is the earliest overt reference to commerce in these goods at Gaeta,[25] has aroused considerable

[15] *CDC* 20. [16] *CDC* 24, *CDC* 26. [17] *CDC* 42. [18] *CDC* 88.
[19] *CDC* 113. [20] *CDC* 125, *CDC* 139, *CDC* 151. [21] *CDC* 163.
[22] *CDC* 141. [23] *CDC* 175. [24] *CDC* 123/4.
[25] Although, as we have seen, others owned, and may possibly have traded in, such valuables.

Sergius

Christopher W
(867)

(2) Anna? = CHRISTOPHER *comes* = (1) ?Herania*

John

Christopher W†
(909–19)

John W
(949)

Christopher W
(981)

Peter
(890)

Leo
(890)

Peter£
?
?

Dilicciosa
(890)

Maria
(890)

Christopher W
magnificus
(939)

Christopher W
(944)

Docibilis W
(980–91)

Ramfus
(972–1041)

Leo W
(991–1026)

Gaetanus$
(1006)

John
(1021)

Marinus
(1006–21)

Maria
(1032)
= Landolf

Drosu
(1032)
= Gregory of Rome

* It is unclear whether Herania and Anna were the same woman known by different name forms, but the quite different name patterns descending from each suggest that Christopher married twice.

+ The unprovable line of descent from Christopher rests on the pattern of lead-names and the sons' continued association with the dukes.

£ If there were two branches of the Christopherii, descended from the count's sons Peter and John, it is possible that the sons' names would be used as the lead-names as often as the founder's; thus Christopher son of Peter probably does belong to the Petrine line.

$ Gaetanus is an unusual name for this clan, but the appearance of Marinus son of Christopher as a witness to his purchase of land in 1006 suggests that they may have been brothers.

Figure 4.2 *The Christopherii family (W = witnesses for the Docibilans)*

interest, and was discussed at some length by Merores.[26] Not only was a member of one of the most prominent families at Gaeta involved in trading activities, but he was also dealing with a man from Rome, an easy trip by sea from Gaeta.[27] This Roman connection may explain why one of Ramfus' nieces, Drosu, was married to a certain Gregory of Rome. If the Christopherii had business contacts there, what better way to secure them than with a marriage?

There is still further interest in the document when we look at why Ramfus was buying the property. He states that his cousin John, who cannot be identified with certainty, had sold the house and land to Ubertus, and so Ramfus was in fact retrieving family property. Here we have a phenomenon which appears frequently in southern Italy at this time; that most 'merchants' were in fact predominantly landowners using their landowning wealth to support their trading activities. Merores used Ramfus to support her argument that merchants achieved high status at Gaeta.[28] In doing so she missed the point that as a member of one of the oldest landed families in the territory, and as the son of a man titled *magnificus*, Ramfus could already claim high status and use it to further his business interests. The popular image of the landless man forced to make his living and rise to prominence through trade is, as I have argued in a previous study, comparatively rare.[29] The problem for the landowners, though, was how to liquefy some of their wealth for commercial investment. Is the document of 1012 an illustration of an attempt to do so? There is always a danger of overinterpretation, but I would propose the following sequence of events.

The Christopherii, in need of capital for either a trading expedition in their own right or, more likely, to finance such an expedition, agreed through their representative John to sell off the house and land to Ubertus in a mortgage arrangement, undertaking to pay him in cash and goods which he could sell at Rome. Their guarantor was Marinus son of count Constantine. The 1012 document as we have it consists first of Ramfus' promise to

[26] *Gaeta*, p. 97.

[27] A trip most recently discussed by V. von Falkenhausen, 'Reseaux routiers et ports dans l'Italie méridionale byzantine (VIe-Xe siècles)', in *I Kathimerini Zoi sto Byzantio* (Athens, 1989), p. 274.

[28] *Gaeta*, p. 99.

[29] P. E. Skinner, *The Mobility of Landowners between the Tyrrhenian City-States of Italy*, unpublished M. Phil., University of Birmingham (1988), chapter 9; the activities of some merchants are discussed below, chapters 7 and 8.

Marinus that he would fulfil the contract with Ubertus, or else Marinus would be compensated with double the amount of goods specified; and then Marinus' promise to Ubertus that he will pay him off as Ramfus has agreed. Once the transaction was completed Ramfus and his kin could reclaim their house and land and the whole process could begin again.

It is perhaps a little surprising, given their close contact in other ways, that the Christopherii are not seen raising the finance they needed from the Docibilans, who as we know could call upon considerable amounts of liquid wealth. But perhaps in their trading activities they were in direct competition with the rulers, or possibly they did not desire to become economically, as well as politically, independent. We must remember though that their landed property must always have remained their more important source of wealth. Without land, how could they trade?

It is unfortunate that we have no evidence at all about how the Christopherii cultivated and/or exploited their landed property. The main points to note are that it was widespread and owned in sufficient quantities to allow the risk of small parts on trading ventures. It was a pattern which was repeated in other families' wealth in the tenth century.

(ii) *The Kampuli*

One clan who seem to have had close connections with the Docibilan family were the Kampuli, descendants of Kampulus the prefect (fl.890–949). They achieved immediate prominence over their contemporaries the Christopherii by marrying into the Docibilan dynasty. Kampulus himself married the daughter of John I, Matrona, and thereby secured the fortunes of his kin, or so it appears. The compliment he paid to his new father-in-law's family by naming a son Docibilis and having another Docibilis and three Johns among his grandsons only serves to reinforce the impression of closeness between the Docibilans and the Kampuli. This impression is further strengthened when we discover that successive generations of the Kampuli clan, like the Christopherii, appear as witnesses to Docibilan documents (see genealogy Figure 4.3), and that they received many pieces of landed property from the rulers. However, the case of the Kampuli clan is somewhat more complex than a direct relationship of patronage by the Docibilans. For, by appearing as their witnesses, and making ties of marriage,

Marinus count

John I of Gaeta

Stephen W[§] (922–36) | Kampulus prefect W (890–949) = Matrona (949)

Kampulus W (963–74) | Docibilis W (957–9) = Drosu | Mirus (950–9) | Dusdedi (930) | Kampulus W (957–80) | Marinus W (959–1020)

Kampulus W (998–1042) | John W (978) | Constantine W (972–84) | Matrona (1004) | Docibilis W (984) | Kampulus W (983–93) | John W (976–96) | Sergius W (991–1071) | John W (972)

Marinus W[$] (1010–59) | Euprassia (1004) | Kampulus* (1028–36) | Mirus (1020) | Kampulus[£] (1064–71) | Constantine Berpamuzza = Gemma[†] (1064)

Leo (1064–89)

§ Stephen's career as a witness for the Docibilans (in 930 alongside Dusdedi), and the existence of Kampulus son of Stephen who is associated heavily with Kampuli and Docibilans between 963 and 974 indicate that this is another branch of the same clan.

$ In 1042 Marinus son of Kampulus received a gift from Leo II of Gaeta (*CDC* 176). Kampulus son of Docibilis witnessed the duke's only surviving document (*CDC* 177); Marinus may therefore have been his son rather than son of Kampulus son of Mirus.

* Kampulus son of John does not specify his grandfather's name to enable secure identification. However, he is twice a witness for members of the Caracci family, to whom Mirus son of John gave land in 1020. The association suggests strongly that he and Mirus are brothers.

+ Gemma, widow of Constantine Berpamuzza, mentions a 'Kampus' as her brother-in-law. This is more likely to be Kampulus son of John rather than Kampulus son of Sergius, because the latter may have died prematurely (see £). If Constantine is a member of the Kampuli clan, his adoption of a surname may indicate a change in the family's status.

£ In 1071 Sergius son of Kampulus made his will. His son Kampulus (identified on the basis of lead-name and the fact that both he and Sergius are associated with the Caracci family) seems to have died before that date, for Sergius left his goods to his wife Gaitelgrima and to the church.

Figure 4.3 *The Kampuli family (W = witnesses for the Docibilans)*

the Kampuli, as a cadet branch of the old ruling house, were lending support *and prestige* to the Docibilans, and they would expect to be paid accordingly. Again there is little direct evidence of Kampuli lands coming from the Docibilans, but like the Christopherii, many of their estates were situated in or near areas where there was public land.

A measure of Kampulus the prefect's standing, as I have already pointed out, can be gained if we look at the type of property he held. In two documents of 937 and 949, we see him handling the most prestigious landed property of all, water-mills.[30] The shares he exchanged could have belonged to his wife, Matrona daughter of *hypatos* John I, but she does not appear in the 937 document, as she should have done had this been the case.

All was not harmony between the two families, however. In 957 Kampulus' eponymous son and the heirs of three others disputed with the natural sons of John I (their uncles/great-uncles) over the estate called Rubeanu or Robiano in Flumetica (near Maranula: see Map 4.2). The contestants agreed to divide the land between themselves.[31] The case was judged by duke John II, nephew to John I's sons and cousin to Kampulus', who must have found it very difficult to make a decision against either party.

From later divisions between the younger Kampulus and his nephews, we know that they also owned land at Marana and some woodland in an unnamed part of Flumetica.[32] There is no inherent problem with the notion that the Kampuli divided amongst themselves land which may have been a gift from the *publicum*. The tendency for such land to be treated as private property was a common theme in this period. It should be noted that not all of the land they held was divided; some they chose to hold communally, presumably because it was easier to exploit that way; perhaps because it was too small to be worth dividing.

Once again we are poorly served with evidence for how the Kampuli exploited their land, or who cultivated it. A valuable document of 922 does, however, indicate that they themselves granted out the land to be cultivated. In that year one Sergius of Cliucurvo (north-east of Traetto) gave a piece of land there to Heligerno son of Constantine to compensate the latter for the fire that Sergius had caused in his cornfield.[33] He did so with the

[30] *CDC* 40, *CDC* 50; for a discussion of mills, see above, chapter 3, section (a).
[31] *CDC* 54. [32] *CDC* 68, *CDC* 69. [33] *CDC* 28.

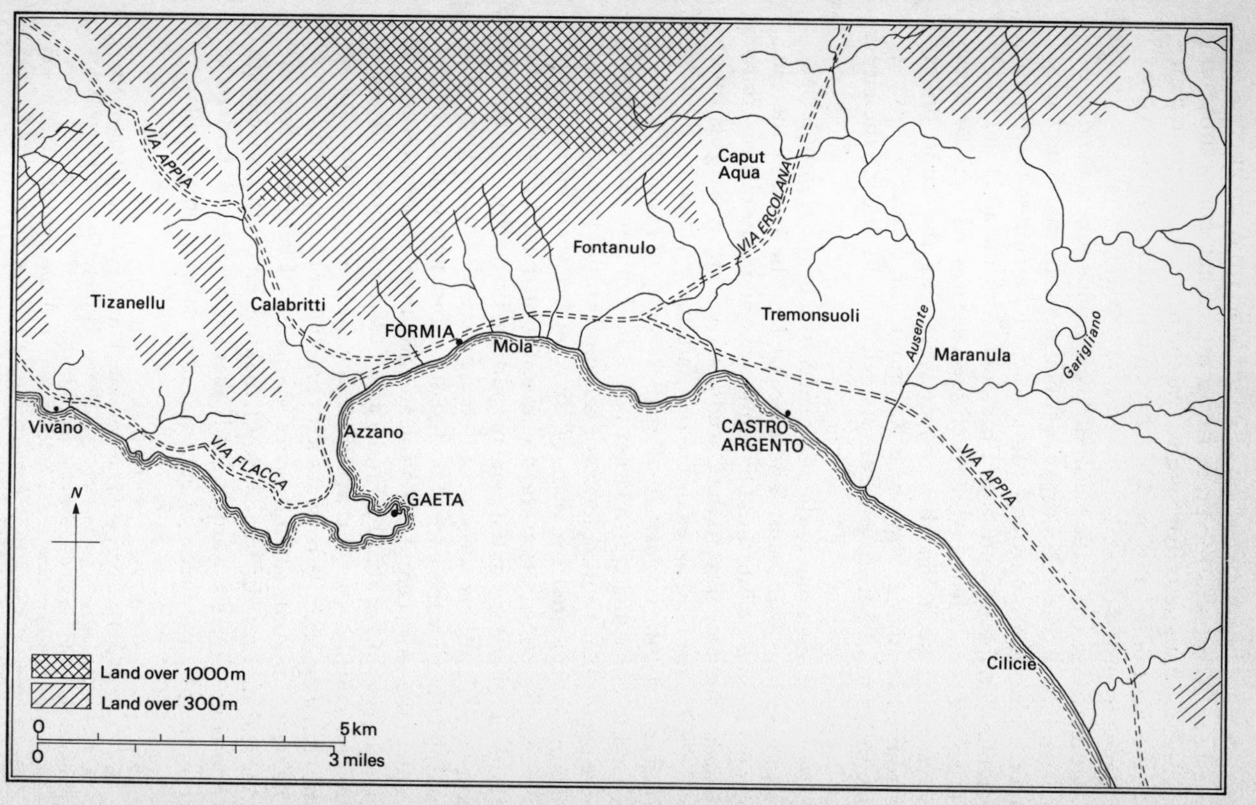

Map 4.2 *Lands of the Kampuli family*

permission of one Stephen son of count Marinus, who appears to have been Kampulus the prefect's brother. That this permission was necessary suggests that Sergius was the manager of, or a tenant on, the Kampuli lands in Cliucurvo, but there is no written evidence to prove this.

More evidence that the Kampuli were frequent beneficiaries of ducal goodwill comes in a stream of documents from 978 onwards. In that year Kampulus and John, sons of Docibilis, received a water-mill in the Ausente river from dukes Marinus and John III.[34] Clearly the family had retained their special status in Docibilan eyes by receiving such valuable property. In 984 the same dukes patronised another grandson of Kampulus the prefect by giving Docibilis son of Mirus some empty public land outside the city walls.[35]

In 991 we meet one of the most successful of the Kampuli clan, Sergius son of Kampulus. The piece of land he bought then in Marana from Docibilis and Leo Christopherii was not large – only 1½ *modia*, but it lay next to the Garigliano river and to Sergius' own land.[36] We see here an example of a familiar practice by the late tenth century, the buying-up of small, possibly uneconomic, plots of land to consolidate into larger blocs. In doing so, Sergius may have been reconstituting pieces of Kampuli family land which had become fragmented by years of division between innumerable heirs. Such reconstitution was not uncommon. Herlihy has noticed it both in other parts of Italy and in southern France by the eleventh century.[37] Toubert too, records the practice of buying up and consolidating on the part of ecclesiastical institutions in northern Lazio in the tenth century.[38] Violante, however, has demonstrated that, in parts of Lombardy, Emilia and Tuscany, family lands were divided zonally, thereby avoiding the uneconomic division of individual pieces.[39] Why was such a practice not adopted in Gaeta? One factor may be the difference in quality of land between one zone and another (discussed below), making fair divisions wellnigh impossible. Thus the Kampuli and others were forced to undertake divisions of some pieces of land and hold others communally.

34 *CDC* 73. 35 *CDC* 84. 36 *CDC* 88.

37 Italy: D. Herlihy, 'The history of the rural seigneury in Italy', in *The Social History of Italy and Western Europe, 700–1500* (London, 1978); France: Herlihy, 'The agrarian revolution in southern France and Italy', *Speculum*, 33 (1958), 33. 38 *Structures*, I, pp. 490–1.

39 C. Violante, 'Quelques caractèristiques des structures familiales en Lombardie, Emilie et Toscane aux XIe et XIIe siècles', in *Famille et Parenté dans l'Occident Médiéval*, ed. G. Duby and J. Le Goff (Rome, 1977), p. 107.

Sergius was certainly a man of substance, as his will dated 1071 illustrates. The document lists only those lands that needed instructions as to their distribution. Along with the Marana land he left properties at Azzano (Arzano), Rubeanu, Maurici (unidentified) and on the Ponzian islands.[40] The Kampuli seem to have had quite an interest in the latter; in 1019 Sergius' cousin, Kampulus son of Docibilis, received public land on Ventotene and St Stefano from duke Leo I, regent for the young John V.[41]

Sergius' aunt, Matrona, is visible in 1004, when she handed over estates in Cilicie (near Mondragone), Faonia (unidentified) and Vivano (S. Agostino), plus land near the Garigliano, moveable goods and property in Gaeta itself to her daughter Euprassia.[42] The latter was to pay her a pension of 20 *modia* of corn, 10 *modia* of beans and peas and 30 jars of wine, and supply Matrona with a slave and such clothes as she might require.

There is much of interest in this document. Matrona was a widow at the time of the transaction,[43] but it is unclear whether Euprassia was married. If not, the gift could be interpreted as a dowry with strings attached to ensure Matrona's well-being for life. Alternatively, Matrona could have been ensuring that the property she wanted to bequeath to Euprassia on her death was already firmly in her daughter's hands. The latter is probably the case, for the lands that Matrona was ceding have a special significance in the history of the Kampuli clan which made their secure transfer to the next generation more important than usual.

The key lies in two pieces of land that Matrona handed over. One was an estate called Faonia, the other land in Vivano. The only other document in which Faonia appears is the lease of 839, when it and an estate called Vivarius (Vivano?) were leased to Constantine Anatolii, the then ruler of Gaeta, by his sister Elisabeth and her Neapolitan son-in-law Theodosius.[44] How had both pieces of land come to be in the hands of Matrona over a century later?

One explanation is that Docibilis I, when he came to power in 867, dispossessed Constantine and his son and co-ruler Marinus of all the lands they were holding, and that the estate came into the hands of the Kampuli family via John I's daughter Matrona, possibly in the form of a dowry when she married Kampulus the

[40] *CDC* 245. [41] *CDC* 135. [42] *CDC* 110.
[43] Her husband was a certain Docibilis *clarissimus*, who is otherwise unidentifiable.
[44] *CDC* 5.

prefect. It may then have come to the younger Matrona via direct inheritance from her father Docibilis, Kampulus' son.

However, rather like a jigsaw with square-shaped pieces, the fragments of evidence we have can be assembled in quite a different way. I suggested in an earlier chapter that Matrona's grandfather Kampulus was the son of *hypatos* Marinus and grandson of Constantine himself. His special treatment by the Docibilans was one indication of this, and his line's continued association with a specifically named estate – Faonia – is an important clue in favour of this hypothesis.

If the memory of their illustrious origins remained strong, the family would take particular care in the transfer of its pre-Docibilan lands, the most tangible evidence of those origins, between successive generations. An indication of the care taken in the 1004 transaction is that one of the witnesses, Ramfus son of Christopher *magnificus*, was a member of another family with pre-Docibilan origins. His presence secured Matrona's gift by guaranteeing its defence by the only other family who could appreciate the importance of the transaction.

The Kampuli and Christopherii frequently appear together as witnesses,[45] but that the two families were particularly friendly with each other is shown by an actual land transaction between them – Sergius son of Kampulus' purchase of Marana land from Docibilis and Leo Christopherii. Whilst witnessing each other's documents is a common feature of all the families described in this and the following chapters, actual transfers of land were very rare. A closer investigation of the witnessing pattern between the Kampuli and Christopherii is a final strong indicator that the Kampuli were the heirs of the former rulers of Gaeta, for it was always a Christopherii witness appearing on their documents, rather than the other way about, and the act of witnessing had the effect of denoting some degree of support for the document's author.

Something quite remarkable occurred in the history of the Kampuli lands in 1020. In that year Mirus son of John received confirmation from his by now elderly grandfather Mirus, son of Kampulus the prefect, of his gift of lands in Castro Argento, Tremonsuoli, Tizanellum (in Calvi), Massa (unknown) and Calabritti (near Tizanellum) to Docibilis, Leo and John the sons of

[45] Co-witnesses: *CDC* 15 (890); Christopherii witnesses for Kampuli: *CDC* 50 (949), *CDC* 67 (972), *CDC* 110 (1004), *CDC* 138 (1020).

John Caracci.[46] This gift may have merely consisted of very small plots of land in many places, but that the younger Mirus required his grandfather's approval suggests that it was somewhat more significant. Why did the transaction take place?

There may be a very simple reason. Just as the dukes of Gaeta may have been expected to be generous with their land grants in order to gain support, then so were their subject nobles. The Kampuli, with their illustrious background, were possibly more concerned than most to build up a clientele of lesser families to enhance their own prestige. Were the Kampuli buying the support of the Caracci in an attempt to gain power at Docibilan expense? It does not appear so; their strength was accompanied by continued support for the Docibilan family even during the eleventh-century crisis of rule at Gaeta.[47] In 1042 duke Leo II issued a document in which he gave Marinus, son of Kampulus, and another man, Gregory, son of John, the whole of the mill Maiore 'in return for their services'.[48] Marinus had witnessed the execution of the will of duke John III in 1010,[49] and was clearly still seen by Docibilans as a valuable ally.

The history of the Kampuli extends beyond the rule of the last Docibilan, Leo II. We have already seen how Sergius son of Kampulus left large amounts of land in his will of 1071, and had he had an heir the fortunes of his side of the family would no doubt have continued to flourish. Another clan member, Kampulus son of John, appears as a witness to a document of duchess Maria and her son duke Atenolf II in 1063,[50] and frequently in documents of other nobles in the period to 1071.[51] If my genealogy is correct, he also owned land at Formia, next to that which his sister-in-law Gemma sold to the abbot of St Erasmus in 1064.[52] Gemma's son Leo appears as a witness in documents until 1089.[53]

What was the secret of the success of the Kampuli clan? It can be summed up in one word, independence. True, they were in receipt of land gifts from the Docibilan dukes, but their history, and presumably their landed wealth, extended further back than 867, the beginnings of Docibilan rule. So, whilst they benefited from Docibilan patronage, they certainly did not rely on it, enabling them to survive after the Docibilans themselves disappeared from

[46] *CDC* 138. [47] For a discussion of this, see below, chapter 5, section (a).
[48] *CDC* 176. [49] *CDC* 120. [50] *CDC* 218.
[51] Kampulus son of John as witness: *CDC* 232, *CDC* 234, *CDC* 235, *CDC* 237, *CDC* 238, *CDC* 240, *CDC* 245 (1066 to 1071). [52] *CDC* 221. [53] *CDC* 232.

view. Meanwhile the Kampuli had also built up their own circle of supporters, among whom were the Caracci. Before the 1020 land transfer described above, we do not hear of the Caracci under that name. If Merores' version of their history is correct[54] then they were of modest origin, and may have owed their rise to Kampuli benefaction. Thereafter, John Caracci's three sons and their heirs were active throughout the eleventh century and into the twelfth. Other families of a similar social level to the Caracci are very difficult to trace in this early period, simply because, as clients, their land transactions are unlikely to appear in documentary form as often as those of their patrons.

The Kampuli and Christopherii are very heavily documented, possibly because their pre-Docibilan origins gave them a head start in wealth over their contemporaries under Docibilan rule. However, we do see other landowners whose families can be traced over one or two generations, and who perhaps more truly represent the nobility under Docibilis and his successors.

(iii) *The Gaetani and the Coronellas*

In 950, for example, one count Gaetanus received a piece of public arable land in Marana from dukes Docibilis II and John II.[55] Gaetanus appears again as a witness to a document issued by duke Gregory in 964.[56] In 998 his son, also called Gaetanus, sold off a piece of land in the Ausente valley below Marana.[57]

One of the younger Gaetanus' witnesses in this sale was one 'Maria' de Coronella. Given that women appear in no other witness lists in our Gaetan documents in this period,[58] I am inclined to think that 'Maria' was in fact Marinus son of John Coronella who, acting as a trustee and will executor in 1000, sold off some land at Grazanu (unidentified).[59] In a court-case of 1109 we learn that this same Marinus had received land from duchess Emilia (fl.

[54] See above, note 5. [55] *CDC* 51. [56] *CDC* 66.

[57] *CDC* 99; the land had been bought from one Maria widow of Mirus, who is otherwise unknown. Although Marana is a territorial area, not a specific, named estate, it is tempting to identify her late husband with Mirus son of Kampulus the prefect, whose sons are known to have owned land in Marana in 974 (*CDC* 68). A tenuous connection between the Gaetani and Mirus can further be made – the document mentioning the elder Gaetanus' land in Marana in 950 was witnessed by Mirus (*CDC* 51).

[58] There seems to be no evidence of women witnessing documents in any part of southern Italy up to *c.*1150. For more discussion of their roles generally, see P. Skinner, 'Women, wills and wealth in medieval southern Italy', *Early Medieval Europe*, 2 (1993), 133–52.

[59] *CDC* 103.

1002–1028) near the Maiore and St George mills, and that he had given it to his slave, Petrocurso.[60] A Marinus Coronella appears termed a noble of Gaeta at three court-cases in the mid-eleventh century.[61] We do not know whether he is the same man as Marinus son of John, nor what his relationship was to Gregory son of John Coronella, who used his wealth to promote a candidate to the bishopric of Gaeta in 1054.[62] Such uncertainty exposes the inadequacies of the evidence. Both the counts Gaetanus and the members of the Coronella family had dealings with the dukes of Gaeta and, in the case of the latter, played a major role in the political history of the duchy. Yet we know very little about them in comparison to the Kampuli and the Christopherii. This raises not only the question of documentary survival again, but also the question of whether association with the Docibilans necessarily brought wealth and power.

This last question must be addressed in the case of a particular group visible in our documents at this time – the witnesses of ducal transactions. Whilst some individuals cannot be linked to landowning, they can be assembled into clans much like the Kampuli or Coronellas. In some cases they can as justifiably be called the nobility of Gaeta as those landed families.

(iv) *A hidden nobility: the witnesses*

An examination of the details of witness lists in documents issued by the Docibilan dukes and their immediate family reveals a very interesting picture. As well as members of the landed families mentioned above (except the Caracci), the Docibilans called upon the witnessing signatures of over eighty other people, less than a quarter of whom can be seen in other contexts as landowners. That is not to say, however, that the remaining three-quarters should be seen as a landless pool of witnesses, merely that our documentary evidence is inadequate to give us indications either way.

Who then were the witnesses? I have already mentioned above the importance of the appearance of Bonus son of count Anatolius as a witness to Docibilis I's first document in 867. Such an appearance, by a member of the old ruling clan, was an important acknowledgement of the new state of affairs. Can any more of the Anatolii be seen performing a similar function? From lead-name

[60] *CDC* 284. [61] *CDC* 180 (1047), *CDC* 187 (1049), *CDC* 195 (1053).

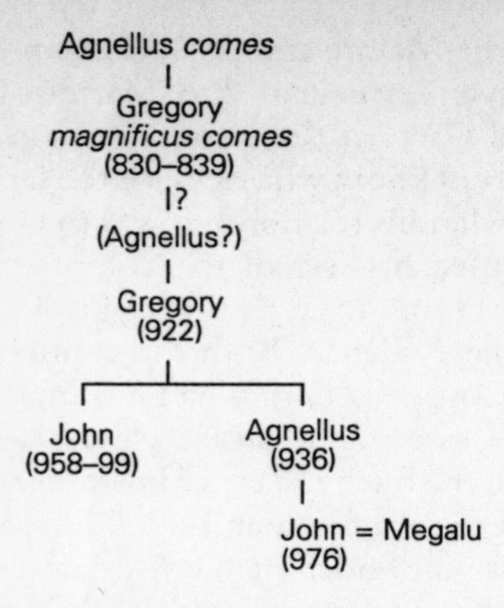

Figure 4.4 *The Agnelli family (based on lead-name evidence)*

evidence and the fact of their continued association with Docibilan documents, Anatolius son of John (witness 890 and 918),[63] Leo son of Anatolius (witness 906)[64] and Anatolius son of Leo (witness 919)[65] can probably be identified as members of the old family.

Another pre-Docibilan family, the Agnelli (see genealogy, Figure 4.4), also seems to have found itself a niche under the new regime. After their initial appearance as landowners and witnesses in the 830s under Anatolian rule, there is a gap of a century before they eventually re-emerge as regular witnesses for the Docibilans. Significantly Agnellus son of Gregory appears in a charter of Docibilis II and John II alongside Stephen son of Marinus the count, brother of Kampulus the prefect.[66] Were the old families sticking together in their activities? It is difficult to tell. Certainly John son of Gregory de Agnello acted as a witness for Kampulus son of Kampulus the prefect in 974,[67] but the continued association of older families could just be symptomatic of the limited number of witnesses available in what was, after all, a small city. John witnessed for Megalu daughter of John I in 958,[68] and was present at a dispute between bishop Bernard of Gaeta and count Dauferius of Traetto in 994.[69] Soon afterwards the Agnelli disappear from view in our documents. If we look at their genealogy, with pre-

[62] *CDC* 197. [63] *CDC* 16, *CDC* 24. [64] *CDC* 19. [65] *CDC* 26.
[66] *CDC* 39. [67] *CDC* 68. [68] *CDC* 58. [69] *CDC* 101.

Docibilan members of the family using titles to denote their noble birth and post-Docibilans not, it may be the case that the Agnelli suffered a dramatic decline in their position during the tenth century.

A third family whose appearances are almost entirely confined to witness lists are the Mauri. They emerged later, during the heyday of Docibilan rule in the latter half of the tenth century. The head of the family, Mauro appears as a witness to three ducal documents in the years 978, 979 and 980,[70] and in one of a great-grandson of Docibilis I, Deusdedit son of Angelarus, in 986.[71] Mauro's services were rewarded in 980 when he and his wife Martha received some public land from dukes Marinus and John III.[72]

Mauro had two sons, one of whom, Mauro, was present at two disputes involving bishop Bernard of Gaeta in 999.[73] His brother Mastalus was also present, and it is he who seems to have continued to mingle in the higher reaches of Gaetan society. He was a witness for John III and John IV in an exchange dated 1002.[74] His co-witness was Landolf, son of the former duke Gregory, and the connection with the Gregorian branch of the Docibilan family continued in 1010, when Mastalus witnessed a sale made by Anna, widow of Landulf's brother Docibilis, to John IV.[75] Mastalus' two final appearances as a witness occur in 1042, when he signed documents issued during the short reign of the Docibilan duke Leo II.[76] Mastalus' activities brought him into contact with members of the major families of Gaeta, for example, the Kampuli[77] and Christopherii[78] and these links, plus his family's presence in ducal documents, may have led him to use the title *magnificus*. If this is the case, we know that he had a son called Bernard who in 1068 acted as an advocate for the church of St Theodore,[79] heavily patronised by the Docibilans, and a natural grandson called John who was the priest of SS Cosma and Damian.[80]

The major lesson to be learnt from the case of the Mauri family is that it cannot automatically be assumed that the aristocracy of Gaeta was made up only of those families recorded as having land. But, whilst the Mauri were aristocratic in the sense that they were part of the Docibilan ducal circle, they may not have had noble

[70] *CDC* 73, *CDC* 74, *CDC* 76. [71] *CDC* 87. [72] *CDC* 77.
[73] *CDC* 100, *CDC* 101. [74] *CDC* 107. [75] *CDC* 121/2.
[76] *CDC* 176, *CDC* 177. [77] *CDC* 110, *CDC* 177. [78] *CDC* 110.
[79] *CDC* 237. [80] *CDC* 211.

origins. We do not, for instance, know the name of the elder Mauro's father, nor is Mauro himself distinguished by a comital or other title. Perhaps the Mauri formed part of the Docibilan clientele as the Caracci were part of that of the Kampuli. In this context Mastalus' title may have been adopted as a means of assimilation into the higher aristocracy with whom he mixed. And, if the Mauri are to be understood to be dependent on the Docibilans, it explains their pattern of witnessing almost entirely Docibilan documents until the fall of that dynasty.

In addition to the ducal witnesses who can be assigned to identifiable families, we have over seventy individuals who appear in the lists, of whom just over half witnessed once only. This suggests that, whilst the Docibilans did favour (or need the approval of) a few noble families, they did not really assemble a well-defined entourage or court of men. The fluidity of the witnessing group was such that in an early document, dated 890, we even have an Amalfitan, Bonus, as a signatory.[81] On the other hand, the witness list of Docibilis I's will of 906 presents a slightly different picture. Along with Docibilis' son John we see Alagernus son of George, who may have heen a member of the old, pre-Docibilan nobility, for his father's name, Greek in origin, was unusual at Gaeta and suggests links with the old Byzantine-influenced and Neapolitan-backed regime. This theory is lent weight by the identity of the final witness Leo, a member of the Anatolii clan. In private documents as well as public ones, the role of the old families in Docibilan life was a prominent one, and it is open to question just how much actually changed at the level of nobility when Docibilis took over at the top.

It may have been to combat such stagnation that men like the Mauri were promoted, and there is evidence of other individual witnesses who seem to have been promoted to the ducal circle in the same way.

The Docibilans may not have had a fixed court, as such, but one Leo son of Bonus' witnessing career – he appears on no less than nine Docibilan documents – suggests that he had some sort of permanent position in their retinue. However, his identity is elusive. In 1012 he is recorded as owning land in the district of Corene close to that of Leo Christopherii, one Anatolius son of

[81] *CDC* 16.

Peter (one of the Anatolii?) and Caruccius son of John,[82] but he cannot be appended to any of the known families of Gaeta, nor does he use a title. Yet like Paul he frequently came into contact with members of the Gaetan nobility. That he may have been raised to his high position by Docibilan patronage is made more likely by the fact that he disappears from view at around the time the Docibilans were becoming weaker, during the minority of John V.

The witness lists are perhaps more revealing than the documents of the noble families who owned land when trying to isolate a Docibilan nobility.

An examination of the men whom the Docibilans raised may, however, provide further clues to the background of their ancestor. From a survey of the personal names used in the Tyrrhenian documents, it is clear that the names of the Mauri family, in particular Mauro and Mastalus, were very unusual at Gaeta, but extremely common in Amalfi. Linking this with earlier evidence that Docibilis I had been ransomed by the Amalfitans from the Arabs,[83] and that an Amalfitan appears as witness to an early document issued by Docibilis and his son John I,[84] it is possible to speculate that Docibilis I was himself an Amalfitan. This would fit well with my suggestion that he was not Gaetan, and that he may have had large amounts of liquid wealth to enable him to seize power. His name is unknown in the Amalfitan documents until the twelfth century, but since only one ninth-century document survives from the city this absence cannot be used as an argument against an Amalfitan identity.

Once securely in power, the Docibilans may have tried to elevate some of their compatriots to positions where they might be termed aristocrats, that is taking part in the political life of the duchy by witnessing the documents of the dukes and possibly receiving land in return for their loyalty. This would explain the appearance of the name Mauro at Gaeta. The rulers could not, however, create a new nobility to replace or exist alongside that which they inherited from the Anatolii. What distinguished these two groups from each other?

[82] *CDC* 125; as we have seen, a possible member of the Caracci family (see above, note 5).
[83] See above, chapter 2. [84] *CDC* 16.

(b) NOBILITY AND ARISTOCRACY: TYRRHENIAN PATTERNS IN THE TENTH CENTURY

Léopold Genicot, making some general comments on the nature of the uppermost stratum of medieval society, defined the nobility as those who were powerful *de iure*, and the aristocracy as those whose position was *de facto* the most powerful.[85] This distinction can be adapted to apply to Docibilan Gaeta; families like the Kampuli, Agnelli and Christopherii, whilst they may not in fact have had any *legal* status, were nevertheless identifiably noble. They had their origins in the pre-Docibilan period, they can be seen to have owned land in the territory and could justifiably be called the nobility under Docibilan rule. Their very 'oldness' was in itself an important contribution to their status. In the words of Schmid, 'even when men no longer knew exactly who their ancestors were, they knew enough to be able to say they were noble'.[86] Our families had not yet reached that stage of vagueness, but it is striking how all three of those mentioned, and the Anatolii as well, derived their status from descent from an early count.[87] An examination of the twelve extant pre-Docibilan documents from Gaeta reveals that no fewer than nine other counts or their sons are mentioned, mostly in witness lists. What did the comital position mean before 867? The evidence is limited, but we find counts witnessing the documents of the three most powerful men in Gaeta at that time – the *hypatos* Constantine, the bishop of Formia/Gaeta, and the rector of the papal patrimony. Some, as I have said, are seen owning lands as well, and this small group might justifiably be termed the landed *aristocracy* of Gaeta whom their *descendants* considered to be noblemen.

Sergi illustrates well this process of change from public officials to private dynasts in northern Italy, taking as as examples the Aldobrandeschi family from Lucca and the Manfredi of Piemonte in the eleventh century.[88] Both were 'noble' families descended from 'aristocratic' men. Aristocratic status though, has its pitfalls, the main one being the deposition of the regime on whom the

[85] L. Genicot, 'Recent research on the medieval nobility', in *Medieval Nobility*, p. 18.

[86] 'Structure of the nobility', p. 48.

[87] Kampuli: count Marinus (pre-890); Anatolii: count Anatolius (*c.*800); Agnelli: count Agnellus (pre-830); Christopherii: count Christopher (*c.*800).

[88] 'La feudalizzazione delle circonscrizioni pubbliche nel regno d'Italia', in *Structures Féodales et Féodalisme dans l'Occident Mediterranéan (XIe-XIIIe Siècles)* (Rome, 1980), p. 252.

aristocrat depends for patronage. In 867 two corners of the triangle of patronage were removed in Gaeta when Constantine was deposed and Docibilis I took on both his rule and that of rector of the papal lands. The Anatolii/Kampuli line survived because Docibilis needed its help, and to a lesser extent that of the wealthy Christopherii. Other counts simply disappear from the witness lists, whilst the family of count Agnellus seems to have suffered a drop in status.

That comital status had merely been a reward for serving the ruler, rather than a mark of noble status linked to landholding, is suggested by the fact that the title was not handed on. Kampulus styled himself *prefecturius*, son of count Marinus; none of count Anatolius' three known sons used the title of their father. Similarly, count Christopher's title was used by none of his descendants; instead alternative indicators of status, such as the title *magnificus*, were used.

The way in which our recognisably 'noble' families traced their descent back to a comital ancestor who may merely have been a service aristocrat is mirrored dramatically in evidence from Amalfi. There also only the founder or ancestor of each family seems to have been distinguished by the title of count, but in this city the counts seem to have lived a century earlier than those in Gaeta. This was illustrated by del Treppo and Leone, using the frequent tendency of Amalfitans in tenth and eleventh century documents to list every generation back to that ancestor and calculating each generation as about thirty years. They found that the earliest Amalfitan counts could be dated to the late eighth century, and suggest that they may have been the original Byzantine governors of the fortress of Amalfi.[89] The nobility may have traced their descent from late ninth-century ancestors with a military role possibly derived from Amalfi's early history as a place of refuge.[90] Such listing is an almost unique feature of the Amalfitan documentation. A list of three or four generations is a very useful tool for building up family genealogies and dating the origins of the families (for the joining together of series of three or four ancestors, in a similar way to joining the patterns of tree rings in dendrochronology, can create longer strings from which to derive a date). One has to use the method with caution, however,

[89] *Amalfi*, p. 100.
[90] G. Galasso, 'Le città campane nell'alto medioevo', *ASPN*, n.s. 38 (1959), p. 16.

for when the list became too cumbersome it seems that one or two intermediate generations were omitted from its citation, so that the line of descent could still include the original comital ancestor. This tells us much about the importance of their origins to Amalfitan noblemen, and also shows that the comital title was not handed down. Thus here again we have early aristocratic ancestors giving rise to a group who, with later land acquisitions and their longevity, came to be regarded as a nobility.

The title of count does not necessarily seem to have brought with it any kind of territorial jurisdiction, although the appearance in early Amalfitan documents of counts associated with place-names does suggest a series of fortified bases protecting the city.[91]

One example of a possible territorial base is the case of a family in Amalfi descended from one 'Mauro *comes* Monteincollo' (fl. late ninth century), whose history illustrates how strong the memory of its prestigious ancestor was. His son Peter appears in a document of 920,[92] and thereafter the family are regularly documented up till 1097, always adding the 'Monteincollo' to their ancestor's name. In that year Gregory and his brother Mauro were still able to list the four generations of descent linking them to the lord of Monteincollo (see Figure 4.5).[93]

Landed property could be built up and bequeathed. Perhaps deriving from their origins as holders of fortified places, and partly due to the fact that Amalfi itself was territorially even more limited than Gaeta, the nobles seem to have been very localised in their landowning. Given the geographical nature of the name Monteincollo, it would seem that it was a territory of some kind, and this finds support in the documentary evidence. All of the documented lands of the Monteincolli family were in Ponte Primaro (see Map 4.3), and they seem to have given their name to a part of this district by 1080.[94] Lands of other families were also tightly clustered, as in the case of the counts of Ferafalcone, which lay along the river Reginnis Maiore.[95] Work on other areas of the duchy has also revealed similarly close-knit landowning, as in the case of Cetara and Vietri, which lay on the fluid border with the principality of

91 E.g. *CDA* 584 (860): Constantine count de Pastina; *CDA* 585 (920): Peter son of Mauro count Monteincollo; *CDA* 2 (922): Leo son of Constantine count de Aprile.

92 *CDA* 585.

93 *CP* 89: Gregory and Mauro 'sons of Mauro son of Gregory de John de Mauro count de Monteincollo'.

94 For example, *CDA* 587 (952), *CDA* 58 (1044), *CDA* 64 (1053). As a placename, *CDA* 75.

95 *CP* 76, *CP* 84.

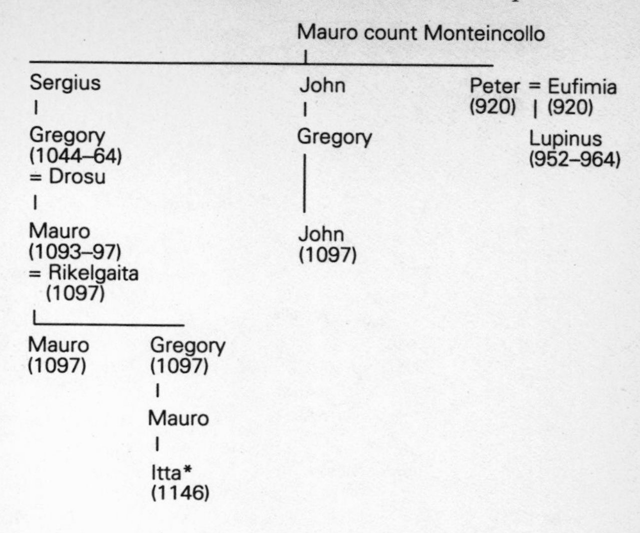

Documents: *CDA* 585, *CDA* 587, *CDA* 7, *CDA* 58, *CDA* 64, *CDA* 65, *CP* 50, *CP* 44, *CP* 38, *CP*42, *CP* 33, *CP* 87, *CP* 89, *CP* 107, *CP* 137, *CDA* 150

The genealogy appears as the documents present the family; however, problems of chronology might be explained by later members of the family skipping generations to their ancestor.

Lupinus appears in 964 as 'Lupinus de Eufimia'; his mother may have been widowed by this time.

* For more on Itta, see chapter 6.

Figure 4.5 *The Monteincollo family*

Salerno. Here other families seem to have carved out territories for themselves, and have formed the subject of close study.[96] They will be discussed in a little more detail in chapter 7, when interactions between the Tyrrhenian states will be examined.

The use of the name Monteincollo provides an easy way to identify those who belonged to this comital clan throughout the tenth and eleventh centuries, and other examples of surnamed comital clans can be added to this one. They include the Scaticampuli clan, whose history stretches back as far as the 860s. They seem to have taken the name of an early member, Kampulus, as their surname, despite the fact that it was Kampulus' son, Ursus,

[96] Figliuolo, 'Gli amalfitani'.

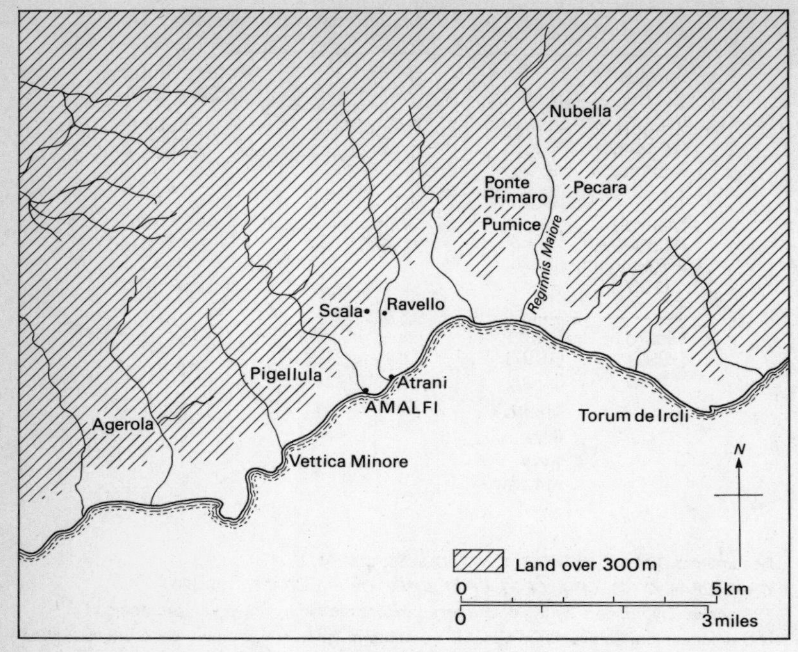

Map 4.3 *Centres of landowning in Amalfi*

who seems to have been their comital ancestor.[97] The family of another count John, distinguished by the surname Neapolitanus, and in all likelihood originating from that city, seem to have settled in Amalfi quite early (Figure 4.6).They are first documented in 939,[98] selling a water-mill on the river Amalfi held in common with the Scaticampuli family. The value of that property itself is an indication of the family's status. Count John's son, Leo, appears in 957 witnessing a charter relating to land in Ponte Primaro,[99] but the family's interests were not limited to the river area. In 1007 John's direct descendant Drosu was able to force the payment of compensation from the bishop of Amalfi for land sold to him in

[97] Leo son of Ursi de Campulo is documented in 920, *CDA* 585; the heirs of 'Urso count Scaticampulo' appear in 939, *CDA* 586. That others belong to the same family is strongly suggested by the recurrence of key names, Kampulus, Ursus, John and Leo, and the fact that their landowning seems, like the Monteincolli, to have been focused on a particular area: mill above Atrani *CDA* 586 (939), house in Atrani *CDA* 8 (970), land near Ravello *CDA* 51 (1039).

[98] *CDA* 586; the transaction in this document is also recorded in *CP* 32, with two names changed (see genealogy).

[99] *CP* 31.

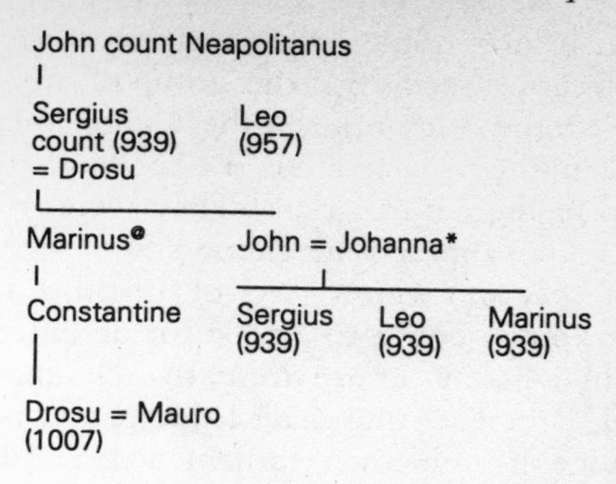

Documents: *CDA* 586, *CP* 32, *CP* 31, *CDA* 21

● Marinus is identified as 'de John count'; the chronology suggests that Drosu, his granddaughter, has omitted a generation in her document. It is unlikely that she was of the same generation as her cousins, documented in 939.

* 'Johanna' in *CDA* 586, 'Norma' in *CP* 32

Figure 4.6 *The Neapolitani family of Amalfi*

Stabia.[100] There is no clear indication of the family's activities after this date. It is possible that in the political upheavals of the eleventh century in Amalfi they returned to their home city.

The Ferafalcone clan, already mentioned, are first documented in 922, when count Leo, who seems to have been the family's ancestor, acted as a witness to a document of another count.[101] However, perhaps because the family's comital status was later in date, Leo's descendants did not trace their origins to him. Rather, they identified themselves in their documents simply by their surname. Ironically, this renders the reconstruction of the family's genealogy more difficult, for, whilst members of the family can definitely be identified, their relationships to each other cannot safely be defined.[102]

This problem recurs with another group of Amalfitans visible in the documents. Relatively early in Amalfi's history other families emerge in the documentation who did not claim illustrious ancestors, simply identifying themselves by a surname. Given the

[100] *CDA* 21. [101] *CDA* 2.

[102] Documented members of the Ferafalcone family to 1100: count Leo (922, *CDA* 2); his son Ursus (943, *CP* 43); Sergius son of Sergius (1004, *CDA* 18); Sergius and Pantaleo sons of Gregory and Marenda (1062, *CP* 76, 1089, *CP* 84); Sergius son of Leo (1090–1097, *CP* 85, *CDA* 88, *CP* 88, *CP* 89).

care with which most noble Amalfitans seem to have cited their illustrious forbears, it seems that this group of surnamed families, which included the Victorini,[103] the Cullonannas,[104] and the Iactabecti,[105] might be characterised as belonging to a different social class from the comital clans. They were still landowners, however, and often appear as neighbours to or witnesses for those clans.[106] The early and wide variety of surnames among families who were not noble points to a need for definite identification, even in a duchy where sheer proximity to each other in the limited city and viable land space must have led to people becoming well-acquainted. Like the noblemen, surnamed clans also seem to have preferred to own coherent, very localised blocks of land. The Rogadeum family are a prime example of this tendency; they based their activities in Ravello, but also had property on the coast at Ercli. These two locations form the focus of their documents.[107]

Turning now to the material emanating from Naples in this period, we can see that in the tenth century there was a group of men distinguished with titles such as *miles* and prefect. The title of *miles* is first documented at Naples in 921, but must have had much earlier origins. Naples' fluid border area with her often aggressive Lombard neighbour, Capua, was from the seventh century known as the *pars militie*,[108] and those later known as *milites* still held estates in the territory.[109] The prestige gained by these men in their role of

[103] *CP* 21 (979), *CDA* 11 (984), *CP* 66 (992), *CP* 73 (1005), *CP* 61 (1039) No further evidence of this family's activities survives.

[104] They appear later, from 1037: *CDA* 48, *CP* 37 (1038), *CodCav* VI/967 (1041), *CDA* 90 (1092), but their period of activity ceases after 1092.

[105] *CDA* 36 (1020), *CodCav* V/777 (1025), *PAVAR* I/11 (1029), *CDA* 57 (1044), *CP* 42 (1053), *CP* 47 (1061), *CDA* 69 (1062), *CP* 46 (1064), *CP* 49 (1067), *CP* 57 (1069), *CDA* 84 (1090).

[106] Other surnamed families, traceable over two or three generations, include the Mazzocculas, landowners in several parts of the duchy: *CDA* 8 (970), *CP* 74 (974, land in Bostopla), *CP* 61 (1039, land in Ponte Primaro), *CP* 70 (1057, land in Paternum Piczulum), *CDA* 70 and *CDA* 80 (1066 and 1086, land in Reginna Maiori); the Cocti of Ponte Primaro: *CP* 33 (1055), *CP* 50 (1061), *CP* 38 (1064); the Benusi of the same place, documented in a variety of forms of their name from 1012, *CP* 72, onwards; and many other families who appear briefly in the documents, including the Falangulas, the Russi, the Gangellas, the Cantalenas, the Cullusigillu, the Dalaquas, the Maioppuli, the Pironti, the Zinziricapras, the Piczilli and the Musceptolas.

[107] Significantly, charters of this family survive in the archive of the bishoprics of Amalfi and Ravello, reflecting the fact that at least one member achieved the latter position: *PAVAR* I/3 (1010), *CDA* 34 (1018), *PAVAR* I/14 (1039), *PAVAR* I/16 (1047), *CDA* 593 (1098), *CDA* 98 (1100).

[108] Galasso, 'Città campane', *ASPN*, n.s. 38, 1959, 18.

[109] For example, Marinus *miles* and Anastasius *miles RN* 7 (921); Kampulus *miles* son of John *miles RN* 36 (937), *RN* 48 (942); John tribune and Lupi *miles RN* 102 (958).

defenders gave them a leading status in Neapolitan society. They were the equivalent of the counts recorded in Amalfi. It is perhaps not surprising then to find that the dynasty who controlled Gaeta in the early ninth century on one occasion claimed descent from Anatolius *miles* rather than Anatolius *comes*.[110]

On the basis of their important military position, I suggest that they founded the families of Naples that we would call noble; that is, the descendents of such men would be proud to claim descent from an ancestor with such high prestige. Unfortunately, it is far less easy to trace these lines of descent. Apart from John *miles* and his clan[111] it is difficult to distinguish them from the rest of the urban population as one can in, say, nearby Amalfi or Gaeta. Because we are dealing here with a far greater number of people, the method of tracing families by lead-names, so effective in the confined area of Gaeta, cannot be used with any safety. Nor did the Neapolitans adopt the Amalfitan style of citing long lists of ancestors to identify themselves. Instead, as in the latter city, the use of surnames appeared early, and is a hallmark of the Neapolitan documents.

It is likely that, as in Amalfi, surnames were used by the nobility of the city. (The anomalous lack of surname attached to John *miles* and his family was probably related to the fact that they were part of the ducal house and therefore needed no further identification.) For example, we see the Isauri family, perhaps deriving its name from its racial origins, documented in the tenth century, and the de Rotunda clan, unusually deriving its name from that of a female ancestor.[112] Over one hundred other surnamed families, who can only be traced through one or two generations, are also visible in the tenth-century Neapolitan documents, and it is possible that one or two were the ancestors of later, similarly surnamed families in the smaller duchies.[113]

The Isauri or Isabri family are first documented in 920, when the widow Maru and her daughter Barbaria gave to their church of St Eufimia in the district Duos Amantes a garden next to it.[114] Maru's

[110] *CDC* I. [111] See above, chapter 2, and figure 2.3.

[112] Isauri: Francesca Luzzatti Lagana, 'Firme', p. 747, note 77, links the name with the Isaurians who accompanied the Byzantine general Belisarius into Italy in the sixth century. De Rotunda family: *RN* 109, *RN* 144, *RN* 299, *RN* 385, *RN* 463, and see below, section (c) for more on Rotunda's clan.

[113] See below, chapter 6, section (a,viii): I am currently in the process of preparing a prosopographical database of Neapolitans recorded to 1139, in order to investigate family patterns in that duchy in more detail. [114] *RN* 6.

brothers John and Gregory owned property bordering the garden. The two women charged the abbot of SS Sergius and Bacchus with seeing that the gift was protected, suggesting that their church was already subjected to the larger foundation. In our next reference, one Peter Isabri is documented as the owner of a house in the *platea* Augustali.[115] Then we have a series of documents issued by different members of the family dealing in rural property, but they show a certain continuity in that many involve the church of SS Sergius and Bacchus as the other party in the transaction.[116] The will of Maria Gemma, wife of Gregory Isabri in 960 began with a bequest to the same church.[117] The Isauri continued to patronise the smaller St Eufimia as well. When Basil gave up his property to SS Sergius and Bacchus in 970, he reserved a *fundus* for the smaller church.[118] Later, in 1002, another member of the family, Andrea, who bore the evocative nickname Pungente, acted as a member of the congregation of St Severus.[119] In their lack of artisanal activity, extensive landowning and connections with a powerful church, the Isauri can safely be characterised as part of the nobility of Naples.

One title which seems to have crossed into usage at Gaeta from Naples was that of prefect. It is difficult to see what function the title had in the latter territory beyond denoting a certain prestige on the bearer's part. It is possible that the title was used by those subject to the duke, but holding the most important centres.[120] (A notable exception to this rule is the count of Cuma, but if this position continued to be held by a cadet branch of the ducal dynasty, its special distinction is understandable). The extreme rarity of ducal documents from Naples means we cannot definitely assign to the prefects a role of witnessing for the duke – a civilian aristocracy to balance the military one – but this seems likely given that these men witnessed the very few Neapolitan documents that we have.[121] The title does not appear to have been hereditary – we have evidence of sons of prefects who do not use the title – and thus may not have indicated landed wealth, but it was clearly thought

115 *RN* 29 (935).

116 For example, an exchange of land in Caucilione in 936, *RN* 34; a gift of Balnearia land to the church in 963, *RN* 131, and another in 970, *RN* 185.

117 *RN* 111.

118 *RN* 185.

119 *RN* 317, *RN* 318.

120 Cassandro, 'Ducato', p. 200; see also the discussion of the title in Brown, *Gentlemen and Officers*, p. 136.

121 For example, Peter prefect son of Sergius and Gregory prefect appeared on an exchange of duke John son of Marinus in 949: *DCDN* 3a.

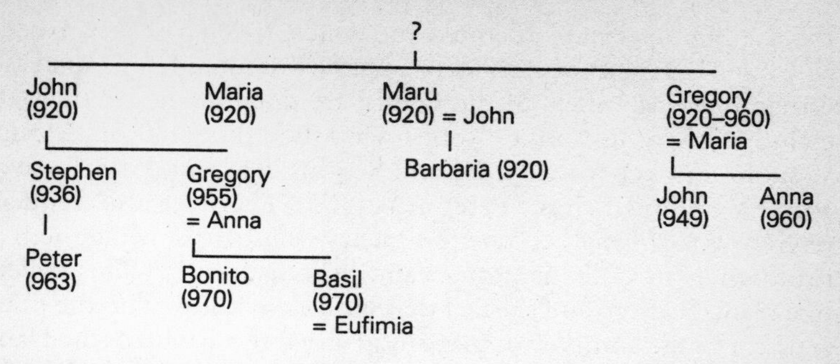

Figure 4.7 *The Isauri family*

an important enough indicator of power (and noble birth?) for the widow of Theodore the count to trace his descent back via his untitled father to his grandfather Aligernus the prefect in 1016.[122]

It may have been the title's perceived importance which led Docibilis I to use it rather than the title of *hypatos* in his first document in 867. Neither title denoted special ruling status, but Docibilis may have wanted to use the title familiar to the nobility of Naples. He soon reverted to *hypatos*, but this was perhaps a reaction to the fact that Kampulus, son of count (or *hypatos*) Marinus, and Docibilis' most potent rival, used the title prefect from his first documented appearance in 890[123] onwards.

I stated earlier that the title of *hypatos* may have conferred honour, rather than a right to rule, on its holder, using examples of its occurrence in other Tyrrhenian states, including Naples. However, in the latter city the title may have become the surname of a family, who must, one assumes, have thought themselves to be noble. The earliest occurrence of the surname or title is in 957, when the heirs of Stephen son of John 'kataypatiae' are recorded in a boundary clause.[124] Taken together with another document of 969,[125] in which one of those heirs, John son of Stephen 'kata domini ypatiae' appears, it seems that the surname developed out of the family's descent from an unnamed ancestor who held the title of *hypatos*, *kata* in Greek meaning 'down' and so translatable as 'decended from'. Thus the family followed a by now familiar pattern of citing their titled forebear as a means of identification.

[122] *RN* 369. [123] *CDC* 15. [124] *RN* 96. [125] *RN* 169.

By 994 the unwieldy formula by which they did so had been jettisoned in favour of the shorter, but no less identifiable, Ipati as a surname.[126] Members of the family are documented until 1038, including Sergius son of John, who bought land on Mount Vesuvius in 1014,[127] Gregory and Sergius in a boundary clause of 1016,[128] and the heirs of Peter in 1038.[129] There are also frequent references to *illi ypati* in other boundary clauses, recording them as landowners in Calbetianum[130] and Pumilianum.[131] This collective identification, and the fact that we do not know who the titled ancestor of the family was, may suggest that those who owned land near them were also not familiar with their neighbours' background. A valuable clue as to why this should be is provided in the will of an Amalfitan resident in Naples, dated 1021. Sergius the Amalfitan appointed as his executors his two uncles, John and Sergius Ipati sons of Marinus 'de Sirrento'.[132] One should perhaps be cautious in using this evidence to assign Sorrentan origins to the Ipati family, particularly since variations of 'Sorrentinus' may again have become a family name at Naples. However, Sergius' careful description of his uncles as 'of Sorrento', and the fact that the title *hypatos* was certainly used there, point to this conclusion. To take the hypothesis a step further, the lack of a name for the Ipati family's ancestor may be because their ancestor was *the hypatos* of Sorrento, and needed no more identification. A final clue supporting the family's non-Neapolitan origins is that after 1038 they disappear from the documents. Either they dropped the name, which is possible, or they returned to their homeland. Unfortunately, the woeful amount of evidence surviving from Sorrento ensures that their fate remains a mystery.

A survey of the noble families of the Tyrrhenian coast has revealed a number of strategies used in identifying themselves, but all seem to have valued the use of titles to add prestige and to reinforce the power brought by their landed wealth. Nowhere is this more apparent than in Gaeta, where the Docibilans seem to have put the title of prefect to a special use during the tenth century,

[126] John son of Peter Ipati bought land in that year: *RN* 287.

[127] *RN* 352.

[128] *RN* 370; they owned land in Campo de Piro, an unknown location.

[129] *RN* 463.

[130] Calvizzano: *RN* 324 (1005).

[131] Pomigliano: *RN* 342 (1011) and *RN* 420 (1028).

[132] *RN* 402; a version of the will published as *CP* 81 is dated 1025, perhaps reflecting a delay in making a copy which was preserved in Sergius' homeland.

as the genealogy below indicates. The title appears to have been held by the youngest son of the *hypatos* or duke. For example, Docibilis I had three sons. One succeeded him as ruler, one became the duke of Terracina and the third, Leo, became known as the prefect. Neither of Leo's two sons actually used the title, but in the next generation both John and Docibilis' sons called their father 'prefect'. And two of John's sons, basking in the reflected prestige of a title which could not, or had not, been passed on to them, styled themselves *magnificus* instead (see Figure 4.8).

The second Leo the prefect we meet in the family again seems to have been a youngest son. His three brothers succeeded each other as dukes of Gaeta, and, whilst the prefecture may not have carried with it any specific role or function, it may have been a sufficiently prestigious compensation for not achieving the higher office. Again one of Leo's sons, Gregory, bears the title *magnificus*. The prefecture may not have necessarily come with landed possessions, although it is difficult to imagine either of the Docibilans named Leo the prefect without land.

It is very difficult to pin down exactly what titles such as *magnificus*, count or prefect signified in Gaeta, but they all pre-dated Docibilan rule there, and because of this could perhaps be taken as indications of noble birth in the tenth century, even if the bearers of such titles, for example Christopher *magnificus*, could really only trace their ancestry back to service counts. But if this was so, how did men of unknown background like Docibilis I, or his family's retainers such as Mauro's son Mastalus come to use such titles?

In Docibilis' case this question has largely been answered in an earlier chapter; he needed to clothe himself in some kind of prestigious identity to obscure his non-noble origins, and titles were one way of doing so. Men like Mastalus, as close to the dukes of Gaeta as their higher-born contemporaries, were merely doing the same, using titles like *magnificus* which were meaningless functionally, but sounded good, to assimilate with the class which they aspired to join.

The Docibilans were successful in creating an aristocratic group of supporters, but could not dislodge or modify the composition of the nobility of Gaeta whose histories were longer than their own. Whilst they had wealth, and could build up a retinue, the latter were ultimately dependent on the fortunes of their benefactors.

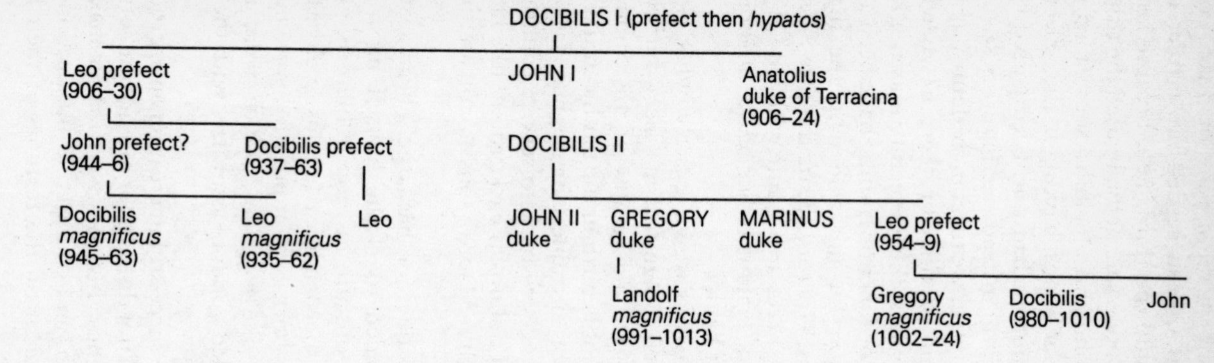

Figure 4.8 *Prefects in the Docibilan clan*

This dependence on the ruler, what the German historians term *Königsnahe*,[133] made the position of the aristocrats of Gaeta precarious, whilst the nobility, friendly towards the Docibilans, but not in need of their patronage, had a solid base of landed wealth to fall back on should political upheaval occur. Whilst there is no direct evidence that this was the case, the use of leading names in the oldest families may have been a means of reasserting the family's hold on particular pieces of land associated with the lead-name ancestor, a phenomenon noted by Werner in his study of Carolingian noble families.[134] Such tight identification may have been useful given the disparate locations of each family's lands. As we have seen, the possessions of such as the Kampuli and Christopherii were scattered throughout the territory of Gaeta, their only common feature being that they were owned by the same clan.

This points to a very strong sense of identity as a clan on the part of each of these families, and their longevity seems to have owed something to very careful husbandry of their lands and, if each family had to look outside itself for business transactions at all, it would look to another similar ancient clan rather than to the newcomers of the Docibilan aristocracy. For this is the crucial point; noble status in the tenth century in Gaeta was not derived from association with the Docibilan dukes, however powerful the latter might have seemed to be. And the Docibilan aristocracy were never wealthy enough to be able to buy their way into closed noble circles.

(c) ROLE OF WOMEN IN THE TENTH-CENTURY NOBILITY

The discussions of family relationships and descent in this chapter have focussed almost exclusively on the roles and relationships of men. However, as mentioned above, at least one family in Naples traced its descent from a female ancestor, Rotunda, and this was by no means an isolated example. Also, the successful continuation of

[133] G. Tellenbach, 'From the Carolingian imperial nobility to the German estate of imperial princes', in *Medieval Nobility*, p. 207, stresses the need aristocrats had to be close to the ruler. W. Metz, 'Reichsadel und Krongutverwaltung in karolingischer Zeit', *Blätter für deutsche Landesgeschichte*, 94 (1968), 11–119, argues that it was the king who benefited from this closeness, a view endorsed by K. F. Werner, 'Important noble families in the kingdom of Charlemagne', in *Medieval Nobility*, p. 176. In Gaeta, both scenarios are valid; the nobility of the city supported Docibilis, and he in turn patronised a new aristocracy.

[134] 'Important noble families'.

the family line relied upon the women who bore the male heir(s); failing these, the blood of the family ran through daughters. How important were the female members of these noble families in cementing relationships?

First, we must establish precisely how many families accorded a primary role to a female ancestor in their histories. A survey of the documents from the three duchies in this early period reveals that several of the Amalfitan nobility's name-chains of descent ended with a female ancestor, titled countess.[135] In addition, all three duchies have evidence of men and women citing descent from a female ancestor without necessarily giving her a title.[136] Why were women cited rather than men in these cases? Several sets of circumstances could lead to a female ancestor being cited rather than a male. Among the nobility, a woman's ancestry might be more illustrious than her husband's. For example, in 1002 one John Papa, who appears in several Gaetan documents of the early eleventh century, gave his mother Maria's name in a document, rather than his father's, which we do not know.[137] Maria was a member of the ruling Docibilan dynasty, the daughter of John II, and John was clearly underlining where he derived his status from. On the latter point, the mother's status could be crucial further down the social ladder. In a court-case of 999, a group of men argued that they could not possibly be slaves of bishop Bernard of Gaeta because their mother had been a free woman.[138]

Widowhood could sometimes lead to a woman's name being

[135] For example, Cristina daughter of Leo son of countess Muscu in 1005, *CDA* 19; John son of Leo the priest son of Urso de Anna countess in 1013, *CDA* 32.

[136] In Amalfi: early examples include count Lupino son of Stephen de Anna, *CDA* 1 (907) and *CDA* 2 (922); Sparanus son of Leo de Mauro de Rosa, *CP* 5 (981) and a possible relative, Mauro son of Constantine de Rosa, *CDA* 34 (1018); later a group of men descended from one Eufimia appear, who may all have been of the same family, Lupinus de Eufimia in 964, *CDA* 7, Leo son of Mauro de Eufimia in 1018, *CDA* 34, and the brothers Fuscus, Mauro and Ursus sons of Leo de Eufimia in 1037, *CDA* 49. It is possible that they were in fact a cadet, or possibly a natural, branch of the Monteincollo family, argued on name evidence. We know from a document of 920 that Peter, son of count Mauro Monteincollo, was married to a woman named Eufimia, *CDA* 585, and their son, named Lupinus, appears in a document of 952, *CDA* 587. Any definite identification, however, is not possible from the surviving evidence. In Naples and Gaeta the evidence for female ancestors is less clear because the lengthy name-chains popular with the Amalfitans were not used. However, at Naples we see Peter son of John de Adelgarda in 987, *RN* 252, Atitio son of Peter Leo de Leoperga in 990, *RN* 267, Andrea son of Gregory de Rosa in 1016, *RN* 367 and Sergius son of Sergii de Mira in 1027, *RN* 412; and at Gaeta Peter de Megalu in 1006, *CDC* 113 and, later, Maria daughter of Leo de Orania in 1068, *CDC* 238.

[137] *CDC* 107.

[138] *CDC* 100; for further discussion of this case, see below, chapter 7.

used by her children. For example, in 1031 one Stephen signed his widowed mother's document at Gaeta as 'son of Sergia', despite the fact that his father's name appeared earlier in the charter.[139] The occurrence of matronymic identification rather than patronymic is well documented in all three duchies.[140] There could, however, be another reason for this, and that is that the parties either did not know their fathers or that they were natural children. This in itself was not necessarily a disablement. The most striking example of a line of descent which may have had these beginnings is that of the counts of Suio in the duchy of Gaeta.[141]

It is possible that the Docibilan rulers of Suio were an illegitimate offshoot (or at least, a natural one) from the line of duke Gregory. We know that count Hugh's father was Docibilis *magnificus*, who may have been the son of Gregory's son Landolf. Docibilis, though, is also recorded by Hugh and in another document as 'son of Pulissene/Polyssena';[142] we know that at the time of the first occurrence of this nomenclature, 1002, Landolf was still alive, and so the citation of Polyssena's name was not caused by her widowhood. The other main reason for citing descent from a woman, that she was the more illustrious parent, also does not seem to apply here. Polyssena is otherwise unknown and Landolf was a fifth-generation member of the Docibilan clan. It seems that Docibilis' birth was not to a married couple. Not that this was any hindrance to his sons; Hugh became lord of Suio and Leo briefly ruled Gaeta in 1042, but it was in the former castle that Polyssena's line became firmly entrenched.

The circumstances in which the family of Rotunda at Naples came to cite her as their ancestor are unclear, but the name itself is unusual enough to be able to link its occurrences. In 916 a gift to St Martin's convent in Naples was received by its abbess, Militu 'named Rotunda'.[143] An abbess was able to enjoy an identity not

[139] *CDC* 160.

[140] In Gaeta: Peter de Musa *CDC* 82 (983), Peter de Megalu *CDC* 113 (1006), Docibilis son of Maria *CDC* 120 (1010), Gregory son of Bona *CDC* 164 (1034); Leo son of Marozza *CDC* 120, 121, 125 (1010–1012) may be the same man as Leo son of Bonus, the regular witness for the Docibilans discussed above, but if so we do not know why he sometimes chose to give his mother's name. In Amalfi: Leo son of Muscu *CDA* 19 (1005), Peter son of Rosa *CDA* 54 and 61 (1041,1051), Leo de Anna *CP* 47 (1061). In Naples: Peter de Matrona *RN* 51 (944), Peter son of Bona *RN* 53 (945), Stephen de Marina *RN* 90 (956), John son of Theotista *RN* 259 (989), etc.

[141] On their history, see below, chapter 5, sections (b,ii) and (c,ii).

[142] *CDC* 108, *CDC* 173.

[143] *RN* 4.

linked with that of a man. She also had high status derived from her abbacy, and, since it was common for religious houses to have links with the nobility throughout Europe at this time, her identity as the laywoman Militu may have gained her equal respect as that of the abbess Rotunda. She is a likely candidate to be remembered with pride. This remembrance could take two forms, however. As well as direct descendants, other members of her family might have named their children after her. Since we cannot be sure whether the abbess had any children,[144] we cannot securely identify the Rotunda documented in 959 as her daughter or granddaughter,[145] but it would be unwise to discount the possibility of a relationship altogether. The second Rotunda and her husband Gregory are recorded in that year as being the previous owners of a piece of land in Anglata (unknown). Significantly, Rotunda is named before her husband, suggesting that she had been the actual owner. Six years later, the 'heirs of Rotunda' are recorded in a boundary clause of land at Miana.[146] Furthermore, the same document records in another boundary the 'heirs of Militum'. Could this possibly be a link to abbess Rotunda, whose lay name was Militu? The hypothesis is persuasive, even taking into account that *militum* could equally mean 'of the soldiers'. But the location of this land in Miana does not correspond with that recognised to be the *pars militie* further afield in Liburia. Either way, the family seem to have found a focus for their landowning in the area north-west of Naples in the tenth century. In 997 one Palumbus the priest bought land for his nephew Bisantius, son of Rotunda, in Maranum.[147] The land had previously belonged to a member of the Caputo family; the same family was earlier documented owning land on the boundary of the Anglata property owned by Rotunda and Gregory. Thus a web of connections tying isolated Rotunda references into a plausible family begins to emerge. Nearby, in Quarto, Gregory de Rotunda is recorded as a landowner in 1020.[148] His wife and children made a charter of security for the *igumenos* of SS Sergius and Bacchus in Naples in 1038 about land which Gregory had leased, and over which there had been a dispute, but we do not know where the land was.[149] Finally,

[144] Although she may have entered monastic life as a widow, a very common occurrence in the Tyrrhenian as elsewhere in this period.

[145] *RN* 109; allowing thirty years per generation, the latter relationship is more likely.

[146] *RN* 144. [147] *RN* 299. [148] *RN* 385. [149] *RN* 463.

Gregory is recorded as a previous owner of land at Antinianum (Antignano), again north-west of Naples, in 1074.[150]

The family of Rotunda do not appear to have been particularly prosperous, to judge by the fact that they were still leasing land as well as owning it in the eleventh century. One might postulate that, if their ancestor was an abbess, they inherited prestige rather than wealth. The bulk of the latter is likely to have followed Rotunda to her convent, especially if she had no children. Nevertheless, her family's continued use of her name illustrate how a woman could be commemorated for over a century.

Having seen the circumstances in which women were cited as the source of the family's lineage, what sorts of activities would they have been expected to undertake? Were they merely caretakers of the dynasty's fortune, or was their role more important?

Starting right at the top of society, the women of the ducal houses are more visible in some areas than others. In the Docibilan family, although daughters seem not to have been considered fit to rule, the women did share in the family's wealth. One effect of this may be the difficulty which surrounds the identification of their husbands in many cases. The latter seem to emerge in the documentation only when widowed and claiming their wives' portions. For example, in 924, when the children of Docibilis I divided up lands which they had inherited, one Rodipert received the portion of his late wife Megalu, Docibilis' daughter.[151] A survey of ducal wives in the three duchies does not provide us with very much information about their backgrounds either. As already noted, Docibilis II was married to Orania of Naples and duke John of Amalfi's wife was Regalis of Salerno, both women members of the ruling houses of their home states, and both bringing property to their husbands.

It is a favourite historical motif to blame the decline of a dynasty's power on the perceived weakness of a female ruler or regent, but the widows of dukes had a crucial role to play in ensuring that their children succeeded to the duchy. Their success or failure depended in large part on the alliances that they had made locally.[152] Only in exceptional circumstances could a foreign duchess use her family connections elsewhere to reinforce her

[150] *RN* 520. [151] *CDC* 31.

[152] For examples of this in the eleventh century, see below, chapter 5, section (a).

power, as for example in the case of duchess Maria of Amalfi, sister of Pandolf IV of Capua, discussed above.[153] A widowed duchess with strong local connections and landed wealth was far more likely to succeed in buying support for her son and maintaining her own position as his guardian. This ties in with the documented activity of noble wives and widows in the former Byzantine coastal cities, who had a legal basis for their position and who seem to have wielded a great deal of economic power and influence.[154]

Marriage was not the only route to such power. For example, Pitru daughter of Kampulus, of the Neapolitan family of John *miles*, had a great deal of economic influence. As a member of a wealthy and powerful family, although not, it now seems, her father's only child (she appears to have had a brother, Peter the curial, but nevertheless seems to have inherited a large share of their father's wealth), she is seen in the tenth and early eleventh centuries exploiting her position to the full. She owned and managed large quantities of land and the family's proprietary church, seems to have totally dominated her husband Stephen to the extent that he retired to a monastery for a while and pursued court cases in Naples on her own behalf, always successfully.

What is interesting is the position of Stephen in relation to his wife, for, although he appears in 968/969 making two leases of Liburia land on his own account,[155] there are ten other documents in which his wife is named first as the author, giving the impression that she was the real controller of their property, or at least that their wealth was largely fron her family, not his. Pitru is the best-documented woman we know from medieval Naples, and was clearly aware of her power; in 963 she apparently acted alone in a court-case to have her neighbour's window, which looked straight into hers, blocked up.[156] The court-case, and a reference in another document to her house in 965,[157] raises the possibility that up to this date she and Stephen lived apart, and that he really was living a monastic life. If so, he apparently lost his vocation between then and 968, when he reappears in the documents as Stephen *miles*.[158] From that point on he no longer used the title of monk, and appears beside his wife in all her transactions (and *vice versa*) until both disappear from view in 977.

[153] See above, chapter 2.
[154] For more on the economic power of women, Skinner, 'Women, wills and wealth'.
[155] *RN* 170, *RN* 171. [156] *RN* 132. [157] *RN* 150. [158] *RN* 170.

Women's roles in pulling together both the noble families in this area and in linking the ruling dynasties have been somewhat ignored hitherto in studies of southern Italy.[159] This section has attempted to introduce the ways in which they did so, and more will be said as the study progresses. One area in which they are often heavily documented is in pious donations to the church. Pitru, for example, was the controller of her family's proprietary church. What significance did such foundations have in the family histories of the tenth century?

(d) NOBILITY AND THE CHURCH: 'EIGENKIRCHEN'

A good relationship with the local church was seen by the dukes of each city as a contributory factor in achieving dignity and respect, and there is evidence that noble families thought in the same way. At Gaeta, an analysis of their transactions reveals that they dealt almost exclusively with the four main ecclesiastical institutions – the bishopric, St Michael at Planciano, SS Theodore and Martin and St Erasmus at Formia. Their activities also show a tendency on the part of both old nobility and new aristocrats to associate themselves with the oldest institutions of the duchy, perhaps another manifestation of the importance attached to age discussed earlier. In addition to these transactions, however, we have evidence that the Kampuli patronised another church, SS John and Paul,[160] and owned a further two, St Gregory at Castro Argento[161] and St Martin at Casa Hortali.[162] This is the only instance we have of a Gaetan family prominent in the tenth century controlling proprietary churches, apart from the Docibilans themselves (those of eleventh-century families are discussed later). In Naples, the family of John *miles* also owned a church, as did the Isabri family, perhaps indicating that this activity was the preserve of the very highest nobility. Such churches existed in some numbers in northern Italy, and from a much earlier date than in the south. In the words of Tabacco, possession of churches 'not only gave the lord a religious insurance and increased his income . . . but

[159] But see Taviani-Carozzi, *Principauté*, pp. 384–409, for a recent discussion of the role of marriage, the 'échange des femmes', in linking the ruling dynasties of Salerno, Benevento and Capua.

[160] *CDC* 208 (1059): Marinus son of Kampulus recorded as having previously donated land to the church.

[161] *CDC* 208.

[162] *CDC* 245.

constituted one of the foundations of the social prestige of the aristocracy'.[163]

It is particularly significant that the only known tenth-century Gaetan family owning churches were the Kampuli. For in establishing these foundations they were not only emphasising their landed wealth and social status, but were also making the very political statement that they, just like the Docibilans, were capable of supporting their own churches as well as making gifts to those of the ruling family.

This attitude of detachment on the part of the Kampuli (and perhaps, other older families) was ultimately very damaging, for by, to a certain extent, remaining aloof from the Docibilans and their patronage, the older noble families of Gaeta indirectly weakened the rulers. They acquiesced to the Docibilan rise possibly because they had not the strength to resist Docibilis I's strong-arm force of Saracen mercenaries, or because the Docibilans were initially so much richer than they were. Having accepted Docibilan rule they received a certain amount of land, and acted as witnesses, but never entirely succumbed to Docibilan patronage in return for their wholehearted support. In refusing to do so they contributed to the fragmentation of Docibilan power, and, ultimately, to their own decline. As will become clear in a later chapter, landed possessions scattered across the whole duchy were only viable if that duchy was peaceful. We have already seen that the Docibilans themselves were running into land problems by the end of the tenth century. For them, and for the landed nobility, as well as for the fledgling Docibilan aristocracy of Gaeta, the eleventh century would be anything but one of peace.

[163] Tabacco, *Struggle for Power*, p. 166, records northern examples from at least the ninth century, although documentary survival must partly explain this difference.

Part II

A TIME OF CHANGE: THE ELEVENTH CENTURY AND BEYOND

Chapter 5

FROM LOCAL DUKES TO NORMAN KINGS

(a) GAETA: NEW REGIMES

The tenth century was one of remarkable continuity and stability in the political affairs of Gaeta. The same ruling family was in power, and the same group of noble families prominent, throughout the century. However, the Docibilans seem to have been experiencing problems maintaining their position by the end of the century, leading to squabbles within the clan over what public land remained in its hands.[1] More significantly, the participants in these disputes identified themselves and their cause with smaller areas of jurisdiction, such as the duchy of Fondi and the county of Traetto.[2] The eleventh century saw a series of regime changes at Gaeta itself, in which much of the old pattern of power and patronage was swept away. This section seeks to illuminate that process from a number of different viewpoints. First, I shall outline the sequence of regime changes in order to provide a framework and background against which to discuss some issues in more detail. Secondly, I shall re-examine the process of the fragmentation of the duchy itself, looking at external pressures and internal developments. The history of Gaeta in this period will then be set against those of her neighbours, to see whether a 'Tyrrhenian' pattern can be established.

The land disputes just referred to between count Dauferius of Traetto and his relatives the bishop of Gaeta and the duke of Fondi, Leo, are significant for the light they shed on the emergence of new areas of territorial jurisdiction within the duchy of Gaeta in the late tenth century. The latter dispute, in 999, was judged at the court of the German emperor, Otto III, who was at that time trying to impose his authority on this part of Italy. His imposition of

[1] See above, chapter 3, section (a).

[2] For example, *CDC* 90 (992): Dauferius count of Traetto v. Leo duke of Fondi; *CDC* 101 (999): bishop Bernard v. Dauferius count of Traetto.

Ademarius as prince of Capua in the same year is a prime example of Otto's heavy-handed, and ultimately short-lived, Italian intervention.[3] Otto, of course, was not the first of his family to entangle himself in Italian politics. After his imperial coronation by pope John XII, Otto I had in 962 issued a privilege confirming the pope's jurisdiction over much of the peninsula. Among the possessions conceded were the cities of Naples, Gaeta and Fondi and the *patrimonia* of Benevento, Naples and upper and lower Calabria. Presumably recognising the political situation as it stood at that time, Amalfi is not mentioned, suggesting that its drift towards Salerno was well known.[4]

The earlier dispute of 992, however, was still submitted to the judgement of the duke of Gaeta, John III, suggesting that the disputants continued to recognise his overall authority. It may have been to preserve that authority that John's father Marinus had succeeded his brothers John II and Gregory in power, despite the fact that Gregory had at least two sons. We do not know the ages of the latter, but it may have been the case that the Docibilans were trying to avoid a minority succession to power, particularly if they were aware that their stocks of disposable public land were running low.[5]

Such fears were well founded. John III died in 1008, closely followed by his eponymous son in 1011/2. This led to a child, John V, assuming the ducal title. Initially this weakness does not seem to have affected the duke's sovereign status; in 1012 a document authorised and received by residents of Castro Argento was still written at Gaeta and dated according to the duke's reign.[6] By 1014, though, the counts of the much larger settlement of Traetto had taken advantage of the fact that Gaeta was being ruled by a minor and his grandmother, duchess Emilia, the widow of John III, to assert their identity as quasi-independent counts. In that year a document recording a dispute between count Dauferius and the abbey of Montecassino was written at Traetto and dated by the rule of its counts, Dauferius, Lando, Ederado and Marinus. Also significant about the case is that it was argued in the presence of the archbishop and prince of Capua, the duke of Naples, the abbot of

[3] Loud, *Church and Society*, p. 28.

[4] *MGH, Constitutiones et Acta Publica Imperatorem et Regum*, 1, ed. L. Weiland (Hanover, 1893), p. 23ff.

[5] See above, chapter 3, section (a) and note 39 for more on the fraternal succession.

[6] *CDC* 125.

Montecassino, the son of the duke of Fondi and the bishop and various noblemen of Gaeta. The duke of Gaeta is noticeably absent. Unless the bishop, Bernard, was seen as the duke's representative (which is likely – documentary evidence suggests a close relationship between Bernard and his sister-in-law, the duchess-regent Emilia), the views of the duke of Gaeta seem to have mattered little to the Traettans.

Matters were not helped by the fact that there seems to have been a power struggle between Emilia and her son Leo for the regency in the following years, revealed by the dating clauses of documents written at Gaeta during this period (see Figure 5.1).

In the period 1017–23 Leo granted out public land to Kampulus son of Docibilis, a member of the powerful Kampuli clan,[7] possibly in an attempt to win over that family's support for his removal of Emilia. The dating clause of a document authorised by a member of the clan, Mirus son of John, in 1020,[8] suggests that he may initially have succeeded in convincing the Kampuli to recognise his position. But Emilia had a far more potent ally in her brother-in-law, bishop Bernard, who gave her land in 1002[9] and whose sole authorised document of the period in question recognised the rule of the young John, without Leo, in 1014.[10] Perhaps it was his support which allowed Emilia to emerge triumphant by 1025, or perhaps Leo had died by that time. Whatever the cause, her victory was not without cost. By that date, Traettan documents had ceased to acknowledge the rule of the Gaetan dukes, and the Sperlongan ones would soon follow.[11]

There is also some evidence to suggest that Emilia and her grandson were losing their authority at Gaeta too. In 1028 they ceded victory in a land dispute to one John son of Constantine, who may have been a descendant of John I via one of the latter's illegitimate sons, Constantine.[12] It is significant also that when duke Sergius IV of Naples sought refuge in Gaeta in 1029, he addressed his appeal for help not only to Emilia and John, but also to all of the Gaetans *magnis et mediocris.*[13] The identity of the latter will be established later in this chapter, but the important point to note is that the duchess and her grandson were not perceived by their Neapolitan counterpart as capable of raising the military force that he needed.

[7] *CDC* 135. [8] *CDC* 138. [9] *CDC* 105. [10] *CDC* 129.
[11] *CDC* 154 (1028) was dated by Leo son of Leo, consul of Fondi.
[12] *CDC* 155. [13] *CDC* 156; see also Cassandro, 'Ducato', 310.

DOCUMENT	DATE	AUTHOR	DATE CLAUSE
CDC 125	1012	Carruccius	Minority of John V
CDC 126	1012	Bernard bishop*	John V
CDC 128	1013	Landolf f. Gregory*	Emilia and John V
CDC 129	1014	Bernard bishop	John V
CDC 131	1014	Marenda	John V
CDC 132	1016	Gregory f. Leo*	John V
CDC 133	1017	Sergia	John V and Leo f. John III
CDC 134	1018	Bona	John V and Leo f. John III
CDC 135	1019	Leo f. John III*	John V and Leo f. John III
CDC 136	1019	John Cecus	no date clause
CDC 138	1020	Mirus f. John@	John V and Leo f. John III
CDC 139	1021	Matrona	John V and Leo f. John III
CDC 140	1021	Alberic abbot+	John V and Leo f. John III
CDC 141	1021	John f. Christopher	John V and Leo f. John III
CDC 142	1023	Hugh count of Suio*	Emilia, John V and Leo
CDC 143	1024	Gregory f. Leo	John V and Leo
CDC 144/5	1024	Leo priest	no date clause
CDC 146	1025	Gregory f. John	Emilia and John V
CDC 147	1025	consorts of S. Peter	Emilia and John V
CDC 148	1025	George f. John	Emilia and John V
CDC 150	1026	Leo f. Marinus@	Emilia and John V
CDC 153	1028	Constantine f. Paul	Emilia and John V
CDC 155	1028	Emilia and John*	Emilia and John V
CDC 156	1029	Sergius duke (Naples)	Emilia and John V
CDC 160	1031	Sergia	Emilia and John V
CDC 161	1031	Maria	Emilia and John V
CDC 162	1032	John f. Constantine	Emilia and John V
CDC 163	1032	Drosu Christopheri	Emilia and John V
CDC 166	1036	Peter	Pandolf and Pandolf

* = Docibilans @ = Kampuli + of St Theodore in Gaeta

Figure 5.1 *Gaetan dating clauses, 1012–1032*

Nor, it seems, was the Gaetan regime capable of defending itself against the attention of the rulers of Capua, Pandolf and his eponymous son. The last documented appearance of Emilia and John V in a dating clause is in 1032.[14] By 1036 Emilia was dead,[15] and from the same year survives the first of five Gaetan documents dated by the two Capuans' reign.[16]

The late 1030s saw a dramatic expansion in the power of prince

[14] *CDC* 163. [15] *CDC* 165.

[16] *CDC* 166 (1036), *CDC* 167 (1036), *CDC* 168 (1037), *CDC* 169 (1038), *CDC* 170 (1038).

Guaimarius of Salerno. By 1038 he is recorded as prince of Capua, and the counts of Traetto were including him in their dating clauses;[17] in 1040 he was named in a Gaetan clause.[18]

That the rule of the Salernitan was by no means welcome is illustrated by the brief appearance of one Leo, son of Docibilis *magnificus*, as duke Leo II in 1042. If his bid for power can be characterised as a revolt of the former supporters of the Docibilans at Gaeta, then the Kampuli family were certainly at the forefront of that movement. One member of the clan, Marinus son of Kampulus, received a portion of the mill Maiore from the duke to share with one Gregory son of John, both men receiving the gift 'in return for their services'.[19] Another family member, Kampulus son of Docibilis, witnessed the duke's other extant document.[20]

The *Codex Cajetanus* furnishes no evidence between the years 1042 and 1045, but in the latter year, the Chronicle of Montecassino records that the Gaetans 'on account of the ill-will of Guaimarius, called out Atenolf of Aquino to make himself their duke'.[21] Were the Kampuli again among the leaders of the discontented Gaetans? Although the documentary evidence is by no means conclusive, it suggests that members of the family achieved a position of honour and prestige under the rule of Atenolf and, later, that of his widow Maria and their son Atenolf II. For example, Sergius son of Kampulus appeared at a court held by Atenolf I at Traetto in 1053 described as a 'noble of Gaeta', and Kampulus son of John witnessed a document issued by duchess Maria and the younger Atenolf in 1063.[22]

Why did men like the Kampuli invite another foreigner to come and take the place of prince Guaimarius' puppet duke Raynulf[23] rather than seize power themselves? I would suggest that, made cautious by the failure of the Docibilan pretender Leo II in 1042, they realised that a Gaetan could not call upon sufficient resources to fend off the attentions of foreign predators, and so sent to Atenolf promising support for his rule if he would leave their position of privilege intact. The wider political scene must also be considered. If, as I argued in the previous chapter, the Kampuli were related to the dukes of Naples, their actions in trying to

[17] *CDC* 171. [18] *CDC* 174. [19] *CDC* 176. [20] *CDC* 177.
[21] *CMC* II, 74. [22] *CDC* 195, *CDC* 218.
[23] *CDC* 203; Amatus, II.32, records Raynulf's tenure of the city, and the choice of his nephew Asclettin by 'li fidel Normant' of Aversa and Gaeta as his successor. The latter, however, does not appear in documents from Gaeta.

remove Gaeta's Salernitan puppet may have been prompted as much by Neapolitan interests as their own.

The evidence suggests that both Atenolf and the nobles found the agreement worked well. The Kampuli continued to prosper, and were joined in Atenolfan witness lists by the Caracci and the Coronellas (though not, interestingly, by the Christopherii). Atenolf seems to have consciously wooed the Docibilan party at Gaeta; it is significant that his only surviving land donation was made to the church of SS Theodore and Martin,[24] the favoured church of the Docibilan rulers. In return for his respect of local political patterns, Atenolf enjoyed sixteen years' rule until his death, and was able to hand on power to his widow and son.

That there was a resurgance of pro-Docibilan sympathy at Gaeta during these years is illustrated by a document of 1054. If the supporters of the Docibilans could not have one of that family as duke, it was possible at least to influence the choice of successor to Bernard, a Docibilan, as bishop of the city, and that, as the document reveals, is precisely what Gregory, son of John Coronella, and one Stephen, son of John de Arciu,[25] did. It appears that when Bernard died, the man in line for the bishopric was Laidulf son of Gregory the magnificent, who is recorded as archdeacon of Gaeta as early as 1024.[26] It is true that he had Docibilan blood, being the great-nephew of three dukes. However, the man who became bishop instead, Leo, was the son of the last Docibilan duke, Leo II, and was perhaps a more immediately attractive candidate to those who supported his father. Leo, moreover, received money from Gregory Coronella and Stephen de Arciu to pay Laidulf off.[27]

Atenolf's death in 1061 signalled the end of the Docibilan 'revival'. In a situation strongly reminiscent of duchess Emilia's reign, his widow Maria was left as regent for a minor, Atenolf II. Like the earlier woman she seems to have required the approval of those about her in Gaeta to carry out transactions, or so her documents suggest. In 1062, her anti-Norman pact with the counts of Traetto, Maranola and Suio also included the people of Gaeta.[28] Maria was here continuing her husband Atenolf's apparent policy towards the Normans, for Gaetans are recorded by Amatus,[29] as having participated in the ill-fated papal expedition against the

[24] *CDC* 203 (1057).
[25] For more on the de Arciu family, see below, chapter 6, section (a,vi).
[26] *CDC* 143. [27] *CDC* 197. [28] *CDC* 215. [29] Amatus III.24.

Normans in 1052. In 1063 she and her son gave public land to St Theodore's with the consent of bishop Leo, Bonus the judge and the Gaetan people.[30] These facts in themselves, however, do not explain the vulnerable nature of her rule. What problems did women like Maria and Emilia face when left as regents?

Although the supposed weakness of female rule cannot realistically be sustained as the reason for the breakdown of a dynasty's power, the role of the prominent women of the duchy of Gaeta during its breakup has never been investigated further. The rule of a woman, even as a regent for a minor, seems to have brought with it a crisis of power at Gaeta under both Emilia and Maria. How was their power viewed in the context of women's roles?

It should be stated at the outset that neither Emilia nor Maria were members of the dynasties ruling Gaeta at the time they came to power, that is, they had married into the ruling family. Their power, therefore, derived wholly from the fact that they were mothers to the rightful heir to the duchy. That the latter had an unchallengeable right to rule was by now accepted totally in the duchy, and the two regencies simply underline that fact. Even when Emilia was challenged by her son Leo, it was only for the right to act as regent for his young nephew, not for the post of duke itself. Significantly, though, Emilia was able to resist the challenge. Why was this?

Several factors may be at work here. The first, as I have indicated, is that Emilia seems to have enjoyed the support of bishop Bernard, whose authority would carry weight not only within the family, but also with the Gaetan people as well. Emilia could also, however, draw upon legal tradition for her role as regent. For, dowager duchess or not, her position as a widow endowed her with a right, in the Byzantine law which prevailed in the duchy, to ensure the upbringing and protection of her children, in this case her son's child.[31] Her daughter-in-law, John IV's widow, who should have exercised this role, is not even known to us by name, suggesting that Emilia was able to supplant her as the senior woman in the family. Significant here may be the fact that

[30] *CDC* 218.

[31] 'A widow shall control her marriage portion and all her husband's property as becomes the head of the family and the household . . . And the children shall not take her place nor claim from her the patrimony, but treat her with all obedience and honour'; Leo III, *Ecloga* II,6, quoted from G. Buckler, 'Women in Byzantine law about 1100 A.D.', *Byzantion*, 11 (1936), 410.

Emilia is the first wife of a duke to have been accorded the title duchess in the documentation, and this may also have been decisive in her fight to rule.

In contrast, duchess Maria does not seem to have faced the type of threat to her regency from within posed by Leo against Emilia, but her rule as regent with the young Atenolf seems to have been fragile from the outset, owing much, perhaps, to the fact that she, unlike her predecessor, had no family to fall back upon at Gaeta for support. Important, too, was the fact that she and her husband had come to Gaeta from Aquino, an area where Lombard law and custom was followed, rather than Byzantine. For, although it was quite common for Lombard men to leave the care of heirs in their widows' hands, women under Lombard law were legally 'incompetent', and so such care was exercised under the tutelage of a male relative, or *mundoald*. At Gaeta, Maria does not appear to have had this male tutelage (which could also, of course, provide support and protection). The Lombard custom in her case may well have been ignored, but it is significant that it was from a city of Lombard law and practice, Capua, that two men came to take advantage of the situation and assume power at Gaeta.

Richard I, prince of Capua, and his son Jordan I took over in 1062 and are recorded as dukes of Gaeta for the first time in the documents from the city in 1064.[32] Dating clauses of that year reveal that for a short time the young Atenolf was permitted to rule alongside them, presumably as a subject rather than a colleague.[33] He soon disappeared, however, and it seems that thereafter Richard and Jordan nominated a series of puppet dukes for Gaeta, whilst they continued to make Capua their base.

One point that seems to be missed in discussions of the weakness of female regencies in the Middle Ages is the strength of challenge they faced, and Emilia and Maria were unfortunate enough to be in power during two periods of Capuan strength and aggression. Maria's action in joining in a pact with Traetto, Maranola and Suio

[32] *CDC* 221; the documents in the *Codex Cajetanus* record Jordan alone as the duke of Gaeta as early as 1058. One, *CDC* 205, has been identified as a forgery from the Register of Peter the Deacon by Loud, on the basis that Richard I is omitted from the date clause during his lifetime, that Jordan's wife in the document, Rapizza, is otherwise unknown, and that the indiction number cannot be reconciled with the date of the document: G. Loud, 'Calendar', p. 111. The other, *CDC* 206, must be regarded with suspicion for similar reasons, although the mistake here may simply be in the date assigned to the document by the editors of the *Codex*, and the fact that it survives only in a seventeenth century copy.

[33] *CDC* 221, *CDC* 222, *CDC* 225.

against the Capuan Normans shows a great deal of political acumen in recognising that the weakness of the duchy lay in its disunity. (I may be mistaken in attributing the idea to participate to Maria, but similarly it is totally unjustified to assume some male 'eminence grise' behind her regency.) However, when Richard and Jordan took over, she was no longer needed as regent, and disappears from the city's documentation. She was not inactive for long, however. Richard handed over the city to his son-in-law William of Montreuil briefly, but after the latter's revolt, in which he repudiated the prince's daughter and sought to marry duchess Maria,[34] less identifiable figures appear as dukes. In 1064/5 the Capuans' choice fell on one Lando,[35] in 1066/7 we see Danimboldus as duke,[36] and then in 1068 a Norman, Geoffrey Ridell, took power.[37] Maria's participation in the revolt is as a shadowy figure, but that she was seen as an essential part of William's attempt to rule suggests that her role as mother of the rightful duke may still have carried influence. The choice of insignificant and now unidentifiable figures to act as puppet dukes from that point onwards underlines the danger that the rebellion had carried with it.

The Ridells, however, were by no means insignificant.[38] Geoffrey was duke of Gaeta for almost twenty years – his son Raynald succeeded him in 1086[39] – but what is remarkable about his reign is the level of detachment he exhibited from the state of affairs at Gaeta. Duke Atenolf had courted the noblemen of the city and had patronised its major church. The only document we have authorised by Geoffrey was written at his castle at Pontecorvo, gave the church of St Erasmus at Formia to Montecassino and was witnessed by two Pontecorvan judges, a man of Isernia and the count of Aquino, Atenolf.[40] Gaeta was no longer a political focus of attention; rather, it was now a satellite of the greater power of Capua and seemingly given to the lords of Pontecorvo simply

[34] William's petition to annul his marriage on the grounds of consanguinity was refused by the pope; Loud, *Church and Society*, p. 12 note 50 and p. 45. Amatus, VI.1, reports that he was joined in rebellion by Lando of Traetto, but it is unclear which Lando is meant here.

[35] *CDC* 228, *CDC* 229, *CDC* 230.

[36] *CDC* 232, *CDC* 233, *CDC* 234.

[37] *CDC* 235.

[38] On their origins, see G. Loud, 'How "Norman" was the Norman conquest of southern Italy?', *Nottingham Medieval Studies*, 25 (1981), 13–34. Amatus, V.9, reports that Geoffrey had led the Norman expedition into Sicily in 1061, a responsibility that perhaps led to his being given Gaeta and Pontecorvo later on.

[39] *CDC* 257.

[40] *CDC* 249; Atenolf is identified by Amatus, V.9, as one of the rebels against Richard of Capua. He had clearly come back into line by this time.

because geographically they were the closest to the newly acquired territory.

This detachment may have been a contributory factor to a renewed Gaetan revolt in 1091, leading to several changes in rule. After the death of prince Jordan I of Capua, the Ridells were ousted from power at Gaeta (Raynald's son Gualganus having died without issue) and were forced to continue their claim to rule from their residence at Pontecorvo.[41]

They were replaced by the last documented eleventh-century duke of Gaeta, one Landolf, who is recorded as being in the second year of his reign in 1094.[42] Merores thinks he may have been a Docibilan, descended from the family of Leo II, since he is recorded in a much later document with the title *senator* by his son Marinus. As she points out, the son of Leo II used this unusual title too.[43] Her argument is strengthened by the fact that only two other documented occurrences of the title at Gaeta in the eleventh century reveal it being used by Docibilans too. The son of duke John III appears as Leo *senator* in 1036,[44] and John's other son Marinus appears to have borne the title too, as his son John appears as John *comes* son of Marinus *senator* son of duke John in 1045.[45] Landolf's reign might, therefore, be a final attempt by the Docibilan party to regain the initiative in the city. It is worth noting that the title *senator* was used as an honorific title within the Neapolitan ducal family, and Neapolitan involvement in the rise of Landolf is highly likely, given the latter city's opposition to Capuan and Norman interests. This theory is given further weight by the fact that Landolf's underage son Marinus appears later in Naples, selling property under the supervision of the Neapolitan duke, John VI.[46] Landolf's attempt to gain power was made during a period when the Capuans were diverted by a feud with Richard de Aquila, count of Pica. In the course of the struggle, Landolf was replaced by another Capuan nominee, William of Blosseville, who is documented as duke in 1103,[47] but by 1105 it was Richard who had gained power and who is recorded as consul and duke of Gaeta.[48] Thereafter, the history of Gaeta's rulers is one directed by the balance of power between the various political

[41] Loud, *Church and Society*, p. 91. [42] *CDC* 269. [43] *Gaeta*, p. 51.
[44] *CDC* 165. [45] *CDC* 179. [46] *RN* 606.
[47] *CDC* 275; but he had been duke from 1101/2.
[48] William is later found documented as a vassal of the de Aquilas; Loud, *Church and Society*, p. 91.

factions holding castles in and around Capua and on the eastern border of Gaeta's territory. As we shall see later in this chapter, the frequent changes of duke in the early twelfth century seem to have had little effect on the internal politics of the city.

A document of 1105 provides a glimpse of the balance of power around the city and its territory in that year, when various local magnates gave security to the bishop of Gaeta, Albert, not to harm ecclesiastical property in the course of their contests. The list of lords included Richard de Aquila, the consul and duke of Gaeta, prince Robert son of Jordan of Capua (his elder brother Richard, the prince of that city, would die the following year), William Blosseville, Richard of Spigno, Leo count of Fondi, Landenolf of Maranola and Marinus of Itri.[49] Dating clauses of the Gaetan documents reveal Richard de Aquila in the fourth year of his rule in 1108,[50] and the following year he held a documented court in the city.[51] From 1112 onwards the city was held by a cadet branch of the prince of Capua's family.[52]

The most successful of these rulers was duke Richard II, who was also the count of Carinola, and, therefore, probably already had quite a detailed knowledge of the duchy's territory. He is first recorded as duke in 1121,[53] having succeeded his nephew Jonathan, who had ruled as a minor from 1112.[54] It is highly likely that Richard had been the regent in the city before he came to power in his own right, for a document of 1117 reveals that at the Capuan court prince Robert's barons included 'duke' Richard son of count Bartholomew of Carinola. Alongside him Leo of Fondi appears again.[55] Richard had achieved even more power by 1123; a date clause at Gaeta records him as prince of Capua, count of Carinola and duke of Gaeta.[56] It is interesting that the three dignities were distinguished during his rule, mirroring the tendency towards fragmentation of jurisdictional areas, even if the same person held all the positions of power. On an even more localised level, it is evident from the documents that the duchy of Gaeta by this date had completely dissolved into separate territories

[49] *CDC* 280. [50] *CDC* 283. [51] *CDC* 284.

[52] Loud, *Church and Society*, p. 12, note 50. [53] *CDC* 296.

[54] Jonathan is recorded as in the fourth year of his minority in 1116, *CDC* 289, and in the seventh year of his rule in 1119, *CDC* 292.

[55] *CDC* 290; Leo appears as *baiuli* of Fondi in a document written at Sperlonga in the same year, *CDC* 291. The power base of Gaeta had therefore shrunk considerably from its height under the Docibilans. [56] *CDC* 301.

concentrated around often fortified settlements. How had this fragmentation occurred?

(b) THE FRAGMENTATION OF GAETA

Much Gaetan historiography blames the fall of the Docibilan dynasty from power and the capture of the city of Gaeta by the Capuans in 1032 on the fragmentation of the duchy into smaller counties. Consequently, it was unable to defend itself against predators.[57] The break-up is usually held to have originated during the reign of duke Marinus (fl.945–84). Guiraud claims that Marinus consciously detached pieces of the duchy from the centre at Gaeta for his sons to rule.[58] Giraud bases his argument on the fact that Marinus' sons Dauferius I, Gregory and Leo were the first documented rulers of Traetto, Castro Argento and Fondi respectively, and has identified a strengthening of localised interests in the duchy in the eleventh century which led to the rise of later fortifications such as Fratte, Suio, Itri, Sperlonga and Maranola.

On the second point Guiraud is undoubtedly correct, but the scenario of Gaeta's fragmentation begins from the mistaken assumption that the duchy had ever been a unified, public entity. It was not: Docibilis I and his clan had divided it among themselves along the lines of a large family estate, and this was how it was ruled. But did duke Marinus deliberately carve up the duchy still further, as Guiraud claims? Or was Gaeta's continuing division into smaller pieces simply a result of being run as a private estate?

The first point to note is that Marinus himself had been duke of Fondi before he achieved power at Gaeta. There seem to have been other forces at work in the Fondi area which go some way to explaining the separate status of that city, where the Docibilans continued in power until the 1070s.[59] The same is true of Traetto and Suio, but there is no evidence that Marinus created the counties deliberately as places for his sons to rule. As late as 981, just three years before his death, he judged a dispute at Traetto as 'duke of Traetto'.[60] The only decision that we know he made was that his son John (III) should succeed him, and he associated the younger man in power with himself from 978.[61] If he did make arrangements for his other sons Leo (duke of Fondi from at least

[57] See, for example, von Falkenhausen, 'Ducato', 352. [58] Guiraud, 'Reseau', 491.
[59] See below, this chapter, section (c,ii). [60] *CDC* 80. [61] *CDC* 74.

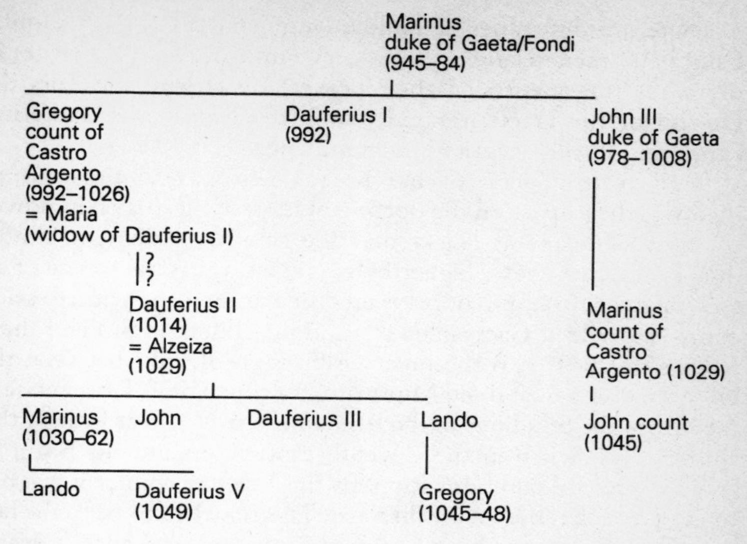

Figure 5.2 *The counts of Traetto*

992), Gregory (count of Castro Argento) and Dauferius (count of Traetto from 992), there is no direct evidence of his actions.

That the idea of distinct counties of Traetto and Suio was strongly entrenched in the eleventh century, however, is indicated by the fact that, even when the Docibilans lost power at Gaeta in 1032, their relatives continued to rule these two centres and Fondi (Castro Argento, briefly a separate county, was early on amalgamated into the growing power of Traetto). Their contact with each other continued even in periods when they had little contact with the larger city. What then were the origins of the counties?

(i) *Traetto*

It was shown in chapter 2 that, as a settlement, Traetto's history was far longer than Gaeta's. Yet, during the apogee of Docibilan rule, some memory must have survived of Traetto as the centre of a jurisdictional territory. It was this, together, perhaps, with an internal disagreement between the Gaetan Docibilans and the cadet rulers of Traetto (see Figure 5.2), which provided the conditions for a reassertion of Traettan power in the early eleventh century. How was this power gained and expressed?

There are difficulties in building up a picture of the comital family and their relations, but a very familiar pattern emerges in the ways they expressed their power. Like their ancestors the Docibilans, the Traettans rapidly adopted a lead-name, Dauferius, expressing its self-identity and confidence.

We have no evidence of churches at Traetto in the tenth century; such was the impact on the documentation of the arrival in power of the Docibilans at Gaeta that the smaller settlement almost disappears from view. Nevertheless, Traetto was the centre of an episcopal see (bishop Andrea is recorded among the witnesses at a court-case held at Gaeta in 992[62]) and the church of St Peter there reflects this fact. It is the most visible sign of links between the hilltop settlement and old Minturno, for much of its fabric was re-used from the buildings of the Roman town. We hear little of this church, and, when in the eleventh century documents begin to appear to record pious donations by the Traettan counts, it was not to St Peter's that they were directed. This may be linked to the fact that Traetto seems to have lost its episcopate after Andrea's death. His last appearance in the documentation was in 999.[63] If he died soon afterwards, his see may have been taken over by the ambitious and capable bishop, Bernard of Gaeta, who lost no opportunity to increase his influence.[64]

The counts of Traetto, like their western neighbours, were active church patrons. Count Dauferius V imitated the policies of his ancestors when he patronised the most prominent monastery in the county, the family foundation dedicated to St Marinus at Coriano.[65] By obtaining the support of the saint, the counts of Traetto seem to have been establishing their right to rule on moral as well as economic grounds, and having no bishop to hand relied on the next best thing. Did such a relationship help them? It would seem so; although relying on Capuan amity as well as divine approbation, they remained in power until 1060, some twenty years after the last duke of Gaeta had fallen, and it was not internal opposition that finally overthrew them.

The clearest indication from our documents that the counts and countesses of Traetto saw themselves as the heirs to Docibilan power is that by 1014 they had their own notary, Peter, and that by

[62] *CDC* 90. [63] *CDC* 100.

[64] On this and later evidence for the see becoming part of the Gaetan bishopric, see R. Castrichino, *Gli Antichi Episcopati di Minturno e Traetto* (Minturno, 1975), p. 28.

[65] *CDC* 188.

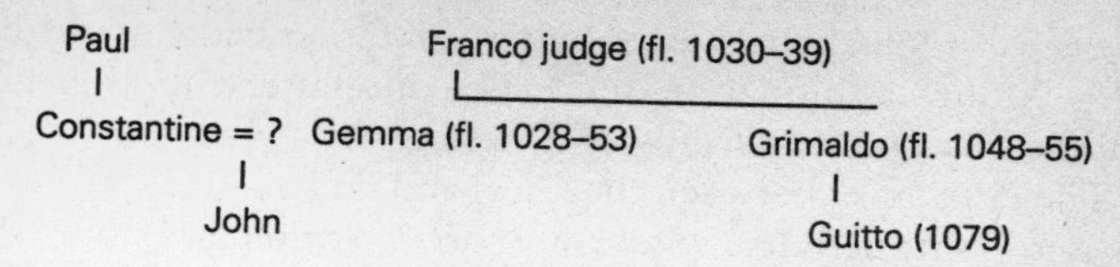

Figure 5.3 *The de Papara family*

1020 they considered the granting-out of public land in the area as their prerogative. Using this power, they may have begun to build up a circle of followers at Traetto.

For example, Peter Giczi, an inhabitant of Fratte, is seen as the beneficiary of four documents issued by various rulers of Traetto. In 1020 he bought some public land in Cirasa from countess Maria, and received part as a gift from her.[66] Five years later, count Ederado gave him some land and a house in Fratte.[67] In 1029 countess Alzeiza gave him more public land in Cirasa,[68] and finally in 1030 he exchanged land in Coriano for a larger amount in Silbakaba (Selvacava) with counts Lando, Marinus and John.[69] Peter's last appearance was as a witness for an otherwise unknown group of inhabitants of Fratte in 1048,[70] but in the same year his son John continued the Giczi family's links with the counts of Traetto when he acted as a witness for the count Marinus.[71]

The Giczi are frequently joined in the documents by another Traettan family, the de Paparas. Franco, the head of the family (see genealogy, Figure 5.3), was a judge, and in this capacity witnessed two comital land transactions in 1030 and 1034,[72] the former being the exchange with Peter Giczi already mentioned. The private side of Franco is revealed in a document of 1039, when he and nine others, including Peter Capomazza and Sicard the notary at Fratte, were accused of seizing land in the area belonging to the abbey of Montecassino.[73] The men came to an agreement with the monastery to rent the land on preferential terms.

Franco's son Grimaldo maintained the comital link when he witnessed a document of count Marinus of Traetto in 1048.[74] Co-witness with him was John son of Peter Giczi, suggesting that the counts of Traetto were indeed creating a permanent circle of aristocrats. Grimaldo is mentioned as the lessee of some land, belonging to the major Traettan monastery of St Marinus in

[66] *CDC* 137. [67] *CDC* 149. [68] *CDC* 157. [69] *CDC* 171.
[70] *CDC* 184. [71] *CDC* 185. [72] *CDC* 159, *CDC* 164.
[73] *CDC* 171. [74] *CDC* 185.

Coriano, at Silbakaba, near to where his father had had the dispute with Montecassino, in 1049.[75] The monastery itself had been founded by count Marinus of Traetto.

The close links between the Giczi and de Papara families – their co-witnessing activity, witnessing for each other and ownership of land in the same place, Silbakaba – may be indicative of a blood or marital relationship between the two families, but none can be detected from the documents. A fragment of extremely circumstantial evidence can be added to the picture if we accept that abbot Giczo of St Marinus at Coriano was a member of the Giczi family. (The name is, after all, almost uniquely confined to this area). Giczo was abbot between 1049 and 1061 as far as we can see. In the earlier year we have already seen Grimaldo son of Franco de Papara leasing the church's land; in 1055 he witnessed an exchange transaction between Giczo and Gregory son of Peter.[76] Whether he did so in the capacity of tenant of the church or relative of the abbot, though, is unclear.

The de Papara clan can be extended in another direction. Franco the judge had a daughter named Gemma, who was in some way connected with Constantine son of Paul. She was left a sum of money in Constantine's will of 1028,[77] and was given the usufruct of his Flumetica estates for life in 1053, when he gave the estates themselves to Montecassino.[78] In the 1028 document, these estates had been originally bequeathed to Constantine's natural son John, and the subsequent donation suggests that the latter died before 1053. One cannot help suspecting that Gemma may have been John's mother, hence Constantine's provision for her from her deceased son's estates.

By virtue of his connection with the de Papara family, John may have been the same John son of Constantine who appears as a *bonus homo* of Traetto, witnessing a dispute between the counts, in 1049.[79]

Another family who witnessed for the counts were the Capomazzas. Leo first appears at Castro Argento in 1006.[80] Thereafter his son Peter witnessed for the counts of Traetto in 1029 and 1030,[81] and in 1039 was among the group of men from Fratte in dispute with Montecassino.[82] The Capomazzas seem to have been displaced by the Capuan takeover of the 1060s and 1070s; they re-emerge further west in Palazzo and Gaeta in the late eleventh

[75] *CDC* 188. [76] *CDC* 201. [77] *CDC* 153. [78] *CDC* 194.
[79] *CDC* 187. [80] *CDC* 113. [81] *CDC* 157, *CDC* 159. [82] *CDC* 171.

and early twelfth centuries.[83] These and the other families mentioned all seem to have made up a court circle around the counts of Traetto, and appear regularly in the counts' documents. However, their status did not solely revolve around their witnessing activities.

The term *bonus homo*, a 'common title for civil officials in the pre-consular period',[84] appears in the documents from Traetto almost fifty years before its first appearance in Gaeta in 1094, when the *boni homines* of that city requisitioned the access to a couple's house in order to build the city wall.[85] This responsibility for building work later belonged to the consuls of Gaeta. There is, however, no evidence of consuls at Traetto. This may be due to the fact that, whilst the settlement was the centre of a district territory, it was never large enough to merit a more sophisticated administration, and remained under the direct control of its counts.

This picture of an independent county is deceptive, however. Whilst the rulers of Traetto seem to have been successful in detaching their territory from the direct jurisdiction of the dukes of Gaeta early in the eleventh century, the evidence suggests that they soon came under increasing influence from their neighbours to the east, the Capuans. Furthermore that influence would lead to the Capuans winning power at the expense of the Gaetans in 1036. How did this situation come about?

(ii) *The expansion of Capuan power*

Early evidence suggests that, after Docibilis I's repulsion of Pandenolf of Capua's encroachment across the Garigliano river in the 880s,[86] relations between Gaeta and Capua appear to have been relatively cordial. This may partly have been achieved by political marriage; Rodipert the *gastald*, who married Docibilis' daughter, Megalu, was certainly a Lombard from his name and title, and is likely to have been a Capuan. This is suggested by a document of 962 surviving in the Gaetan collection, recording the exchange of slaves between Landolf *gastald* son of Pandolf and Pandenolf son of Rodipert *gastald*, written at Capua.[87] Its survival at Gaeta, when it

[83] *CDC* 171, *CDC* 265, *CDC* 299. Although they appear as landowners in these documents, they do not seem to have achieved any prominent position in Gaetan life.
[84] J. K. Hyde, *Society and Politics in Medieval Italy* (London, 1973), p. 51.
[85] *CDC* 271. [86] See above, chapter 2. [87] *CDC* 60.

contained no reference to Gaetan lands or people, makes it highly likely that this is Rodipert's son. Rodipert himself benefited from his marriage by inheriting his wife's portion of the lands of Docibilis I, in the division of 924.[88]

Two documents of 983 and 984 reveal another Capuan marriage, between Sikelgaita, daughter of John I, and an unnamed Capuan prince.[89] In the latter year her grandson, Landolf, is seen living in Gaeta and making a gift of his lands there to Marinus son of Constantine, and receiving *launegild* or a countergift according to Lombard law.[90] These documents provide clues to the identity of the people named in a document of 981, issued at Suessa across the Capuan border. In it, the same Marinus received from one Atenolf son of Atenolf, who can probably be identified as Landolf's nephew, more lands in Gaeta. Atenolf stated that he had inherited the lands, which are not named in any detail, from his *visabia* (great-grandmother), princess Sikelgaita, who may fairly safely be identified as John's daughter. Marinus again handed over *launegild*.[91]

Sikelgaita's marriage appears, therefore, to have opened the way to Docibilan landowning in the Capuan principate. In a memo of 962 it is recorded that duke John II of Gaeta received land at Cilicie (near modern Mondragone) from the late prince Landolf of Capua.[92] His distant relative Matrona, granddaughter of Kampulus the prefect, gave property there to her daughter Euprassia in 1004.[93] Another Gaetan apparently owning land in the Capuan dominions was Benedict, mentioned in a document written at Carinola in 1013. Unfortunately it is unclear whether the city property mentioned in the document was in Gaeta and owned by Carinolans or in Carinola and sold by them to a Gaetan, Dauferius the priest son of John.[94] The evidence is still valuable testimony to exchange between inhabitants of the duchy and the principate, however.

A focus for some of this exchange, not surprisingly, was the area known as Flumetica, along the Garigliano river. The river itself seems to have formed a boundary between the two areas of jurisdiction, but one which was only loosely adhered to. In 984 Veneroso son of John the Lombard bought Flumetica land from

[88] *CDC* 31. [89] *CDC* 83, *CDC* 85.
[90] *CDC* 85; see also Rothari 175, ed. Drew, *Lombard Laws*, p. 83.
[91] G. Caetani, *Regesta Chartarum*, I (Perugia, 1925), p. 6. [92] *CDC* 61.
[93] *CDC* 110. [94] *CDC* 127.

the Gaetans Leo and Gregory;[95] and in his will of 1024 Gregory, grandson of Docibilis II, stated specifically that he owned land on the 'other side' of the Garigliano, including property at Suessa.[96]

Given its proximity to the border area, it is perhaps not surprising that Traetto should exhibit signs of Capuan influence. What evidence we have suggests the Lombards had become a potent force within the county long before it ceased to be ruled by the Docibilan line in 1062. Merores, for instance, comments on the frequent occurrence of Lombard names among the Docibilan counts of Traetto.[97] The influence seems to have gone further, however, and during the first half of the eleventh century we find several Lombard landowners in the county. For example, in 1026 Landolf son of Astolf drew up a document at Capua selling land at Passignano near Traetto to countess Maria of Traetto. His cousins Landolf and Guaimarius sons of Guaimarius also owned land there, and he sold his portion 'according to Roman law' for 11 pounds of silver.[98] Other Lombard landowners recorded in the county include Farrolfo at Silbakaba in 1049[99] and Ratteri at Cozara in 1055.[100]

Another development is visible in 1029, when men with Lombard names acted as witnesses for countess Alzeiza; Maienolf and Leodemar signed in that year.[101] Whether they were native Lombards or simply Traettans taking Lombard names is unclear, but an indication that the counts and countesses were actually encouraging such men comes in another document of 1047, which Maienolf's son Lodoico signed.[102] Lodoico also received public land from count Marinus in 1048.[103] The latter transaction was signed by Grimaldo, son of Franco de Papara, whose name also seems to reflect a growing Lombard influence. Perhaps the culmination of the foreigners' infiltration is seen in 1059, when the judge of Traetto alongside count Marinus was one Roctio.[104]

It would seem that Lombards, most likely Capuans, were welcomed to Traetto. In the years prior to 1032, it is possible that they were befriending the Traettans in order to facilitate their takeover of Gaeta. Traettan co-operation with the Capuans is suggested strongly by the dating clauses of 1034 and 1036. These

[95] *CDC* 86. [96] *CDC* 143.

[97] *Gaeta*, p. 34; but see Toubert, *Structures*, I, p. 693, for a timely warning against relying on personal names as an indication of ethnic origins. [98] *CDC* 151.

[99] *CDC* 188. [100] *CDC* 199. [101] *CDC* 157. [102] *CDC* 182.

[103] *CDC* 185. [104] *CDC* 210.

show that whilst Pandolf and his son Pandolf took over and ruled Gaeta directly, the Traettans were allowed to rule themselves.[105] The separateness of Traetto is further emphasised by a dating clause of a document of 1039. By that time prince Guaimarius of Salerno had taken over Capua, and he is named alongside the counts of Traetto in the document, written at Traetto.[106] That the latter place was recognised by the prince as a completely separate entity from Gaeta is revealed by documentary evidence after his takeover of Gaeta. Initially he is named in Gaetan dating clauses (for example in 1040[107]), but after the brief appearance of the apparently Docibilan duke Leo II in 1042, Guaimarius' nominee Raynulf is seen ruling Gaeta as its consul and duke,[108] whilst the Traettan counts continue to appear as rulers of their own territory. Their relationship with their neighbours across the Garigliano continued too. The counts of Suessa and Carinola are visible at Traetto in 1047,[109] and count Peter of Suessa was present at a court-case there in 1049.[110] The appearance of Atenolf I of Gaeta holding court at Traetto in 1053[111] might suggest that he was able to reassert Gaetan control over the castle, but this is deceptive. Throughout the period of his reign and that of his widow and son we have many documents written at Traetto and dated by the reign of its counts, not that of the Gaetan duke.

Traetto, then, had gone its own way, but it was not the only settlement to have counts of its own during the eleventh century. Let us turn now to the history of another, Suio.

(iii) *Suio*

Suio, lying on the banks of the Garigliano river, may originally have been a Capuan fortress. Our first sign that the castle had come into Gaetan, or rather Docibilan, hands, is in a document of 1023 in which count Hugh transferred ownership of half the castle to the abbey of Montecassino.[112] The donation itself will be discussed a little later – it does not seem to have had very much practical effect at this date.

The counts of Suio were particularly active (or rather, their

[105] *CDC* 164 (1034) and *CDC* 167 (1036), issued at Traetto, are dated by the rule of the counts, whilst contemporary Gaetan documents *CDC* 166 (1036), *CDC* 168 (1037) and *CDC* 169 (1038) are dated by the Capuans. [106] *CDC* 171. [107] *CDC* 174.
[108] *CDC* 178. [109] *CDC* 180. [110] *CDC* 187. [111] *CDC* 195.
[112] *CDC* 142.

documents increase in number) around the middle decades of the eleventh century, and their transactions include several sales of land. There is no clear evidence that by such transactions the counts were building up a circle of followers (although a document of 1079, discussed below, does suggest that Suio had a distinct aristocratic group). What is clear is that they, like the counts of Traetto, had their own notary, John, by 1063.[113]

The last appearance of the de Papara and Giczi families of Traetto occurs in 1079, when Guitto son of Grimaldo and John son of Peter Giczi co-witnessed a document of the Suian count John, son of Hugh.[114] Their appearance at Suio is relatively simple to explain, since Traetto had been taken over by the Norman princes of Capua in the previous decade. The Docibilan counts cease to be documented after 1062, and presumably their regular companions saw the neighbouring Docibilan fortress of Suio as an attractive place of refuge. However, when the counts of Suio were deposed by the Capuans, the Giczi and de Papara families also disappear, indicating the insecurity of their position. It is ironic, given its probable origins as a Capuan fortress, that Suio's history is one of a castle staunchly loyal to the Docibilans and their successors as dukes of Gaeta. For example, even though he was distant enough in terms of blood and location to act independently during the Gaetan power struggle of the early eleventh century, we still find count Hugh's charter of 1023 dated by the rule of duchess Emilia and dukes John V and Leo.[115] This was at a time when the Traettans were already dating by their own comital rule. Such loyalty may have been prompted by economic concerns as much as political ones – John son of Hugh, for example, is documented as the owner of parts of mills in the Gaeta area.[116] We must remember too that it was from this branch of the family that the short-lived duke Leo II of Gaeta came, and that his line also provided the bishop of Gaeta, Leo, in the mid-eleventh century. These close and continuing connections with Gaeta may explain why two members of the Suian comital line, Leo and Landolf, married two daughters of the Gaetan Cotina family in the 1060s.[117]

In 1062, however, it appears that all the rulers of petty castles in the area, regardless of their previous loyalties, were beginning to

[113] *CDC* 217; John wrote five documents for the comital family, including three for count Raynerius, *CDC* 223, *CDC* 224, and *CDC* 243.
[114] *CDC* 252.
[115] *CDC* 142.
[116] Maiore and Zoppella in 1056, *CDC* 202.
[117] See below, chapter 6, section (a,viii).

feel threatened by the growing power of the Normans at Capua. In 1058 Capua had been taken by the Norman count of Aversa, Richard, who was confirmed as prince by pope Nicholas II in 1059.[118] That this event caused some disquiet in the duchy of Gaeta is illustrated by the agreement made by the counts of Traetto, Maranola and Suio with duchess Maria and duke Atenolf II of Gaeta not to make any pact with the Normans for one year.[119] That separate parts of the duchy found it necessary to make a documented agreement with each other, rather than acting together naturally, illustrates the degree of localisation present by the late eleventh century. That localisation was not merely focussed on large settlements like Traetto and Suio, however.

(iv) *Incastellamento in the duchy of Gaeta*

In his study of the appearance of the castles in the duchy of Gaeta, Guiraud listed Traetto, Castro Argento, Fratte, Suio, Itri, Sperlonga and Maranola as new fortifications. We should perhaps remove Traetto and Suio from this list in view of their histories and add the 'castello Conca' recorded in 1064.[120] It is possible too that the existence of a *casale* Capomazza and a *torre di Cotina* foreshadowed later castle-building on the part of those families.

What was behind this assertion of local power? Two issues emerge. The first is that of people's perception of the world around them. If we examine the way in which residents cited individual towns and villages in their documents we find their identity was a very localised one. They had little stake in describing themselves as citizens of the duchy of Gaeta, or county of Traetto or any similar polity.

An analysis of these citations of residence indicates a gradual shift away from residence in Gaeta between the tenth and eleventh centuries. Gaeta had been the centre of Docibilan power in the tenth century, and it was perhaps politically wise for those who wished to gain favour to live there. After 1000, however, new centres of power offered other opportunities. Gaeta was still the dominant centre, but her residents made up a smaller proportion of the total of people declaring their place of residence. By 1050, the proportion had dwindled still further, and the documented

118 Loud, *Church and Society*, p. 38. 119 *CDC* 215.
120 Guiraud, 'Reseau'; *CDC* 227.

residents of Gaeta had dropped slightly from their tenth-century levels.[121]

This picture of a dispersal of population parallels that of a dispersal of power, which perhaps caused the decline of the old Gaetan landowning nobility. In the new atmosphere of localisation, those whose fortunes were based on estates scattered throughout the duchy of Gaeta may have faced problems of control over lands that were now in areas of separate political jurisdiction.

The issue of localisation and how, in the late tenth and early eleventh centuries, it came to be translated into the development of concentrated settlements or castles (a process known by the Italian term *incastellamento*) is one which has attracted a considerable amount of attention from historians of this and other parts of Italy. What lay behind the development of such centres in the territory of Gaeta?

In his substantial study of Latium during the medieval period, Toubert addressed the problem of *incastellamento*. However he admitted that it is difficult to get at the origins of castle-building in the southern half of the area because, unlike the north, new concentrations of population were not being created. Instead, old Roman sites were merely being re-used.[122] In addition the tenth- and eleventh-century documentation for southern Lazio is not nearly so detailed as that for the north, and so Toubert's study concentrated on the latter, particularly the collection from the abbey at Farfa. Here, *incastellamento* could be seen to accompany the abbey's policy of opening up new lands for cultivation and the creation of new peasant settlements, which was largely a tenth-century phenomenon.[123] An increase in population in the tenth century in the area provided the settlers for the abbey's new centres.[124]

The abbey of Montecassino, too, had to take similar action to repopulate its territory after devastation by the Saracens in the ninth century. Encouraged by his Capuan allies (whose own principate was witnessing the growth of new castles in the tenth century, controlled by castellans who co-ordinated their local agrarian economy[125]), abbot Aligernus presided over the

[121] For more on this, see below, chapter 7, Map 7.1. [122] *Structures*, I, p. 315.
[123] *Ibid.*, p. 526. [124] *Ibid.*, p. 313.
[125] N. Cilento, *Le Origini della Signoria Capuana nella Langobardia Minore* (Rome, 1966), p. 41.

construction of the castles of St Angelo in Theodice, St George and Rocca Janula in the 960s.[126] These castles did not merely provide protected habitations for peasant cultivators. It appears that some had more than one function. Cilento and Fabiani both comment on the particularism and turbulence of subjects of Capua such as the counts of Teano and Aquino, and view the Capuan princes' encouragement of Cassinese castle-building as insurance against the unruly *gastalds* extending their spheres of influence too far.[127]

Guiraud sees both of these evident functions as reasons for *incastellamento* in the territory of Gaeta, and cites the reclamation of forested land in Flumetica as one of the incentives for new settlements in the east in the eleventh century.[128] Fratte, he says, was of strategic importance in that it lay near to the borders of Cassinese territory.[129] This is true, but a document of 1030 already mentioned above may point to Fratte as a base for new agricultural enterprise as well. In that year Peter Giczi exchanged 30 *modia* of land at Coriano for 44 *modia* at Silbakaba with the counts of Traetto.[130] Peter at this time lived at Fratte, and the fact that his acquisition bears a name derived from the Latin for woodland (*silva*) and that he obtained a larger quantity of it suggests that he intended to clear it.

Suio, too, might have been a centre for new cultivation, lying as it does at the edge of the Flumetica region. Its function was also military – a border post on the rather indefinite border between Gaeta and Capua, and a post which seems to have changed hands during Docibilan supremacy at Gaeta. Such strategic fortresses are known also in Campania, though this time they were built as defences against the Normans in the eleventh century.[131] Some in time became centres of administration for the incoming rulers, and local officials were based at both Itri and Maranola by the early twelfth century.

A defensive posture against the Normans of Capua is increasingly apparent in the duchy of Gaeta in the eleventh century. Besides the anti-Norman pact mentioned above, a series of documents in the *Codex Cajetanus* suggests that the counts and

[126] L. Fabiani, *La Terra di S. Benedetto*, I (2nd edn., Montecassino, 1968), p. 56.
[127] Cilento, *Origini*, p. 38; Fabiani, *Terra*, p. 56. [128] 'Reseau', 500.
[129] *Ibid.*, 505. [130] *CDC* 159.
[131] P. Toubert, 'La terre et les hommes dans l'Italie normande au temps de Roger II; l'exemple campanien', in *Histoire du Haut Moyen Age et de l'Italie Mediévale* (London, 1987).

dukes who signed the pact were none too confident of resisting the Capuans on their own. Instead, it seems, they turned to a neighbour whose political stature was growing by the mid-eleventh century, namely the abbey of St Benedict at Montecassino. In doing so, they were not the first to have dealings with an external power.

(c) GAETA'S EXTERNAL RELATIONS

So far the history of the city-state of Gaeta has been characterised by its intensely internalised administration and family-based rule. Little has been said to place the duchy in its wider Italian context, yet the establishment of Docibilan power and, arguably, the 'golden age' of Gaetan statehood would hardly have been possible without Neapolitan goodwill and Roman, or more strictly papal, land donations. Later, the influence of Montecassino would come to dominate the area. This section will attempt to illustrate how external factors were influential in developments at Gaeta, and to examine their role in the collapse of the independent duchy.

(i) *Naples*

Gaeta's history is intertwined with that of Naples from the very start of the documentary evidence. That close political links were maintained between the two states is shown by two early eleventh-century documents. In 1014 duke Sergius of Naples appears as an observer at a court-case held at Castro Argento.[132] Then in 1029 he is seen at Gaeta itself. A fragmentary Gaetan document of that year, issued by the Neapolitan duke in the presence of duchess Emilia of Gaeta, her grandson John V and the Gaetan *magnis et mediocres*, promises them that, given help to re-enter his city (he had been deposed by Pandolf IV of Capua), he would allow Gaetans to come into his territories on business and not pay any tolls to the *seniores*, judges or *portolani*.[133] His offer was clearly acceptable, for with help from the Gaetans and Norman mercenaries he was soon restored to power. His exile had not lasted long – we have only four documents, all of 1029, dated by Pandolf's rule at Naples.[134]

Whether the help of the Gaetan navy signified that the smaller state really was strong militarily is open to question, for Gaeta itself

[132] *CDC* 130. [133] *CDC* 156. [134] Cassandro, 'Ducato', p. 312.

fell to the depredations of the Capuan in 1032, and the fact that its weakness was almost contemporary with Naples' suggests that neither duchy was really in a position to resist. The motive for Sergius' appeal to the Gaetans may not have been entirely military, however. Amatus of Montecassino states that the duke of Naples' sister was the widow of the duke of Gaeta, and that when Sergius was restored to power in Naples with the help of the Norman, Raynulf, he gave Raynulf his sister's hand in marriage in 1030.[135] The chronicler does not name this sister, but the obvious candidate is John IV's wife, mother of John V. Opinions differ, however. Amatus' statement, that Sergius' sister was 'novellement estoit faite vidue par la mort de lo conte de Gaite' ('newly widowed by the death of the count of Gaeta') in 1030, has prompted speculation that she had been the wife of Leo, the regent, for John IV had died in 1012.[136] However, Leo himself disappears from the documentation by 1025. Neither candidate, therefore, can be definitely proven as the late husband of Sergius' sister. But neither John's widow nor Leo's may have found life especially comfortable at Gaeta under Emilia's regency. The former seems to have been totally overshadowed by her formidable mother-in-law at Gaeta, and, with Emilia in control of her son, may have seen the marriage with the Norman as a means of escape. As the widow of Emilia's former adversary for the regency, Leo's wife may have found it expedient to return to Naples after the death of her husband. Whatever the case, neither woman is anywhere recorded in the charter evidence.

The fall of the Docibilan dynasty did not signify the end of the relationship between the dukes of Gaeta and Naples. After a period of instability, discussed above, the city was taken over by the Normans in 1068. Geoffrey Ridell, who attempted to found his own ruling dynasty at Gaeta by associating his son Raynald in power, married off his daughter to John VI, duke of Naples. Some two hundred years after Gaeta had become a state in its own right, the close link with the larger city still exerted a great influence.

(ii) *Rome*

If Naples can be credited with supporting the establishment of Docibilan power at Gaeta, then Rome played an equally suppor-

[135] Amatus I.42. [136] On the debate, *ibid.*, p. 53.

tive role. It is necessary at the outset to point out that 'Rome' in this context indicates the papacy, and that the receipt of control of 'Roman' lands by the Docibilans in the late ninth century should be understood to refer to the papal patrimonies and their rectorship. There is some evidence that Roman laymen attempted to intervene in the politics of the Gaetan duchy, but certainly not on the immediate and grand scale of the pope's actions.

Cassandro interprets the transfer of the Byzantine title of imperial patrician to John I of Gaeta, on the eve of the 915 campaign to rid the Garigliano estuary of its Arab settlement, as a means of obliging the Gaetan ruler to fight.[137] Alternatively, the transfer may have functioned as a public gesture that Gaetan power, if only loosely, was ultimately derived from the goodwill of the Byzantine emperor. Cassandro's statement could have been applied equally well to the relative positions of John I, his father Docibilis I and the popes after the conferring of the patrimonial rectorships. In this case some way of obliging the new rulers to serve Rome was being sought. If the popes responsible, John VIII and John X, were thereby hoping to maintain control of the Gaetan patrimonies using the Gaetan *hypatoi* as their agents, they appear to have underestimated the ability of Docibilis and John to take over the lands for their own benefit rather than that of the popes.

Nevertheless, some parts of the former patrimonies maintained a more 'Roman' character than others. For example, from documents of 906 and 924 we know that Docibilis I's son Anatolius was the holder of the title duke of Terracina.[138] We also know that Docibilis II's son Marinus, before becoming the duke of Gaeta, held the post of duke of Fondi.[139] After the fall of the Docibilans from power at Gaeta, however, these two cities followed a different course from those of Traetto and Suio. Whilst the latter provide us with documents dated by the rule of their counts[140] or not at all, those from Terracina are dated by the reigning pope.[141] The evidence suggests that Terracina's position oscillated between being part of Gaeta and loyal to Rome, and is worth further investigation.

Terracina had a long history of being under papal control, and it appears that after a period of Docibilan rule, following the papal

[137] 'Ducato', p. 126. [138] *CDC* 19, *CDC* 31. [139] *CDC* 46.
[140] Suio for example, *CDC* 217; Traetto for example, *CDC* 201.
[141] For example, *CDC* 172, *CDC* 186.

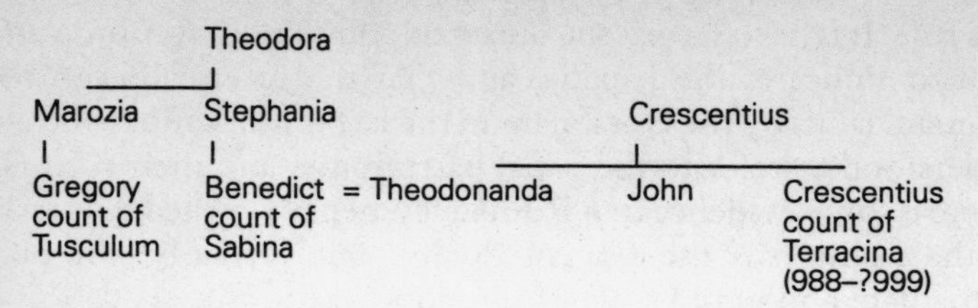

Figure 5.4 *The family of Count Crescentius*

concessions of the late ninth to early tenth centuries, the city reverted to Roman masters. This is at least how historians have interpreted the appearance of Crescentius 'excellentissimus vir et omnium Romanorum senator atque gloriosus comes'[142] as ruler of the city in fragmentary evidence from the years 988 and 991. The first appearance, from a document surviving only in an eighteenth-century copy of a thirteenth-century inventory of documents, reveals that Crescentius received the city and province of Terracina from pope John XV.[143] From detailed research, Gerstenberg illustrated that this Crescentius may have been related to several noble Roman families. His father led the revolt in Rome in 974 which could only be put down with German intervention. By his sister's marriage, moreover, the Terracinan count was related to the counts of Sabina and Tusculum (see Figure 5.4).[144]

In 1000, Terracina passed to the control of count 'Daiferius', being ceded to him by pope Sylvester II, with the approval of the German emperor Otto III.[145] It is now generally accepted that this man was a member of the Gaetan family of Docibilis. Likely candidates are either Dauferius I or Dauferius II of Traetto. Toubert sees the cession of Terracina to him as a way of curbing the growing power of the family of Crescentius and, at the same time, pulling Gaeta into the Roman political sphere.[146] The family history of the Crescentii lies outside the scope of this study. Relations between Gaeta and Rome must remain open to question. Certainly the fact that one of their number was now directly answerable to the pope does not seem to have had much impact on the Docibilans outside Terracina; documents at Gaeta, for instance,

[142] 'most excellent man and senator and glorious count of all the Roman people'.
[143] Biblioteca Apostolica Vaticana, *Cod. Vat. Lat.* 12632; see also *IP*, II, p. 120.
[144] O. Gerstenberg, 'Studien zur Geschichte des Römischen Adels am Ausgange des 10. Jahrhunderts', *Historische Vierteljahrschrifte*, 31 (1937–9), 1–26.
[145] Giorgi, 'Documenti', p. 65.
[146] *Structures*, II, p. 1101.

did not begin to be dated by the pope's rule. Due to the lack of much Terracinan documentary evidence, we cannot in any case determine how long 'Daiferius' was in control of the city. By 1042 we see one Teodald, bishop, consul and duke of Terracina giving out land there,[147] although a Daiferius *magnificus* – possibly a son of the former ruler – witnessed a Terracinan document of 1049.[148] What can be said, if dating clauses on documents are any indication, is that the city remained under papal influence. In 1092 a document issued in the city was still using papal dating.[149] Pope Leo IX was also able to intervene directly in 1052, returning the church of St Stephen at Terracina to the abbey at Montecassino.[150]

Churches from near Rome also had interests in the area. We know that SS Basil and Scholastica at Subiaco controlled a cell in the territory.[151] As a final indication that Terracina largely lay outside the sphere of Gaetan rule, it is apparent from a prosopographical study of surviving documents from the city that the landowners and witnesses of both cities were moving in totally separate circles. As in Gaeta, it is possible to connect fathers with sons in the witness lists of Terracinan documents (although, of course, on a much more limited scale), and to find the same men on more than one document,[152] but we never find the same person on a Terracinan and a Gaetan document, as (perhaps) we might expect if Gaeta and Terracina were closely linked. A culmination of the two cities' detachment from each other might be seen in a treaty of the twelfth century, made between Gaeta and Monte Circeo against Terracina.[153]

Far more overlap can be found between evidence from Terracina and Fondi. Several of the inhabitants mentioned in the documents were landowners in both areas. For example, in 1039,[154] one Constantine son of Leo, an inhabitant of Fondi, had fallen ill whilst visiting his father-in-law in Terracina, and in gratitude for his recovery with the aid of holy water gave the estate 'ad Flexu' at Portelle, mid-way between the two cities, to the bishop of Terracina. In 1093, the same estate was given – probably

[147] Giorgi, 'Documenti', p. 82.
[148] *CDC* 186.
[149] Giorgi, 'Documenti', p. 84.
[150] *CDC* 192.
[151] *Regesto Sublacense*, eds. L. Allodi and G. Levi (Rome, 1885), p. 60.
[152] For example, Giorgi, 'Documenti', p. 80 has a document dated 1011 featuring Marinus son of Palumbus *magnificus*; in 1049 Marinus' son Bonizzo is documented, *CDC* 186.
[153] G. Falco, 'L'amministrazione papale nella Campagna e nella Marittima', *ASRSP*, 38 (1915), 704. For more on this, and other Gaetan pacts of the twelfth century, see below, chapter 8.
[154] *CDC* 172.

confirmed – to the bishopric by Leo, count of Fondi.[155] In 1049, Adilasci of Terracina gave property there and in Fondi to the monastery of St Magnus outside the latter city.[156]

The position of the rulers of Fondi, who like the Terracinans used the title duke, is worth further investigation. It is first necessary to establish their relationship to the Docibilans at Gaeta, and to clarify some kind of genealogy, since that given by Amante and Bianchi seems somewhat confused.[157] Part of the confusion arises from the assumption by these two authors that men with different mothers cannot possibly have had the same father, which has led to rather more men named Leo appearing in their genealogy than mine (see Figure 5.5). In a society where remarriage on the part of widowers was the norm, it is not an unlikely scenario to expect to find men with children from more than one marriage or by concubines.

The first duke of a distinct territory of Fondi was Docibilis II's son Marinus. Under his son Leo the separation of Fondi from Gaeta and its counties became more acute; in 992 we see Leo in open dispute with Dauferius, his brother and count of Traetto, over the boundaries between their respective territories.[158] This dispute, which Leo lost, may give a false impression of the relationship between the dukes of Fondi and their relatives further east, for, unlike the rulers of Terracina, the dukes (often also called consuls) of Fondi can be seen regularly present at courts in Gaeta. For example, Marinus II and Leo II were witnesses in 999 to their uncle Bernard, bishop of Gaeta's dispute with Dauferius,[159] and in the same year Marinus witnessed another between Bernard and a group of men trying to prove they were not slaves of the bishopric.[160] The continued involvement of the Fondi branch in their family's affairs at Gaeta is also attested to by the fact that Leo II executed the will of his brother John III of Gaeta.[161] Leo II's son John was the next member to represent Fondi as a witness to a dispute at Gaeta in 1014 between Dauferius II of Traetto and the abbey of Montecassino.[162] Such interest in the affairs of another branch of the Docibilan clan is perhaps understandable when both had Gaeta as a meeting place of their interests; but it is striking that the relationship of witnessing continued between the Fonditans

155 *CDC* 267. 156 *CDC* 186.
157 B. Amante and R. Bianchi, *Memorie Storiche e Statutarie del Ducato di Fondi* (Rome, 1903), p. 88. 158 *CDC* 90. 159 *CDC* 101. 160 *CDC* 100.
161 *CDC* 120. 162 *CDC* 130.

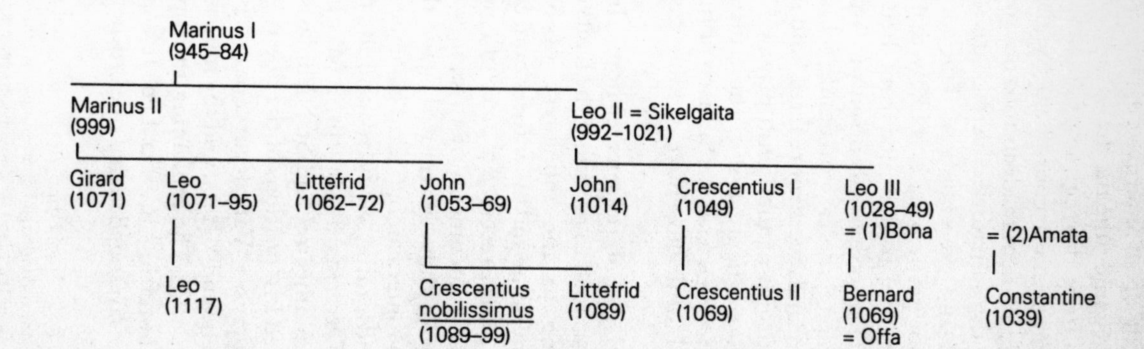

Figure 5.5 *The dukes of Fondi*

and Traettans even after their family had fallen from power in the central city. Thus Leo III and Crescentius I are present at Traetto in 1049, during the settlement of an internal quarrel between the counts of Traetto.[163] At the same time the dukes of Fondi seem to have distanced themselves from the regime of Atenolf of Gaeta. They are noticeably absent from a court held by the duke in 1053.[164] Similarly, in the agreement made in 1062 not to make any pacts with the Normans, the signatories were Maria duchess of Gaeta, her son Atenolf II and the counts of Traetto, Suio and Maranola.[165] Fondi did not participate: it is likely that its rulers' continued interest in Traettan affairs stemmed from their interest in Traettan lands; the dispute in 992 had centred on lands around Ventosa and Apranum, far to the east of Fondi. This is hardly surprising, since the eastern lands were more fertile and productive than the uncontrollable swamp of the Fondi plain.[166] The river plains may even have aroused the interest of those further north; we have an eleventh-century charter from Subiaco noting a gift to the church of land in Flumicello 'next to the casale called Aprano'.[167]

The dukes of Fondi also had interests nearer home. In 1028, for example, Leo III was accustomed to receiving the fruits of the land near Sperlonga belonging to the monastery of St Michael Planciano in Gaeta. In that year he and his wife renounced this right to the monastery, and in return received a piece of land.[168]

More informative are two documents of 1072, in which dukes Girard and Littefrid, sons of duke Marinus II, gave their Fondi property to the abbey of Montecassino. Girard gave the monastery of St Magnus with its lands, mills, vineyards and in addition the churches of St Andrea in Terracina, St Maurus, St Martin in Tirille, St Maria 'next to the amphitheatre' and St Nicholas ad Fossa in Rome.[169] Littefrid donated his 'portion' of the duchy – a third of the city, the castles of Aquaviva, Valledecursa, Ambrise, Pastena, Lenola and Campu de Melle and Vetera, and the monasteries of St Archangel and St Anastasia.[170] The remaining third presumably belonged to Girard and Littefrid's brother Leo. It would appear that the donations were pre-arranged in that one brother gave most

163 *CDC* 187. 164 *CDC* 195. 165 *CDC* 215. 166 See below, chapter 7.

167 *Regesto Sublacense*, p. 219. In a similar context, it is interesting to see that the church of St Nicolas in Rome had an interest in the island of Zannone: its representative disputed property there in Rome with the abbot of St Magnus, Fondi, in 976, *CDC* 70.

168 *CDC* 154. 169 *CDC* 247. 170 *CDC* 248.

of the churches and another gave the fortified places, but by the late eleventh century the dukes had extended their interests well inland, perhaps to compensate for the unpromising marshland of the plain (see Map 5.1).

Fondi's relationship with Rome was far looser than Terracina's, however, and its rulers were more eager to extend their contacts eastwards. It is in this context that consul Bernard of Fondi's marriage to the count of Suessa's daughter Offa in 1069 can be placed.[171] Following the unsuccessful claims in the tenth century to Traettan land on the Gaetan side of the Garigliano discussed above, the marriage could perhaps be seen as an attempt to gain some friendly relations on the Capuan side. Bernard's contract to marry Offa was guaranteed by his cousin, the *consul* Crescentius II of Fondi, son of Crescentius 'the prefect'. Is it merely coincidence that this most Roman of names should begin to occur with some frequency in the ducal family of Fondi during the eleventh century? It is striking that the dynasty should begin to include the name only fifty years after the disappearance of count Crescentius of Terracina, who was of Roman origin. Could his family have continued to wield power in a more indirect way in southern Latium by marrying into the family of the dukes of Fondi? There is no direct evidence, but another Crescentius comes into view in 1089, witnessing a dispute between a group of Normans and the Terracinan monastery of St Stephen at Fossanova, alongside his brother Littefrid.[172] This fusion of the Crescentius name and one known in the Fondi dynasty raises further the possibility of a union between the two families. This Crescentius seems to be the same man as Crescentius *nobilissimo* son of John, inhabitant of Rocca de Montecelli (modern Monte S Biagio, near Fondi) who in 1099 sold a house site in the castle of Asprana to one Docibilis Gattula.[173] Another Crescentius, titled *miles* and son of Marinus, sold some Gaetan land to one John Mancanella son of Stephen in 1121, and may be another member of the Fondi dynasty if his name is any indication.[174]

Does this possible union between a Roman family and the Fondi rulers, and later transactions with men whom we shall see were members of leading Gaetan clans, indicate a growing closeness between the Roman aristocracy and the duchy of Gaeta? We

[171] *CDC* 239. [172] *CDC* 262.

[173] *CDC* 274; on the Gattula family, see below, chapter 6, section (a,xii).

[174] *CDC* 298; on the Mancanella family, see below, chapter 6, section (a,iii).

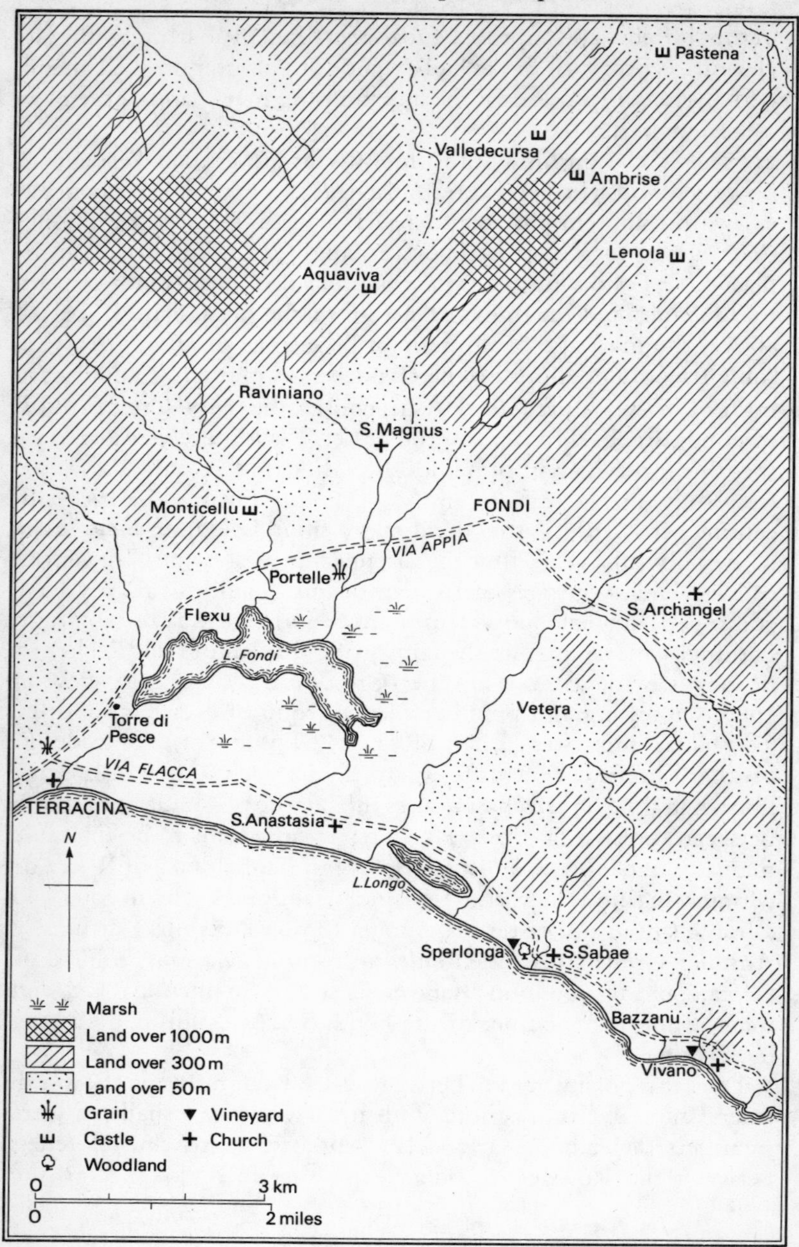

Map 5.1 *The plain of Fondi*

cannot discount the idea, particularly since there is further circumstantial evidence of intermarriage, and direct evidence of exchanges between the two.

The possibility that the Crescentii had aims further afield than Fondi is suggested by the name, or rather the title, of duke Leo II of Gaeta's wife, Theodora *senatrix*.[175] The only other occurrence of this name and title in the area had been that of the wife of duke John III of Naples in the tenth century, and she is securely identifiable as a Roman. It can remain only a possibility that Leo's wife was similarly a member of the same family.

Sporadic direct relations between Gaetans and Romans are documented, however, such as the example of Ramfus son of Christopher's trade transactions with Ubertus the Roman in 1012 discussed at some length above.[176] The Gaetan bishop Leo is recorded as present in documents issued at the Lateran in 1050 and 1059.[177] It was in the late eleventh century and the early twelfth that more significant contacts began to be made, however. If a document of 1093 written at Rome is at least partially genuine, a former duke of Gaeta, Lando, was resident there. Lando's donation of all his lands in Gaeta to the abbey of Montecassino may be interpolated, as the document is contained in the Register of the notorious Peter the Deacon, but Peter had no reason to invent Lando's presence in Rome.[178]

Most revealingly, a document of 1105 shows that members of the Cotina, de Arciu, Salpa, Baraballu, Boccapasu and Lazaro families of Gaeta had co-invested in a ship with Gregory count of Tusculum.[179] The Tusculans were loosely related to, although permanently in dispute with, the family of count Crescentius of Terracina, but it may be significant that their partners in the shipping venture came from almost every active noble family at Gaeta apart from the Gattula and Mancanella clans, whose members we have just seen dealing with Crescentii. It is possible that two powerful Roman families were trying to establish toeholds in the duchy of Gaeta. Gaeta's worsening relationship with Terracina in the twelfth century may be a result of this rivalry.

Another family, the Conjuli, seem to fit in with the increasing

175 Her son Peter uses this title of her in 1055, *CDC* 200.
176 See above, chapter 4, section (a,i).
177 *IP* VIII, p. 9, document no.4 and p. 11, document no. 12.
178 *CDC* 268. 179 *CDC* 278; on these families, see below, chapter 6.

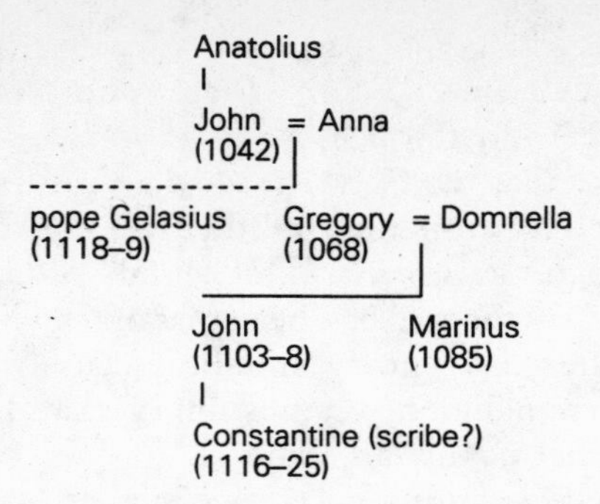

Figure 5.6 *The Conjulo family*

pattern of interaction with Rome and emerge in the eleventh century.

In 1042 John Conjulo son of Anatolius bought a piece of empty land (*terra vacua*) in the city of Gaeta from Domnella, widow of Sergius.[180] John's son Gregory (see genealogy, Figure 5.6) obtained more empty land in the city in 1068, but this time it was a gift from the abbot of SS Theodore and Martin to make a tomb, in return for all the services that Gregory and his wife Domnella had rendered to the church.[181] There is no information about these 'services', but they can possibly be understood as allusions to one or several donations of land made by the couple to the church.

The only other references to the Conjuli's landowning come in twelfth-century material. In 1119 the heirs of Marinus Conjulo, son of Gregory, are mentioned as owning a cellar in Gaeta,[182] and in 1125 Marinus' nephew Constantine son of John borrowed 20 *solidi* for three years from Leo son of Radi, secured on a *medialoca* or warehouse in the city.[183] This transaction and the modest nature of the family's landed property suggests that they were engaged in some commercial activity. If so, they seem to have moved in different circles to the consortium mentioned above, and this is perhaps reflected in the lack of a Conjulo among Gaeta's consular aristocracy during the early twelfth century. The witnessing activities of members of the clan show a similar detachment.[184] If Fedele is correct, however, the Conjuli were participants in much

[180] *CDC* 178. [181] *CDC* 233. [182] *CDC* 292. [183] *CDC* 307.

[184] Marinus son of Gregory, his brother John and nephew Constantine all appear for, and with, a number of men who are otherwise unidentifiable in 1085 (*CDC* 259), 1103 (*CDC* 295), and 1116 (*CDC* 289) respectively.

wider political events, and one of the family became pope in 1118 with the name Gelasius II.[185] He issued a document to the people of Rome from Gaeta in that year.[186] Although his reign was brief – he died in 1119 – the event should warn against supposing that Gaetan families under Norman rule were content to pursue their political ambitions within the city walls. An alternative hypothesis might be that the Conjuli were in fact a Roman family who decided to enter the Gaetan land market, but who remained on the periphery of the city's political life. The fact that they do not appear in the remaining twelfth-century evidence from the city supports the latter possibility.

The hypothesis that Gaeta and Rome moved closer together does not necessarily mean that relations between their respective citizens were always cordial. In 1124 the consuls of Gaeta were in dispute with Bello of Rome, son of Bobo, and his sons, over a ship and its goods which he was captaining on behalf of a Roman consortium. It is significant that pope Calixtus called the case to Terracina to be settled by cardinal Matthew in the presence of John count of Terracina. Still more significant is that Bello could call upon one Nicolas de John de Fasano among his witnesses to testify for him and, ultimately, win the case.[187] For Nicolas was from Sperlonga – at least his father had bought land there,[188] and his testimony on behalf of a man who should have been regarded as a foreigner to Gaetan soil suggests that Romans had contacts deep within Gaetan boundaries by this time. The impotence of the Gaetan consuls in this situation in the face of stronger outside influence should be noted, and one could almost see the case as a triumph of landed aristocracy with connections over the administrators of what was a very much less powerful city. The contrast here is apparent; a Roman citizen could call upon the full weight of Rome to back him, yet the consuls of Gaeta, whose overlord by this time was Richard, prince of Capua, and who should have been able to call on his support, were left to deal alone with what was viewed as an internal matter. Richard's appearance in our discussion reminds us that Gaeta no longer stood alone.

(iii) *Montecassino*

So far little has been said about Gaeta's relationship with Montecassino. Until 982 there is no sign in the documents that the

[185] P. Fedele, 'La famiglia'. [186] *IP* I, p. 180. [187] *CDC* 302. [188] *CDC* 233.

abbey's territory did border on that of the duchy. Yet the late tenth- and eleventh-century evidence from the *Codex Cajetanus* detailing the monastery's exchanges with the Gaetans indicates that their contact was frequent and, ultimately, had a profound effect on the history of the duchy.

It is not the intention here to take up the history of Montecassino in these centuries. Such ground has been covered more than once in studies by Fabiani, Cowdrey and Bloch.[189] It should be noted, however, that when it comes into view at Gaeta, the monastery was entering a phase of territorial expansion and was of sufficient political (and ecclesiastical) stature to lead the German emperor Otto II to decide in its favour in a land dispute with duke Marinus of Gaeta in 982.[190] Particularly significant is Otto's dismissal of Marinus' evidence – a document recording pope John VIII's gift of the lands, which lay near Aquino, to the *hypatoi* of Gaeta; the Cassinesi produced an even more aged gift charter from Charlemagne. The precedent having been set, another court of 1014 also accepted the Carolingian evidence against charters of John VIII and John X when Montecassino complained that Dauferius II of Traetto was trespassing on the same lands.[191] The north-eastern border of the territory of Gaeta seems to have been a constant theatre of conflict between its inhabitants and the abbey. In 1039 we see abbot Riccherius in dispute with a group of men from Fratte,[192] and in 1047 Sergius of the Kampuli clan acted as a guarantor in a settlement between Riccherius and count Marinus of Traetto, made in the presence of Atenolf duke of Gaeta and the counts of Suessa and Carinola.[193] Finally, in 1064, the counts of Suio gave a guarantee that they would come to an agreement with the abbey over further border disputes in the Garigliano area.[194]

The fact that Montecassino won all of these disputes is a good illustration of the monastery's growing prestige. Rulers like Otto wished to be seen patronising the abbey, as a means of gaining a political toe-hold in the area as well as winning spiritual favour. Such protection brought the monastery wealth in terms of land and valuable moveable wealth,[195] and so was mutually beneficial.

[189] Fabiani, *Terra*; H. Bloch, *Montecassino in the Middle Ages*, (Cambridge, Mass., 1986); H. E. J. Cowdrey, *The Age of Abbot Desiderius* (Oxford, 1983).
[190] *CDC* 81.
[191] *CDC* 130.
[192] *CDC* 171.
[193] *CDC* 180.
[194] *CDC* 227.
[195] For a description of the latter in the ninth century, H. Willard and A. Citarella, *The Ninth Century Treasure of Montecassino in the Context of Political and Economic Developments in Southern Italy* (Montecassino, 1983).

In this context, and given their proximity to the Cassinese territory, it is perhaps not surprising that inhabitants of Gaeta feature in some of our documents recording gifts to the monastery. Thus, for example, Constantine son of Paul made a bequest in his will of 1028[196] and made another gift before becoming a monk in the abbey in 1053.[197] The abbey also had property in the city itself. In 1024 the church of St Salvator in Platea Maiore was under its control,[198] and in 1027 abbot Theobald arranged for an exchange of lands so that the abbey's cell of St Scholastica was not overshadowed by a wooden house.[199]

Four years previously, however, Theobald had received a much more substantial gift: half of the castle of Suio and its lands donated by its count, Hugh.[200] Taken at face value, this was a pious donation (albeit a large one) on account of Hugh's ill health, which he mentions. However, taken into the context of the events mentioned above – the political instability at Gaeta, Capuan encroachment and the overt detachment of Traetto – could not the gift also represent an attempt by Hugh to gain a protector, or at least an ally, in a time of insecurity? Montecassino was, after all, not far from the castle, and, as a foundation regularly patronised by the Lombard princes, may have acted as an intercessor on Hugh's behalf. The gift appears to have worked – Hugh is recorded as the count of Suio even after the Capuan takeover of Gaeta. In 1040 he reiterated his gift, this time to abbot Riccherius and in more detail, reserving half of the castle for his son John,[201] who remained in possession until 1079.

It may have been fear of the Norman princes of Capua, who were keen to be seen as friends of Montecassino, that prompted the counts of Traetto to follow their relative's example in 1058/9. In those years Marinus count of Traetto issued three documents handing over a quarter of his county, half of the castle of Spigno, a quarter of Fratte, the monastery of St Marinus at Coriano and a quarter of the monastery of St Martin near Maranola in 1058/9.[202] These donations were, in the words of a 1059 document, made for the souls of Marinus and his wife Oddolana, but there is no doubting the political intent behind them. Having been friends of the Lombards at Capua, the Traettans could expect no sympathy

[196] *CDC* 153. [197] *CDC* 194. [198] *CDC* 144. [199] *CDC* 152.
[200] *CDC* 142. [201] *CDC* 173.
[202] *CDC* 204 addressed to abbot Stephen; *CDC* 209/10, the same donation repeated to abbot Desiderius.

from the Normans unless they gained some representation from an institution whose word held weight. In 1058 Richard of Aversa, the conqueror of Capua, had been received at Cassino 'as a king',[203] and the close relationship between him and abbot Desiderius indicates that Marinus did well to try to win the latter as a friend. The lack of success of his gift is, unfortunately, self-evident; he and his relatives disappear from our documents after 1062. John son of count Hugh's gift[204] of half of the castle of Suio in 1079 plus his portion of the church of St Erasmus in Formia was similarly unsuccessful; again the count disappears from view. His gift was made in slightly different circumstances, for the year before prince Jordan of Capua, Richard's son, had confiscated the castle from John's relatives, the other counts.[205] It looks as if it was the prince whom John was trying to win as an ally rather than the abbey, by transferring his portion of the castle into Cassinese hands.

Two documents issued by the abbot of Montecassino, Desiderius, are particularly interesting in this context. In the first he promised the Traettans in 1061 that he would allow them to keep their houses and land, would do them no injustice and would not demand service or any payments except one tenth of their large pigs and one fifteenth of their small ones. In a final clause he promised he would not take their wives – a statement of which the significance has yet to be discovered.[206] To named men of Suio in 1079 he promised exemption from service, which they had enjoyed under the counts; the other inhabitants owed one day seeding, one day reaping and one day winemaking.[207] These agricultural practices confirm both Traetto and Suio as centres of cultivation. The named group of men at Suio also indicates that there was a recognisable group of aristocrats in the fortress, although these were not evident in the other documentary material from the castle. Conversely, the named men and families we have seen as forming a favoured group around the counts of Traetto were clearly not perceived as the leading citizens of that place by outsiders. The documents do not show the growth of a communal spirit in these castles. To interpret them as such ignores the donations preceding each document, and is at the very least an overinterpretation of the documentation.[208]

Noticeably absent from our documentary evidence after their

203 Loud, *Church and Society*, p. 39. 204 *CDC* 252. 205 *CDC* 251.
206 *CDC* 213. 207 *CDC* 253.
208 See, for example, Loud, *Church and Society*, p. 42; Cowdrey, *Age*, p. 7.

gifts are the counts themselves. Marinus' Traettan transaction and John son of Hugh's donation of Suio in 1079 mark their last appearances. The same is largely true of the counts of Fondi, who also handed over large areas of their territory in 1071/2. Leo, consul of Fondi, however, appears in a document of 1117,[209] suggesting perhaps that this branch of the Docibilan clan was not quite so easily removed. Why did the Docibilans disappear elsewhere?

In the case of Suio, a document of the incoming prince Jordan of Capua provides a clue. Dated 1078, it relates that count Raynerius and his consorts *culpam fecerunt* (loosely, 'had done blameworthy things', that is, rebelled) and were deprived of their castle.[210] At Traetto, it is possible that Marinus was the last of his line to rule there, and that his donation was intended to secure the safety of himself and his wife, both of whom must have been quite elderly by 1062. In neither case is there any hint from the charters that the counts were allowed to continue living in their castles as private citizens.[211]

I have presented the wholesale handover of large chunks of the duchy of Gaeta as a move initiated by the various counts out of fear of the Normans. The agreement of 1062 illustrates apprehension at least. Given that Montecassino had a long history of interaction both with Capua and Gaeta, and that its abbots were keen to expand their landed territories (abbot Desiderius' use of Suio as a port to bring building materials from Rome by water illustrates how valuable parts of the duchy could be to him[212]), might it not conceivably be the case that the Cassinesi and the Capuans came to some agreement whereby the monastery would act as a friend to the isolated counts, encouraging them to seek protection and smoothing away resistance to the Capuans? The case of Suio, for instance, is striking – one branch of the comital family (Hugh and son) seem to have acquiesced to Capuan rule, whilst the others rebelled and were consequently deposed. Taking this a step further, if Montecassino were seen as a benign ally, might not the word have spread between different branches of the Docibilans that handovers of territory were a good idea, encouraging the Fonditans, who ostensibly had no need to seek protection as early as they did, to follow the example of their relatives? This may be overinterpreting the actual content of the documents and ascribing

209 *CDC* 290. 210 *CDC* 251.

211 In a rare appearance of a Docibilan as a private citizen, however, Raynerius' eponymous son witnessed a charter in 1125 (*CDC* 307). 212 *CMC* III, 26.

to Montecassino and Desiderius a deliberate policy which did not exist. The possibility, though, remains, and is worth further investigation in a separate study.

How can we sum up the pattern of Gaeta's relations with her neighbours? Throughout the period in question, the duchy seems to have been split in two between the two great powers, Rome and Naples, with the Neapolitan party in the ascendance at Gaeta through the rule of the Docibilans. The split dated from as early as the ninth century, when Naples seems to have controlled the fortress of Gaeta itself and Rome the lands around it. Later, the Neapolitans may have been responsible for Atenolf I of Aquino taking power at Gaeta in 1044. They do not appear to have been capable of sustaining Docibilans in control there. But the Romans, strongly entrenched in the western part of the duchy, were similarly unable to take advantage of the mid-eleventh century instability in the city, in order to reaffix it firmly to the formerly papal lands. The beneficiaries of this indecisive contest were, ultimately, the rising powers of Norman Capua and the increasingly assertive abbey of Montecassino, the wholesale transfer of Gaetan lands to the latter ensuring that the documents enabling the reconstruction of the history of the area were preserved.

The ideas set out in this section prompt a revision of the picture of the duchy of Gaeta. Historians in the early years of this century, many from the city itself, presented it as a small, proudly independent state. This image cannot now be realistically sustained. At various points in its history Gaeta was formally subject to larger states, and, even during its period of supposed independence, outside influences were at work. Good relations with larger neighbours were necessary for Gaeta's political and economic well-being, and its naturally sheltered coastal position would make it an attractive possession for Rome, Naples or Montecassino.

That Gaeta's political life was subject to more external influences than was previously thought, should come as no surprise, given that its commercial life seems always to have brought it into contact with other states.[213]

This section has examined the border areas of the duchy of Gaeta, where exchange with external powers is most marked. Such exchanges, however, could have far-reaching effects at the centre of the duchy. The eleventh century saw the Capuans take over at

[213] On Gaeta's commercial life, see below, chapters 7 and 8.

Gaeta twice, but these events were only part of a much larger process of change. It is to Gaeta's internal development during the eleventh century that we must now turn.

(d) ROUTES TO POWER: SCRIBES, JUDGES AND CONSULS AT GAETA

Throughout the period under examination in this study, Gaeta was ruled by a duke, whether independent or subject to the sovereignty of others. However, from the early eleventh century onwards the administrative functions within the duchy seem to have been carried out by the duke's officials, some of whose roles increased in importance as the power of the Docibilan dukes waned. The documentary evidence highlights three particular posts as worthy of further investigation; the scribes and notaries in the duchy, the judges and, finally, the emergence of consuls at the beginning of the twelfth century.

(i) *Scribes and notaries*

Scribes, by their very function, appear in the Gaetan documentation from our first surviving document onwards. It is likely that in this part of southern Italy the level of lay literacy was quite high, and that many of the participants in the transactions recorded could read, but that fewer were able to write.[214]

Early documents were almost exclusively written by clerics, and there is evidence of a pride in the ability to write not only Latin, but Greek as well.[215] By the middle of the tenth century, there is a visible tendency on the part of the dukes of Gaeta to have their documents written by the current archdeacon of the city. Thus Marinus the archdeacon acted as scribe for Docibilis II on four occasions between 939 and 946, and the other four documents written by him all involved other members of the Docibilan family.[216] Martin the archdeacon wrote Docibilis II's will in

[214] Skinner, 'Women, literacy and invisibility'.

[215] Three clerics, Leo (fl.909–26), John (fl.922–59) and Peter (fl.935–45), describe themselves as 'Greek and Latin priests and scribes'. All three were based in Gaeta, and dominate the Gaetan documents from 909 (*CDC* 21) to 935 (*CDC* 38).

[216] For Docibilis II: *CDC* 41, *CDC* 45, *CDC* 46, *CDC* 49; for Gregory son of Docibilis II, *CDC* 42; for bishop Marinus in dispute with Peter, natural son of John I, *CDC* 47; for the heirs of Kampulus the prefect in dispute with the natural sons of John I, *CDC* 54; for the natural sons themselves, *CDC* 56.

954,[217] and Lordemanno the archdeacon was used by both Docibilis, son of duke Gregory, and bishop Bernard.[218]

The archdeacons did not have exclusivity as scribes at Gaeta, however. Other clerics also performed the role, and there was a growing number of lay notaries by the middle of the tenth century (at least, they give their occupation simply as 'notary' or 'scribe' and do not append that of 'cleric').[219] John, the protonotary and scribe, was one of the first lay notaries, and seems to have enjoyed a prolonged career at Gaeta between 958 and 999.[220] As Docibilis II had patronised Marinus the archdeacon, so John seems to have been favoured by dukes Marinus and John III, writing three documents for them.[221] Again, he was also used by other members of the Docibilan family, writing for Megalu, daughter of John I, in 958; Leo, duke of Fondi (at Gaeta) in 995; and bishop Bernard in 997.[222] During the same period Leo the scribe was also active at Gaeta, again writing a mixture of ducal and noblemen's documents, and it is possible that he was John's deputy.[223]

Despite this slight indication of a rise in lay literacy, no surviving document from any part of southern Italy seems to have been written by the participants: the intervention of a notary to write down the record was universally required. Why was this so? The first and most obvious reason might be that neither party in the transaction could read, but each wanted a written record in case of future dispute over the exact terms of their agreement. The main problem with this argument is that many relied on the memories of the witnesses to a verbal transaction, and did not see a document as necessary. The proof of this is furnished by the numerous court-cases in which testimony was accepted as sufficient to decide the argument in the form of oaths.[224] There is also the occasional document which proves that charters were not always drawn up immediately after the time of the transaction they record. Thus in 968, the daughters of John Sirrentino drew up a document at Naples recording his sale, in the past tense, to Peter the freedman,

[217] *CDC* 52. [218] *CDC* 79 (981), *CDC* 97 (997).

[219] On the ambiguity of the status of scribes and notaries elsewhere, in this case in the St Gall charters, see R. McKitterick, *The Carolingians and the Written Word* (Cambridge, 1989), p. 116.

[220] Given that no notary thought it necessary to use a patronym or other identifier beyond his title, it is always possible that there was more than one John. But the title protonotary was unusual enough in this period to allow that the same man is indicated throughout.

[221] *CDC* 74, (979), *CDC* 75 (980), *CDC* 84 (984). [222] *CDC* 58, *CDC* 94, *CDC* 96.

[223] Leo's documents: *CDC* 55 (957), *CDC* 62, *CDC* 63, *CDC* 65, *CDC* 72, *CDC* 80 (981).

[224] See above, chapter 1, section (d) and chapter 3, section (e).

because John had failed to do so.[225] Perhaps Peter was now contemplating selling the land, and needed written proof of his ownership. The fact that he was of lowly social status possibly increased his need to prove his title to the land. It is unclear whether John was still alive at the time of his daughters' document, and because of this it cannot be asserted that he originally had thought a charter unnecessary. Perhaps he had died very soon after the sale, before he and Peter had reached a notary. As long as the witnesses to the original transaction could be assembled, there was no problem in delaying the process of redaction.[226]

However, evidence from Gaeta and other parts of the Tyrrhenian littoral seems to show an increasing preference for written proof in court-cases. In Naples, the almost universal use of oaths in the tenth century gave way to a mixture of oaths and documents in the eleventh. There is also a certain amount of care shown in a document of 994 from Gaeta, replacing a charter which may have been lost or whose terms might have changed.[227] This indicates that memory was no longer sufficient to secure a transaction.

As this tendency towards written evidence grew, the role of scribe changed from simply producing a record of an agreement, to someone who had a responsibility to see that that record was accurate. The scribe had always had a legal function as an extra witness to the transaction; now he might be the first person to whom parties in a disagreement might appeal before taking their dispute to court.

Scribes and notaries could have a wider role to play than simply writing their communities' documents. Politically, the fact that Traetto had its own notary by 1014, Peter, and that other local centres followed suit in the troubled middle years of the eleventh century, indicates that public power now no longer emanated solely from Gaeta. It is striking that, unlike the situation at Gaeta, where clerics still wrote the majority of documents,[228] the new

[225] *RN* 168.

[226] Rosamond McKitterick, *Carolingians*, pp. 94–8, discusses this process from the evidence of the St Gall charters. [227] *CDC* 93.

[228] Scribes active at Gaeta: Ranerius the deacon (978–84), Constantine the priest (986–98), John the priest (1002–16), Leo the priest (1006–60), Constantine the priest (1008–9), John the priest (1021–38), Dauferius the priest (1041–2), John the deacon (1047–61), Marinus the deacon (1058–84) and Peter the deacon (1089–96). Leo the priest's long career may have been linked to the fact that he was the priest of SS Salvator and Benedict in the central Platea Maiore in Gaeta, which he held from the abbey of Montecassino. In 1024 he gave half of the church back to the abbey; unfortunately, although he gives his father's name, Dominicus, in this document, it provides no further clues to his family background, *CDC* 144.

local notaries were almost all laymen. After Peter at Traetto came Sicard (fl.1029–49),[229] Gregory (1036),[230] Giczo the priest (1047–8),[231] and Benignus (1050–87).[232] Notaries appear for the first time in Castro Argento in 1029,[233] Maranola in 1045,[234] Pontecorvo in 1058,[235] and Suio in 1063.[236]

From the trust placed in them in legal matters, it was a short step for a notary to become a judge, and we have evidence of this progression in a man's career. For example, Venerius, who wrote a document for Girard, consul of Fondi, in 1071, gives his title as judge and scribe.[237] John Caracci, who in 1085 is recorded simply as a scribe, then as a scribe and judge, appears finally as a judge in 1116.[238] The early role of judges has already been examined, but how did the position develop in the eleventh century onwards?

(ii) *Judges*

In 981, for the first time, the nobles of Gaeta judged a dispute between the two sons of duke Gregory. The ruler of Gaeta at that time was duke Marinus, and the case represents a departure from the norm in that it was not referred to him for a decision.[239] In the eleventh century, men titled *iudex* appear far more frequently in the documents. One, Gregory, appears in court-cases alongside the duke, and at the head of witness lists to land transactions between 1021 and 1037,[240] indicating that he made a career out of this function. Such expertise did not require that he be of noble birth, and we never find out who his father was. To be a judge was a position of status in itself, as the care with which one witness named John in 1054 cited his father as John the judge illustrates.[241]

Unlike the tenth-century evidence, however, the eleventh-century documents reveal judges in wider roles than simply witnessing. For example, in a dispute of 1053, Raimari the judge acted as advocate for two men contesting land with Leo, the bishop

[229] *CDC* 157, *CDC* 159, *CDC* 164, *CDC* 171, *CDC* 184, *CDC* 185.
[230] *CDC* 167.
[231] *CDC* 182, *CDC* 183.
[232] *CDC* 189, *CDC* 199, *CDC* 201, *CDC* 204, *CDC* 209, *CDC* 214, *CDC* 215, *CDC* 216, *CDC* 258.
[233] Lando the priest, *CDC* 158; a layman, Stephen, appears as the notary of Castro Argento in 1071 and 1086, *CDC* 246, *CDC* 257.
[234] John the notary and scribe, *CDC* 179.
[235] Littefrid the notary, *CDC* 207, *CDC* 249 (1075).
[236] John the notary, *CDC* 217. He appears frequently until 1070: *CDC* 220, *CDC* 223, *CDC* 224, *CDC* 242, *CDC* 243, *CDC* 244.
[237] *CDC* 247.
[238] *CDC* 259, *CDC* 275 (1103), *CDC* 289.
[239] *CDC* 79; Merores, *Gaeta*, p. 115.
[240] *CDC* 140, *CDC* 147, *CDC* 150, *CDC* 162, *CDC* 168.
[241] *CDC* 196.

of Gaeta. When documentary proof of the men's case was demanded by duke Atenolf, it was Raimari who produced it. Despite the fact that his party lost the case, the record provides rare and valuable evidence of the judge's representative function.[242]

A Bonus *iudex* appears in another role beside duke Atenolf I in 1057, and beside his widow and son in 1063, in the latter case consenting to Maria's land donation.[243] The 1063 document is particularly important, for we have previously seen that one of the roles of dukes was that of consenting to the transactions of a minor, which was the work undertaken by Bonus here. The legal authority of the duke had, therefore, been taken over by specialists. In 1109 one John the judge is recorded at a court of Richard, duke of Gaeta, and again in documents of duke Richard son of Bartholomew in 1121 and 1123.[244] In the latter document he appears listed in order of prominence before the four named consuls, and again in 1124.[245] Was this John the same man as John Caracci? It is unclear, but highly likely, and the later documents illustrate just how a man of humble origins could achieve one of the highest positions of power at Gaeta.

As in the case of notaries, there is some evidence to suggest that the increasing localisation of political power in the eleventh century led to individual centres having their own judges. Franco, the judge at Traetto recorded between 1030 and 1039, was an active and prominent member of the community living in the Flumetica area, and the presence of Roctio in the same settlement has already been noted above. A document of 1064, recording the end of a dispute between the counts of Suio and the abbot of Montecassino, was witnessed by three judges, all of whom stated their local affiliations.[246]

Judges had been a familiar part of Amalfitan life in the tenth century,[247] and there is plenty of evidence to suggest that their role became more important in the eleventh. The role of witnessing ducal documents has already been discussed, but what other functions can we see judges performing? A survey reveals that, despite the odd appearance as landowners,[248] the overwhelming

[242] *CDC* 195. [243] *CDC* 203, *CDC* 218. [244] *CDC* 284, *CDC* 297, *CDC* 301.
[245] *CDC* 302.
[246] *CDC* 227, witnessed by Giso, the judge of Mortula, Peter, the judge of *castello* Conca and John, the judge of Fondi. [247] See above, chapter 3, section (e).
[248] In 1028 the children of John the judge are recorded as landowners in Supramonte, *PAVAR* I/10; John the judge owned a house in the same place in 1043, *PAVAR* I/15; the son and daughter of Manso the judge owned Capri land in 1059, *CP* 75; Constantine Piczilli the judge is also recorded as a landowner in 1099, *CDA* 96.

majority of judges are recorded as witnesses to transactions, as they did for the dukes of Amalfi. Not all transactions were thus witnessed, but the high number of instances suggests that, like the presence of notaries described above in the Gaetan context, the presence of a judge was often seen as added insurance in case of dispute. A strong link between the two roles is provided by the case of a man recorded in 1059 buying land, who gives his name as John 'judge and curial'.[249] He appears as a witness in 1087,[250] again with the twin titles. It is likely that the notariate was the entry point to becoming a judge, and an indication of how the process worked is given in 1062,[251] when Leo son of John the judge completed a document written by his son Leo. It is likely that the elder Leo was himself a scribe, allowing his son to learn the trade under his supervision, and that he aspired to his father's position as a judge. The Amalfitan evidence thus supports the picture from Gaeta that judges often began their careers as scribes.

The identity of the judges is difficult to pin down, but several general points can be made. The majority, as at Gaeta, do not seem to have been of noble origins, but there is the odd exception.[252] Several give their fathers' names, but many conformed with the Gaetan pattern of simply giving their title; this was identity enough for many men, and a survey of the eleventh-century sample shows that the judges of Amalfi may have been limited in number, for the same names recur with some frequency.[253] They may be the group of *boni homines* recorded as witnessing the settlement of a dispute in 1092.[254] The continued shortage of court-case evidence from Amalfi, however, does not allow us to see whether judges managed to take over the handling of disputes generally.[255] Even a cursory

[249] *CP* 57. [250] *CDA* 81. [251] *PAVAR* 1/19.

[252] For example, John the judge recorded in 1028 was a descendant down three generations from one Sergius the count, *PAVAR* 1/10, *CDA* 10.

[253] They include: John, *CDA* 10 (977), *CP* 9 (993), *CDA* 28 (1011); Lupinus son of Pantaleo, *CP* 80 (998), *CodCav* v/826 (1030), *CP* 39 (1033); Sergius, *PAVAR* 1/4 (1010), *CP* 39 (1033), *CDA* 46 (1036), *PAVAR* 1/14 (1039); and John son of Niceta, *PAVAR* 1/4 (1010), *CodCav* v/826 (1030), *CDA* 591 (1033), *CDA* 42 (1035), *CP* 36 (1039). Two other judges, Constantine and Anthimus, also appear regularly, together on three occasions, but the date of their first appearance in 986, *CP* 11, must be open to doubt given their subsequent cluster of appearances in the later *eleventh* century (together in 1059, *CP* 65, and 1062, *CP* 76; Constantine in 1062, 1067 and 1068, *CDA* 69, *CP* 49, *CP* 48; Anthimus in 1064, *CP* 46).

[254] *CDA* 89.

[255] The cases we have from the eleventh century break down as follows: two were settled by the duke, *CDA* 590 (1023) and *CP* 33 (1055); two by the 'court', which is likely to have been ducal, *CDA* 21 (1007) and *CDA* 49 (1037); one was settled with a payment *PAVAR* 1/5 (1011) and one by sharing the disputed property, *PAVAR* 1/25 (1094).

survey of the evidence, however, reveals that the main function of judges in the twelfth century remained that of witnessing documents, and again their number may have been limited.

It is possible to analyse the roles that judges performed in the Tyrrhenian cities of the South as those of service to their communities. They were, in some sense, representatives of the law to their fellow citizens, and men appear for long periods making a career out of performing this duty. However, as in contemporary England, there is no sense as yet of professionalism on the part of judges, nor of a legal profession as such.[256] That is, if men performed the role of judges, be it as witnesses, ducal deputies or representatives, they did so as respected members of their communities and not (overtly, at least) for regular payment. The advocates who sometimes appear in the documents performed a similar representative function, and again do not seem to have received payment.

Only in the twelfth century is there any indication at all that legal practice was becoming the preserve of suitably qualified men, and the evidence comes not from the Tyrrhenian states, but from Bari, the other major city of the South. In 1180, Bisantius made his will prior to travelling to Bologna to study law. That his case is applicable to other parts of the South, however, is suggested by the fact that he was a notary: again, the link between the notariate and the law is apparent.

(iii) *Consuls*

Another position of power at Gaeta was that of *consul*. The families who held the consulate in the city will be discussed in more detail in chapter 6, but it is worth looking at the number of recorded consuls in the documents, and the distribution of the posts among various families, to try to get some idea of how the consulate actually worked.

Hagen Keller recently furnished a timely warning against assuming that the first documented evidence for the presence of consuls necessarily indicates the creation of a commune.[257] He was referring to Lombard cities, but the relevance of his warning

[256] Paul Brand characterises England before 1150 as 'a land without lawyers': P. Brand, *The Origins of the English Legal Profession* (Oxford, 1992), chapter 1.

[257] H. Keller, 'Gli inizi del comune in Lombardia; limiti della documentazione e metodi di ricerca', in *L'Evoluzione delle Città Italiane nell'XI Secolo* (Bologna, 1988), p. 47.

1123	Docibilis Mancanella, Jacob Maltacia, Anatolius Castanea, Constantine Burdo Gattula
1124	Constantine Burdo Gattula, Gregory son of Marini Castanea
1125	?
1126	?
1127	Stephen Mancanella, Marinus Boccapasu
1128	?
1129	Docibilis son of Marinus Mancanella, John Bonus Mancanella, Jacob Maltacia, Matthia Madelmo de Arciu, John son of Leo Castanea, Constantine son of Constantine Gattula
1130–33	?
1134	John son of Leo Castanea, Constantine son of Docibilis Gattula
1135	Hieronymus son of Hieronymus Maltacia, Gualganus son of Leo Castanea
1136–48	?
1149	Bonus son of Boni Maltacia

Figure 5.7 *The consuls of Gaeta*

becomes apparent if we remember that most members of new families at Gaeta had appeared, and were influential in the political life of the duchy, at least fifty years before some achieved consular status.

The appearance of the consuls in Gaeta may have been facilitated by the fact that the city's Norman rulers, based in Capua, were too preoccupied with their own political struggles to worry too much about the city on the coast. Nevertheless, there is no evidence to suggest that the Capuans disapproved of the development of the consulate. Rather, they seem to have been happy to allow the Gaetans to regulate their own internal affairs. Only when their subjects overstepped the mark, as in the case of the Suian rebels mentioned above, did the princes of Capua actively intervene.

Several comments can be made about the Gaetan consulate from the evidence of the list of consuls. It seems that initially there were four consuls, and that this may have risen to six in the late 1120s. However, we must remember that the Gaetan year ran from September to September for dating purposes, and so the high number of consuls recorded for 1129 may represent two sets. There is no indication of the process by which the consuls were chosen, but it is almost certain, looking at the incumbents, that no one was allowed to serve for two years running. This did not prevent a man from becoming consul more than once in his lifetime, however, as the appearance of John son of Leo Castanea in 1129 and again in

1134 proves. It is quite striking that all the recorded consuls belonged to the new, surnamed aristocracy of Gaeta, and that some families were extremely successful in raising different members to the post in different years, thereby securing a political dominance in the city.

In addition to specific factors such as their wealth and the entry into the aristocracy provided by the professions of scribe and judge, the rise of the new families was helped by the instability of the ducal throne throughout the eleventh century. The focus of attention on the dukedom drew the spotlight away from the fact that new men were encroaching in the aristocratic circles once dominated by the old nobility. It was also greatly to the advantage of the new men that the rulers of Gaeta from 1064 onwards had their main centre of power at Capua. Unlike the Docibilans, men like the princes Richard I and Jordan I had no need to cultivate the older noble families, and seemed quite content to allow the internal power structures at Gaeta to develop however they would. Only when their new subjects acted against them, as in the case of the counts of Suio in 1078, did the Capuans take direct control. Otherwise, an air of co-operative autonomy prevailed at Gaeta. In the words of Loud, 'In spite of its supposed subjection to Capua, Gaeta continued to act as it pleased.'[258] This is well illustrated by a document of 1123, in which duke Richard promised the judge and consuls at Gaeta that he would leave the coins known as *follari* as they were.[259]

This agreement is evidence of one of the public powers of the consuls of Gaeta, that of regulating its financial and commercial concerns. This function is apparent again in a document of the following year when the consuls were in dispute with the Roman merchant, Bello.[260] In 1125 a merchant of Salerno, Peter Sfagilla, acknowledged the return of his ship and his goods from the consuls of Gaeta, who had seized it during a war between the two cities.[261] Of course, although these documents present the consuls acting as public representatives of Gaeta, private interest may also have influenced their actions. For example, Miro son of Leo, consul of 1124, may have been a member of the Baraballu clan, to which Girard, consortium member of 1105, belonged. To such men, any change of Gaeta's coinage, which they used beside the ubiquitous

[258] *Church and Society*, p. 15. [259] *CDC* 301.
[260] *CDC* 302; see above, section (c,ii); see also chapter 8. [261] *CDC* 308.

Pavian *denarius*, could have proved financially problematic, perhaps even invalidating contracts they had made.

Other consular functions seen in the surviving documents included the regulation of building work at Gaeta. In 1124 Docibilis son of Gregory de Anatolii promised to the consuls that he would build his house only to the height of his nephew's house and no taller, and would roof it 'according to the laws'.[262] Again there may be a certain amount of self-interest involved here. As one of the features of the civic elite at Pisa during the same period, Bordone has isolated the fact that urban prestige was expressed by the ownership of towers, the taller the better.[263] This phenomenon is by no means uncommon; Hughes illustrates how each family's house and tower in Genoa in the eleventh and twelfth centuries went to the eldest son, thus identifying the family with its fortification from generation to generation.[264] Could the regulation of house heights in Gaeta by the consuls therefore represent an attempt to maintain their pre-eminence or to prevent anyone else from gaining it? It is possible. That Gaeta may have witnessed a period of intense tower-building is suggested by a sculpted panel of the thirteenth-century paschal candlestick in Gaeta's cathedral, representing the city during the sculptor's lifetime and positively bristling with tall, stylised towers.

This concern with the regulation of the city's internal life is reflected in another example of the consuls' work in 1129. In this year they declared that whatever profit should come from the Jewish dye-works or other work, including salt-pans, in the city should be devoted to the city's use.[265] Unfortunately they do not specify what uses they had in mind for the money (nor, for that matter, what cloth the Jews were dyeing and what other work the Jewish community did). However, we can speculate that the two main concerns so far highlighted, building work in the city (perhaps of churches as well as defences?) and commerce, probably received some of this profit. A more illuminating document of 1135 reveals that 'the Gaetans' (including a judge and seven consuls) had decided to tax the sale of olive-oil, and that the revenue would be used to light the cathedral.[266]

[262] *CDC* 305.

[263] R. Bordone, 'Le "elites" cittadine nell'Italia communale (XI–XII secolo', *MEFRM*, 100 (1988), 51.

[264] D. Hughes, 'Urban growth and family structure in medieval Genoa', *Past and Present*, 66 (1975), 10.

[265] *CDC* 317.

[266] *CDC* 327.

External relations continue to be the area in which the consuls were most active in the first half of the twelfth century. In 1129, they made peace with a group of named Neapolitans who had had their ship stolen by unnamed Gaetans.[267] This, and another document of the same year, in which the Gaetans and Sergius, the duke of Naples, made a ten-year peace,[268] suggest that relations between the two cities had suffered a considerable souring in the latter half of the eleventh century. Such a breakdown is probably most easily explicable in terms of the takeover by the Lombard, and then Norman, princes of Capua, with whom Naples had never enjoyed peaceful relations. In the context of events in the late 1120s and early 1130s, the peace can be understood to be a holding gesture on the part of the Neapolitans, who were still engaged in resisting the might of the Normans, and would successfully do so until 1139. If so, it clearly failed at some point during the cease-fire period, for in ?1137 a letter from the consuls of Pisa warned those of Gaeta that the Pisans would take measures against anyone who harmed their ally, Naples.[269]

There is some evidence to suggest that the Gaetans were not averse to conflict. In 1132, Geoffrey de Aquila made peace with 'the Gaetans', over what dispute we do not know.[270] Geoffrey was lord of Itri, just above Gaeta, and so the most likely cause of acrimony was probably the latter city's by now very cramped territory. One of Geoffrey's barons recorded in a document of 1135 was William Blosseville, the former duke of the city.[271] In 1134 the Gaetans are seen making a treaty with the lord of Monte Circeo, Marinus Formosus, against the city of Terracina.[272] Four years later a group of Atranians confirmed that they had received compensation for the 8 ounces of gold they had 'lost' in Gaeta whilst on their way to ransom men of their city from the Pisans.[273] All of these documents have implications for the history of Gaeta's commercial life, and will be discussed more fully in a later chapter.[274]

It is likely that had the history of the proto-commune of Gaeta been allowed to continue, we should have seen similar commercial and territorial ambitions to those of contemporary northern cities (Pisa itself being a notable example). Duke Richard II seems to have been content to allow internal autonomy on the part of the consuls during his rule, which lasted until his death in 1134/5. However, its

[267] *CDC* 319. [268] *CDC* 318. [269] *CDC* 331. [270] *CDC* 323.
[271] *CDC* 329. [272] *CDC* 325. [273] *CDC* 332.
[274] See below, chapter 8.

life seems to have come to an end soon afterwards. A document of ?1140 contains a formulaic oath of the duke of Gaeta to king Roger and to his sons duke Roger and prince Anfusus of Capua, and one of the following year an oath by the Gaetan people to the man nominated to rule them, Atenolf count of Spigno.[275] Thereafter, apart from one isolated reference to a man titled consul and *baiulus* in the city in 1149 (and these titles might well relate to a function within the Norman hierarchy, as the dating clause of the document cited king Roger's rule[276]), the documents are largely silent about the internal administration of the city and its territory.

It is clear that Gaeta underwent some dramatic changes in its internal administration in the eleventh and early twelfth centuries, mirroring the external turmoil that accompanied the rise of Norman power. How did the duchies of Amalfi and Naples fare during this period, and did their political lives develop in the same way?

(e) AMALFI IN THE ELEVENTH CENTURY

(i) *Changes of rule*

After the upheavals of Capuan rule in the mid-eleventh century, discussed earlier, the ducal line of Amalfi was restored to power. However, its tenure of the duchy was not to last very long. In 1073 duke Sergius died, and, mindful of the problems encountered when a minor came to power, the Amalfitans seem to have preferred to take their chance with a new political force in Campania, the Norman Robert Guiscard. The city placed itself under his protection in that year.

The history of the Guiscard's rise is long overdue for re-examination, but is not directly relevant here. A shrewd politician, one of his main tactics in extending his influence seems to have been marriage. His first wife, Alberada, was repudiated on grounds of consanguinity in 1058, and Robert took as his second wife Sikelgaita, the daughter of the prince of Salerno. She succeeded in promoting her son by Robert, Roger, over his half-brother Bohemond, and it is Roger whom we see as co-ruler of Amalfi with his father by 1077. He subsequently became sole ruler on the death of his father, and is recorded as being in his first year as duke in 1089.[277]

[275] *CDC* 334, *CDC* 335. [276] *CDC* 340. [277] *CP* 64, *CP* 84.

Sikelgaita herself may have been instrumental in the Amalfitans' decision to submit to Robert. Amalfi had a long history of exchange with Salerno, as we shall see in a later chapter. Certainly in 1079 Sikelgaita showed distinct political sensitivity when she gave land to the church of St Trophimenus, the patron saint of Amalfi and Atrani,[278] and Roger followed her example in confirming the gift in 1091.[279]

For all their efforts, however, Amalfi was not entirely subdued, and on a wider front both the pope and Byzantium were becoming alarmed by the rise of Norman power in the South. It may have been the efforts of the latter that led Amalfi to rebel. Between 1092 and 1097 the lack of dating clauses on surviving Amalfitan documents is indicative that the Normans had run into problems, and the ruler documented as in his first year in power in 1097, Marinus *sebaste*,[280] clearly owed his position to Byzantine backing.

As with all Byzantine intervention in southern Italy, however, this period of rule was not able to resist Norman pressure. Marinus' need to have his actions witnessed by the public judges of Amalfi in 1098, when he made a gift to the bishop of Ravello, may itself point to a feeling that his position was by no means secure.[281] By 1102 the dating clauses of Amalfitan documents reveal duke Roger back in power, in the second year after his restoration.[282] He was succeeded by his son William as duke in 1110, although the latter is identified in an isolated date clause as prince and duke as well.[283] He asserted his authority in 1113, when he confirmed to the monastery of SS Ciricus and Iulicta all the lands which the monastery had bought by the river Reginna Maiori at the sea-shore from duke Marinus *sebaste*.[284]

William died in 1127/8. In the latter year a document dated by duke Roger reveals Williams' successor.[285] In 1130 the creation of the Norman monarchy in southern Italy led to Roger, now king, requiring the authorities of Amalfi to submit to his rule. When they refused he sent an army to impose his terms forcefully. As a result the Amalfitans and the Neapolitans submitted.[286]

This issue of resistance is worth investigating. It is at least hinted at in the failure of many Amalfitans to acknowledge the current ruler in their documents after 1100. Why, after thirty years of continuous Norman rule, did they balk at Roger's request in 1130?

[278] *CDA* 592. [279] *CDA* 87. [280] *CP* 89. [281] *CDA* 593.
[282] *CDA* 100. [283] *CP* 98 (1115). [284] *CDA* 114. [285] *CP* 119.
[286] Matthew, *Norman Kingdom*, p. 38.

The answer may lie in the internal history of the duchy during this period.

(ii) *Internal administration*

Amalfi's political life in the late eleventh and early twelfth centuries seems to have followed a different line from that of Gaeta, reaching much earlier the situation of direct rule by a Norman nominee, and never experiencing the embryonic consular rule that Gaeta had been allowed to enjoy. This might be explained by the difference of styles between duke Roger and prince Richard, the latter having less power to enforce his rule, and therefore working on the basis of leaving the existing power structures of Gaeta intact with simply a nominal duke at their head. Roger, on the other hand, dealt directly with the Amalfitans. In 1104 a document issued by the duke to his *fidele* Sergius the judge, of the Piczillo family, granted land near the sea-shore in Amalfi in return for his service.[287] There are several issues to examine here. The first is the terminology which the document uses, which was by now a standard Norman practice throughout the South. Further, that Roger's favour fell on a faithful judge suggests at least some deputisation of power within the city. This is supported by the fact that the land granted, on the *plano Amalfi*, had a long history of ducal association, and would be the natural choice of a sovereign wishing to indicate that the recipient was a man of some standing.

The document collection from Amalfi in the twelfth century reveals other public officials in the city. In two documents recording land exchanges in 1115 between SS Ciricus and Iulicta and Peter son of John Viscatari, both witness lists include one Mauro *protonobilissimus* and one Mauro *coropalatus*, both of the Comitemaurone family.[288] The latter re-appears in another document of 1120, which he both wrote and witnessed.[289] Given that we have previously noted the rise of curials to positions of responsibility and power in the duchy of Gaeta, could this be another layer of internal power under the sovereignty of the Norman dukes, with judges and men with various titles actually running the city and its territory subject to ducal approval? It is possible, and the fact that the two Mauros are listed as the witnesses to a further document of 1129 suggests that their presence may

[287] *CDA* 595. [288] *CDA* 117, *CDA* 118. [289] *CP* 106.

have lent authority or validity to the transaction.[290] The title of *coropalatus* persists sporadically in the Amalfitan documentation throughout the twelfth century.[291]

Much later on, there is evidence of more titles of this type emerging at Amalfi, and from the middle of the twelfth century we have documented examples of men known as the *stratigotus* of Amalfi and of Ravello.[292] The latter is seen in 1177 authorising the seizure of goods in repayment of a debt, witnessed by two judges, and so is clearly the official who was delegated to ensure justice and smooth local administration. This is lent weight by the fact that the *stratigotus* of Amalfi in 1183 was also titled judge, and is recorded acting in the presence of the *boni homines* of the city.[293] Alongside what can probably be described as the civil authorities in the latter half of the twelfth century, there is some evidence that the Norman kings organised military authority as well, with isolated references to the *castellani* of both Amalfi and Turris Maioris.[294]

It is probable, therefore, that there were local officials at Amalfi under the control of the Norman dukes, and that they had the responsibility of day-to-day administration of the city. It is likely that this was the more usual pattern of power under Norman rule, and that the nascent commune at Gaeta, which added an extra layer to the chain of command, was an anomaly which developed in a period of weakness for the Capuan princes. However, Roger's request in 1130 for the keys of Amalfi suggests, if only symbolically, that he intended to intervene in the internal life of the city. At this point, the Amalfitans refused to co-operate, with predictable consequences.

(f) *Naples*

The history of Naples is the most stable throughout the period from the mid-eleventh to the mid-twelfth centuries, in that it

[290] *PAVAR* I/36. [291] *PAVAR* II/73 (1170), *PAVAR* I/55 (1177).

[292] *Stratigotus* of Amalfi: *CDA* 597 (1145), 219 (1186) and 244 (1200); of Ravello: *CDA* 153 (1150), *PAVAR* II/58 (1159) and *PAVAR* II/85 (1177).

[293] *CP* 173; a survey of published documents from elsewhere in southern Italy confirms the role of the *stratigotus* as a chief judge in each city under Norman rule. The appearance of the title earlier in the far South (men with the title are documented in Messina (1110, *NSK* 3); Terlizzi (1123, *PCT* 42); Conversano (1128, *PC* 78); Stilo (1128, *Théristes* 13); Troia (1130, *Troia* 56), Corato (1135, *Corato* 36); Barletta (1138, *Barletta* 41); Trani (1139, *Trani* 37) and Lesina (1141, *Tremiti* 103)) may reflect a swifter acceptance of Norman administration there than in the cities of the Tyrrhenian littoral, such as Amalfi and Salerno, which had been more used to autonomy. (See Abbreviations for full references). [294] Amalfi: *CDA* 231 (1193); Turris Maioris: *PAVAR* I/64 (1188).

enjoyed the continuous rule of its ducal dynasty and experienced very few internal changes to its administration. The only significant break came in the late 1020s, when Pandolf IV of Capua briefly seized the duchy and expelled its duke, Sergius. The hiatus was short-lived, however, to judge by the minimal effect the rule of the Capuans had on the dating clauses of Neapolitan documents written during their supremacy,[295] and Sergius was able to call in Norman reinforcements to restore him to power. His use of these mercenaries in the 1030s, however, is seen as a turning-point in the history of the area, for, in giving them the settlement of Aversa as their base, Sergius legitimised their military presence within his borders, and allowed the Normans to see the fragility of the duchy's security. It is during the rule of the Normans at Capua that a letter survives from pope Gregory VII to John, archbishop of Naples. Gregory urged him to avoid the *magister militum* and the other Neapolitans and prince Jordan of Capua, for they were anathema.[296]

The history of Naples' resistance to the Normans spans sixty years. In 1077 the city was besieged by Robert Guiscard and his brother, but the death of the latter led to the siege being lifted. A document written in the city in 1078 illustrates the insecurity and disruption that the siege had caused. It records a dispute between Peter, the abbot of the monastery of St Gregory in the Furcillense district of the city, 'which monastery has no congregation as the monks have left the city on account of the war with the Normans who surround the city', and Andrea, the abbot of the monastery of St Felix, outside Naples at Pumilianum. Peter claimed that during the war Andrea had allowed two *sorole* to be dug from St Gregory's land and moved to Pumilianum. Andrea claimed that he had bought them from Lidolf the viscount, and that it was Lidolf who had dug them up. Andrea now paid 32 Amalfitan *tari* to Peter for the *sorole*, suggesting that in the uncertainty of the war unscrupulous men like Lidolf relied on the disruption being caused by the Normans to attempt illegal sales of this type.[297]

When the siege was lifted, Naples seems to have enjoyed a respite as the Guiscard's successors concentrated their efforts elsewhere, but pope Anacletus is seen as sealing the city's fate in 1130. Raising Roger II to the status of king, he granted him the

[295] A document from Capua dated 1029 refers to the rule of Pandolf IV and his son at Naples: T. Leccisotti, *Abbazia di Montecassino: I Regesti dell'Archivio*, x (Rome, 1976), p. 362. [296] Capasso, *Monumenta*, I, p. 261 document 19. [297] *RN* 528.

'honour' of Naples, thereby implicitly endorsing any action that the king might have to take to win the city. When Roger gained entry to Amalfi in that year, Sergius VII of Naples submitted too. The rumour of Roger's death which swept the South when he withdrew to Sicily to mourn his wife's death in 1135, however, led to the reversal of Naples' position. The city became the focus for opposition to Roger, and, as reinforcements arrived from the German emperor Lothar, it was able to withstand the Norman's forces for two years. Some indication of the pressures to which the city was subjected can be gained from a document written there in 1136. It records a sale of land between two former inhabitants of Calbetianum (Calvizzano) who were now inhabitants of Naples, presumably because they were unable to leave. The vendors used the 10 *solidi* raised to live on (*opus et necessitates eorum*) and also to pay off their debts, citing the siege as the reason (*pro ista guerra ubi modo sunt*).[298] Clearly their enforced stay in the city was causing them hardship. The siege was lifted in the face of pressure elsewhere in 1137, but just as it seemed that the German efforts would bear fruit Lothar fell ill, and the army withdrew. Sergius, aware that his position was precarious, immediately submitted to Roger a second time. His submission was accepted, but he did not have long to enjoy his renewed position of favour; he died on campaign with Roger soon afterwards.

The two years between these events and the formal submission of Naples in 1139 deserve further study. For, deprived of a duke, the Neapolitans seem to have experimented with the kind of consular rule that their neighbour Gaeta had enjoyed. Although the title *consul* was not used, by 1139 there are isolated references in the sparse documentation to the 'most noble men' as authorisers of actions. The two examples that survive both show them allowing minors to undertake land transactions, a role which the duke of the city had previously performed. What is especially interesting, however, is that the *nobiliores homines* seem to have acted on a regional level within the city. That is, they did not have jurisdiction over the entire city, but acted within areas of it. Thus the first transaction, of 20th March 1139, was permitted by the noblemen *de regione S. Pauli*, and the second, on 20th May, by those of the *regione Nilo*.[299] Both groups appointed representatives for the young authors of the documents. In the first document, even the witnesses signed 'with the permission of the noblemen'.

[298] *RN* 666. [299] *RN* 680, *RN* 681.

Who were these noblemen? Most histories of Naples have left this question unasked, but the assumption seems to have been that the Neapolitans maintained their independence from Norman rule for the two years to 1139. This is based mainly on the formal act of submission that took place in that year. I am not entirely convinced of this. That the Normans could have set up an informal administration for the city, whose capture was prized, is more than likely. After all, they had a long history of proximity to the city, holding Aversa. There is also the odd reference to Norman landowners in the Neapolitan documentation after 1137.[300] A Norman identity would perhaps explain why the 'noblemen' are not named in the two examples which we have. To accept Norman intervention in their daily lives did not compromise Neapolitan dignity, since their duke had already submitted to the foreigners. Another factor to consider is that, unlike Gaeta, Naples does not seem to have witnessed a dominant group of noble families around the duke. The ducal family was at the forefront of Neapolitan society. The fall of its head left a vacuum. It is possible that the noblemen were the remnants of that family, though this would surely have been stated. The same is true if the *nobiliores homines* had been members of families known at Naples. Certainly there is no reticence about identification in the documentary evidence as a whole.

If we accept that the Normans were able to take over in 1137, the letter of the Pisans to the Gaetans in that year, advising them not to harm Pisa's allies at Naples, must be explained.[301] The Pisans were certainly no friends of the Normans at this date. The letter may well relate to the Pisans' involvement in the force which had raised the siege of Naples in that year, that is, before duke Sergius' submission. If so, it illustrates that the Gaetans were by this time acting as loyal subjects of Roger. Whatever the case, Pisan help does not seem to have been able to sustain Naples' independence for long.

According to the chronicler Falco, when the Neapolitans submitted in 1140 each existing Neapolitan knight was given 5 *modia* of land and 5 *villani*.[302] Again the identity of the knights poses a problem. Was the grant a sweetener to those Neapolitans who had always held the rank of *miles* and their followers, or are we here witnessing the share-out of the spoils to the invading army?

[300] For example, Rupert Lorvangno, documented in 1138, *RN* 674.
[301] *CDC* 331. [302] Matthew, *Norman Kingdom*, p. 146.

Possibly both scenarios are correct. Naples was now part of a larger political entity, and a certain amount of harmonising of locals and incomers may have occurred. The history of the city after this date, however, is outside the scope of the present study.

CONCLUSION: A TIME OF CHANGE?

The eleventh century saw great upheavals in the regimes of the three Tyrrhenian cities under discussion, also a widening of their horizons as outside forces sought to gain control of southern Italy. Yet the impact of the Normans has perhaps been exaggerated. In the Tyrrhenian cities many administrative offices continued to function just as they had under their old rulers, and dukes continued to rule at Gaeta and Naples, albeit with Normans filling the ducal post. The stability represented by this continuous pattern requires an explanation. I would suggest that to find one we must return to the population of the cities, in particular their noble families. How well did these weather the storms of the eleventh and early twelfth centuries? Was their survival a key factor in the survival of patterns of rule in the cities?

Chapter 6

THE EMERGENCE OF NEW FAMILIES

(a) GAETA: A NEW ELITE

We have seen in the previous chapter that, despite the upheaval of the mid-eleventh century, a few of the older Gaetan families continued to be prominent after 1032. Although that date is seen as a watershed in the history of the duchy of Gaeta by many writers, it did not signal the end of Docibilan power, which continued to be supported actively by clans such as the Kampuli and Coronellas. However, the instability led to the disappearance of the Christopherii from our documents after 1041, and those whom I identified as a new tenth-century aristocracy patronised by the Docibilans, such as the Gaetani and Mauri, also fared less well. The former disappear after 998, and, whilst members of the Mauri family are present in our documents right up until 1109,[1] they suffered a period away from court between the fall of duke Leo in 1042 and the end of the eleventh century. Even the Kampuli, who may have owed their longevity to their enormous wealth, disappear after 1071.

But the survival of their erstwhile patrons until the 1070s may explain why the Caracci continue to appear in the documents throughout the eleventh century and into the twelfth.

(i) *The Caracci*

After their initial receipt of lands in the more western parts of the duchy and at Caput Aqua,[2] the three brothers, Docibilis, Leo and John Caracci, in 1036 expanded their interests into Flumetica,

[1] Atenolf son of Bernard appears as a witness at the court of Richard in 1109 (*CDC* 284), and the rarity of the name Bernard makes it likely that he was the son of Bernard son of Mastalus Mauri. Atenolf is associated in the document with Gregory son of Constantine Salpa; Bernard had been associated with the latter in 1071 (*CDC* 245).

[2] See above, chapter 4, section (a,ii).

when they exchanged an unknown piece of land (there is a lacuna in the document) for property at Vellota (see Map 6.1).[3] It is interesting that their opposites in this transaction were from the city of Carinola, which lay well within the boundaries of the principate of Capua. This fact may simply be seen as a result of the Capuan take-over at Gaeta (the transaction is dated by the rule of Pandolf and Pandolf his son), but even when Gaeta and Capua had been separate political entities their boundary does not seem to have been a bar to economic exchange.[4]

The progress which the three Caracci brothers made in building up their Flumetica holdings is well illustrated by the will of one of them, Leo, in 1067.[5] In it he left lands in Vellota and Costranu as well as other property in Conca, Tremonsuoli and Pedemonte (unknown). He seems to have died childless; his wife Matrona is named as his main heir, and on her death the lands were to be divided between the churches of St Theodore, St Angelus and SS George and Salvator in Gaeta, and St Martin Aqua Mundula near Maranola. Leo's benefaction of the church of St George was later copied by his nephew Peter, son of John, in 1069.[6] The land given by Peter lay in Marana, another indication of Caracci family interests in Flumetica.

There is no apparent reason for the family's choice of this church to receive their donations. Its documented history stretches back as far as 887, relatively early by Gaetan standards, but the only notable feature is that it was not a church which enjoyed the patronage of the dukes of Gaeta. Unlike their contemporaries and patrons the Kampuli, the Caracci did not have a place among the highest ranks of Gaetan society.

It was precisely at the time the Kampuli disappear from our documents that the Caracci seem to have suffered some disruption in their landowning activities. After his land donation of 1069, Peter son of John only appears as a witness in 1089 and 1091.[7] Similarly modest in his activities in the 1080s was Peter's cousin John, possibly a son of Docibilis. He is first recorded as a scribe in 1085 and again in 1087.[8] The fact that his customers in these two documents were not, as far as we can tell, noblemen, fits in well with the idea that the Caracci were themselves of relatively modest origins. John rose above these however. In 1103 he is described as a

[3] *CDC* 166. [4] For a discussion on this exchange, see above, chapter 5, section (b,ii).
[5] *CDC* 234. [6] *CDC* 240. [7] *CDC* 261, *CDC* 264.
[8] *CDC* 259, *CDC* 260.

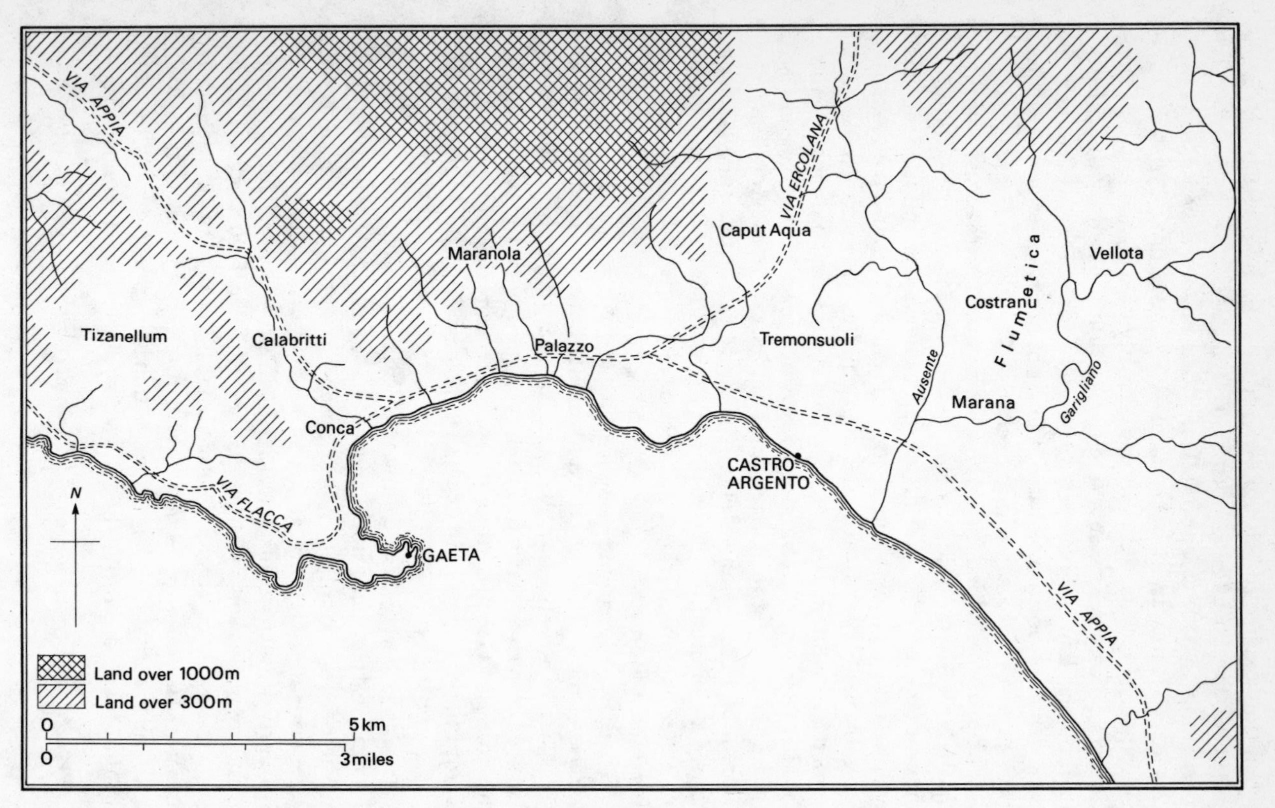

Map 6.1 *Lands of the Caracci family*

scribe and a judge, writing and witnessing a document for one Alferius son of John.[9] In 1108 he did the same for Bona, widow of Anatolius Cotina.[10] By 1116 John owned land at Palazzo and was designated by the title of judge only.[11] This indicates a recovery in the Caracci fortunes, and in 1125 the family was still active at Gaeta. In that year Maria, widow of Docibilis Caracci and her son Kampulus ('Kampus') sold a cellar in the city to Leo son of Radi.[12] The occurrence of the name Kampulus in the Caracci family genealogy should be noted. Whilst they were now independently wealthy and enjoyed some prominence, they had perhaps not forgotten their erstwhile patrons. Their prominence may not have lasted much longer, however, as our last record of the family is the appearance in a witness list of 1128 of one Constantine son of John Caracci.[13] Thereafter the evidence reveals no more Caracci members, although a change of surname (through marriage into a more important clan, for example) might obscure them from view.

I said earlier that other families on the same social level as the Caracci may be difficult to see in the tenth century precisely because their origins were modest and their land transactions may not have been significant enough to record in writing or to keep for posterity. But in the first half of the eleventh century a whole group of families emerge in our documents who, like the Caracci, used surnames and do not seem to have traced their origins back to a noble ancestor.

(ii) *The Coronellas*

The Coronella family have already been mentioned within the context of the 'old' aristocracy at Gaeta, but perhaps fit more comfortably into this group, in view of their surname and obscure origins. They really only rose to prominence in the mid-eleventh century, by courtesy, it seems, not of the Docibilans, but of the Atenolfan dukes. Marinus Coronella was a 'noble of Gaeta' in documents of 1047 and 1049,[14] and the disappearance from view of the family for over forty years after the death of Atenolf I suggests that their elevated status owed much to his patronage.

[9] *CDC* 275. [11] *CDC* 289. [12] *CDC* 309.

[13] *CDC* 314: Constantine son of John witnesses the execution of Docibilis Frunzo's will by Bonus Pedeacetu and the sons of the count of Suio and Constantine Gattula son of Munda. [14] *CDC* 180, *CDC* 187.

Nevertheless, the Coronellas were clearly a wealthy family – Gregory son of John Coronella was able to put up half of the 20 pounds of silver required to buy off the candidate for the bishopric of Gaeta in 1054.[15] But the essential point to note here is that the wealth was in the form of cash, not land, which perhaps goes some way to explaining their rather ephemeral appearance in what is largely a documentary collection of land transactions. This image is reinforced by the only other reference to the family in a document of 1128. In it, the deceased John Coronella is recorded as having lent $4\frac{1}{2}$ pounds of *denarii* to bishop Leo (the same man the family had earlier helped to power) against a mortgaged mill, which he subsequently gave to his son Marinus as a dowry. Now, Marinus' son-in-law, Marinus son of Landulf, returned the mill to bishop Richard, who paid off the debt.[16]

(iii) *The Mancanellas*

Similarly limited were the landowning activities of the Mancanella family. They are first recorded in 1000, with property at the unidentified estate Mallianum.[17] Like the Coronellas, it was under the rule of dukes Atenolf I and Atenolf II that a family member achieved prominence, for John Mancanella seems to have been favoured as a scribe under Atenolf I[18] and his eponymous son and successor.[19] Unlike Marinus Coronella, however, he did not disappear after the Atenolfan fall, but seems to have come under the protection of the Gaetan church of St Theodore. He had written the donations of the dukes to the church,[20] and acted as a scribe for the abbot of St Theodore in a dispute in 1068.[21] In the same year, we discover he had a tomb plot within the church precincts.[22] This connection leads me to suspect that John was himself a cleric. Alternatively it may be the case that the Mancanellas had made substantial donations to the church to earn the tomb plot; if so, no evidence survives.

A thirty year gap ensues before we meet the Mancanellas again. Their prolonged absence from the documentation is partly attributable to the patchy nature of the latter; very few documents issued at Gaeta survive from this period, when the Capuan Normans took control of the city.

[15] *CDC* 197; see above, chapter 5, section (a). [16] *CDC* 313. [17] *CDC* 104.
[18] *CDC* 203. [19] *CDC* 218, *CDC* 222. [20] *CDC* 203, *CDC* 218.
[21] *CDC* 237. [22] *CDC* 236.

That the takeover did not affect the status of the Mancanella family as modest landowners with a place at the ducal courts is shown by our evidence from the late eleventh and early twelfth centuries. Bonus Mancanella is mentioned in 1098 as owning land in Scauri.[23] In 1109 we see John Bonus Mancanella acting as a witness at a court-case brought before duke Richard of Gaeta.[24] Some indication of John's status, apart from the very fact of his presence, can be gained by examining the other people mentioned in the document; his co-witnesses included Docibilis Caracci and one Gregory Salpa. The dispute to be judged was between the church of St Erasmus and one Constantine Gattula, and was recorded by Leo Baraballu. We have already traced Docibilis' family connections, and we shall soon see that the other three named men were all members of prominent families. John Mancanella was in very good company.

In 1121 we see another John Mancanella, son of Stephen, buying a piece of land in Planciano (Monte Orlando) just outside Gaeta.[25] Although comparisons are not without their problems, it seems that John was charged a very high price for his new property. The 100 *solidi* of Pavian *denarii* that he spent was the price of four cellars in Gaeta in 1119.[26] A loan of that sum would have required security of five warehouses in Gaeta in 1125.[27] It is unfortunate that there are not directly comparable land transactions, but the Planciano sale can be put in some sort of context if we look at a sale in 1104 of another piece of land, which lay in Dragoncello and sold for just one-twentieth of the price.[28]

Why was the Planciano land so valuable? Its proximity to Gaeta was a major factor; the Mancanellas' activities largely centred around the city. It is possible that the city itself was expanding at this time, and that the family were speculatively buying up land in the only possible direction of expansion along the narrow Gaetan peninsula.

However, the point is surely not how valuable the land was *per se*, but how much the Mancanellas were prepared to pay for it. Like their contemporaries the Coronellas, they may have been seen as having large amounts of disposable wealth, causing vendors to raise the price accordingly. It is also important to remember that the Mancanella clan could not boast any titled member among

[23] *CDC* 273. [24] *CDC* 284. [25] *CDC* 298. [26] *CDC* 292.
[27] *CDC* 307. [28] *CDC* 276.

their number. They had wealth, but they had little status in the eyes of others if they could not tie that wealth to landed property. In this context, what better land to buy than a piece of property in the old heartland of Docibilan power? Although only John is named as the purchaser, his action must have met with the approval of the rest of the clan, for another member, Docibilis son of Bonus Mancanella, appears as a witness. The latter's name, repeated in other eleventh-century clans may represent another facet of the family's attempt to 'age' itself; it could, after all, claim a history extending back into the period of Docibilan rule. At the very least the more frequent occurrence of the name Docibilis in Gaeta in the eleventh century may represent a political statement on the part of the families who included it in their genealogies, or proof that the former rulers of the city had had a profound effect on that city's memory.

As far as the Mancanellas' attempt to create an impression of semi-nobility is concerned, their association with the Caracci family in 1109 and 1121[29] cannot be coincidental, for the latter too are traceable from the Docibilan period and, of course, had themselves been associated with (or more precisely, patronised by) the noble Kampuli.

The social aspirations of the Mancanella appear to have paid off by 1123. In that year one Docibilis Mancanella son of Marinus (note again the occurrence of the Docibilan lead-name) is numbered among the *consules et maiores* of Gaeta.[30] Other members of the family, Stephen in 1127 and John Bonus in 1129, also achieved the consular office, and Docibilis himself is named as son of Marinus the *consul* in the latter year.[31] In 1132 Docibilis son of Bonus Mancanella acted as a judge in a dispute between two members of another prominent family, the Gattulas (see below), and it is reasonable to assume that he did so with the same or even a greater degree of authority as the consuls.[32] This group of men seems to have been responsible for running the internal and commercial affairs of the city under the sovereignty of the princes of Capua.[33]

This political prominence was mirrored by evidence of an increase in the wealth of the family, if the case of Mira Mancanella, widow of one Peter Aderradi, can be taken as any indication.

[29] *CDC* 284, *CDC* 298. [30] *CDC* 301.
[31] *CDC* 311, *CDC* 319, *CDC* 317 respectively. [32] *CDC* 322.
[33] On judges and consuls, see above, chapter 5, section (d).

Becoming a member of the cathedral community,[34] she surrendered all her lands to the bishopric of Gaeta. These included: houses in the city, a shop, a cellar, land in Casaregia, Mola, Flumicello, Fondi, Capua, Teano, Aversa, Carinola, Traetto, Itri, Maranola, Spigno, and Fratte.[35] The ownership of lands outside the old borders of the duchy of Gaeta is the most obvious result of the new political situation from the late eleventh century onwards. Mancanella interests in commerce even further afield are illustrated by a later piece of evidence. In 1190 one Bonus 'Manganella' witnessed a contract written at Genoa.[36]

A final piece of evidence from the seventeenth century indicates that the Mancanellas did eventually achieve the status of nobles of Gaeta. Onorato Gaetani d'Aragona relates how the development of an urban patriciate of Gaeta, or Sedile, culminated in a series of royal charters in the sixteenth and seventeenth centuries, listing those families who were officially recognised as noblemen of Gaeta. From the list of 1660 we see that the 'Manganella', by then extinct, had been classed among these noblemen.[37]

(iv) *The Maltacias*

Alongside Docibilis Mancanella in the 1123 document appears one Jacob Maltacia, also titled *consul* and *maior*. The Maltacias are present in our documentation from 1006. In that year Marinus son of Anatolius de Maltacia appeared as a witness for the otherwise unknown Leo son of Gregory.[38] Throughout the eleventh century all we see the Maltacias doing is acting as witnesses. Marinus' sons Leo and Constantine are both visible in this role, the latter achieving the status of a witness for duke Atenolf II and his mother duchess Maria in a gift to the church of St Theodore in 1063.[39] In 1064 he appears alongside Peter Caracci and John Mancanella in a witness list for one Peter son of Sergius.[40] The family's next appearance was in 1124, when Bonushomo Maltacia's house in Gaeta was used as a point of reference in a boundary clause.[41] The

[34] Perhaps in the same way as the *conversi* of the North in the same period: D. Osheim, 'Conversion, *conversi* and the Christian life in late medieval Tuscany', *Speculum*, 58 (1983), 368–90. [35] *CDC* 321.

[36] D. Abulafia, *The Two Italies* (Cambridge, 1977), p. 179. On the external contacts and commerce of Gaeta, see below, chapter 8.

[37] Gaetani d'Aragona, *Memorie Storiche*, p. 95.

[38] *CDC* 112. [39] *CDC* 218. [40] *CDC* 222. [41] *CDC* 305.

history of the Maltacia family at Gaeta does not end there, however. Both the Caracci and Mancanella families continue to appear in the twelfth-century documentation, and the Maltacias seem to have formed part of their circle of associates, reaching a similar level on the social scale with the elevation of Jacob to the consulate in 1129.[42] Other families too associated with the Maltacias: Docibilis son of Marinus Cotina co-witnessed with Leo son of Bonus in 1128,[43] and the execution of Jacob's will in 1135 reads like a *Who's-Who* of Gaetan society. It was executed by Leo, just mentioned, and reveals that Jacob's concubine (*amabili*) was a Capomazza, Matrona.[44] The execution was witnessed by a Gattula and a Boccapasu.[45] The will itself reveals much about Jacob's life. He left 40 *solidi* of Pavian *denarii* for his soul, and 3 pounds each to Matrona and to his daughter Bona. Matrona received his bed and bedclothes as well, but no other property from her former lover. The church of St Maria at Sperlonga benefited from a bequest of land in Valle Caprina and Vetera, and the church of St Angelus, where Jacob was buried, received land at Bazzanu. Apart from another bequest at 'Cepopa' (Cecropa?), the executors were ordered to sell the remainder of Jacob's property and, having paid his debts, divide the cash between Bona, Jacob's nephews and the daughter of Matrona Capomazza. The will is quite reticent about Jacob's landed estate, suggesting that he had other property which did not need to be distributed in a will.[46] It also shows the importance of liquid wealth to the Gaetan aristocracy at this time, although it is notable that land had to be sold before debts could be paid.

Other recorded property of the family includes a vineyard at Vendici given to Marinus son of Leo by his uncle Constantine son of Gregory in 1132.[47]

The family's history continues throughout the twelfth century, with various members achieving prominence. The otherwise unknown Hieronymus son of Hieronymus is recorded as consul in 1135,[48] and another member of the family, Bonus son of Bonus,

42 *CDC* 317. 43 *CDC* 316.

44 On the Capomazzas, see above, chapter 5, section (b,i). 45 *CDC* 328.

46 If Jacob had other children, especially sons, for example, it would be automatically assumed that they would inherit most of his property. His wife must have been dead by now: there is no indication that Jacob's daughter Bona was by Matrona.

47 *CDC* 324. 48 *CDC* 327.

achieved that dignity in 1149, although the status of the latter is open to question.[49] He and his brother Marinus are seen in that year receiving a tomb in the cathedral 'next to that of duke Docibilis'. What they had done to gain such an honour is unclear, although the likelihood is that they had contributed to the fabric or finances of the church.[50] It is certain that the family had risen to the highest rank of Gaetan society, and it is probably the same Marinus who acted as advocate in a dispute of 1157.[51] The culmination of the family's history was the elevation in the late thirteenth century of one Bartholomew Maltacia to the position of bishop of Gaeta. He was a close associate of king Charles I of Anjou, and was responsible for the construction of the bell-tower on top of Gaeta cathedral.[52] Finally, 'perche vivevano nobilmente',[53] the Maltacia family are included in the 1660 list of the prominent families of Gaeta as 'substitute nobles' (*nobili surrogati*). Like the Mancanellas by this time, the family is described as extinct.

(v) *The Salpas*

The origins of the Salpa family were almost as early as those of the Maltacias in the documents. The first member we meet, Gregory son of John, witnessed a dispute between count Dauferius of Traetto and the abbot of Montecassino, Atenolf, in 1014.[54] The court-case was held at Traetto, and this marries well with the districts in which Gregory owned land. His donations to the church of SS John and Paul at Gaeta are recorded in 1059 as lying in the districts of Flumicellum (the Ausente valley) and Scauri.[55] Five years later one John Salpa, who is not securely identifiable, is mentioned as having offered land in Maranula (between the Ausente and Garigliano rivers) to the church of St Erasmus at Formia.[56]

The Salpas are documented as frequent church patrons. Not only do we hear of their gifts to the churches mentioned above, but also a document of 1052 shows that the heirs of John Salpa had a tomb plot at the church of St John the Baptist at Gaeta,[57] and later

[49] I suggested above, chapter 5, section (d,iii), that by this date the function of consul might have been as part of an incoming Norman hierarchy.
[50] *CDC* 340; the document is witnessed by their relative Gregory son of Pero.
[51] *CDC* 344. [52] Gaetani d'Aragona, *Memorie Storiche*, p. 359.
[53] *ibid.*, p. 97. [54] *CDC* 130. [55] *CDC* 208. [56] *CDC* 222.
[57] *CDC* 191.

evidence of their activities does indicate that, whilst their landowning interests were concentrated in the east around Traetto, much of their political activity took place in Gaeta. It also indicates that they were of a similar aristocratic standing as those clans already discussed. In 1071 Constantine son of John Salpa was present when Sergius son of Kampulus the prefect drew up his will.[58] Quite apart from the fact that he was witnessing for a member of the prestigious Kampuli clan (whose last appearance in our documents this is), Constantine was co-witnessing with Bernard son of Mastalus the magnificent (of the Mauri family) and members of another prominent family, the Lanciacane, of whom more presently.

Constantine's son Gregory, the last of the Salpa family to appear in the period under discussion, seems to have had an even wider circle of contacts. In a remarkable document of 1105 he is listed as one of a Gaetan consortium in dispute with Ptolomeus, consul and count of Tusculum, over the co-ownership of a ship.[59] One of his partners was a Leo Cotina,[60] and Gregory renewed his association with that family in 1108 when he witnessed a document for Bona, widow of Anatolius Cotina.[61] The following year he was present at a dispute between the church of St Erasmus at Formia and one Constantine Gattula, son of Christopher.[62] His co-witnesses were highly respected men at Gaeta, and included John Mancanella, Leo Baraballu,[63] and Docibilis Caracci. With Constantine's disappearance from the documents, the Salpas vanish too.

(vi) *The de Arciu/Maulottas*

The de Arciu/Maulotta family, too, had external contacts, two of their number being included in the consortium who disputed the ship with Ptolomeus of Tusculum in 1105. However, one member of the family had been very heavily involved in influencing the internal pattern of power at Gaeta, putting up the silver to buy the bishopric for Leo in 1049. The fact was acknowledged by Leo in 1054, when he granted to Stephen and his partner Gregory

[58] *CDC* 245.

[59] *CDC* 278; to settle the dispute, the Gaetans seem to have bought out the Tusculan share – they paid 24 pounds of Pavian *denarii* and received the ship.

[60] See below, section (a,viii). [61] *CDC* 283. [62] *CDC* 284.

[63] See below, section (a,xi).

Coronella the profits of the episcopal water-mill called de Ferruccio, for as long as he and his brother Docibilis owed them the silver.[64] Two years earlier, Leo had given Stephen a site for the de Arciu family sepulchre in the church of St John the Baptist at Gaeta in return for his 'services and building work'.[65] Whether Stephen had literally been involved in the building work for the bishop, or whether he had patronised the work monetarily is unclear. 'Some noble Gaetans' are recorded as contributing 5½ pounds of silver in 1008 towards the building work to Bernard, the bishop at that time.[66] We do not know if Stephen was among them, but, given the evidence that he could produce a substantial amount of liquid wealth in the middle of the century, he had probably made a similar donation.

Unlike some of their contemporaries, the de Arcius do not appear to have been concerned to turn their liquid wealth into land. In 1087 Stephen's heirs are mentioned as owning a house in Gaeta,[67] and, even after a marriage between Benedict son of John de Arciu and Maria Maulotta, the lands of the combined clan did not extend beyond Casa Regula (modern Casarevole?), less than 5 kilometres from Gaeta.[68] This pattern continues in the twelfth-century evidence. We know that one 'Matthia Madelmo' was consul of Gaeta in 1129, and on the basis of the occurrence of the unusual name Madelmus he may have been a member of the family.[69] Similarly, one Docibilis son of Madelmus appears as a witness in a much later document, dated 1167, but we know nothing of the family's landed possessions in this period.[70] An explanation for this, and for the isolated appearances of the de Arcius, might be found if we pursue the connection with the authors of the latter document, the Gattula family. For in 1179 Marucza de Arcia is recorded as the widow of one John Gattula, and her son took his father's name.[71] The history of the Gattulas will be discussed presently, but, if the de Arciu clan were less wealthy or politically important, they might have found it difficult to acquire property without 'disappearing' into the families with a higher profile at Gaeta. It is significant that they do not appear in the later lists of Gaetan noble families, and we should probably characterise them as one of the client families in the city at this time.

[64] *CDC* 197. [65] *CDC* 191. [66] *CDC* 115. [67] *CDC* 258.
[68] *CDC* 272. [69] *CDC* 319. [70] *CDC* 348. [71] *CDC* 358.

(vii) *The Boccapasus*

Similarly limited were the landed interests of the Boccapasu family, who had a representative, Leo, in the consortium of 1105. They are the most poorly documented of the families under scrutiny, yet they fall into what is becoming a recognisable pattern of clans with modest landowning interests, some commercial activity and, as a document of 1059 illustrates, a desire to give to the church. In that year Marinus, the priest of the church of SS John and Paul in Gaeta drew up a list of its possessions.[72] Among them was land at Fontanulo (near Mamurrano) given by Docibilis Boccapasu and Maru wife of Agnellus Boccapasu. Leo's experience of dealing within a Gaetan consortium may represent the family's attempt to achieve a network of contacts with other families at Gaeta, and Marinus Boccapasu benefited from this when he became consul in 1127.[73] But the appearance of Gregory son of Leo Boccapasu as a witness to the execution of Jacob Maltacia's will in 1135 probably confirms the Boccapasu family's status as clients, and they disappear from the sources after this date.

(viii) *The Cotinas*

It is in the role of donors to the church that we can see the next family to emerge in the documents, the Cotinas. In 1064 John Cotina, son of Nicephorus gave his family's church foundation dedicated to St Mary at Gruttelle in Flumetica, plus some land, to the church of St Erasmus in Formia.[74] The family's interests seem to have largely centred on the Flumetica district, in particular Suio. In 1056 John Cotina had acted as a witness for John son of Hugh, count of Suio,[75] and in the 1064 transaction we learn that his two daughters were married to two brothers descended from a cadet branch of the Suian comital dynasty, (see genealogy, Figure 6.1). This close relationship with the Suians was disrupted soon afterwards, however. In 1078, as we saw earlier, prince Jordan of Capua had confiscated the castle from count Raynerius and his consorts, and taken away their goods.[76]

The effects of this upheaval can be seen on the pattern of Cotina documents thereafter. All the recorded activities of the family from

[72] *CDC* 208. [73] *CDC* 311. [74] *CDC* 225.
[75] *CDC* 202. [76] *CDC* 251; see above, chapter 5, section (c,iii).

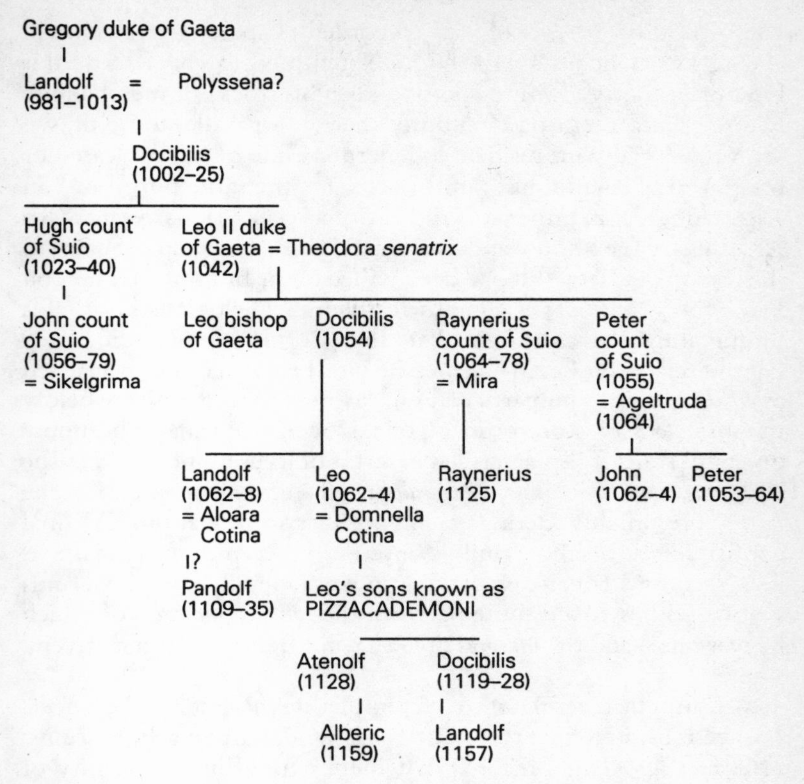

Figure 6.1 *The counts of Suio and their descendants*

1079 onwards were centred around Gaeta. In that year Anatolius son of Gregory Cotina witnessed a sale of Mola land recorded in the city.[77] Perhaps the clearest indication of the direction of Cotina interests after the fall of the Suian dynasty is a document issued by the widow of John Cotina, Marenda, in 1089. In it she states that she is resident in Gaeta, and gives land at Scauri to the church of St Theodore in the city.[78] Her sons, John and Anatolius, gave their consent to the transaction.

It is unfortunate that later members of the Cotina clan cannot be related with certainty to their earlier ancestors, but their activities can still be said to have been Gaeta-based. Leo Cotina, son of Docibilis, was the family's representative in the Gaetan trading

[77] *CDC* 254. [78] *CDC* 261.

consortium of 1105. Leo's only recorded property was a cellar in Gaeta, mentioned in 1119.[79] One is tempted to characterise this kind of property as somewhere to keep his stocks of merchandise before selling them on. Certainly there is a parallel to be drawn with the Amalfitans resident at Salerno, some of whom leased or bought very small houses in that city for the same purpose.[80] In 1108 another member of the Cotina clan, Bona widow of Anatolius, gave a house and a *pothega* in Gaeta and land in Scauri to the bishop of Gaeta.[81] It had been willed to the bishopric by her son Leo, who was now buried in the cathedral. The document itself is illuminating; it confirms that the Cotina family did keep commercial premises in Gaeta – the word *pothega* can be translated as warehouse.[82] This particular one lay next to the sea-shore below the *medialoca* or storeroom of one Docibilis Purina. The house given by Bona is also described in terms of its usefulness: it was, she said, made up of a cellar, a *medialoca* and a *ventum* or top floor, the latter presumably acting as living accommodation. A final confirmation of the family's interest in commercial affairs is furnished by a court-case of 1124, when Docibilis son of Marinus Cotina witnessed a dispute between the *consuls*, *maiores* (of which he was one?) and the *minores* of Gaeta and Bello the Roman over a ship.[83]

We must be careful not to overemphasise this interest, however. For we must note that the Cotinas had land, particularly, it seems, in Scauri. De Santis records that there existed in the vicinity of Traetto in the fourteenth century a Terra or Torre di Cotina, which could very well refer to the family's lands or fortified house in Scauri.[84] This evidence is a timely reminder that very few men in this period could make a living from trade alone. Individual members of the family continue to appear as witnesses to documents throughout the twelfth century,[85] but we have no further evidence about their property or political activities.

Unlike most of the other families under discussion in this section,

[79] *CDC* 292. [80] See below, chapter 8. [81] *CDC* 283.

[82] It is derived from the Greek word *αποθηκη*, meaning storehouse. Given that Gaeta had previously strong links with Naples, the adaption of a Greek term into Latin should perhaps not surprise us. [83] *CDC* 302.

[84] A. de Santis, 'Centri del basso Garigliano abitati nel Medioevo e abbandonati nei secoli 16 e 17', *BISI*, 75 (1963), 394.

[85] *CDC* 316 (1128): Docibilis son of Marini co-witnesses with a Maltacia; *CDC* 348 (1167): Girard son of Leo witnesses a Gattula document, suggesting clientage again; *CDC* 344 (1157): Pandulf witness to a dispute.

we may be able to postulate where the Cotinas came from. Two documents from Naples, dated 1027 and 1038,[86] include references to members of the 'Cutina' family who owned land in the Piscinule district north-east of Naples and had strong connections with the church of Sorrento. Nothing but the similarity of their name relates the Neapolitans to the Gaetan clan, but one should not discount the possibility that the former were the ancestors of the latter.

(ix) *The Castaneas*

One of the consuls of Gaeta named in the dispute with Bello the Roman in 1124 was Gregory, son of Marinus Castanea. In the same year, and in the same capacity, he appears again receiving a guarantee from Docibilis son of Gregory de Anatoli[87] that the latter would not build his house above a certain height. Gregory, however, was not the first of his family to achieve the position of consul: his relative (in what capacity we do not know) Anatolius is named as one of the consuls of 1123,[88] and other members of the family, John son of Leo (twice, in 1129 and 1134) and Gualganus son of Leo, possibly his brother (in 1135) also achieved this dignity. Add to this the fact that Anatolius son of Anatolius Castanea witnessed a ducal document in the city in 1134,[89] and the picture is of a family who were at the centre of Gaeta's political life.

There is very little documentation from which to ascertain the reason for the powerful position of the Castaneas in the early twelfth century. We know from a document of 1059 that Marinus Castanea, Gregory's grandfather, owned land at Fontanulo,[90] and that Gregory's father Marinus, son of Marinus, had been witness to a settlement between bishop Raynald of Gaeta and one Leo Trituru in 1091.[91] But the latter association was surely a result of a now undocumented prominence in the eleventh century, rather than a cause of their prominence in the twelfth? If we examine other pieces of twelfth-century evidence, the power of the Castaneas is apparent. In a rare document, perhaps conforming more to contemporary northern Italian examples, they are recorded in 1131 as owning a tower in the city,[92] itself a statement of their ambitions. Association with other powerful families followed, or

[86] *RN* 412, *RN* 470. [87] *CDC* 305. [88] *CDC* 301. [89] *CDC* 326.
[90] *CDC* 208; Marinus' vineyard lay next to land belonging to the Boccapasu family.
[91] *CDC* 264. [92] *CDC* 321.

perhaps contributed to, this rise: Munda Castanea is recorded as the widow of Christopher Gattula in 1132,[93] and her gift of a shop by the Salini gate of Gaeta reveals that the family still had commercial interests.

It seems that the rise of the Castaneas did not end, for the 'Castagna' family are recorded as nobles in the patriciate list at Gaeta in 1587.[94] By the seventeenth century, however, like other families we have met in this chapter, their line died out.

(x) *The Lanciacani*

Association with the older nobility may explain the brief period of prominence of the Lanciacane family, from 1067 to 1084. They appear exclusively as witnesses during that period, but the social status of those for whom they witnessed suggests that the Lanciacane clan do belong among the families under discussion here. John Lanciacane and his sons Marinus and Kampulus all appeared as witnesses for Sergius son of Kampulus the prefect in 1071,[95] and both John and Kampulus were associated more than once with Peter son of John Caracci.[96] The most likely explanation for the Lanciacane family's appearance in our documentation is that they, like the Caracci, were patronised by the powerful Kampuli. But, whilst the Caracci were able to use a strong land base to survive the rise of new families at Gaeta, the Lanciacane do not seem to have had that degree of security, and so faded back into obscurity when the Kampuli were no longer powerful. No further evidence for them survives.

(xi) *The Baraballus*

The Lanciacani could not have been helped by the rapidity with which some families emerged to challenge the old order. Such a family were the Baraballus, who are first recorded only in 1071. In that year, we learn, Mirus son of Constantine Baraballu owned a house in Gaeta.[97] This family, too, had a member, Girard, involved in the Gaeta trade consortium of 1105, and he is recorded earlier as a landowner at Curallum just outside Gaeta in 1085.[98] Perhaps the clearest indication of where the Baraballus centred

[93] *CDC* 322. [94] Gaetani d'Aragona, *Memorie Storiche*, p. 95. [95] *CDC* 245.
[96] *CDC* 240, *CDC* 241. [97] *CDC* 245. [98] *CDC* 259.

their landed wealth is given by a document of 1091, in which John son of Landulf Baraballu sold land in Palazzo near Formia to his daughter Sergia and her husband John son of Peter.[99] Other landowners in the area included Mirus, who was John's nephew, another nephew (or niece?) Beneincasa, and John's sister-in-law Matrona Mancina. Just over a mile further down the Via Appia lay Scauri, and in 1098 John divided land here with his brother Leo son of Landulf.[100] In this context Girard Baraballu's commercial outing of 1105 seems to be the action of a man whose family had a strong landed base and could afford to risk some capital on less secure money-making enterprises.

The Baraballus had contacts with many of the other aristocratic families of the period. As witnesses we can link Mirus son of Constantine with the de Arciu/Maulotta family in 1096,[101] and his brothers Gregory and Leo with the Caracci and Castanea clans in 1091.[102] In 1109 Leo son of Constantine mediated in a dispute between the abbot of St Erasmus and Constantine Gattula, in the presence of many prominent men of Gaeta including John Mancanella, Gregory Salpa and Atenolf of the Mauri family.[103]

With such contacts, one might expect a member of the Baraballus to achieve the dignity of consul of Gaeta, as the other families had done, but we have no record of this happening.[104] This, though, is perhaps the fault of the documentation, for there was nothing wrong with the family's credentials to hold office. In a document of 1120 we see they had expanded their formerly localised landed base. In that year six descendants of the earlier Baraballus (see genealogy, Figure 6.2) divided up communally held land. As might be expected, property in Palazzo was included, and the document reveals an expansion westward into Mola. But, far from conforming to the pattern of compact landholdings that has emerged from the evidence of other families, the Baraballus also now had land at Paniano near Itri, and in the Ausente valley.[105]

Despite the lack of consuls on the family, it is not surprising to find the wealthy Baraballus in positions of responsibility in Gaeta in the twelfth century. Particularly worthy of note is Docibilis son of Leo, who appears as a witness to a Mancanella document

[99] *CDC* 265. [100] *CDC* 273. [101] *CDC* 292. [102] *CDC* 264.
[103] *CDC* 284.
[104] Although Mirus son of Leo, consul in 1124, may have been a Baraballu on account of his fairly distinctive name. [105] *CDC* 295.

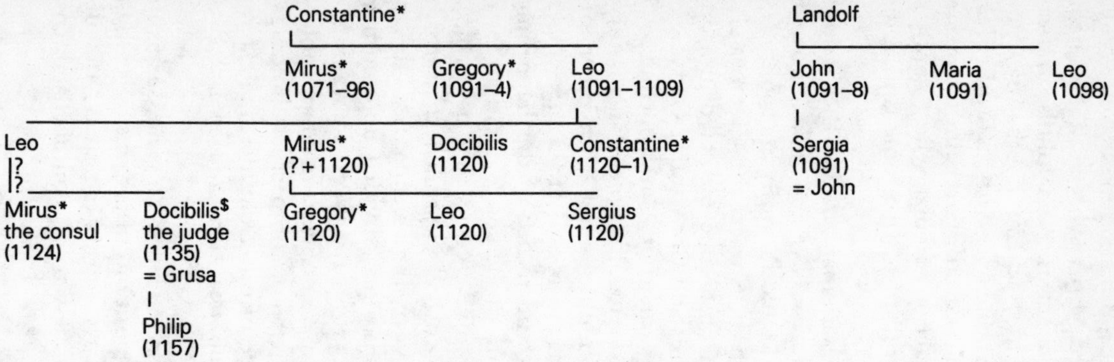

Constantine*

Mirus* (1071–96) | Gregory* (1091–4) | Leo (1091–1109)

Leo | Mirus* (? + 1120) | Docibilis (1120) | Constantine* (1120–1)

Mirus* the consul (1124) | Docibilis$ the judge (1135) = Grusa

Philip (1157)

Gregory* (1120) | Leo (1120) | Sergius (1120)

Landolf

John (1091–8) | Maria (1091) | Leo (1098)

Sergia (1091) = John

Other members: Girard (1085–1105), Bonus (+ pre 1091), Beneincasa (1091), Gemma (1159)

The family is traceable down two distinct lines: perhaps Landolf and Constantine were brothers.

* Although the Baraballus identified themselves with a surname, lead-names seem to have persisted.

$There is no direct evidence for the identity of Docibilis' father; I have suggested that he was the son of this Leo on the basis that nephews were often named after uncles.

Figure 6.2 *The Baraballu family*

alongside a Gattula in 1131[106] and perhaps should be identified as the same man as Docibilis the judge. In 1134 the latter acted alongside the consuls of Gaeta.[107] In the same year Docibilis son of Leo witnessed a ducal document issued by duke Richard.[108] It is likely that the two Docibilis' were the same man, for Docibilis the judge continued his association with the duke's nominee, William Blosseville, in the following year when he and his wife Grusa bought land from William.[109] The position of judge may then have been equivalent in honour to the consulate, but with a specifically legal function. It may simply be coincidence that the sole appearance of Docibilis' son, Philip, occurs as a witness to a dispute in 1157,[110] but by citing his father's occupation Philip added greater authority to his presence.

Records of the family's wealth and connections continue in the twelfth century. In a rare example of its type, a document of 1171 records that Pasca widow of Constantine Baraballu and her sons John and Nicolas had provided a dowry for her daughter Trocta to marry.[111] The groom, Bonus Campello, acknowledged receipt of 8 pounds of Amalfitan *tari*, some silk and a pair of gold earrings. Contemporary evidence from elsewhere in the South reveals this to have been something of a standard trousseau: the appearance of Amalfitan coinage will be discussed a little later. In 1159 Gemma Baraballu, daughter of Mirus and widow of John Gattula, mortgaged land in Paniano to the abbess of St Martin, Scholastica.[112] Apart from revealing a continued link with the Gattula family, this document may also suggest a reason for the earlier rise of the Baraballu family to prominence. For Gemma states that she had bought the land from Aloara 'Glossavilla', her mother. The similarity between this surname and that of the rulers of Gaeta suggests strongly that the Baraballus had close links with the latter, although these are now obscured by the lack of documentation. The Baraballu rise clearly continued, however. In 1290 Matteo Baraballu became bishop of the city,[113] and the family are listed among the highest ranks of the Gaetan patriciate in 1660, although by that date their line was extinct.[114]

106 *CDC* 321. 107 *CDC* 325. 108 *CDC* 326.

109 *CDC* 329 (1135); the couple subsequently received a guarantee of loyalty from William's vassals on the land: *CDC* 330 (1136). 110 *CDC* 344.

111 *CDC* 352. 112 *CDC* 346. 113 Ferraro, *Memorie*, p. 210.

114 Gaetani d'Aragona, *Memorie Storiche*, p. 95.

(xii) *The Gattulas*

Similarly highly honoured were the Gattula family, who are again a late addition to our circle of Gaetan aristocrats, and who have featured prominently in the histories of other families so far mentioned. As the Gattolas, they appear in the 1660 patriciate list as the lords of Sperlonga,[115] and among their descendants in the eighteenth century were don Erasmo Gattola, historian and abbot of Montecassino[116] and Girolamo Gattola, author of an incomplete history of Gaeta conserved in manuscript form in the archive of Montecassino.[117]

What were the origins of this illustrious family? When we meet our first member in 1091, he was already exhibiting a degree of authority. Constantine Gattula son of Constantine appears as a guarantor of the settlement of a dispute between Raynald, bishop of Gaeta, and one Leo Trituru.[118] In the twelfth century, using the additional name Burdone, we see Constantine as a consul of Gaeta alongside Mancanella and Castanea family representatives.[119]

Other members of the family appear in landowning context. Leo Gattula was a neighbour of the Baraballus in Palazzo,[120] and in 1099 Docibilis Gattula bought a house site in the castle of Asprana[121] from Crescentius lord of Rocca de Monticelli.[122] Although tenuous, this interest in the extreme west may indicate the beginnings of the Gattula family's rise to the position of lords of Sperlonga.

Other members of the clan had interests closer to Gaeta. In 1109 Constantine Gattula son of Christopher disputed and lost land near to the mills of St George and Maiore, near Mola, to Ursus, the abbot of St Erasmus at Formia.[123] It is interesting to look at the background of this case, which was judged at the court of duke Richard in the presence of Mancanella, Salpa, Baraballu and Caracci family representatives. Constantine claimed that the land had been given to his ancestors by the parishioners of St George 'in the time of duke John I', and showed the charter recording the gift. Ursus in response produced charters showing how duchess Emilia

[115] *Ibid.*, p. 96. [116] See above, chapter 1, section (c).

[117] At least the manuscript was preserved there in 1887; *CDC*, 1, preface p. xii.

[118] *CDC* 264. [119] *CDC* 301 (1123), *CDC* 302 (1124). [120] *CDC* 265.

[121] For the location of this castle: V. Bartoloni, 'Indagine preliminare del sito di Asprano', *BISALM*, 12 (1987), 174.

[122] *CDC* 274. Monticelli lay on the site of the modern Monte S. Biagio: Amante and Bianchi, *Memorie*, p. 3. [123] *CDC* 284.

of Gaeta had given the land to Marinus Coronella, who had given it to his slave Petrocurso, who had subsequently given and sold it to St Erasmus. In addition, Ursus swore to his case, whilst Constantine was unwilling to do so, and so St Erasmus was adjudged to own the property.

This case in effect shows up the way in which members of the newly prominent families at Gaeta were eager to associate themselves with the older order – the lands around Mola, rather like those at Planciano bought by the Mancanellas, had strong Docibilan ducal connections. Whilst the Gattulas mingled freely with other new families – as well as being neighbours of the Baraballu clan, Girard Gattula witnessed the division of the Baraballu lands in 1120[124] – they also seem to have tried to 'age' themselves. This tendency is illustrated perhaps by the occurrence once again of the name Docibilis in the family, but more particularly by Constantine's assertion that Gattula claim to the St George land stretched back 200 years. It is noticeable, though, that he was not prepared to swear to the veracity of his claim. Another way of suggesting that the family were more established than they actually were was the association with older clans. We see evidence of this in two documents of 1119 and 1125. In the first Maria, widow of Docibilis Caracci, bought a cellar in Gaeta. In the second she resold it at a profit.[125] Witness to both was Christopher Gattula son of Docibilis. Since the Caracci by this time could claim to have the longest family pedigree at Gaeta, the Gattulas perhaps saw them as useful patrons or associates. The association certainly did them no harm, as their subsequent history illustrates. Whilst the Caracci fade from view, Gattula documents dominate the twelfth-century evidence from Gaeta.

Before examining this evidence in detail, a problem of identification arises. It is clear as the century progressed that the use of a surname became acceptable in itself as a means of identification, sometimes allied with a secondary surname (Constantine Burdo or Burdone, mentioned above, is a good example of the latter). However, whilst the surname became the norm, families tended to retain the idea of a lead-name as well, Constantine being the favourite of the Gattulas. The result is that there are several Constantine Gattulas present in the documents who are difficult to distinguish from each other, especially when they do not give their

[124] *CDC* 295. [125] *CDC* 292, *CDC* 309.

fathers' names. This causes a problem in trying to follow the careers of individual members of the family, but the inability to do so may not be a particular drawback. The power of the Gattulas lay in their number, and in the fact that they seem to have been represented in all the important spheres of influence in Gaeta at this time. Acting as a group, just as earlier the Docibilans or the Kampuli had done, the Gattulas were able to assert themselves as one of the most influential families at Gaeta, arguably the most powerful. How is this reflected in their twelfth-century documents?

One feature of Gattula documents that is immediately apparent is the number of links the family had with other clans in the city. We have already seen some evidence of this, but further examples occur in the later documents. Thus Constantine son of Munda executed the will of Docibilis Frunzo in 1128 with a member of the Pizzacademone family.[126] Another Constantine, son of Leo, was present at the execution of Jacob Maltacia's will in 1135.[127] In 1131 Constantine son of Constantine co-witnessed a document of a member of the Mancanella family with a representative of the Baraballus.[128] If we could safely connect this Constantine with the consul of the same name visible in 1129,[129] his appearance as a witness might be connected with his office. However, the Gattulas might have had a more personal relationship with both the Mancanellas and the Baraballus. In a rare dispute between members of the family in 1132, it was to a Mancanella that they went to resolve the problem.[130] Later evidence reveals that John Gattula had been married to one Gemma Baraballu.[131]

The consulate was an office which the Gattulas seem to have been keen to dominate. Given the breadth of action and power that the Norman sovereigns of Gaeta seem to have allowed the consuls, this is not surprising. Besides Constantine Burdo (1123/4) and Constantine son of Constantine (1129), another Constantine, son of Docibilis, held the office in 1134.[132]

Another position of influence with which the family developed a close association was the bishopric of Gaeta. Leo son of Christopher acted as a witness on an episcopal document of 1128,

[126] *CDC* 314, and see below, p. 236. [127] *CDC* 328. [128] *CDC* 321.

[129] *CDC* 317, *CDC* 319.

[130] *CDC* 322: Constantine son of Constantine the consul disputed with Christopher, Girard and Burdo (another Constantine?) sons of Constantine over a shop by the Salini gate. Another member of the family, Leo son of Christopher, witnessed the settlement.

[131] *CDC* 346 (1159); Gemma was by this date widowed. [132] *CDC* 325.

and Matrona the widow of Iaquintus, and Constantine and Marinus sons of Constantine contributed in 1152 to the cost of building steps for the bishopric.[133] This interest may be connected with the Gattulas' property-owning in the city, for the shop by the Salini gate that had formed the subject of the dispute of 1132 seems to have lain near the bishopric. It or other shops owned by the family near the same gate are described as near to the episcopal building in a later document.[134] The Gattulas seem to have had several similar properties in the same area.[135]

The family continues to be documented at Gaeta throughout the twelfth century,[136] but it may have been their commercial activities which lead the Gattulas to look outside the former duchy for exchanges. Munda, daughter of Christopher Gattula, is mentioned in 1175 as about to marry in Rome.[137] In the same decade, Gattulas begin to appear in some numbers in Amalfitan documents,[138] and here a far stronger case can be made for their involvement in commerce.

(b) A NEW ELITE: DEFINING FEATURES

I have discussed above different families, with different names and different economic interests, but it is striking how similar many of the histories sound. The adoption of surnames is a similarity between these clans in itself, and will be discussed presently. Also, most of the families can be shown to have had only limited amounts of land, concentrated in particular districts. Of course, the

[133] *CDC* 313, *CDC* 341. [134] *CDC* 360 (1182).

[135] Later evidence of such ownership includes *CDC* 358 (1179): Marucza de Arcia widow of John Gattula, and Constantine Gattula her son promise not to claim a shop owned by Richard Burdo, their relative. Further family interest is indicated by the presence of Christopher de Thoma, another Gattula, as a witness; *CDC* 360 (1182): Ugotonis Gattula son of Marini and Marenda his wife offer their shop near the bishopric near Salini gate to Montecassino. His cousins, the heirs of Iaquintus his uncle, own a shop nearby. Again a family member, Constantine son of John, witnesses the document.

[136] *CDC* 324 (1132) Christopher owns land at Vendici (boundary); *CDC* 327 (1135) Constantine son of Constantine the consul features; *CDC* 347 (1166) John Dallacerca son of Littefrid Gattula judges a dispute; *CDC* 348 (1167) and *CDC* 354 (1175) Tomaula wife of Christopher gives property to her sons and then to her husband; *CDC* 359 (1180) Marinus son of Christopher gives land to St Maria Casaregula; *CDC* 365 (1197) Marocta is abbess of St Maria and Gregory son of Adenulf witnesses her document.

[137] *CDC* 354; this marriage may have nothing to do with commercial ties, but it does at the very least illustrate that the Gattulas had established links there.

[138] Gattulas in Amalfi: *CDA* 182 (1172), *CDA* 194 (1177), *CDA* 196, *CDA* 203, *CDA* 215, *CDA* 216, *CP* 158 (1176), *CP* 175 (1184), *PAVAR* 1/54, *PAVAR* 1/63, *PAVAR* 1/64. See below, chapter 7.

phenomenon of the smaller landowner was nothing new at Gaeta; about a sixth of the Gaetan documents record modest landowners who may only appear once, and who cannot be related by transaction or birth to any well-known place or person.

Bearing in mind that the new families of the eleventh century could have owned far more land than our documentation reveals, the evidence available shows one major difference between these families and earlier 'small' landowners. That is that most of the new clans played an active role in the public life of Gaeta, either being present at the courts of post-Docibilan dukes or, after 1123, appearing as consuls. How had these men risen from their humble origins to achieve the status of representatives of the Gaetan people?

It became apparent from the story of the landowning nobility of Gaeta in the tenth century that noble birth usually conferred a position of prominence and aristocratic status, but that the aristocracy was not merely confined to those of noble birth. The rise of the Docibilans to the summit of power illustrates that wealth could sometimes compensate for lack of birth. However, it is also clear that they tried to establish marital links with the older nobility to disguise their origins still further, and ultimately these shaky foundations of their power crumbled beneath them.

The position of the new families of the eleventh century was a similar one; they had no noble ancestry to call upon, and their efforts to associate themselves with the remnants of the Docibilan nobility indicate that they were well aware of the fact. Did these links with the old order, however tenuous, help the rise of the new families? Probably not: by the time we see them buying up land and rubbing shoulders with the Kampuli and Caracci, they had already reached a certain status. They had done this through the liquidity of their wealth. Most of the families seem to have had commercial interests, and they used the profits shrewdly. The prime case is the overt buying of the bishopric at Gaeta in 1049, in outright defiance of the anti-simoniacal rumblings emanating from Rome at this time, by Stephen de Arciu and Gregory Coronella. Other transactions of the eleventh century, however, suggest that if the papal disapproval of simony was largely ignored at Gaeta, the new families did begin to heed warnings about proprietary churches. The Caracci received St Gregory from the Kampuli in 1020, and the social prestige attached to church ownership seems also to have been realised by the Cotina family, whose foundation of St Mary at Gruttelle is recorded in 1064. In that year, however, John son of Nicephorus Cotina is seen relinquishing control of the church of St Erasmus at Formia.[139] Boyd notes a trend in the eleventh century for Italian families to begin releasing their churches from family control,[140] and her evidence from northern Italy is mirrored by examples from Gaeta. As early as 1025 a consortium relinquished its share of the income of St Peter's in Scauri,[141] and in 1061 one Bonushomo son of Marinus freed his family's church of St Augustine at Vivano.[142] He did, however, make the proviso that the church was to take no other patron. Clearly if his family (who are unknown to us) could not enjoy the prestige of ownership of St Augustine's, no other family was going to either.

(c) SURNAMES

If the new families of Gaeta could express their identity through wealth, some landowning and positions of political power, what function did their surnames perform? Elsewhere, surnames were usually derived from a prominent ancestor (as I have created the surnames Kampuli or Christopherii) or from the place where the family lived or had large landholdings. Such a 'residence' surname is unknown at Gaeta. The surnames of the new elite at Gaeta did not fit in with these characteristics at all. Why should this be?

The first reason is that such surnames denoted landed wealth or noble birth, and very few of the new men, when they emerge with surnames, had either, relying instead more on liquid wealth. Their names were a peculiar mixture of meaningless words and words which derived from often colourful nicknames, neither conferring status on their bearers, nor denoting descent from a noble ancestor or ownership of land. So why did they use them at all?

The answer may lie in the occupation of these families. Most were engaged in some kind of commercial activity. Also it is a fact that a very small pool of personal names was used at Gaeta; a large proportion of the male population bore the names John, Leo, Gregory and, in the eleventh century especially, Docibilis. The essential need in a commercial transaction, particularly if it was going to be written down, was surely to be easily identifiable – to

139 *CDC* 225.
140 C. E. Boyd, *Tithes and Parishes in Medieval Italy* (New York, 1952), p. 125.
141 *CDC* 147.
142 *CDC* 212.

call oneself John son of Leo was not sufficient.[143] This may account for the unusual, but memorable, surnames being used by the newly prominent men of Gaeta. As we have seen, similar names of identification can be found among the Amalfitans and Neapolitans, although the former also solved the problem of identification by resorting to lengthy, confusing and instantly forgettable lists of their ancestors. A second reason may be that, faced with the incoming foreigners taking up estates and positions as a new nobility, the names of the Gaetans were adopted almost as a reaction to the Norman Ridells, Hautevilles, or Blossevilles, to put the administrators of Gaeta almost on an equal footing with the retinue of their new rulers.

A notable example of this phenomenon involves one line of the former counts of Suio who, deprived of that position, appear in the late eleventh and early twelfth century as a surnamed family, the Pizzacademoni. After they lost the county, the family seem to have moved to Gaeta and are seen acting very similarly to the other 'new' families there. Thus the first document to mention them overtly under their new identification shows Docibilis Pizzacademone (note the continuation of their ancestor's lead-name) as the owner of a *medialoca* or warehouse in Gaeta in 1119.[144] However, not all of the former comital family was content to make a new life and identity, as the witnessing of 'Raynerius son of Raynerius count of Suio' (the latter having been named as one of those deposed in 1078) to a document of the Conjulo family in 1125 attests.[145] The Pizzacademone name seems to be associated with the line of Docibilis, son of duke Leo II of Gaeta, a generation after Docibilis' sons Leo and Landolf are documented marrying into the Cotina family. The document of 1119 shows that Docibilis Pizzacademone's *medialoca* lay above Leo Cotina's cellar in Gaeta. Once established in the city, the family forged links with other clans. In 1128 Docibilis and his brother Atenolf were among the executors of Docibilis Frunzo's will, together with individuals from the Gattula and Pedeacetu families.[146] In 1157 Docibilis' son Landolf is documented as the judge of a dispute at which a Maltacia acted as advocate for one of the disputants and where a Baraballu and a Cotina were witnesses. Finally in 1159 Atenolf's son Alberic co-witnessed a Baraballu document with another Pedeacetu.[147]

143 Although the further a man was from home the more likely it was that the use of 'Gaetanus' or 'de Gaeta' would be sufficient identification.

144 *CDC* 292. 145 *CDC* 307. 146 *CDC* 314. 147 *CDC* 346.

Certainly, in the attempts to associate themselves with older forms of nobility and status at Gaeta there seems to have been a collective consciousness on the part of the new families of preserving their Gaetan identity in the face of the Norman takeover. That many of the families survived as nobles of Gaeta into the sixteenth century, to be listed alongside a new influx of foreigners, the Spanish, is testament to the success of their attempts.

(d) NEW FAMILIES: SPHERES OF INTERACTION

Although hampered somewhat by the less than consistent availability of evidence for the period 1000 to 1139, it is possible not only to build up a picture of the individual families who emerged at Gaeta during this period, but also to try to reconstruct some of the political and economic groupings that occurred between them. In the twelfth century especially, when some families achieved commercial prominence and the position of consuls of Gaeta, relationships are clearly traceable. This is hardly surprising in a city which remained small, and whose nobility saw urban residence as essential (the tower-house mentioned earlier is the most overt evidence of this). In the twelfth century we see at least three examples of intermarriage between the clans, with Maria Maulotta marrying a de Arciu, Munda Castanea being the wife of Christopher Gattula in 1132, Gemma Baraballu the widow of John Gattula in 1159 and Marocza de Arciu marrying and being a widow of John Gattula in 1179. That many should involve the Gattula family is not surprising. Although the clan emerged relatively late in the eleventh-century political life of Gaeta, it swiftly gained a strong and permanent position in the city's life, and is ever-present in the documentation from the city in the twelfth century. It is notable that in all of the marriages, despite the fact that the woman in each remained identified by her surname, her offspring took the name of their father. Thus we hear nothing more of the Maulottas after they married into the de Arcius, and many of the 'Gattulas' we meet in the twelfth century may well be the last surviving members of other families who had become integrated into the Gattula clan.

If we examine the histories of the families a little further into the twelfth century, the complete disappearance from the documents of a large number of families in the 1130s and 1140s becomes apparent. This cannot but be related to the change in the nature of

Norman rule at about this time, discussed in the previous chapter. I argued there that the rule of the consuls, the identity in which many of the prominent families appear in the twelfth century, only lasted as long as the Capuan supremacy over Gaeta, when the princes of Capua were too concerned with their continuing struggles nearer home to worry too much about what was going on in the smaller city. The fact that many of the families who benefited from this *laissez-faire* approach to the government of Gaeta disappear after 1140 only serves to reinforce the impression of a new regime sweeping in with a different attitude towards the rule of its subjects. Some were able to come to an arrangement with the Norman king and his nominees, and continued to play important roles in the life of the city; others simply fade from view.

How did developments in Gaeta compare with those in the surrounding area? The following section provides some local context for the trends discussed in this and the previous chapter.

(e) ELEVENTH-CENTURY FAMILIES IN NAPLES AND AMALFI

(i) *Naples*

In Gaeta, the advent of the surnamed families in the late tenth century signalled a threat to the older established nobility. Eventually the latter were eclipsed as the new clans took advantage of the instability of rule at Gaeta to build up their own positions in the eleventh century and on into the twelfth. In Naples, too, we have surnamed families, too numerous to list. Far from replacing the nobles, they emerged at the same time in the documentation, that is, in the 930s. Like the Gaetans, the Neapolitan surnamed families appear to have been fairly localised in their landowning.[148] Although the surnamed families here seem to have been more securely land-based than at Gaeta, there are one or two slight indications that commercial exchanges took place. For example, we see in 959 that Sergius Pictuli son of John was obliged to transport the wine produced on his leased vineyard by sea.[149] Where he had to take it is unclear, but it illustrates that he had access to shipping.

[148] The Millusi family, (*RN* 79, *RN* 289), of whom more in a moment, the Bulcani family (*RN* 289), the de Piperas (*RN* 312, *RN* 427, *RN* 470), all exhibit this pattern.
[149] *RN* 104.

The need for definite identification in commercial contracts was proposed as a reason for the use of surnames at Gaeta. Although commerce does not seem to have played such a great part in the lives of the Neapolitans, the need for identification remained. The territory itself, was larger and the choice of Christian names was even more limited. A survey of named individuals in Naples to 1050 reveals a total of just under 2,900 men and women. Of these, about 500 were women, almost half of whom were named Maria or its variant, Maru. Of the *c.*2,400 men, a quarter were named John, 272 Peter, 237 Stephen, 229 Gregory, 216 Sergius and 160 Leo. Or, to put it another way, three-quarters of the Neapolitan male population was named one of these six names. This is only a rough indication of the problem, however; the limited pool of names, many without surnames in the documents, makes secure identification of each individual for the purposes of listing well-nigh impossible. Being a larger area and more populous, and with such a limited pool of names, the need for identification in the duchy of Naples emerged earlier than in Gaeta.

With the small amount of Neapolitan ducal evidence available to us, it is difficult to see whether the surnamed families became part of the nobility of Naples. I suggested in an earlier chapter that many of them, such as the Isauri and Ipati families, were probably recognised as nobles of the city: the appearance of a count among the ranks of the Millusi in 1036 supports this view.[150] As at Gaeta, more links may have occurred between individual families than are now visible.[151] The artisan families of the city, however, seem not to have mixed very much with those of a higher social status. One identifiable group, the smiths, seem to have concentrated their activities in one street in the city and to have intermarried gradually, creating a clan centred around a profession.[152] Their insularity suggests that there was very little opportunity for social mobility in Naples. This must be largely due to the fact that apart from a brief hiatus around 1029, when we find duke Sergius of Naples taking refuge at Gaeta having been ousted from power by the aggressive Capuan Pandolf,[153] the Neapolitan duchy was

[150] *RN* 458.

[151] For example the double surnames of Gregory Cutina son of John de Pipera (*RN* 470), John Miscino son of Romani Pappadeum (*RN* 428) and Sergius Pictulo son of John Pappadeum (*RN* 428) suggest a great deal of intermarriage, and the appearance of Gemma daughter of Stephen Pappadeum and wife of Stephen Cannabari (*RN* 218) illustrates it.

[152] For more on the smiths, see Skinner, 'Urban communities'.

[153] *CDC* 156.

politically very stable. The rule of its dukes was continuous up until the 1130s, when the Normans finally conquered the city, and so the power vacuum which contributed to the rise of the new aristocrats at Gaeta never occurred in the larger city.

(ii) *Amalfi*

In Amalfi, too, the distinction between the nobility and the group of surnamed families was not always clear cut. It is true that the former group, distinguished by their ties of descent to a comital ancestor, provided witnesses for the dukes more frequently than the latter.[154] If landowning patterns were the only criteria, however, little would distinguish the nobility from the surnamed families of Amalfi. Both owned land in localised areas, as we have seen in a previous chapter, and the nobility took on surnames as an additional means of identification in their unwieldy name strings.

One family which did this, the Monteincolli, continues to feature in Amalfitan documents of the eleventh and twelfth centuries. They appear to have remained close to their landed base in Ponte Primaro, as the heirs of Mauro 'Monsincollu' feature in a boundary clause there in 1126.[155] Their neighbours were the Benusi family, and in 1122 John Benuso and his wife sold a vineyard in the same place to one Sergius son of Urso Campanella and Itta, his wife.[156] From later evidence it is possible to identify Itta as a member of the Monteincollo clan.[157] Her will, executed in 1146, reveals that both Sergius and her daughter Gaitelgrima had predeceased her: her son-in-law Constantine was one of her executors. In that year her entire bequest at Ponte Primaro, which she and Sergius had received as dowry from her mother Sikelgaita, was sold off, and the 210 *solidi* raised donated for her soul.[158] It may be because of Gaitelgrima's premature death that the Monteincolli disappear from the Amalfitan documents at this point. The possibility that they may have become Campanellas on Itta's marriage (assuming that she was the only surviving member of the family at this time) does not find support in the written records.

[154] For example Leo, a member of the Scaticampuli family, witnessed for duchess Regalis in 986 (*CodCav* II/386). A member of count Sergius' family, Sergius de Lupo, witnessed the same document. His brother Constantine witnessed for duke Manso in 988 (*CDA* 588) and 1004 (*CDA* 18). The latter document also features Sergius Ferafalcone.

[155] *CDA* 128. [156] *CP* 107. [157] See above, Figure 4.5.

[158] *CDA* 150; the purchasers of the land, Manso son of John Capuani and Anna his wife, later gave the land to the convent of St Laurence: *CP* 137 (1153).

Another noble, surnamed family were the Ferafalconi, whose switch to that surname was discussed in chapter 4. They feature in documents of the early twelfth century, but seem to have disappeared by 1120.[159] Sergius son of Gregory, who featured with his brother Pantaleo in documents of 1062 and 1089,[160] and witnessed a sale of 1100,[161] had died by 1102. In the latter year, his widow Maru sold land in Reginna Maiore to her brother-in-law, Pantaleo. She acted on behalf of her son Lupinus, whom she stated was away at the time of the transaction.[162] It is easier to trace and recreate the Ferafalcone genealogy in the twelfth century than the eleventh, for Pantaleo and his children were much more conscious of their origins than were previous members of the family. Pantaleo named his son and daughter Gregory and Marenda, after his parents' names. Although it is less apparent than at Gaeta, the use of lead names is certainly discernible among Amalfitan families, and would reward further investigation. The most interesting feature of the documents of Gregory and Marenda, however, is that they reverted to the use of long name-chains, and thus allow us to trace their descent from the ancestor of the Ferafalcone clan, count Leo.[163] It is likely that this reversion was prompted by the instability caused by the Norman takeover of the duchy, causing people to define their status *vis-à-vis* the newcomers. If this was so, it does not seem to have had the effect of securing the family's position. In 1115 Gregory and Marenda sold all their inherited land in Reginna Maiore to one Mastalus Pizzillo.[164] They are recorded in 1118 as having sold another piece to Ursus Falangula, who subsequently also sold it to Mastalus.[165] It looks as if the Ferafalconi were under pressure from another family in their favoured area

[159] *CP* 92 (1100): Sergius Ferafalcone; *CDA* 101 (1102): Maru daughter of Lupini Scirice, widow of Sergius son of Gregory Ferafalcone, and Pantaleo her brother-in-law; *CP* 98 (1115): Gregory and Marenda son and daughter of Pantaleo de Gregory de Sergio de Urso de Leo count Ferafalcone; *CP* 102 (1118): Gregory son of Pantaleo (as 1115).

[160] *CP* 76, *CP* 84. [161] *CP* 92. [162] *CDA* 101.

[163] *CP* 98: Gregory and Marenda, son and daughter of Pantaleo de Gregory de Sergio de Urso de Leo count Ferafalcone. However, the date of this document, 1115, suggests that they may have omitted two or even three generations of the family (working on del Treppo and Leone's calculation of thirty years per generation) in order to link themselves with count Leo, who is documented in 922 (*CDA* 2). A further problem arises on reading the document, for they sell land which was bought by their father from Maru, his sister-in-law, widow of Sergius *son of Sergius their grandfather* (*sic*). This reveals a misreading in this document, for other evidence strongly suggests that Maru's husband and Pantaleo's brother was Gregory, not Sergius. The two names are easily confused in script form, but such errors illustrate the care needed to establish accurate genealogical lists. [164] *CP* 98. [165] *CP* 102.

around Maiori. Their disappearance after this date supports that view.

The Rogadeum clan owned land in Ircli, but lived in Ravello, where a member of the family became bishop.[166] However, the family appears to have suffered some disruption to their fortunes in the unstable conditions of the early twelfth century. Although plenty of documentary material survives from the diocesan archive from the period, they do not appear between 1100 and 1172. Thereafter they once again feature prominently in the charter material.[167]

The Iactabecte family appear to have weathered the storms of the Norman takeover, only to disappear in the late 1120s.[168] In their period of prominence, however, one of their number, John, had achieved the post of judge in the city, which carried its own prestige.

(f) GAETA IN CONTEXT: POINTS OF COMPARISON

What do the documents from Naples and Amalfi demonstrate? The first point to make is how different the development of the political and social pattern of each was from that of Gaeta. Neapolitan society seems to have been somewhat static; the documents of Amalfi and Gaeta reveal far more social mobility. I think there must be at least some link between this and the fact that the latter two cities suffered more upheaval as far as the rule of their dukes was concerned, particularly during the mid-eleventh century.[169] At Gaeta the effect was to allow new families into the aristocracy, whilst at Amalfi there were many families competing for land and position. The result in the latter city is that it is difficult

[166] For early references to the family, see above, chapter 4, note 107; Constantine son of Leo Rogadeum, bishop of Ravello: *CDA* 98.

[167] *PAVAR* II/73 (1170): Urso son of Leo de Mauro; *PAVAR* II/75 (1172): his sons Leo and John 'de Urso de Leo de Monso Rogadeo' (this name-chain at least proves that the family had an idea of its continuity, even if the documents do not reflect it); *PAVAR* II/102 (1186): Landulf son of Mauri Rogadei; *PAVAR* II/109 (1188): Leo son of Urso Rogadio; *PAVAR* I/67 (1193): Rogadio; *PAVAR* II/116 (1195): Urso son of Mauro Rogadeo. All of these documents reveal that the family continued to base their activities in Ravello.

[168] *CP* 104 (1120): Maria daughter of John de Constantine de count Marinus, widow of Sergius son of John judge Iactabecte; *CP* 109 (1124): land recorded as having been bought from Sirgia and Gemma daughters of Gregory Iactabecte; *CDA* 126(2) (1125): Pantaleo son of John judge Iactabecte.

[169] See above, chapter 2, and chapter 5, section (a).

to trace many families over more than three or four generations, or that the histories we can trace exhibit breaks, such as that seen in the case of the Rogadeum family. These could be interpreted perhaps as periods of political exile. (The city-states of northern Italy frequently used this method to curb the ambitions of their prominent families; the presence of Norman sovereignty in the South does not preclude the possibility that such a sanction was available to the citizens of individual cities.[170]) Unlike Gaeta, a communal-type internal structure does not appear to have developed at Amalfi, making the development in Gaeta even more interesting. It is clear, though, that some families were able to maintain their position as landowners over a long period. They did so by concentrating their holdings into one specific area. This mirrors Gaetan evidence, where the localised new aristocratic families were able to displace the nobility. The latter's widespread estates were no help to them when the lands lay in separate political jurisdictions.

In making this point, we return to a constant factor in the lives of aristocrats and noblemen, their role as landowners in the Tyrrhenian world. How could land be exploited to produce political power? And why did some of the wealthiest landowners not survive into the twelfth century?

[170] On this phenomenon in the northern cities, see D. Waley, *The Italian City-Republics* (3rd edn., Harlow, 1988), p. 154ff.

Part III

THE ECONOMICS OF POWER

Chapter 7

LANDOWNERS AND EXCHANGES IN THE TYRRHENIAN

So far this study has focused on the political life of the three ex-Byzantine duchies of the Tyrrhenian, but in the narrative it has become apparent that landed wealth and commercial exchange may have been crucial to individual and family power. This and the following chapter explore the economic life of the area in a little more detail. Firstly, the local and landed bases of wealth will be examined, and then the picture will be widened outside the immediate area of the Campanian and Latin coast to investigate the evidence for the effects of long-distance trade connections on the political life of the duchies.

(a) GAETA

The natural features of the territory of Gaeta clearly dictated the economic life of the duchy and shaped its political history. At its widest extent, the duchy of Gaeta spread from Terracina to the Garigliano river, and inland as far as Valledecursa (Vallecorsa) and Fratte (Ausonia).[1]

At their highest the mountains rise to some 1500m. At its lowest the plain is several metres below sea-level. In some places one gives way to the other so suddenly that the sheer scarps formed have still not been tamed for agricultural use. Nor has it been necessary to do so, for since the nineteenth century a programme of drainage has opened up large areas of the flat land to the type of intensive cultivation seen also in the English fenlands.

The rivers of the duchy present a contrast too. Those rising in the mountains behind Gaeta and Formia flow swiftly down steep inclines and disgorge into the sea in some cases only a few kilometres from their source, whilst the main river of the duchy,

[1] All placenames used are those in the medieval documents. Where there is a modern equivalent it follows in brackets.

the Garigliano, meanders slowly across its plain, fed by other rivers, before finally reaching the sea.

This dichotomy between mountain and plain is one key to understanding the territorial ambitions of the dukes of Gaeta as manifested in the documentary evidence, and their subsequent successes and failures. For the Aurunci mountains split the duchy into three distinct areas: the plain of Fondi and Terracina, the central highlands around Gaeta and the plain of the Garigliano to the east.

The plain of Fondi was once much wetter than it is now. It is no accident that the Via Appia, which crossed the Pontine Marshes further north, skirted around those of Fondi, and is still recorded as having been flooded during the late Roman period.[2] We have no references to the Lago di Fondi during our period, but its greater extent would provide some explanation for the total lack of documented medieval placenames in the centre of the plain today. All the habitation centres recorded in our period were located on its edges, either in the lower, fertile hill slopes, as in the case of the town of Fondi itself and the estates called Portelle, Raviniano, Flexu and Vetera; or on the coast, for example Sperlonga and Terracina. The coastal area does not seem to have been as waterlogged as the interior. Another Roman road, the Via Flacca, ran along the coast and passed the monastery of St Anastasia[3] midway between Sperlonga and Terracina.

The Gaetan documents are singularly unhelpful when it comes to describing how the lands of Fondi were exploited. This is partly due to a comparative lack of Fonditan material, but also to the lack of lease documents in the entire *Codex Cajetanus*. These are the documents which would have been most useful in a discussion of land use, specifying, as they frequently do, rent as a fraction of the crops.

Although much changed from its medieval state, some aspects of the landscape of the plain of Fondi remain largely unaltered. The two main communication routes through the plain still follow the lines of the old Roman roads, and, despite the arrival of intensive soft fruit cultivation on the fertile, drained land, the agricultural exploitation of the peripheral areas perhaps follows older patterns. For example, olive trees grow along the Via Appia between

[2] M.-R. de la Blanchère, *Terracine: essai de Histoire Locale* (Paris, 1884), p. 184, reports an inscription of king Theoderic recording his work to de-flood the road.

[3] *CDC* 248.

Terracina and Fondi, and the Via Flacca, with cereals, vines near Lago Lungo and reeds. The latter crop was as important in medieval households as food crops, being used for a variety of domestic purposes including lighting. Contemporary evidence from Amalfi shows that reeds were deliberately cultivated there,[4] and it is likely that the Fonditans exploited the marshland in the same way. We have seen that lake Lungo was a valuable resource to the dukes of Gaeta, who obtained fish as rent from its tenants.[5] The larger Lago di Fondi may also have been exploited; the name of the later Torre di Pesce on its shores about two kilometres outside Terracina suggests that recognised fisheries were known in the area.

To add a little to our picture of the land use on the plain we are fortunate to have three documents from Terracina.[6] Two are transactions in marshland outside the city, one a sale dated 1011, the other a gift of ?1042, from which fish and eels could be caught. The third is a lease dated 1092 of arable land, 'at Lianum outside the city' (probably the foothills of Mt Leano), made by Peter, bishop of Terracina, to Rico son of John. Rico and three generations of his heirs were ordered to improve the land, growing grain, but paying a rent in cash. This perhaps illustrates the uncertainty of revenue from land which, to judge from the length of the lease, was going to take a long time to bring up to its full potential. An unpublished document from Terracina surviving in the archives of Montecassino seems to confirm that land near the city needed much care to bring it into production. In ?917 John, the abbot of St Stephen there leased land to be improved with vines to one Lea and Stephen the priest for three generations, again at a cash rent.[7]

The plain of Fondi was linked to the central area around Gaeta by the Via Appia, running through the foothills of the Aurunci mountain range near Itri, then descending to emerge on the coast at Formia, and the Via Flacca, which followed a cliff-top route along the coast from Sperlonga and then cut through the Valle Helena. The hills between these two roads are rolling and hospitable. The Flacca's cliff-top route is interrupted at intervals by small caves where streams rising in the hills reach the sea. Further east the

[4] Skinner, *Mobility*, p. 42. [5] *CDC* 55; see above, chapter 3.

[6] Giorgi,'Documenti', 80, 82, 84.

[7] Montecassino, Archivio, *Aula* II, *Caps.* LIII, *fasc.* 1, no.1. Vines were also grown at Pallari (unknown), as another document of 973 from the same archive illustrates: no. 3.

Gaetan peninsula and hinterland are made up of limestone and have no rivers, but modern military maps show many perennial wells and springs.[8] There is no reason to suppose that these did not exist in medieval times, making the settlement of these areas possible. It is at Formia that the character of the central highlands changes. Foothills give way to steep mountain slopes, rising behind the city and continuing southwards. Forcing the road and most human habitation into a narrow strip of coast which only widens at Scauri, the scarp then turns inland, forming a steep western edge to the Ausente valley as far as Silbakaba (Selvacava). This mass effectively creates a barrier between the eastern and western parts of the duchy. No roads run across it, and the major communication line is still the Via Appia. Much of this mountainous area was, and still is, barren, infertile scrubland, but the documentary evidence shows us that those areas below 300 metres in height were intensively cultivated during the Middle Ages, particularly along the coast and up the Itri valley. In the west, we know that the coastline between Sperlonga and Gaeta was dotted with vineyards.[9] We find some more vines above Mola at Saraquiano (unidentified), at Mola itself (Formia, suburb),and further east on the widening coastal plain at Fontanulo (near Castellonorato).[10]

Although there was other vegetation present,[11] the evidence from the documents points to an almost exclusive cultivation of vines. No grain is recorded, which is striking given the number of mills recorded in the same area.

The tight control exercised over the milling facilities in the duchy has already been discussed.[12] The question must now be raised as to the source of the grain processed by the mills of the central area of Gaeta's territory. In the absence of evidence of cultivation in the central area, we must examine the eastern part of the duchy; to transport it from here to the Formian mills would have been considerably easier than transporting any grain from the Fonditan plain.

The eastern part of the duchy of Gaeta is dominated by two great river systems, the Ausente and the Garigliano. The Ausente cuts

[8] Istituto Geografico Militare, *Carta d'Italia*, 1:25,000, F.171 IV SO.

[9] At Sperlonga: *CDC* 154, *CDC* 228; Vivano: *CDC* 19, *CDC* 228; Serapiano: *CDC* 52; Casa Regula: *CDC* 272, *CDC* 294; Mt Conca: *CDC* 234; and Ciceriniano: *CDC* 52.

[10] Saraquiano: *CDC* 31; Mola: *CDC* 221; Fontanulo: *CDC* 208.

[11] We have frequent references in this area to woodland, for example, at Sperlonga, Paniano, Cirasa and Maranola: *CDC* 1, *CDC* 15, *CDC* 137, *CDC* 175.

[12] See above, chapter 3, section (a).

past the eastern flank of the Aurunci, forming a valley up which the Via Ercolana wends its way to Cassino. It flows into the Garigliano about $1\frac{1}{2}$ kilometres from the sea, and together the rivers form a flat, marshy estuary.

The Garigliano is formed by the joining of the Gari and Liri rivers near Montecassino, and descends through the ever-widening valley towards its confluence with the Ausente. On its way it is fed by at least ten minor rivers. Small wonder then that this area was known in medieval times by the name Flumetica, whose sense is roughly 'river-land'. The Ausente, itself no minor stream, was in comparison to the Garigliano sometimes called Flumicellum, or 'little river'. Often the additional name Frigido was used of it, a description echoed by the nineteenth century traveller Keppel Craven when he recorded that the Ausente was 'of such icy coldness, that it was impossible to keep the hand in it for more than half a minute'.[13] Doubtless if he had put his hand into other rivers and streams he would have achieved much the same result, but it is possible that he was testing the aptness of a local name for the river which had persisted since medieval times.

Unlike the marshy plain of Fondi, the river valleys and coastal land from Scauri to the Garigliano were heavily cultivated. There are signs today of some drainage channels on the low-lying coastline between Scauri and Castro Argento but the area's apparent tendency to wetness does not seem to have deterred its medieval cultivators, who grew vines and grain, tended woodland and built mills on the Caput Aqua river.[14]

This picture of mixed land use was repeated up the intensively farmed Garigliano valley, with grain and vines being grown in an apparently random pattern. Again there was woodland, and one mill is recorded on the river.[15]

We are slightly less well furnished with information about the Ausente valley. Again one mill is recorded, although both the Ausente and the Garigliano must have had more. At Cocciaria (Cozara) we have evidence of grain cultivation and the rearing of pigs.[16] Further up the valley, woodland and vines covered the more hilly terrain.[17]

The eastern area of the duchy was thus considerably different in character from the central highlands. Whereas the latter grew only

[13] K. R. Craven, *Excursions in the Abruzzi* (London, 1838), p. 70.
[14] *CDC* 138, *CDC* 146. [15] *CDC* 96. [16] *CDC* 10.
[17] *CDC* 125, *CDC* 188.

vines, as far as we can see, Flumetica was an area of mixed, and possibly deliberately integrated, cultivation. The grain fields were never far from a mill; but if, as is most probably the case, the mills of the Ausente and Garigliano could grind the grain from the surrounding district (an assumption which depends greatly on two unknown factors – how much grain was produced and the capacity of the mills to grind it), there was no reason to transport it to the mills of Mola and Pontone near Formia and Gaeta. What then did these latter mills grind? Either we must reappraise our view of what was grown in the central highlands, and hypothesise that grain was cultivated there which does not appear in our documentation, or we must conclude that Gaeta had to import some of its grain. The latter seems more likely, and the problem will be discussed presently.

Whether Flumetica can be regarded as the granary of the duchy or not, it is clear that the land here was regarded as economically important by the Gaetans. The Docibilan family, which provided the rulers of the duchy for over a century, and other major families of Gaeta all owned land here. Flumetica was also valued by the Capuans, with whose state the Garigliano formed a loose border. Capuan encroachment in the area was part of the process which led to the fall of the Docibilans from Gaetan rulership.

Could control of much of the land where food was grown and a monopoly of the milling facilities of the area explain the Docibilan supremacy for over a century and a half? Was enough food grown in the duchy to support its people? We have little idea of just how many people lived in the duchy – an attempt to show at least a distribution of its population follows in the next section. But there can be no doubt that the holding by one family of large areas of Flumetica may have reinforced its political power.

(b) PRODUCERS AND CONSUMERS IN GAETA

This picture of the landed resources of the duchy of Gaeta gives us some idea of what was grown, but who was responsible for the actual work of cultivation? Was the resultant produce sufficient to feed the inhabitants of the duchy?

One obstacle to producing a satisfactory answer to the first question is the comparative lack of leases to cultivators in the *Codex Cajetanus*. Of over 300 documents from the ninth century to the twelfth, less than 20 are leases. This total is cut when we exclude those leases that were clearly not made to the eventual cultivators of the land, or were made against a cash rent, leaving the identity of the cultivator open. This leaves us with just 7 leases to consider. The identity of the lessors suggests very strongly that in Gaeta at least only the church used written lease agreements.

A clue as to why we have so few Gaetan leases emerges if we look at the length of the tenancies recorded. Most span at least two generations, and Merores suggests that written renewals to each generation were thought unnecessary.[18] This would indicate a very static land lease market at Gaeta, with the same families holding pieces of land over many generations, which may reflect the relative stability of Gaetan political life. If the same noble families owned land over several generations, there would be little reason for them to seek new tenants for their lands, assuming the existing holders had children willing to take over the lease.

The wide distribution of the dating of the seven surviving lease documents allows us to postulate that free cultivators formed a part of Gaetan society throughout our period. Their obligation to their landlords extended only to producing the required rent; they did not have to remain on the land for the full lease period, but the lessors guaranteed a secure tenancy. Rents varied enormously; perhaps the most interesting is the very high amount of grain demanded from Merco son of Andrea when he was given control of a mill.[19] This clearly reflects its elevated value, thrown into relief by the fact that only a fifth of the rental amount for the mill was demanded for the land leased along with it.

If most lease agreements in the tenth- and eleventh-century Gaeta were made orally in the presence of witnesses, we cannot now assess what proportion of cultivators in the duchy were free tenants. That bishop Bernard could specify the terms of a lease of 1047 as 'the usual rent' suggests that leases were very common and fairly uniform in their terms.[20]

There is some evidence, however, to suggest that not all cultivators were free. We would not expect unfree tenants to be able to make documents themselves, but in 906 Docibilis I freed a number of slaves in his will, among whom were Leo the *vicedominus* or farm manager, Petrulus the miller and Lupulus the swineherd. He endowed them with land or livestock, but it is likely that they remained as free workers on his lands.[21] Almost fifty

[18] *Gaeta*, p. 92. [19] *CDC* 96 (997). [20] *CDC* 181. [21] *CDC* 19.

years later his grandson, Docibilis II, freed over thirty more slaves in his will, including a swineherd, pack-horse handlers, a groom and a herdsman.[22] More revealing still is the fact that many of the slaves' names were followed by their place of residence. The widespread distribution of these, mirroring the locations of the Docibilans' property, suggests that the family preferred to use unfree labour, at least in specialist functions, and perhaps also to cultivate their lands. This is not to say that all the Docibilans' workers were unfree; they may well have leased out some of their land in verbal transactions. Or, if Merores' theory is correct, the relative stability of the ducal lands over a long period might have rendered written leases unnecessary as tenants' children took over their holdings. The duke could, in either case, call upon some fairly powerful witnesses to ensure that terms of the leases were closely observed.

Slavery in the duchy of Gaeta was not just a tenth-century phenomenon. In 1067 the will[23] of Leo Caracci left 3 *modia* of land in Tremonsuoli and a small piece outside the city gate to John Gutium, his *clientulus* or client. John was to serve Leo's wife Matrona for her lifetime, and would be freed on her death. Here we can see that in the mid-eleventh century a man could be tied to serving another; that John's origins were lowly is indicated by the diminutive ending of his title. He was not necessarily a cultivator of Leo's land, but his case and those of others whom we find manumitted in the tenth- and eleventh-century wills[24] illustrates that servility was by no means uncommon.

One group who may have been cultivators were John and Anatolius sons of Passari Caprucce and their relatives, who in 999 disputed their status with the bishop of Gaeta, Bernard. They were referred to as *famuli*; he claimed they were his slaves, they that they were free, and the title had no definite meaning to decide the matter. After failing to persuade them Bernard called in the *missus* of emperor Otto III, Notticher, requesting that he should accompany him to Gaeta, Traetto and Castro Argento and enforce the bishop's authority over his workers. Notticher, with Otto's authority, ordered that John and Anatolius, who were also acting on behalf of their relatives, should prove their case in trial by combat. This was highly irregular, such proof being unknown in Gaetan courts, and not surprisingly neither John nor Anatolius

22 *CDC* 52. 23 *CDC* 234.

24 E.g. *CDC* 143 (1024): two male and three female slaves freed; *CDC* 153 (1028): two female slaves freed; *CDC* 168 (1037): one male slave freed.

were prepared to submit. Instead they offered to swear oaths to the effect that their mother, Benefacta, had been free, and that their father Passari had not been obligated to the bishop. This oath, plus payment of a pound of gold, secured their freedom.[25]

The cash payment probably had far more influence in gaining these men's freedom than the oath. It is striking that men whose status teetered on the brink of servility could raise a pound of gold between them, a fact remarked upon by Wickham as an indication of the rise in status of slave cultivators.[26] But if his interpretation is correct, some explanation for this wealth and rise in status must be attempted.

To explain this particular case, it would help if more were known about the labour situation in Gaeta at this time, and whether the Caprucci went on to work for Bernard as free men after the case. Bernard's plea to the emperor himself suggests that he was more than a little disturbed at the prospect of losing his workers, particularly since their discontent seems to have been widespread (suggested by Notticher's itinerary through three areas, Gaeta, Traetto and Castro Argento). It would make sense, therefore, that he exacted a hefty price for their freedom.[27] If labour were short in Gaeta, the gold could quite feasibly have come from another wealthy landowner, eager to secure the services of the bishop's disgruntled men in return for buying their freedom. This must remain merely a hypothesis in the absence of any other documents featuring the Caprucce family, but the case does illustrate that the status of cultivators in Gaeta was often open to question. It may also reflect the growing instability of the Docibilans' hold on their lands at precisely this time. We saw earlier that disputes had begun to break out among different members of the family, including Bernard, over their landed properties. This may have encouraged men like the Caprucci, whose status before the trial is unclear, to question the authority of the family and perhaps, if they had originally been slaves, to challenge that status. That they won is a clear indication of the weakening of Docibilan power.

Were the goods produced by the cultivators sufficient to feed the population of the duchy? To offer an answer to this question, it is

[25] *CDC* 100. [26] Wickham, *Early Medieval Italy*, p. 152.

[27] The case is unusual in itself; one wonders why Bernard did not ask for the help of his brother, duke John III.

necessary to address the thorny matter of food production and its relation to population numbers.

With regard to produce, it is clear that the documentary material from the duchy gives a far from complete picture. For example, the plain of Fondi had limited potential for arable farming and viticulture, but we cannot say whether this deficiency was compensated for by keeping herds of animals. The area today produces large quantities of dairy products, but it cannot be assumed that the medieval plain was grazed by cattle and buffalo. Other, more general problems, exist for the duchy as a whole. There is a notable lack of references to animal husbandry. Those that we have often refer to the modest stocks kept by the priests of churches.[28] Yet some of the uplands must have been grazed by sheep, and pigs and possibly cattle were kept in Flumetica.

Grain and vine products are certainly present in our documents, but the other corner in the Mediterranean diet triangle, olive oil, does not appear at all. If olive trees were grown, as they are still today in some places, not in groves, but dotted along the edges of vineyards, they might not show up in land transactions.[29] That oil was used in the duchy, however, is clear from a few documents in which churches charged a measure of oil for lighting whenever a body was buried in one of their crypts.[30] Gaetan householders may have supplemented their diets from kitchen gardens – houses were often sold along with small plots of land.[31] But was the produce of the duchy sufficient to feed the population?

Any attempt to quantify the medieval population of any district is fraught with hazards. All documented males could perhaps be counted and multiplied by a factor of 4 or 5 to account for their families, but this is unsatisfactory, particularly if we remember that in Gaeta the first 3 Docibilan rulers had 7, 11 and 9 offspring respectively! A straight head-count of documented names would also severely underestimate numbers. The small sample of the actual population of Gaeta and its territory can be used in a productive way, however, if the distribution of named inhabitants of different places is plotted onto a map and compared with the distribution of food resources studied earlier (see Map 7.1).

[28] For example, in 1061, St Augustine's at Vivano (S. Agostino) owned a cow and a sow *CDC* 212.

[29] A feature noted by Toubert in northern Lazio: *Structures*, I, p. 261.

[30] *CDC* 191.

[31] Mola seems to have been an area popular for this type of cultivation; gardens (*hortus*), are recorded here in 1025 (*CDC* 146), 1055 (*CDC* 200), 1071 (*CDC* 245), 1120 (*CDC* 295) and 1124 (*CDC* 303).

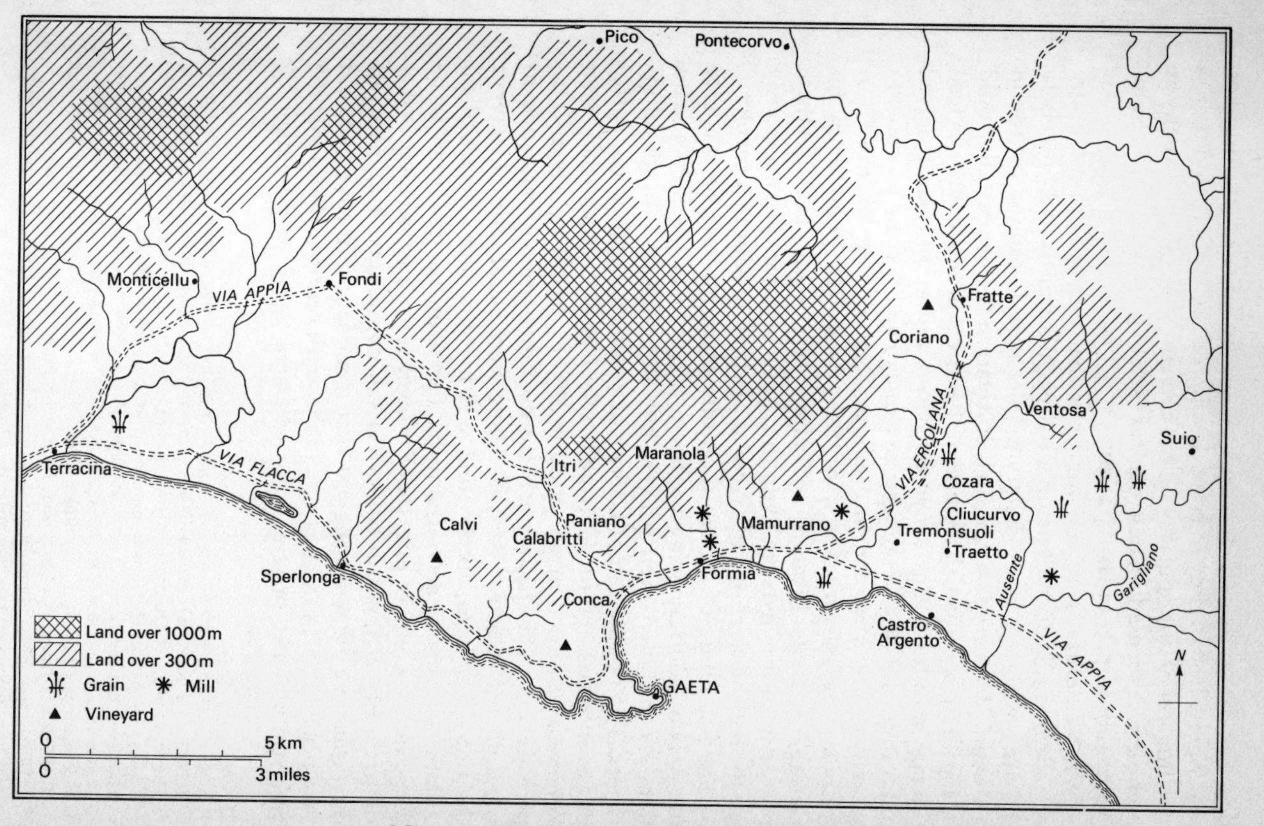

Map 7.1 *Population centres and crops in Gaeta*

Between the ninth and tenth centuries, there is a rise in the number of people who say they lived in the city of Gaeta itself, and then a levelling-off of its population in the eleventh as that of the duchy as a whole was focused on new centres such as Castro Argento, Suio, Fratte and, in particular, Traetto.

What emerges from this survey is that throughout the entire period the bulk of the documented population lived in precisely the area where a basic dietary staple, cereal, cannot be found growing. With evidence of such cultivation further east, it would be logical to speculate that some of the cereal produce went to feed Gaetan mouths. When *hypatos* Constantine of Gaeta leased unlocated lands in Gaetan territory in 839 and 866, he was able to actually export the rent, in grain, to Naples.[32] His example was followed by Aligernus son of Leo, who had grain from his Garigliano estate brought to Naples too.[33] Just because these powerful landowners could do this, however, does not necessarily mean that the territory of Gaeta as a whole produced a surplus.

The beginning of the tenth century seems to have been a time not only of political change, as the new regime of Docibilis and his family established their power, but also of economic developments. The population of Gaeta had, it seems, quadrupled, partly due to an influx of refugees from the Saracen raiders who had razed Formia and settled at the mouth of the Garigliano river. This period also heralds the arrival in the documentation of references to the mills at Mola near Formia. These were clearly meant to serve the needs of Gaeta, for Formia was in ruins and Gaeta had no suitable streams to drive the mills. For so many new ones to be constructed would require that the level of production increased as dramatically as the number of Gaetan consumers. Fragments of documentary evidence suggest that some land improvement did take place in the Flumetica area in the tenth century,[34] and that the area continued to provide some of Gaeta's grain requirements,[35]

[32] *CDC* 5, *CDC* 12. [33] *CDC* 53.

[34] E.g., at Sozzione, a grain-growing area, a piece of land called a *pastinum* is recorded in 954 (*CDC* 52). Another is recorded at Mola in the same document, and another at Rubiano in Flumetica in 972 (*CDC* 67). Contemporary evidence from elsewhere shows that to take on land to 'pastinate' it was to improve it for crop growing. *RN* 189 (971) requires tenants to cultivate vines and wheat in Naples; *RN* 198 (973) specifies only vines. That the phrase *ad pastinandum* was more usually associated with the latter crop is suggested by Salernitan and Amalfitan examples *CodCav* II/230 (965), *CodCav* II/393 (987) and *PAVAR* I/11 (1029). See also Lizier, *L'Economia*, p. 77.

[35] *CDC* 96 (997): bishop Bernard of Gaeta demanded a total of 120 *modia* of grain per year as income from a mill and land near the Garigliano.

but a large increase in production is not apparent. It seems, then, that Gaeta did have to import some of its grain.

Unfortunately, there is no tenth-century evidence at all for such importation. The only clues we have come from the twelfth century, with a document of 1125 recording a Salernitan merchant who had been hired to bring grain from Tunis to Gaeta,[36] and king Tancred of Sicily's promise in *c.*1191 that Gaetans would not be prohibited from bringing grain from Sicily to Gaeta, unless a general prohibition on exports from the island was in force.[37] It is very hazardous to try to stretch twelfth-century evidence to cover the inadequacies of the tenth-century material, but if importation, be it from Africa, Sicily[38] or even just along the coast from Naples, did take place in the tenth century, several points raised so far fall into place. The appearance of new mills becomes logical, processing grain from outside the duchy which was now needed. (Grain travelled better if left unmilled; flour would have gone bad if transported any great distance). The high value of mills, out of all proportion to their construction costs, can be explained in terms of their function; the provision of a lifeline to the city population. The political power of Docibilis and his family may, therefore, have derived from the controls that they were able to exert through their monopoly of the milling process.

(c) AMALFI

The problem of limited amounts of grain was one which concerned the rulers of Amalfi even more. The city of Amalfi lies at a point on the coastline where the gorge through which its river runs opens out to the sea. Hemmed in by cliffs, it has been unable to expand much beyond its medieval size, and access to it is still much easier by sea than by the winding coastal road. The mountainous terrain of the duchy is punctuated by fast-flowing rivers, and these had been harnessed by the tenth century to provide the power for water-mills.

As at Gaeta, Amalfitan mills were bought and sold in portions expressed in terms of months.[39] The divisions of mills in some cases

[36] *CDC* 308. [37] Abulafia, *Two Italies*, p. 40.

[38] That these areas were by the tenth century Arab strongholds did not prohibit the possibility of exchanges with Gaeta: here the duchy's economic life reflected the political situation.

[39] For example, John son of Mauro bought a month of a water-mill in Amalfi to make his share up to one third in 971: *CP* 63.

were not as simple as a whole or half month. In 1013 John, son of Leo the priest, rented four months and seven and a half days of an Atranian mill from Leo son of Constantine. John would hold this time for four years, at an annual rent of 46.75 *modia* of corn.[40] In 1034 Maria, daughter of John, gave her father two months minus five days of a mill in Atrani.[41] With such complex divisions it is difficult to avoid the conclusion that specific times of use were being referred to. Just how the times were allocated is not specified, nor who was responsible for allocating them.

The value of mills appears to have restricted their ownership to the upper classes of Amalfi, including noblemen, describing their ancestors as counts, or Amalfitan churches such as the wealthy foundation of SS Ciricus and Iulicta. Such exclusivity is again likely to be linked with the control of the grain supply.

There is no documentary evidence of any kind of cereal-growing in the duchy except for a piece of 'seed-land' (arable) at Carniano (unknown) owned by SS Ciricus and Iulicta.[42] Nor have I been able to find much evidence of Amalfitans investing further afield in order to provide themselves with grain.[43]

Vera von Falkenhausen has proposed that the Amalfitans bought in their grain,[44] and in the apparent absence of self-sufficiency either within the duchy or through external landowning she is probably correct. Citarella's citation of Liutprand of Cremona's assertion that 'the merchants of Amalfi . . . need our wheat to live' may not necessarily support his argument that they needed it to export to North Africa,[45] but certainly supports the idea that they imported it. Loud concurs that the presence of Amalfitan colonies at S. Germano, Aversa and Capua in the latter's principality 'represented the search for foodstuffs and local products to underpin Amalfitan overseas trading'.[46] The role of the Amalfitans as merchants will be dealt with more fully later.

In contrast to the situation at Gaeta, however, individual ducal

[40] *CDA* 32. [41] *CDA* 40. [42] *CDA* 41.

[43] An oft-cited document recording men of Atrani buying up unusually large tracts of land near Paestum in the principate of Salerno may well indicate that such investment took place, but does not specifically state the purpose for which the land was being purchased. See below, note 78. [44] 'Ducato', p. 342.

[45] Citarella, 'Patterns', 540. The translation of the relevant passage from *The Embassy to Constantinople* by F. A. Wright, in *Works*: 'Amalfitan traders . . . by bringing [silk cloths] support life by the food we give them' (chapter 55), does not support the idea that the food was sold on. On silk, see below, chapter 8. [46] *Church and Society*, p. 21.

families at Amalfi were unable to enforce the type of monopoly held by the Docibilans over milling and, by implication, some of the grain importation. This may have been one cause of the political instability in the duchy, as no early family was able to rise far enough above the others in terms of economic power to enjoy a sustained period of rule.

The limestone massif of the Lattari mountains supports little agriculture even today, and the rocky slopes can have been no more productive during medieval times. Those centres of cultivation whose placenames can be located lay almost exclusively along river valleys or, less often, on high plateaux such as that of Agerola. The vine was certainly the most widely cultivated crop in Amalfi, and wine-presses are often recorded in the documents.[47] The area around Ponte Primaro on the river Reginnis Maiore is still predominantly vineyard, as it was in frequent documentary references to it from 957 to 1044.[48] Apples were also grown here, and it is interesting to note references to the deliberate cultivation of reeds. A reed-bed was specifically mentioned in a sale of 957,[49] and other similar references indicate the importance of reeds and willows in domestic life.

The rest of the river valley of the Reginnis Maiore appears to have been under similar crops to Ponte Primaro. Nubella was an apple-growing area, as a sale of an orchard there in 1037 illustrates.[50] Paternum Piczulum (unknown) had vineyards, one of which formed a wedding gift from Leo son of Peter to his daughter Drosu and son-in-law Ursus in 1007.[51] The land around Pecara is described as vineyard and woodland.[52] Minule, which lay above the river, was described in 1038 as having deserted vineyards and apple orchards converted to vine cultivation.[53] The latter example is particularly significant, since it suggests a certain flexibility in Amalfitan agriculture. It was possible to grow apples in the area, but the landowner in question, Leo Rufolo, had deliberately changed to vines. Del Treppo and Leone have suggested that such changes occurred to meet market demands,[54] and certainly it seems likely that the Amalfitans may have exported their surplus wine, probably in exchange for grain. Lizier was in no doubt about the eventual destination of one of the products of these estates: 'i

[47] For example, *CDA* 5 (939) and *CDA* 7 (964).
[48] See, e.g., *CDA* 20, *CDA* 58, *CP* 31, *CP* 73, etc. [49] *CP* 37. [50] *CDA* 50.
[51] *CP* 55. [52] *CDA* 22, *CDA* 584. [53] *CP* 37. [54] *Amalfi*, p. 42.

paesi musulmani, che non producevano vino, consumavano quello dell'Italia meridionale'.[55]

A variety of crops were sometimes grown in what was apparently a limited area. In three documents of 1010, 1039 and 1047, the Rogadeum family divided, bought and leased out vineyards, chestnuts and apple orchards, woods and uncultivated land at Torum de Ircli.[56] In other areas cultivation appears to have been more specialised, as on the plateau of Agerola, where chestnut seem to have been the dominant crop.[57]

Surprisingly, given the fact that most landowners in Amalfi seem not to have cultivated their property themselves, there are very few examples of leasing out to cultivators. Amalfitan landlords appear to have come later to written leases than their Salernitan or Neapolitan counterparts. The distinct lack of documents of this type reflects the Gaetan model, and, despite Amalfi's rather more eventful political life, may still reflect a basic stability at the level of landowning and tenancy. The first written lease from Amalfi is dated 1029, when Drosu widow of Leo gave a piece of empty land in the *castellum supramonte* (unknown) to the son of Ursus Calvelli to cultivate with vines for four years at a rent of 2 *solidi* a year.[58] It is clear that leasing had been happening before this date, since in 1036 Leo son of Sergius de Palmola received an apple orchard which his father before him had tended.[59] The survival of documents from this date may be accidental, but I would suggest that at a time (the mid-eleventh century) when the duke of Amalfi was under constant pressure from Pandolf of Capua,[60] the recording in writing of agreements between landlord and tenant may have been perceived as a prudent defence against future instability.[61]

To sum up, Amalfi offered a living to those who could exploit its difficult terrain and produce wine and fruit either for home consumption or export, but the most basic sustenance in the form of grain had to be bought in. Those in control of this were of necessity wealthy, since both bulk importation and the ownership

[55] 'the Muslim countries, which did not produce wine, consumed that of southern Italy': Lizier, *L'Economia*, p. 147. [56] *PAVAR* 1/3, *PAVAR* 1/14, *PAVAR* 1/16.

[57] *CDA* 31. [58] *PAVAR* 1/11. [59] *CP* 35. [60] See above, chapter 2.

[61] Taviani-Carozzi, *Principauté*, p. 577, makes the point for Salerno that land disputes and the signatures of judges on documents from that city increased dramatically when there were crises of rule in the principality. People trusted to the law to preserve their possessions in periods of instability; it is likely that Amalfitans thought in the same way.

[62] *CDA* 586/*CP* 32 (939).

of whole or divided mills was expensive. Some early mill-owners were Neapolitan counts,[62] until their wealthy Amalfitan counterparts took over. Yet the limited amount of land available in Amalfi made it difficult for any one family to assert its dominance or have a permanent presence in the documents. Survival of evidence also makes it difficult to reconstruct the patterns of Amalfi's internal economic life. One very visible phenomenon, however, is the movement of Amalfitans and Atranians towards Salerno, and their investments in the neighbouring principality. It seems clear that such activity was caused by economic necessity, but it may also have reflected political changes within the duchy. This movement and investment will be discussed in more detail presently.

(d) LAND TRANSACTIONS AS A MEANS OF COHESIVENESS

It has become apparent that in their landscapes and the types of property owned, Gaeta and Amalfi are quite similar. The relatively limited amount of land available seems to have encouraged the rapid development of wealthy elites in both duchies, with a high level of social mobility based partly on economic influence. Commerce featured strongly in the lives of many families discussed so far, and the striking parallel between the two cities over mill ownership suggests that the inhabitants of both viewed property ownership in a similar way to each other. Limited land, it seems, artificially inflated the value of other kinds of property. When associated with a shortage of grain, the value of mills as a means of processing imported foodstuffs shot up. There is, however, another factor which I should like to explore, and that is the significance of mill-owning to the family-based social patterns we have witnessed in the two smaller duchies.[63]

Family unity seems to have been preserved among the clans of Gaeta, especially the Docibilan house, by means of a remarkably high number of documents detailing exchanges of land within the clan. This pattern is repeated among the noble families to a lesser extent, and seems to work in Amalfi as well, from the limited investigation that is possible from the evidence. Another way in

[63] An earlier version of the discussion which follows was first presented as a paper, 'Mill ownership and social status in medieval southern Italy', at the conference *Medieval Europe 1992*, held at York in September 1992. There are, regrettably, no plans to publish the proceedings.

which a family could express its unity, common throughout Europe in the early Middle Ages, was by founding a family church (*Eigenkirche*), an option which was taken up by some families.

However, given the lack of land in both duchies, even the richest families may have found it difficult to satisfy the demand from within the clan for portions of the family property. I would suggest, then, that the emphasis placed upon mills and their inflated value was because they were built precisely to satisfy this need. With the potential to be divided into as many as 365 portions (though none seems to have achieved this level of fractioning), a mill could act as the focus for a family's exchanges. In itself the property was modest, but, because it was the medium through which different lines of the same extended clan could communicate their willingness to co-operate, it had a symbolic value far outweighing its physical construction. As a result, portions were given high prices, in part to avoid their alienation outside the family.

Significantly, I have found no evidence of this type of fractioning anywhere else in southern Italy at this time. Where land was plentiful, there was no need for what was in effect an artificial property exchange, and the difficulty in reconstructing Neapolitan noble families may be precisely because they did not indulge in so many land transactions. This lack of exchanges, so necessary to reinforce social and familial ties in the other two duchies, reflects the basic stability of Neapolitan political life throughout most of the period in question.

(e) CROSS-BORDER MOVEMENT: AMALFITANS AND ATRANIANS

One aspect of the history of the three duchies of Gaeta, Amalfi and Naples which has never been examined in much detail is the amount of cross-border movement and investment that went on between them, and their interaction with their Lombard neighbours in Salerno and Capua.[64] Yet there was much exchange across the border between Gaeta and Capua, perhaps prompted by a need for foodstuffs, and certainly motivated by political considerations. Amalfi, too, clearly needed a source of grain to import, and seems

[64] The cases which have been most discussed are those of Amalfitans who migrated to Salerno, see e.g. Kreutz, *Before the Normans*; del Treppo and Leone, *Amalfi*; Figliuolo, 'Gli Amalfitani'; Taviani-Carozzi, *Principauté*, pp. 800–35.

to have looked to Salerno. The inhabitants of both small duchies, therefore, had regular contact with their Lombard neighbours.

There is evidence to suggest that a large number of Amalfitans and Atranians took a further step, leaving their homeland to go and live in the principate of Salerno. A large number of them went to live in the city of Salerno itself, renting plots of land on which to build houses, often from the church of St Maximus, or buying houses in the St Trophimenus area which, significantly, was close to the harbour.[65] None of these immigrants appears to have held land elsewhere, and with no other apparent means of support – none, for example, is surnamed with an occupational title – it is possible that they too acted as middlemen in the food trade or as sailors on ships plying along the Tyrrhenian coast and to the Arab countries.

Relevant in this context is a transaction of 1006, in which Peter the Amalfitan son of Ursus paid 2 *tari* to Disigius son of Ingnelgardus for permission to cut wood from Disigius' slopes of Mt Falerio outside Salerno in order to build a ship.[66] Given the abundance of wood available in Amalfi, it seems that Peter must have been based permanently in Salerno, and was probably either a merchant or one who built boats for the mercantile community.

Many of the Amalfitan and Atranian immigrants gained their toe-hold in Salerno by taking on leased land, and the fact that they agreed to cultivate it or build houses on it indicates that they did take up residence. They focused their activities in three main areas apart from Salerno itself: Vietri and Cetara on the coast towards Amalfi, and Lucania, south of Salerno.

Lease lengths ranged from six to twelve years, but were probably renewable without further documentation. There was a pattern of varied cultivation for periods up to life,[67] repeated all over the principate, and the terms of the leases, which usually demanded a portion of the crops grown, allowed the cultivators to make their own living. Among the tenants in Cetara we can identify several dominant families, whose histories are traceable through two or more generations. One family which appears to have lived on the land they owned was that of the Atranian Marinus the judge. In 980 in a sale of lands in Fonti, his sons stated

[65] Leases from St Maximus to Amalfitans/Atranians include: *CodCav* II/331 (981), *CodCav* II/372 (984), *CodCav* IV/705 (1018); St Trophimenus street: *CodCav* II/315 (979), *CodCav* II/377 (985), *CodCav* VI/1033 (1044).

[66] *CodCav* IV/587.

[67] *CodCav* II/362.

that their father had received land from prince Gisolf,[68] indicating perhaps that the de Marini had begun life in the principate as tenants.[69] Significantly, though, such families do not appear among the clans whom we have seen active in the Amalfitan hinterland. Nor do any of the latter appear to have invested in Salerno, and it is likely that the division between them reflected the shifting political life of the duchy.

In some cases the tenants went on to own the land they had initially rented and, renting it out in turn to cultivators, they often moved back to Amalfi. This is illustrated by the case of Amalfitans and Atranians in the district of Fonti near Cetara, where the de Rini family were able to establish themselves as tenants of the bishop of Salerno.[70] The rent on the episcopal leases, moreover, was demanded in cash, possibly indicating that the bishops thought that their new tenants were well able to pay in this way rather than in a share of their crops, and that the bishops had a use for cash. They probably did not cultivate their lands themselves, unlike Mastalus son of Leo Roibuli, another Amalfitan tenant of the bishop, who paid half the wine from the vineyards he leased.[71] By 972 the bishops were beginning to sell land to the foreigners as well as lease it out. In that year a former tenant, Peter de Lupeni de Rini, bought the church of St Felix at Fonti and its land with his nephew Leo.[72]

Hardly any of the Amalfitans or Atranians owning land in Salerno appear to have had land in Amalfi, and, although many were clearly resident in the latter city, their landholding in the duchy may not have been great. The major difference between these landowners and the immigrants was that the former were wealthy enough not to have to cultivate their own land, and often, as already stated, moved back to, or remained in, Amalfi. Many of these lessors appear to have been engaged in the kind of entrepreneurial landowning mentioned above in an Amalfitan context, by which crops were grown specifically for the market. In

[68] *CodCav* II/326.

[69] The de Marini and other clans who moved to Vietri and Cetara are discussed in Skinner, *Mobility*, pp. 16–24; see also Figliuolo, 'Gli Amalfitani'.

[70] In 940 bishop Peter leased out the church of St Felix and its lands to be restored and worked by three Amalfitans including Ursus de Rini: *CodCav* I/169. Another member of the de Rini family received half the church and its estates in 966, the other half going to Sergius Calendola: *CodCav* II/242. On the history of the church itself, see Taviani, *Principauté*, pp. 625–7. She and Figliuolo, 'Gli Amalfitani', 74, disagree, however, on the reconstuction of the de Rini family. I tend towards Figliuolo's interpretation.

[71] *CodCav* II/303.

[72] *CodCav* II/270.

1024 Leo son of John leased to Peter son of Amorus an apple orchard in Fonti in which Peter was to plant chestnut trees for ten years.[73] Such cultivation must have produced high profits to be worth a ten-year investment. Leo also owned, and possibly exploited for the market in the same way, vineyards and reed-beds in Fonti, exacting the very high rent of two thirds of the crops (against the norm of a half) from his tenant Marinus son of John.[74]

Another manifestation of growing to demand are those leases by which land was given *ad pastinandum*, that is, to cultivate from new land. The amount of uncultivated land brought under crops in this way was significant, and the leases must have proved very profitable for the landowner. He could buy 'empty land' cheaply, specify the crop to be grown, take his share as rent and then sell off the land at a profit as an established vineyard or orchard. The fertility of such land must have been higher due to the fact that it had lain fallow,[75] and rendered pastination leases even more efficient.

The need for land certainly seems to have prompted some Amalfitans and Atranians to invest or live in Salerno. Those who went as tenants were probably attracted by the fact that many leases led to the eventual ownership of some of the land leased, usually half. This type of arrangement suited both the landowner, who needed labour, and the tenant, whose shortage of capital meant that he could not buy outright, and whose only obligation on becoming the proprietor of his holding was to give first refusal on any sale of the land to his former landlord.

Those who were wealthy enough to invest in foreign land were possibly also affected by the shortage of it at home, having the money to buy, but little land available to purchase. Cheaper land prices in Salerno may also have attracted investment there, especially if the buyers were engaged in the production of crops for the market, as their heavy investment in vineyards indicates, and so needed to extract the greatest profits possible. Once established as landlords, they exploited their estates almost ruthlessly, with relatively high rents demanded. There is evidence to suggest, however, that the Amalfitans and Atranians came to be in Salerno through a deliberate policy of encouraging immigration.

The early history of their arrival in the principate was linked to the capture of Amalfi by prince Sicard in the ninth century, and his

[73] *CodCav* V/755. [74] *CodCav* II/363. [75] Lizier, *L'Economia*, p. 79.

subsequent transfer of a group of Amalfitans to his own city.[76] It is probably true that Sicard wanted to bring Amalfitan money and trade to his state, but royal involvement in the lives of the foreigners certainly did not end with his death. In a document referred to in a court-case of 1065/6 and published in paraphrase, prince Guaimarius conceded to Guttus the Atranian son of Peter some lands in Albole (unknown). Cherubini attributes the document to Guaimarius II, and thus dates it to between 913 and 923.[77]

Later on, in 957 and 977 John, the bishop of Paestum, had to ask prince Gisolf's permission to sell Lucanian land to a group of Atranians.[78] Gisolf appeared posthumously in a document of 980, when Ursus the Atranian confirmed the sale of some land at Fonti, which the prince had conceded to his father Marinus the judge, and gave the documents relating to the history of the land to the purchaser, John the Amalfitan son of count Mauro.[79]

Even when the Capuans took over Salerno in 974, the Atranians seem to have maintained good relations with the rulers, if the claim made in a dispute of 985 by Ligori son of John, that he had received a house in St Trophimenus street from Pandolf Ironhead and his son Pandolf, can be believed.[80] Unfortunately, because Ligori and the other litigant were ordered to swear to their cases at a later date, and the document recording that event has not survived, the outcome of the case is not known.

The sale of a piece of land, almost 4 miles (approximately 6.5 kilometres) square, near Paestum in Lucania, by the bishop of Salerno to a group of men from Atrani in 977, was certainly the largest single investment made by them in the principality, but it was not the first. Ligori son of John the Atranian had paid the bishop 12 pounds of silver in 957 for a piece of uncultivated land here.[81] What he and his compatriots in 977 were planning to do with their property is unclear, but it seems likely that it was destined for grain cultivation. Significantly, some of the 977 group were described as being at sea, suggesting either mercantile activities or, closer to home, that these men were actively involved in bringing foodstuffs to their home city.

It is significant that all records of either the princes' or bishops'

[76] M. Berza, 'Amalfi preducale (596–957)', *Ephemeris Dacoromana*, 8 (1938), 360.

[77] P. Cherubini, 'Nuovi documenti dei principi di Salerno in parafrasi', *ASPN*, 3rd series 19 (1980), 45ff.

[78] *CodCav* I/197, *CodCav* II/296, *CodCav* II/299.

[79] *CodCav* II/326.

[80] *CodCav* II/377.

[81] *CodCav* I/197.

transactions with the foreigners end in this year, and only resume in 1035 with a document freeing Iannaci the Atranian's church of SS Maria and John in Vietri from episcopal control, for which archbishop Grimoald exacted a payment of 2 pounds of silver.[82] Although the unpredictability of documentary survival must be taken into account, it is surely no coincidence that records of princely interest in the immigrants end precisely as a new dynasty assumed power in Salerno. Certainly records of a foreign presence continue throughout the period, but given that he had deposed an Amalfitan to win his throne, John of Spoleto was unlikely to show the Amalfitans and Atranians under his rule any favours.

Why though do the princes of Salerno after 984 appear to have ignored such a source of income? The answer lies in the nature of the documentary evidence, which for the most part records transactions in land. Perhaps by the late tenth century the task of attracting foreign settlement by means of land grants was seen to have been achieved by the rulers of Salerno, and so the number of documents recording such grants would tail off. The benefits to the state provided by the existing foreigners may also have made more immigration unnecessary.

Less well documented are the activities of the Amalfitans in Naples, but their presence in the city seems to have been constant. In 946 John the monk, son of Leo, bought a strip of rural land for 48 *solidi* from the abbot of SS Sergius and Bacchus in the city, and in the same year donated it to the abbot as a gift. It is likely that he did so on entering the monastery, as the gift document records him as 'monk of SS Sergius and Bacchus'.[83] In 984 Leo son of Gregory and Peter son of Leo, both from the city of Amalfi, made a gift of land and their ruined church of St Peter in Ercica (unknown) to the Neapolitan monastery of SS Severinus and Sossus, but on condition that the monastery paid them an annual rent in kind from the land.[84] There is little further information in this document to work out the background to the Amalfitans' links with SS Severinus and Sossus, nor is it clear whether Ercica lay within the duchy of Amalfi or that of Naples.[85] What is unusual is that the Amalfitans were receiving some income from the monastery, rather than simply making a pious donation. This case and that of John the monk reveal similar patterns to Amalfitan

[82] *CodCav* 1/98. [83] *RN* 56, *RN* 57. [84] *RN* 82.

[85] Other documents featuring the placename, *RN* 237 (982) and *RN* 301 (997) provide no further clues, except perhaps to tip the balance in favour of a Neapolitan location.

movement and investment in Salerno, in that the church may have acted as a major conduit in both areas. In this respect, however, the 'ecclesiastical filter' at work must be taken into account, in that most of the surviving Neapolitan evidence comes from SS Sergius and Bacchus and St Gregory, and so these two houses will inevitably seem important.

This impression is reinforced if we examine other documents from Naples. In 956 the church of St Euthimius in Naples divided rural land with Leo son of Ursus the Amalfitan.[86] In 970 the land of Cesarius the Amalfitan is included in the boundary clauses of land in Mesanum (unknown), where the monastery of SS Severinus and Sossus also had property.[87] Mauro the Amalfitan is cited as the previous owner of land in Piscinule (Piscinola, 5 kilometres north of Naples) which was sold in 1027 to the convent of St Gregory.[88] In the same document several members of the Cutina family are recorded as previous owners too; I have already raised the possibility that they should be identified with the later Cotina family of Gaeta. One Sergius de Sillicta of Amalfi is mentioned in the boundary clause of land on which wheat and wine was produced in 1034 at Malitum (unknown) in Naples.[89] The convent of St Gregory features again in a document of 1050, in which one Anna became a nun, and gave all of her land in Clibo Galloro (unknown), which she had partly obtained from her nephew and niece, children of Leo the Amalfitan, to the convent.[90] It does not seem to be the case that Leo was Anna's brother; she mentions that some of the land had also come from her own brother and sister, and would surely have provided that information in Leo's case. Leo's presence in the document, therefore, arises from the fact that he had married into Anna's family.

Intermarriage seems to have taken place quite frequently between Neapolitans and Amalfitans, though it is unclear whether it led to, or was the result of, the movement between the two cities. In 1022 land bought in Casole (unknown) had previously been owned by John Pappamaurontum and his wife, Maria Amalfitana.[91] That Maria's origins are stated suggests that her husband was Neapolitan.

Maria was a rarity: a woman who had come from her home city

[86] *RN* 90; frustratingly, the location of the land, in the *fundus* Turandi, is once again unknown. [87] *RN* 183. [88] *RN* 412. [89] *RN* 448.

[90] *RN* 485; the land was bordered by that of Ademarius the Amalfitan as well.

[91] *RN* 397.

to a different one. It is likely, though all too easy to assume, that she had come to Naples as John's bride. That is, the initiative for her move had come from the fact that he had travelled to Amalfi for some reason and met her there. Alternatively, Maria may have been the daughter of an Amalfitan already settled in Naples. In either case, her presence in the latter city probably stemmed from men's actions. Although Amalfitan women had considerable freedom of action at home, the general restriction on female activity visible in southern Italy at this time makes it unlikely that Maria had travelled to Naples independently.

Marriage occurred more frequently between women of Naples and men of Amalfi, where it was the men who were the travellers. Mauro the Amalfitan's wife Drosu, who had to contest some of his Stabian property whilst he was at sea in 1007, was of Neapolitan stock.[92] Anna Millusi, documented in 1085 in Naples and certainly of a Neapolitan clan, was the widow of Leo the Amalfitan, imperial *protospatharius*.[93]

One man who seems to have frequently travelled between Amalfi and Naples was Sergius the Amalfitan, son of Pardus, whose will survives in two copies. The first, dated 1021, was preserved at Naples.[94] The second, dated four years later, survived in the collection of charters from the church of St Laurence in Amalfi.[95] Although Sergius had houses in the city of Naples, his main land base remained in the duchy of Amalfi, including some property on Capri. Most of his bequests, however, were in money, and reveal his connections in the larger city. It is likely that the St Gregory included in the list of beneficiaries was the church of that name in Naples, and, in common with other Neapolitan wills, Sergius' last bequest was a *tremissus* to the church of Naples for candles. This may reflect a strong notarial practice in the city, but the fact that Sergius allowed his will to be expressed within this framework suggests that he was attuned to that practice. Sergius appears to have had two daughters. The first, Marenda, was a nun, and a bequest was made to her convent. To his other daughter, Blacta, Sergius left a rich array of plain and embroidered cloths, in linen and silk, including one piece worth 4 ounces of gold alone.[96]

The detail with which the cloths were described indicates strongly that Sergius may have been in the textile trade. His interest in linen partly explains his presence in Naples, for that city was

[92] *CDA* 55. [93] *RN* 537. [94] *RN* 402. [95] *CP* 81.
[96] *pannum sericum unum balientum uncias quactuor de aureum.*

famed as a centre of linen production. Indeed, an Arab writer of the tenth century stated that the city based its wealth on linen.[97] He may have exaggerated somewhat, since there are only two references to linen cultivation in the entire Neapolitan document collection,[98] and one of these refers to the growing of the crop in Capua.[99] Possibly linen cultivation was sufficiently profitable to make transactions in its land comparatively rare. Alternatively, the production of the cloth may have been a Neapolitan state monopoly, so that the lands where its raw material was grown were tightly controlled and rarely available on the open market. Direct evidence for manufacture of the cloth comes in 1083, when three millers promised to work a mill co-owned by the convent of St Gregory and others. The millers undertook to make a chute (*sfosario*), and after six years to soak and mature 250 *faschios* of linen and spread them out free of charge for the convent each year.[100]

Because it has proved impossible to locate most of the places where Amalfitans appear in the territory of Naples, it is difficult to decide whether, as in Salerno, their landowning exhibits any areas of particular concentration. However, because they seem to have arrived from Amalfi in a far less structured way, it is likely that there was no real preference for one area of Neapolitan territory over another. In an urban context, however, the limited evidence does suggest a faint concentration of Amalfitan interests and connections with the western area of the city. Sergius the Amalfitan owned houses in the *vicus* Nilum. This lay very close to the *vicus* Sol et Luna, the street in which the church of St Euthimius, divider of lands with Leo son of Ursus, lay. On Salernitan evidence, it might be expected that the Amalfitans would congregate near the sea-shore in Naples, but much of the harbour frontage seems to have been monopolised by the palace and property of the dukes of Naples. They do not seem to have actively encouraged Amalfitan settlement in the same way as the princes of Salerno.

(f) CROSS-BORDER MOVEMENT: GAETANS

Investment by Gaetans in Naples must have been relatively easy due to the long-standing political ties between the two states. I have

[97] Abu al-Qasim Muhammed ibn Hawqal, The Book of the Routes and the Kingdoms, extract trans. R. Lopez and I. Raymond, *Medieval Trade in the Mediterranean World* (London, 1955), p. 54. [98] *RN* 233, *RNAM* 208. [99] *RNAM* 208.
[100] *RN* 532.

already suggested that members of the Docibilan house at Gaeta may have spent time in the larger city.[101] They were joined there by several of their compatriots. Drosu Maria, daughter of Leo the Gaetan, appears in 960, receiving repayment of a loan made by her aunt to Eupraxia, mother of one Leo, from Leo's wife Anna the nun.[102] Anna repaid the debt of 21 *solidi* in land, but again its location cannot be ascertained. From the similarity of his name to that of the river Garigliano, a previous holder of the land, one Marinus de John de Curilianum, should possibly also be identified as Gaetan.

Another Gaetan woman, Anna the nun daughter of John,[103] bought land in Quarto Maiore (probably near modern Madonna di Quarto) and Pausillipense (Posillipo), both west of Naples, in 1013. She was the widow of one Gregory Millusi, and that family's documented unions with both a Gaetan in this case and with an Amalfitan man, already mentioned, indicates far more activity on the part of that clan than is now visible. Anna's widowhood, however, does not seem to have resulted in her return to Gaeta. Freed of the authority of her husband she was able to engage in this land transaction completely alone; there is no evidence to suggest that as a nun she was buying land on behalf of her convent.

There is a gap of over sixty years before another non-Docibilan Gaetan appears in the Neapolitan charters. In one of the most detailed wills left by a woman to have survived from eleventh-century southern Italy, a certain Maria made her bequests in the presence of her husband, John 'Gaytani'.[104] It may be significant that one of her landed bequests to him lay in Posillipo, where Gaetan property-owning is documented. John is also recorded as having given to Maria houses in the Furcillense[105] district of the city of Naples, and these reverted to his ownership in the will. Cash bequests were made to Maria's nephews, the sons of John's brother Peter.

It is likely that these Gaetans and others from their city came to Naples as a result of flourishing trade exchanges between Gaeta and its larger neighbour. These are now not visible in the documents, but a clue that they existed is provided by the document issued by Sergius IV of Naples when he was overthrown from the duchy by

[101] See above, Figure 2.2. [102] *RN* 115.

[103] Although it is tempting to do so, there is no evidence to identify this Anna with the nun mentioned in the previous document. [104] *RN* 523.

[105] In the eastern part of the city.

Pandolf IV of Capua in 1029. In it he promised many commercial concessions to the Gaetans if they would help him to retake the city.[106] Such an offer must have been significant either to have been made or accepted, and so continued good relations benefited more than just the rulers themselves.

It is difficult to gauge whether members of the prominent families of Gaeta engaged in such trading activities, as none of those Gaetans visible at Naples can be identified with any certainty. From the documentary evidence from Amalfi, however, a rather different picture emerges. Here, in the twelfth century, there is limited evidence of a Gaetan presence which can be linked into the Gaetan documents.

The most obvious example, already signalled in the previous chapter, was the sudden appearance of the Gattula surname in Amalfitan material from 1137 onwards. In that year Ursus son of Sergius Gattula and his wife Ciuzza bought a chestnut grove and vineyard in the Transmonti district between Amalfi and Naples.[107] Much later, in 1172, Matthew Gattula is documented in a boundary clause of an unlocated chestnut grove.[108] The buyer was Ursus Castallomata, who may also have been the purchaser of land in Pogerola in 1176. That transaction was witnessed by Sergius son of Mauro Gattula.[109] The following year Sergius witnessed three further documents, one involving the archbishop of Amalfi, the second a lease of Transmonti land and the third yet another purchase by Ursus Castallomata.[110] The latter man was named in a will of 1180 as the intended purchaser of half of Sergius da Tabernata's property, and once again Sergius Gattula acted as witness.[111]

Four years later, Sergius appears in the witness list of another sale of land in Pogerola, and in another document that gives us the first real clues about the Gattulas' background in Amalfi.[112] In the latter, Sergius and his brother Matthew (almost certainly the man documented in 1172), and their nephew Sergius sold off land bequeathed by the younger Sergius' brother Mauro. All three vendors provide a long list of their ancestry, in the tradition of Amalfitan noblemen. Matthew and Sergius were the sons of

106 *CDC* 156. 107 *CDA* 141. 108 *CDA* 182. 109 *CP* 158.
110 *CDA* 194, *PAVAR* 1/54, *CDA* 196. 111 *CDA* 203.
112 *CDA* 216, *CDA* 217 (published also as *CP* 175). No other information is available; Sergius went on to witness two further Amalfitan documents in 1186 and 1188, *PAVAR* 1, documents 63 and 64.

Mauro Gattula, son of Pantaleo de Leo de Pantaleo de Leo de Pantaleo de count Iusto. Their nephew did not use the Gattula surname, giving his pedigree as 'son of John de Pando de Sergius de count Ursus de count Pardo'. The names look very Amalfitan, and the Gattula surname is used on top of the precise ancestry list given. It is likely, from this combination and the fact that their nephews do not appear to have been Gattulas, that the Gaetans had married into an Amalfitan line. Given that we have very little information about their landed property in Amalfi, and that no real pattern is visible in their witnessing activities, it seems that the Gattulas were trading in Amalfi, but did not settle there.

Earlier compatriots of the Gattulas do seem to have come to Amalfi to settle, though. In 1133 the Amalfitan monastery of SS Ciricus and Iulicta leased land in Transmonti to one Palumbus son of Palumbus de Garofalo 'da Gete'.[113] The land was bordered by a piece belonging to Leo 'da Gete'. A pair of leases issued by the monastery in 1139 granted out more land, to Lupino son of John 'da Gete' and Stephen son of Palumbus 'da Gete' respectively. These two tenants had adjoining plots.[114] Again we see the church actively participating in transactions with outsiders. That these men were Gaetans and not all members of the same family (though Stephen and Palumbus were probably brothers) is suggested by the use of the word *da*, which like the modern Italian had already come to mean 'from' in the Latin of southern Italy.

Perhaps the most intriguing indication of a Gaetan presence in Amalfi comes in a document of 1164, in which the abbot of SS Ciricus and Iulicta leased out land near Lettere, again in the Transmonti area, to Athanasius son of Ursus 'de Docibile'.[115] This is the sole occasion on which the name Docibilis occurs in the Amalfitan documents, but, given that Athanasius was leasing land in the same district as earlier Gaetans, there is a very strong case for suggesting he was one too. It cannot be suggested that he was related to the Docibilans of Gaeta, since many families used the name Docibilis for their sons. It is striking, however, that we cannot trace the Docibilans at Gaeta after their final pitch at power in the late eleventh century. If, as I have tentatively suggested, Docibilis I was an Amalfitan, might not his line have chosen to return to their homeland, or to have always retained property there? Endless speculation is possible, but it would make sense for a family ousted from power to do so.

[113] *CDA* 137. [114] *CDA* 144, *CDA* 145. [115] *CDA* 176.

(g) CROSS-BORDER MOVEMENT: NEAPOLITANS

Although the flow of immigration between Gaeta, Amalfi and Naples is always likely to have been dominated by movement from the smaller cities to the larger, there is some evidence of Neapolitans choosing to invest or make their homes in the smaller duchies, such as the family of John the Neapolitan count, resident in Amalfi.[116] Further research among the surnames of other families in the smaller duchy reveals several of John's compatriots there.

For example, there is a number of references to a family descended from one Cunari. In 984 the latter is described as being of Capri.[117] However, in another document featuring the family dated 1031, Cunari is described as being 'da Marmorata' (from Marmorata).[118] Marmorata was the name of an urban district of Naples. Neapolitan origins cannot definitely be assigned to the Cunari family, and an explanation might be that one of the clan had moved from Amalfi to Naples. However, some contact had clearly been made.

There seems to be no doubt that the creation of the Norman kingdom led to a greater degree of movement and exchange between the inhabitants of its constituent duchies. Certainly there is a marked increase in the number of Neapolitans recorded in Amalfi after 1130. Thus Drosu daughter of Guainerii de Aldemariscu of Naples and her daughter sold land in Transmonti in 1138,[119] and the heirs of one Sergius Guindazzi of Naples are recorded as owning a portion of the church of St Sebastian above Amalfi in 1151.[120]

More evidence of Neapolitans becoming involved in the internal life of Amalfi comes in the documents of the Cacapice clan of Naples. They had a long history in their home city, being

[116] See above, chapter 4, section (b).

[117] *CDA* 11: the document records a sale by Ursus and Manso sons of Leo 'de Cunarene' to Leo the priest son of Sergius de Leo de Cunari of Capri of the ground floor of a house in Caput de Crucis near Amalfi.

[118] *PAVAR* 1/12: the document records a sale of property in Supramonte by Gemma wife of John son of Cunari 'da Marmorata', Drosu widow of Mauro son of Cunari for her son Cunari, and Drosu wife of Stephen son of Cunari for her son John. Clearly there are chronological problems in fitting these and the personnel featured in the 984 document into the same family, but the recurrence of a very unusual name suggests that they were related in some way.

[119] *CP* 130.

[120] *CDA* 154; the Guindazzi are recorded in Naples in 1016 and 1026, *RN* 370, *RN* 408.

documented from 935.[121] In 1127 they appear in Amalfi, with John son of Gregory and his wife selling off their entire inheritance in Reginna Maiori to Sergius, her cousin, and Sergius' wife Gaitelgrima, daughter of Ursus Cacapice.[122] Even more significantly, both John's wife, Marocta, and her cousin Sergius were from the Agustarizzo family, prominent in Amalfitan documents throughout the twelfth century. It seems that a double marriage had accompanied the Neapolitans' internal investment in Amalfi. Another marriage is documented in 1171, with Truda daughter of Leo recorded as the widow of Gregory son of Sergius Cacapice. In that year she and her children Leo, Rachel and Redentiana sold land bought by her father in Nubella.[123] They acted on behalf of their sisters in Naples, and Pantaleo son of Sergius Neapolitani signed the document as witness.

It is unclear whether this Pantaleo, and others with names ending in 'Neapolitani', can safely be identified as coming from Naples. It could be argued that, since Pantaleo was in this instance associated with a Neapolitan family, he himself was probably Neapolitan. Three years previously, however, he had appeared as a witness to a charter where none of the participants in the transaction had any Neapolitan links.[124] Furthermore, a document of 1172 records Pantaleo and his brother John, the judge of Amalfi, receiving land and wooden houses in the *iudaica* of Salerno for themselves and their brother Sergius, to hold for two years and spend 100 ounces of Sicilian *tari* building there.[125] In 1176 the three brothers divided the houses they had built with the heirs of the original lessor of the land, Marinus.[126] Clearly the Neapolitani were active entrepreneurs and prominent in both the political and economic life of Amalfi. Two valuable documents of 1169 and 1174 may provide more information about their possible Neapolitan origins. The first records John the judge as co-executor of a will with one Cesarius, deacon and abbot and son of Gregory Brancatii of Naples.[127] As in the case of the Cacapice above, association with another Neapolitan family does strongly suggest that John and his brothers were from Naples. In 1174, in settlement of a dispute over the *iudaica* houses, John made his agreement with Ebolus, son of

[121] *RN* 28; thereafter they appear frequently in the Neapolitan documents throughout the eleventh century: *RN*, documents 241, 259, 331, 350, 419, 423, 485, 516, 520, 528, 555.
[122] *CDA* 131.
[123] *CP* 149; the land was subsequently sold on in 1193, *CDA* 231.
[124] *CDA* 177.
[125] *CDA* 183.
[126] *CP* 161.
[127] *CDA* 180.

Marinus the Neapolitan royal justiciar.[128] The name Ebolus recurs as one of the heirs mentioned in the 1176 division, and is so unusual that identification as the same man is fairly secure. Thus the lease reveals not only the Neapolitani, but also their landlord in Salerno, as Neapolitans investing in that city.

Ebolus' brother Matthew appears in another document of 1176, receiving confirmation from Truppoald, the judge of Salerno, of a document recording a sale of lands and houses in the city by the seashore to Matthew's father Marinus in 1171.[129]

The Brancatii family, mentioned above, are again documented at Naples from the tenth century.[130] Although less well documented at Amalfi, they again seem to have invested in the smaller duchy in the twelfth century. Anna, daughter of Cesarius 'Brancazzi', is seen selling land near Agerola in 1138.[131] She does not reveal her Neapolitan background, but her father's name recurs again in the family in the 1169 document when Cesarius the abbot identifies his father's family as Neapolitan.

The increase in Neapolitan activity in Amalfi and Salerno is quite notable after 1130, and perhaps requires some explanation. It could be argued simply that movement became easier between one state and another when all were subject to the king of Sicily, but in fact there is little evidence to prove that it had been difficult before. The frequent political and economic exchanges in the tenth and eleventh centuries between Gaeta and Capua, and Amalfi and Salerno, make it unlikely that travel and migration between Naples and Amalfi were difficult. Also, it is clear that Amalfitans had been settling in Naples before 1130. What is striking about the migration pattern I have just described is that (a) it was from the larger city to the smaller, and (b) it does seem to have been concentrated in the latter part of the twelfth century. I would suggest that the emigration from Naples took place partly as a result of the city's previous, longstanding resistance to Roger. Although it is impossible to recreate the internal political patterns of the city in the early twelfth century, might not the families found in Amalfi and Salerno after 1130 represent those who found the incoming (and presumably hostile) regime uncomfortable to live with, and who preferred to transfer their livelihood to the nearby cities where the Normans had ruled for much longer, and

[128] *CP* 155. [129] *CDA* 192.
[130] *RN* 119 (964); an earlier appearance may be in 934, when Marinus 'Brancii' is recorded, *RN* 26. [131] *CDA* 142.

where life had therefore stabilised somewhat? This issue, and much of the twelfth-century history of those under Norman rule, must await further study.

(h) CROSS-BORDER MOVEMENT: CONCLUSIONS

The large number of emigrants and cross-border landowners encountered in the documents suggests that to move to, or invest in, a foreign land was relatively easy. This may have been partly due to the fact that borders between the states do not seem to have been firmly delineated or controlled. Areas such as Liburia (between Naples and Capua) and Stabia (between Naples and Amalfi) had no firm political identity, and subjects of different states lived here side by side.[132] There is documentary evidence that other borders may have been similarly fluid. For example, although Cetara was part of the principate of Salerno, many of the landowners there were Amalfitan and authorised their Cetara land transactions from Amalfi. Land in S. Marzano (unknown), which again was Salernitan, formed the subject of a sale between two Neapolitans at Naples in 941, with the boundary clauses including the land of the 'Langubardi'.[133] The confusion as to whether the participants in the sale of a garden in Mairano[134] were Salernitan or Neapolitan, since the document was written at Naples, but preserved at Salerno, may be caused by the fact that this area again appears to have lain on the border between the two states.

Thus immigrants found it easy to move from one territory to another, even if they had few resources to help them in their new homes. Sergius Calendola was clearly free to cross the border between Amalfi and Salerno in order to act as an agent for Lupenus of Atrani.[135]

From this section, it can be seen that various motives made men invest in, or move to, other lands, but all were linked in some way or another. The initial need for land in Amalfi, for example, led many to take up property in Salerno, forming a community of landowners and merchants who found the coast between the two cities an ideal base for their activities, with both sides benefiting as a result. For those who ruled the states, landowning elsewhere was a

[132] In 933 the fluidity of Liburia's status is illustrated graphically by an agreement made between Naples and Capua over the terms by which they shared it: *MGH* II,ii, p. 144, quoted in Taviani-Carozzi, *Principauté*, p. 289.

[133] *RN* 44.

[134] *CodCav* IV/640.

[135] *CodCav* II/408.

secure manifestation of good political relations. These relationships at the highest level benefited their subjects, whose right of passage into other states was made easier if cordial relations existed.

The movement of people may have had another significant economic result. A survey of the coinage used in the documented transactions of the three duchies[136] reveals that Amalfitans almost constantly used their own city's *tari*, at a rate of 4 to the *solidus*, and began in the twelfth century to use Sicilian *tari* as well.[137] As the century progressed, the use of the latter became more and more common; Amalfi's political subjection to the Sicilian monarch was thus matched by increased economic adherence.

In Gaeta the situation was a little different, in that the city only minted its own bronze coinage. After a cluster of very early documents mentioning *tari*,[138] presumably Arabic, Gaetan prices were expressed in Byzantine *solidi*, or gold or silver by weight. The latter was the most common throughout the eleventh century, and seems to have given way smoothly to the use of Pavian silver *denarii* in the early twelfth century.[139] However, there are a couple of isolated examples later in the century of the use of Amalfitan *tari*,[140] suggesting that these two cities had frequent enough economic contact to enable free circulation of the latter's coinage, even if it did not replace the use of silver. Taken together with the instances of Gaetans documented at Amalfi in the late twelfth century, it is clear that far more contact took place between the two cities than is now visible.

It is in Naples that there is perhaps the most surprising use of coinage, for from an early date the *tari* dominates as the currency in which sales and a few other transactions were negotiated. It seems likely that the *tari* used were Arabic; an early document refers to *solidos siculos* (Sicilian *solidi*, perhaps a way of expressing the use of Arabic *dinars*, of which the *tari* was a quarter).[141] Alongside the *tari*, Byzantine *solidi* also feature as a unit of currency, and from 987

[136] The survey was based on coinage mentioned in actual transactions, and ignored the formulaic use of the Byzantine *solidus* in penalty clauses. It is also acknowledged that the prices and rents quoted may have been expressed in coinage of account, yet paid in much smaller denominations. The coinage of account can, however, tell us much about political and economic affiliations.

[137] First use of Sicilian *tari*: 1138 (*CDA* 142).

[138] *CDC* 25, *CDC* 29, *CDC* 32, *CDC* 38.

[139] First mention of Pavian *denarii*: 1105 (*CDC* 278).

[140] *CDC* 346 (1159), *CDC* 352 (1171).

[141] Capasso, *Monumenta*, I, p. 267, document 5 (882).

references to the exchange rate of 4 *tari* to the *solidus* begin.[142] This rate remained constant throughout our period, despite a reference in a document of 1027 to *tari* in 'good old money', suggesting a debasement had occurred which might be expected to affect the value of the coin.[143] More overt evidence to such fluctuations in the coinage available comes from 1063. In that year, a garden of the convent of St Gregory in Naples was leased to its tenant for life, at an annual rent of 25 *solidi* at a rate of 4 Amalfitan *tari* – the first direct evidence of coin from that city in Naples. However, this arrangement would last only as long as Amalfitan coinage continued to circulate in Naples. If it was replaced by better coinage, the rent would decrease to 20 *solidi*, but only if the convent agreed to accept the new coins.[144]

It is not stated whence this new coinage might come, but, given that Amalfi had just emerged from thirty years of political upheaval at this date, it is perhaps not surprising that the city's mint may have been disrupted. The Amalfitan *tari* continued to circulate in Naples throughout the remainder of the eleventh century, but it is perhaps indicative of its varying quality that another document of St Gregory, dated 1072, again stresses the uncertainty of supply of Amalfitan coin.[145]

The interchangeable use of coin visible in the documents of the three cities under consideration reinforces the impression of free movement between them. Movement was not merely limited to neighbouring states, however. In the final chapter I shall consider briefly the issue of the long-distance trading activities of the three duchies under investigation. This will not encompass a detailed examination of Amalfi's activities, which are already well documented, but will instead seek to set that city in its Tyrrhenian context and to examine the less well known commercial life of Gaeta and Naples.

[142] *RN* 251. [143] *RN* 412. [144] *RN* 493. [145] *RN* 512.

Chapter 8

LOCAL EXCHANGE AND LONG-DISTANCE CONTACTS: THE NORMAN KINGDOM AND THE NORTH

Urban residence offered political advancement in all three of the duchies under consideration. The presence of the aristocracy stimulated the towns economically, creating a market for the produce of the surrounding countryside and for the outward trappings of wealth and status, including imported luxury goods. The role of Gaeta as a centre of exchange is very visible. Its *forum* or market-place lay near the palace,[1] and the city's commercial life is evident from documents recording *medialoca* or warehouses. From their name – 'middle places' – these seem to have been constructed above open shops and below living accommodation in three-storey buildings.[2] Gaeta's variety of trades is reflected in the inhabitants recorded in her documents. Not only the duke, his retinue and clergy, but also lime-burners, goldsmiths, a master smith, a painter and a teacher can be seen.[3] In 906, the carpenters of the city were to be found congregated in the *platea* near the church of St Salvator.[4]

Hints of early trading activity may be found in the presence of inhabitants of other cities in Gaeta. As early as 890, an inhabitant of Amalfi, Gaeta's more famous commercial neighbour, appears as a witness to a document of the ruling family,[5] and one Bonizzo the Pisan is recorded as having owned a warehouse in the city in a document of 1040.[6]

The evidence for Amalfitans travelling long distances to trade is fairly well known, their presence being attested in Cairo,[7] Pavia,[8]

[1] *CDC* 82. [2] *CDC* 14, *CDC* 174.

[3] *CDC* 167, *CDC* 92, *CDC* 80, *CDC* 140, and *CDC* 8 and *CDC* 140 respectively.

[4] *CDC* 19. [5] *CDC* 16. [6] *CDC* 174.

[7] In 978 Leo, a member of the de Rini family, who owned land and may have produced some of his own exports, confirmed an exchange made by his wife Anna while he was away in Babilonia, the pre-Arab name for Cairo: *CodCav* II/300. See also A. Citarella,

Jerusalem,[9] Palermo,[10] and Constantinople.[11] The bronze doors of many major Tyrrhenian churches were brought from the latter city, itself indicative of regular exchange.[12] The Amalfitans also feature in documents from other parts of southern Italy, though not directly in a trading context.[13] Here, however, identification becomes a problem, in that Amalfitans can be confused with Melfitans. The confusion was already apparent in the eleventh century, as Amatus of Montecassino explains:

et est a noter que il sont II Melfe, quar est Melfe et Amelfe: Melfe est en la confine de Puille, et Amelfe est vers Salerne et Naple.[14]

(it should be noted that there are two Melfe, which are Melfi and Amalfi: Melfi is in the district of Apulia, and Amalfi is near Salerno and Naples.)

Less well known is the fact that the Gaetans, too, appear to have engaged in a variety of trading activities. The possibility that Docibilis I was an enterprising Amalfitan merchant who took advantage of the political situation in Gaeta to make himself ruler must remain only speculation. Gaetans, however, are recorded at Pavia alongside the Amalfitans in the tenth century, arriving in the city *cum magno negotio* (literally, 'with great business'), and paying one-fortieth of its value to the Pavian treasury.[15]

Gaetans are also recorded in Constantinople. A letter to the bishop of Gaeta, Leo, dated 1064, relates the death in the Byzantine capital of the Gaetan John son of Peter de Benedict. John had bequeathed a substantial amount of money to various churches in

'Scambi commerciali fra l'Egitto e Amalfi in un documento inedito della Geniza di Cairo', *ASPN*, 88 (1971), 141–9. In the latter half of the tenth century, many of the Amalfitan community in Fustat (old Cairo) were massacred on suspicion that they had burnt some ships: A. Citarella, 'Patterns in medieval trade: the commerce of Amalfi before the crusades', *Journal of Economic History*, 28 (1968).

[8] *Honorantie Civitatis Papie*, ed. C.-R. Brühl and C. Violante (Köln–Wien, 1983), p. 20.

[9] Matthew, *Norman Kingdom*, p. 123.

[10] *Ibid.*, p. 75; evidence for the Amalfitan community in Palermo, and the fact that they had a 'master' at their head, comes in documents of 1172 and 1183, *Cusa* 117 and *Cusa* 146.

[11] A. R. Lewis, *Naval Power and Trade in the Mediterranean* (Princeton, 1951), p. 215: by the middle of the eleventh century, the Amalfitans had a permanent quarter in the city.

[12] On those of Montecassino, Amalfi cathedral and others, Bloch, *Montecassino*, pp. 140–55.

[13] See, for example, evidence for Amalfitans in Monte S. Angelo on the Gargano peninsula: *Barletta* 30 (1112) and *BN* 6 (twelfth century); the house of Ioannaci the Amalfitan appears in a document from Tricarico in 1148, Naples, Archivio di Stato, Sezione Politico-Diplomatica, *Inv*.99, no.39; an Amalfitan also witnesses a document from Lecce in 1198, *SGL* 16. Saints' lives also provide valuable evidence for Amalfitan activities in the South, as A. Cerenza illustrates: 'Amalfitani in Calabria e Siciliani ad Amalfi in epoca prenormanna', *Rassegna del Centro di Cultura e Storia Amalfitana*, 3:5 (1983), 175–9.

[14] Amatus, II.7, p. 65.

[15] See note 8.

Gaeta, and the bishop was asked to send someone to collect the cash.[16] The letter is endorsed with Leo's agreement to do so, suggesting that contact between Gaeta and Constantinople was frequent enough by this time to enable prompt action. The evidence of Liutprand of Cremona supports the idea that Gaetans had long been a familiar sight in the imperial city. He reports a speech by the two sons and deposers of emperor Romanus, saying that their opposition had consisted not only of Greeks, but also of foreigners, including Amalfitans and men of 'Caieta'.[17] Whilst the speech itself may be a fabrication, the presence of Gaetans and Amalfitans in the city must have been a credible notion.

One commodity that was certainly brought from Constantinople to the West was silk. A survey of the documents of the noble men and women of the Tyrrhenian states in the tenth and eleventh centuries reveals that silk cloths formed a valued part of their moveable property.[18] Liutprand of Cremona explicitly states that the silk worn by 'street-walkers and conjurors' in the West came via the Amalfitans.[19] Amatus of Montecassino also characterises Amalfi as 'rich in gold and cloths'.[20] The Amalfitans, as members of a state nominally subject to Byzantine overlordship, probably received the same treatment as provincial Greeks, who could buy and export from Constantinople any kind of silk fabric except that worn exclusively by the emperors.[21] This concession could equally well have applied to the Gaetans. However, if we can trust a reference to 'Gaetan silk' in a will from 1028,[22] it seems that the latter city was engaged in the manufacture of the cloth.

From an eleventh century source we learn that as early as the ninth century Gaeta had a Jewish community.[23] This community seems to have played a very important part in Gaeta's commercial life by the twelfth century. We have already met a document of

[16] *CDC* 219. [17] Liutprand of Cremona, *Antapodosis*, V, 21.

[18] For example, the wills of the Gaetan rulers Docibilis I and Docibilis II, *CDC* 19 (906), *CDC* 52 (954), and of Sergius, an Amalfitan resident in Naples, *CP* 81 (1025), all contain references to bequests of silk. Other documents featuring silk cloths (*panni serici*): *CDC* 66 (964), *CDC* 143 (1024), *CDC* 153 (1028), *RN* 482 (1045), *CodCav* II/382 (986), *CodCav* III/528 (999), *CodCav* IV/582 (1006), *CodCav* IV/688 (1015), *CodCav* V/738 (1022), *CodCav* V/812 (1029), *CodCav* VII/1096 (1046).

[19] Liutprand of Cremona, The Embassy to Constantinople, chapter 55, in *Works*, p. 268.

[20] Amatus, II.7, p. 65.

[21] R. Lopez, 'The silk industry in the Byzantine Empire', *Speculum*, 20 (1945), 38.

[22] *CDC* 153.

[23] Ahimaaz ben Paltiel, *Chronicle of Ahimaaz*, trans. M. Salzmann (New York, 1924, repr. 1966), p. 63.

1129, in which the consuls of Gaeta declared that profits from the Jewish dye-works or other arts should be used for the benefit of the city.[24] The other 'arts' referred to seem to have been olive oil and salt extraction. The Jews thus had a vital role to play in providing the city's necessities of life, as well as dyeing its cloth, and this may have prompted the consuls' concern to control the trade in some way. Jewish communities in the cities of the South were well used to such supervision of their activities, and there are many charters granting control of entire communities to local noblemen or rulers.[25]

Given the early and continuing involvement of the Tyrrhenian cities with the Arabs of North Africa and Sicily, Jews may have been used as middlemen in trade with these areas. Certainly there is evidence to suggest that they rose to prominent positions at Muslim courts.[26]

One area in which Jewish middlemen might have been used was in the slave trade of the South. Slavery continued in southern Italy until at least the mid-eleventh century. An early document from Naples reveals an inhabitant of that city who had bought three slaves from the Saracens and was now freeing them.[27] Given the general condemnation of Christians who owned slaves, it may well be that the Neapolitan bought the slaves, all women, in order to free them. However, the widespread occurrence of slave-ownership among the documents of the southern cities suggests that such scruples were largely ignored.

[24] *CDC* 317.

[25] See, for example, a document of 1086, in which duchess Sikelgaita, widow of Robert Guiscard, gave all the Jews in the city of Bari to Urso, archbishop of the city. She had received them as her dowry: *Codice Diplomatico Barese*, I–II, ed. G. B. Nitto de Rossi and F. Nitti di Vito (Bari, 1897–99), document no.30. In 1107 countess Adelaide, wife of count Roger of Sicily, gave to the monastery of St Bartholomew at Lipari the tithe of the Jewish community at Termas: *Codex Diplomaticus Regni Siciliae*, II, I, Rogerii II Regis Diplomata Latina, ed. C.-R. Brühl (Köln, 1987), document no.1. In 1136 king Roger exchanged the dye-works of Bibone, Leo the Jew and all his family, plus various other property and a number of villeins, for two churches belonging to the abbey of St Trinity at Mileto: *ibid.*, document no. 42. Closer to Gaeta, Taviani-Carozzi, *Principauté*, p. 448–9, cites an important document from Capua dated 1041 and listing the obligations of the Jews of that city to the fisc; in Salerno, the Jews, who lived in a defined *iudaica* near St Trophimenus street, were subject to the control and financial demands of the archbishop: C. Carucci, 'Gli ebrei in Salerno nei secoli XI e XII', *Archivio Storico della Provincia di Salerno*, I (1921), 74–9. See also A. Marongiu, 'Gli ebrei di Salerno nei documenti dei secoli X-XIII', *ASPN*, 52 (1937), 3–31.

[26] The eleventh-century writer Ahimaaz ben Paltiel's ancestor became master of astrology at the Fatimid court: Ahimaaz, *Chronicle*, p. 22.

[27] *RN* 15 (928).

The Neapolitan document does provide concrete proof that trading between Christian and Muslim occurred. To this other fragments of evidence can be added from the Amalfitan evidence, in so far as it supports general points about the relationship of the Tyrrhenian cities with the Arabs. Some references to exchanges are fairly explicit. In 978 Leo, a member of the de Rini family, who owned land and may have produced some of his own exports, confirmed an exchange made by his wife Anna while he was away in Babilonia, the pre-Arab name for Cairo.[28] The Amalfitan documents reveal other men away at sea or 'not in this land', with their wives and mothers handling their business at home.[29]

If the East provided the source of luxury goods for some Amalfitans, Salerno probably acted as the point of exchange for the agricultural goods that the Amalfitans and Atranians needed to sell in order to buy such luxuries, and for the grain they needed to buy to eat. The focus of Amalfitan and Atranian activity in the city was in St Trophimenus street, near the harbour. Mercantile activities there may be indicated by the leasing out by Leo the Atranian son of Ursus of his house for the very short period of eighteen months in 1044.[30] This may have been the duration of a trading expedition. It is possible that some of the city-dwellers spent very little time in the houses they bought or leased, viewing them rather as *pieds-à-terre* to be used between trips. It appears that from a very early stage the immigrants in Salerno had reserves of spare cash. In 932 Iohannelgarius son of John the Atranian lent 16 *tari* to Magelgardus for a year, secured on Magelgardus' land. After a year the repayment would consist of the money plus five barrels of wine, a healthy rate of interest and a shrewd form in which to obtain it if the Atranian was in the wine trade, although whether he was a merchant lending out a small amount of his profits is unclear.[31]

In Gaeta we saw that individual noblemen had commercial interests, but that the newer families were far more heavily involved in trade. In Amalfi it was the former group whose members are cited as being at sea or abroad most often; I would suggest that in the duchy where any landed property was at a premium, it was the nobility who could amass more to use as collateral against commercial loans. For example, the family descended from Cunari (fl.late ninth century), had two members,

[28] *CodCav* II/300; Cairo: Citarella, 'Scambi commerciali'.

[29] See, for example, *CDA* 42, *CDA* 45, *CDA* 48.

[30] *CodCav* VII/1033.

[31] *CodCav* I/152.

Cunari son of Mauri and John son of Stephen, at sea in 1031.[32] The sons of Lupus de Sergius de Lupo de Sergius *comes* were at sea four years later,[33] and Mauro Monteincolli went abroad in 1097.[34] Such evidence does somewhat dispel the idea that the Amalfitans became a great maritime people because they were forced into trade through lack of land.

Later in the Gaetan evidence, it is possible to see a growing commercial exchange, sometimes reinforced with marriage ties, between the great families of Gaeta and Rome.[35] Some of the aristocratic families clearly owned shops and *medialoca* in Gaeta, perhaps to support trade further afield.[36] Although we have little idea of the commodities traded, the economic ties may have led to the political interest of the Tusculani and Crescentii families in the northern part of the duchy. Also, the pattern of certain families in Gaeta trading with the former Roman house, and other families trading with the latter, may reflect not only competition between the Romans, but also a growing factionalism in Gaeta itself.[37] This is not explicitly expressed in the Gaetan documents, but there was presumably a certain amount of competition to gain the consulate in Gaeta when the consuls' powers covered many aspects of Gaeta's economic life.

Most of the documents illustrating these powers deal with Gaeta's external relations, and provide a fascinating glimpse of the constant need for negotiation in a world of fast-developing commercial cities. This was the period in which the northern city-states, particularly Genoa and Pisa, were staking a claim to both local and long-distance trading rights, and the twelfth century can be characterised as one in which the cities of the South were forced to fight for their continued place in the commercial world of the Mediterranean. The fate of Amalfi is most often studied as evidence of this phenomenon. As the power of the northern cities grew, however, Amalfi gradually lost ground compared with its

[32] *PAVAR* 1/12. [33] *CDA* 42. [34] *CP* 89.

[35] The first evidence is the document of Ramfus Christopheri, see above, chapter 4; on later links, see above, chapter 6.

[36] Shops were owned in Gaeta by the Mancanella family (*CDC* 321, 1131), the Cotinas (*CDC* 283, a 'pothega'), the Castaneas and the Gattulas (*CDC* 322, 1132). Other families, such as the Coronellas (in 1054 and 1128, *CDC* 197 and *CDC* 313) and the de Arcius (in 1054, *CDC* 197) seem to have had large amounts of liquid wealth at their disposal, again indicating that they were active in trade.

[37] I have developed this image of factions at Gaeta further in P. Skinner, 'Politics and piracy: the duchy of Gaeta in the twelfth century', *Journal of Medieval History*, forthcoming.

previously dominant position.[38] The rivalry between the Campanian city and its northern competitors culminated in the famed Pisan sack of Amalfi in 1136/7.[39] Gaeta, on the other hand, whilst not having such extensive trading contacts (at least, no evidence has survived if it did), does not seem to have suffered such a dramatic decline as its neighbour,[40] and its history provides a rather different picture.

Although little evidence survives for Gaetan commercial activities before the twelfth century, external sources, such as the isolated references cited above, reveal that Gaetan traders were known from an early date in both northern Italy and other parts of the Mediterranean. Gaeta's flourishing commercial life does not seem to have been adversely affected by the fall of its independent dukes and their replacement in 1062, after a period of rule by the duke of Aquino, by the Norman princes of Capua. In the twelfth century the external sources for the city's trading activities become fuller, in particular the archives from Genoa.

The Gaetans and Genoese seem to have had an ambivalent relationship. In 1128 a Genoese commune tariff list showed the respective payments of the Gaetans, Neapolitans, Amalfitans and Salernitans at Genoa for each person on board their ships docking at Genoa as 12 *denarii*, 18, 18 and 18.[41] Thus the Gaetans enjoyed a favoured position over merchants from the other three cities, and over inhabitants of Rome, who also paid 18 *denarii*. Such a concession suggests that the Gaetans already had a longstanding relationship with the Genoese which is not now visible. The only circumstantial clue, before the twelfth century, is that a Gaetan ship took the mission of monks from Montecassino to the island of Sardinia in 1063.[42] The significance of this fact is simply that the island was colonised by both the Pisans and the Genoese, raising the possibility of Gaetan-Genoese meetings or exchanges there.

[38] A. Citarella, 'Il declino del commercio marittimo di Amalfi', *ASPN*, 3rd series 13 (1975), 9–54.

[39] Bernardo Maragone, *Annales Pisani*, ed. M. L. Gentile (Rerum Italicarum Scriptores, IV, ii, Bologna, 1930), pp. 9–10 (1136).

[40] There has recently been a revision of the picture of Amalfi's commercial 'decline', summed up by David Abulafia in 'Southern Italy, Sicily and Sardinia' (see above, Introduction, note 16).

[41] *Codice Diplomatico della Repubblica di Genova*, ed. C. Imperiale, I (Rome, 1936), p. 61; Abulafia, *Two Italies*, p. 74 has the amounts as 12d, 12.5d, 10.5d and 10.5d, and therefore comes to a rather different conclusion about the respective relationships of the four cities with Genoa.

[42] Loud, *Church and Society*, p. 51.

It is not known when the consulate in Gaeta came into being (using the term consulate as an executive power in the city, not the title of *consul* which the dukes of Gaeta often used), but, if we compare the date of its earliest appearance – 1123 – in the documents to the datable references to consulates in northern cities, Gaeta falls in the list of the 'more precocious cities' to use Waley's term.[43] More significantly, Genoa is known to have had consuls by 1099. Did the trading links between this city and Gaeta influence the development of the consulate in the latter city? It is highly likely; the Gaetans did not have any similar southern example to model their institutions on. It is important, however, to bear in mind that Gaeta had a long history of exchanges with Rome. That city's consuls and senators appear in a Gaetan document of 1127, conceding safe passage by boat to a group of monks,[44] but I am inclined to prefer Genoa as a source of the political patterns that developed at Gaeta on the grounds that Rome's political structures were always exceptional. The strong link between the consuls and the commercial life of the city also suggests external influence.

However, in 1140 the Genoese annals of Caffaro show that relations had soured somewhat:

adhuc in eodem consulatu galee II Gaitanorum ad depredandum Ianuenses Provintiam venerant. Ilico galee II Ianuensium armate fuerunt, et eas sequentes apud Arzentarium invenerunt, et unam preliando ceperunt, et cum hominibus ac cum tota preda quam fecerant Ianuam adduxerunt.[45]

(In this same consulate two Gaetan ships came to plunder the province of Genoa. So two Genoese ships were armed, and following them found them at Arzentarium, and captured one, taking its men and all its plunder back to Genoa.)

It is unclear where Arzentarium was, but perhaps it could be identified with Castro Argento on the Gaetan coast.[46] What is particularly interesting about this account is the stress on the Gaetans as the aggressors. The raid may not necessarily have reflected commercial rivalry, however. In the political upheavals

[43] Waley, *Italian City-Republics*, p. 35, tentatively lists six cities with consuls before 1100, and a further seven between 1100 and 1125. [44] *CDC* 312.

[45] *Annali Genovesi di Caffaro e de' suoi Continuatori*, ed. L. T. Belgrano, I (Genoa, 1890), p. 30.

[46] It could also, perhaps, have been Monte Argentario in Tuscany, given that the Genoese would have been more concerned to defend their own coastline (personal communication D. Abulafia: I thank him for pointing this out).

of the creation of the Norman kingdom in the South, northern states often intervened, and this raid might have been to warn the Genoese not to become involved in the internal matters of the kingdom. Documents issued at Gaeta in the first half of the twelfth century, however, give a clear indication of the links between politics and commercial interests.

The striking feature of these documents is the number of occasions on which the consuls of Gaeta are seen making peace and restoring goods to foreign merchants in the city. Again the political background must be taken into account, but confiscation of goods, an economic weapon, seems to have been a favourite tactic of the Gaetans. Thus in 1124 Bello of Rome son of Bobo and his sons won a dispute against the consuls over a ship and its goods which he was captaining on behalf of a Roman consortium.[47] In the following year, Peter Sfagilla of Salerno, who had arrived from Tunis, acknowledged the return of his ship and its cargo of grain from the consuls of Gaeta, who had seized it during a war between the two cities.[48] Sometimes such seizure may have come close to outright piracy, as a document of 1129 reveals. In this year a group of named Neapolitans[49] acknowledged the return of a ship which had been stolen by 'men of Gaeta', and made peace with the consuls.[50] Similarly, in 1138 a group of named Atranians received compensation for 8 ounces of gold 'lost' in Gaeta while they were on their way to ransom captives in Pisa.[51]

Whatever the political situation, however, commercial life seems to have continued, and by the latter part of the twelfth century we again find Gaetans in Genoa. It may be significant, however, that the individuals recorded were integrated into Genoa's commercial life, and in two cases signed up as crew on a Genoese ship. In 1190, for example, Peter son of Leo Gaetanus made a contract at Genoa in July, and John Gaetanus and Ricardus Bonus Fides Gaete signed up as crew on a Genoese ship.[52] Does this indicate that Gaeta's own fleet was now less frequently seen in the northern port? It is possible that the Gaetans had been forced off the routes to Genoa and had to seek other markets. The city was now part of the Norman kingdom, of course, and this perhaps opened up new trading opportunities. Matthew makes the valid point that

[47] *CDC* 302. [48] *CDC* 308.

[49] Including one Constantine de Ranuzzu Pisanu, whose surname belies his origins.

[50] *CDC* 319. [51] *CDC* 332. [52] Abulafia, *Two Italies*, p. 179.

much of the southern cities' most significant trade had been with areas outside the new kingdom.[53] However, it is clear that, while Amalfi found conditions more difficult, Gaeta flourished in the new markets. This at least is the impression given by other evidence from the late twelfth century. Several members of the Gaetan Gattula family, for example, begin to appear in Amalfitan documents in the 1170s, suggesting that they may have been seeking internal markets to replace trade lost outside the kingdom.[54] In *c.*1191, king Tancred of Sicily promised that Gaetans would not be prohibited from bringing grain from Sicily to Gaeta, unless a general prohibition on exports from the island was in force.[55] Nevertheless, fragments of evidence show that Gaeta had not entirely abandoned their northern connections. In 1198 the Doge of Venice apologised to Gaetan merchants whose goods had been seized.[56]

That Gaeta's relationship with the northern cities underwent changes in the middle of the twelfth century is perhaps not surprising when political events are taken into account. It seems that much of the stimulus for the city's period of intense trading activity in the first half of the century came from the patriotic and sometimes piratical members of the consulate, in imitation of northern models. When Roger became Norman king in 1130, he set about establishing his authority. His most vigorous opposition came from the princes of Capua, allied with the dukes of Naples, and he did not succeed in crushing this resistance until 1137. More telling, however, is the fact that the last record we have of consuls in the city is in 1135.[57] Nevertheless, at least two acts of Gaetan aggression occurred after this date: the apparent seizure of the Atranians' ransom money and the raid on the Genoese coast. The latter occurred in 1140.

Thereafter, Gaeta's leaders became part of the Norman hierarchy. The same families are still visible, but the cavalier confiscations and raids that had characterised the period of the consulate, together with treaties with other southern cities,[58] were

[53] *Norman Kingdom*, p. 73.

[54] Gattulas in Amalfi: *CDA* 182 (1172), *CDA* 194 (1177), *CDA* 196, *CDA* 203, *CDA* 215, *CDA* 216, *CP* 158 (1176), *CP* 175 (1184), *PAVAR* 1/54, *PAVAR* 1/63, *PAVAR* 1/64.

[55] Abulafia, *Two Italies*, p. 40.

[56] Abulafia, *Two Italies*, p. 10.

[57] *CDC* 327.

[58] For example, a ten-year peace with Naples in 1129, *CDC* 318, and a treaty with the lord of Monte Circeo against the Terracinans in 1134, *CDC* 325.

no longer left to their discretion. The Mancanellas, however, may have taken advantage of their commercial contacts to leave Gaeta for a while: Bonus 'Manganella' appears in Genoa as a witness to a contract in 1190.[59]

This chapter and the preceding one have dwelt at some length on the commercial lives of the Tyrrhenian cities and their inhabitants, at both a local and international level, in order to illustrate the level of movement that there was between them, and the effect this might have had on their internal politics. Naples has not featured very heavily in these discussions. It is no coincidence that of the three cities under examination, Naples was the one with the most stable history, perhaps because it was rather less receptive to any external influences that the merchants of Amalfi and Gaeta brought back to their own cities. Certainly this is suggested by the static nature of its political life and in the unchanging character of its documents.

Movement was vital to the existence of these two smaller states, however, for neither seems to have been able to support itself from its landed resources. We might speculate that a man like Docibilis I was already involved in the supply of foodstuffs or luxury items to the Gaetans when he perceived that the city could be taken over politically.

It is difficult to judge the importance of commercial exchange to any of these cities when the source material under scrutiny is concerned far more with land transactions. This fact in itself is significant, for, as I pointed out earlier, much trade could not have taken place without landed resources from which to raise the capital. Land was the most important factor in assessing the power of the families and individual rulers that this study has examined, but the trade connections that are visible force a scrutiny of these cities in their wider context. Amalfi and Gaeta are all too often characterised as petty states with little significance in the history of southern Italy. Their history is ignored in favour of that of the larger, Lombard principalities. Yet, as we have seen in this chapter, their links with other parts of the peninsula and with the East suggest that they may have been far more important to their trading partners (and perhaps to the economy of the South) than can now be ascertained. The histories of these states, furthermore, can illuminate a number of general problems in medieval European history.

[59] Abulafia, *Two Italies*, p. 179.

CONCLUSION

What contribution can an examination of a tiny duchy like that of Gaeta and its neighbours make to our understanding of early medieval political and economic life? Does its history have a significance beyond southern Italy, let alone the borders of Italy as a whole?

The history of the duchy of Gaeta is one of contradictions. Documents of the tenth century present the image of a duke whose territory, if not large, was united and firmly ruled by his powerful family. Yet, as we have seen, the base from which he chose to rule had never been the natural centre of that territory. It was chosen because of the need for a defensive site in the face of Arab incursions and, perhaps, because the Docibilans were making a deliberate break with the old centres of papal administration for the area, Fondi and Traetto. This created internal tensions and led ultimately to the reassertion of the older pattern of a fortress on the peninsula and two separate jurisdictions. The major achievement of Docibilis and his clan is that for a century they were able to paper over these natural divisions and forcibly create a duchy.

What though, did the creation of the duchy of Gaeta entail? The answer to this question is to be found in the surviving documentary evidence from Gaeta, which is so unusual as to be worthy of examination by medieval historians working in other areas. This evidence, unlike much of that from southern Italy, does not seem to have been produced or preserved by an ecclesiastical institution before Montecassino received it in the late eleventh century. It is full of documents authorised by laymen, particularly members of the remarkable Docibilan family. Numerically their transactions predominate; suggesting either that they must have had more property to administer, or that they were seen as so important by their contemporaries and successors that their documents were thought worth preserving. A third factor may also be at work, and that is the importance attached to the written evidence of their actions by the Docibilans.

It is unlikely that the value placed on charters was introduced by the family, however. The strong patterns of local continuity with a Byzantine and late Roman past meant that some vestige of their tradition of written administration probably survived throughout the 'dark ages' of the sixth to the eighth centuries. And, unlike other parts of Italy or Europe, the Tyrrhenian coastal cities were not taken over by incoming Germanic rulers; one might imagine, therefore, that their tradition of writing records of legal transactions remained relatively unaffected during the Lombard invasions of the South. Only the preservation of such material, once the work of the *gesta municipalia*, seems to have been disrupted.[1]

The Gaetan evidence shows early medieval rulers acting like private citizens, managing the *publicum* of Gaeta in much the same way as they would their own lands, and frequently blurring the distinction between the two. Gaeta's identity as a duchy seems to rest solely on the fact that during its history it had documented dukes. Prior to the Docibilans' rise, the ruler of the castle had been a *hypatos* and the governor of the territories surrounding it was called the rector. The Docibilans themselves used these titles before adopting the ducal one; little seems to have changed perceptibly, except perhaps in their self-esteem, when the Docibilans began to style themselves dukes.

It may not be entirely coincidental, however, that the rule of the first duke coincided with the first documented use of the term *publicum* or public land, at Gaeta. Perhaps the Docibilans were trying to formalise their position, clothing their *de facto* power in more legalistic phraseology. This reveals a need to legitimise their position. The documentation reveals that a 'state' did not necessarily have to have formalised institutions to run it, but could rely upon different members of the ducal family performing loosely defined functions which, after a while, came to be centred on settlements other than Gaeta.

It is in relation to the problem of their public power that the documents of the Docibilans become less informative. We have seen that the duke controlled land termed public, and that he sometimes held courts to judge disputes. It is difficult, however, to

[1] Compare R. McKitterick, *The Carolingians and the Written Word* (Cambridge, 1989), p. 82 on the survival of written culture in Alemannia and Rhaetia, where 'It may . . . be due to the assertion of familiar written modes of record by one section of an early medieval community, drawing on its Roman past, that we owe the gradual adoption of written modes by other [Frankish] sections.'

gauge the territorial limit of his jurisdiction. Nor were there any publicly appointed officials or a formal court circle. Hints of the latter can be gained from analysis of ducal witness lists, but there is no indication of the type of palace circle familiar to historians of northern Europe (particularly Carolingian France) or recently identified in other parts of Italy, as in the Salernitan example investigated by Taviani-Carozzi.

Taviani-Carozzi attempted to survey the early offices visible in the Salernitan documents, such as treasurer, count of the palace, and *referendarius*, but was unable to define their functions beyond the distinction they brought to members of the prince's own family. In Gaeta, Naples and Amalfi the situation was much the same, with titles other than that of the ruler having no real power or function attached to them.

Nor do public officials appear to have had any fixed function. Judges, one of the few groups for whom there is substantial evidence, seem almost universally to have had a witnessing function, validating documents with their presence. They are hardly ever seen deciding the outcome of disputes, but they may occasionally have deputised for the duke in other roles, particularly the supervision of minors.

A public treasury is documented in the early twelfth century under Norman rule, but none seems to have existed under the Docibilans. Whether the family did impose any controls over the financial affairs of the duchy is unclear; I suggested that they may have tried to monopolise milling activities in the territory. They may conceivably have attempted to enforce other restrictions on the economy of the duchy, but if so there is no documentation of these. It is essential to note that such activity did not have to be the public action of the rulers, but may simply have been the aggressive tactics of a particularly powerful private family. The absence of any Docibilan public legislation supports this view.

The Docibilans' use of informal networks of power was their major weakness, however, in that there was no secure foundation for their cosmetic changes at Gaeta. By virtue of their wealth they were able to dominate in the duchy itself, welding together historically separate pieces into a whole. But their failure to secure that with any military provision or administrative framework, together with the fact that the territory itself was still only a tiny area, meant that the duchy was easy prey to outsiders.

Paradoxically, the absorption of Gaeta into the lands ruled by the Norman princes of Capua did not so much signal the end of the duchy as the creation of an entity far more public and state-like in its nature. Since the duchy had fallen under the control of the Norman princes of Capua before the latter succumbed to the power of king Roger, its history in the early twelfth century is often obscured by their actions. Its Norman dukes, with other territories to control besides Gaeta's, delegated the internal running of the duchy to those men whose families had gained prominence during the latter half of the eleventh century. Suddenly, formal, governmental processes become visible in our documents – a fisc, the permanent consular posts filled each year by different men, public control by these consuls of Gaeta's trade activities and, crucially, some kind of legislative activity. This latter is suggested by the case of the consuls' imposition of a limit on the height of buildings in the city; there must have been a point at which a decision was made and thereafter stood as a precedent for future cases.

The informality displayed by the Tyrrhenian states in their administration until the late eleventh century is reflected in their loosely defined boundaries. Stabia, between Naples and Amalfi, Liburia, between Naples and Capua, and Flumetica, between Capua and Gaeta, all seem to have been fluid border areas in which the inhabitants of one state might frequently interact with those of another. A fourth area, the district of Cetara and Vietri between Amalfi and Salerno, seems to have witnessed almost complete integration between inhabitants of those two cities. Given the evidence set out in this study, it is difficult to sustain the idea of all these small states as discrete and separate from one another.

Gaeta can certainly no longer be viewed as an autonomous or unified duchy. Even before the Capuan/Norman takeover it was subject to external influence, and may have been more closely attached to Naples in particular. This position, which can be described as 'detached subjection', may also have been the lot of another minute state in this area, that centred on Sorrento. The latter, however, is so poorly documented that Sorrentan historiography has not created the myth of a separate state. Again we return to the question of relative documentation – would the duchy of Gaeta be so prominent if its charter collection had not contained such a large number of transactions authorised by its dukes? The rise of the Docibilan family to power was dramatic and quite sudden, as far as we can see, but their power was ephemeral in comparison to that of the families who provided later rulers of the city, and the families who surrounded them without ever providing a ruler.

Detailed prosopographical and genealogical analysis does not seem to have been widely employed by historians working on the southern Italian documents, yet the use of these methods is common in northern Italian and German studies. As I have shown, prosopography and genealogy can be used profitably in research into the political structures of southern Italian states. Real power was often held in the hands of local noble families, who have not been studied at all. There is considerable potential for similar studies in other areas of the South.

Clearly the approach must be modified in each individual case. For example, tracing genealogies in the Lombard states of southern Italy might present problems when men stated only their own name without a patronym (this is the case, for example, in a large number of the documents from Cava). The Lombards, a Germanic people, may potentially reveal clearer lines of descent through the lead-name method. Certainly the sheer confusion of Pandolfs, Paldolfs and Landolfs visible as rulers of Capua suggest that the repetition of ancestral names was a feature of Lombard family tradition. The gratifyingly large number of Salernitan documents, both published (in the *Codex Cavensis*) and unpublished, may provide a useful database on which to test this theory in some detail.

There is a copious amount of documentary evidence for the history of southern Italy before the coming of the Normans, yet it has never been systematically explored. The area has previously suffered from a lack of study due, no doubt, to the poverty of documents about the various rulers. If we look instead at the rulers' subjects, however, a whole new vista opens out, which may necessitate a reappraisal of the political life of the whole area.

Even taking a small sample of the documentation available in the South can provide much information on its history. By breaking down Gaeta's population into smaller power groups, we have seen that this area was not so much a state as a loosely knitted collection of smaller political units, family estates and public land which, during the period under review, was united under Docibilan rule, fell apart in the eleventh century and then reunited as a part of the Capuan and Norman territories in the late eleventh and early twelfth centuries. By focusing on the subject families rather than the rulers at Gaeta, the true political patterns of the petty states are revealed.

The major implication of all this is fairly disquieting. If even tiny states such as Gaeta and Amalfi cannot justifiably be treated as political units, where does that leave our perception of the other southern Italian 'states'? Giovanni Tabacco calls the tenth and eleventh centuries in Italy the period of political anarchy. It would seem that the image of southern Italy as made up of small, but recognisably unified, states identified by the titles of their rulers (duchies, principates, etc.) has endured so long in the historiography simply because historians of the area felt the need to impose some order on what may have been an area of total political incoherence.

It might be argued that Gaeta's territory lay too far north really to be counted among the cities of southern Italy at all. Its history reveals it to have been something of a border area between Rome to the north and Byzantine and Lombard territories to the south. Its political life in the early twelfth century reveals the influence of contact with the northern cities. Freed of the restrictions apparently in force under Docibilan rule, Gaeta seems to have flourished economically under the Normans, with documented commercial exchange with other parts of Italy and the Mediterranean. Such interaction may explain why a city some seventy-five miles south of Rome began to act in a way more commonly associated with cities in the North, that is have consuls at all. Here there is (as far as I am aware) the unique situation of a southern city displaying communal characteristics, whilst at the same time being under the sovereignty of a greater power. It is a phenomenon which requires that we reconsider the division of Italian history into 'North' and 'South', and begin to look at the features common to both the northern city republics and the southern kingdom.

The development of an aristocracy with consular titles is certainly an unusual one, and pulls Gaeta more firmly into the northern half of Italy. Yet its political life was profoundly affected by southern powers, and the level of exchange with Naples and Amalfi, and Gaeta's eventual identity as part of the southern kingdom of Naples, mean that its southern identity cannot be jettisoned too quickly. Its unique position may make it an exceptional case, therefore, but until we re-examine the histories of some of its neighbours in more detail, we cannot be sure.

For a short while the city of Gaeta had, to all intents and

purposes, behaved in exactly the same way as the more famous northern communes. The essential difference to remember is that the Gaetan consuls were always subject to the overlordship of the princes of Capua. The latter condoned the consuls' activities by entering into agreements with them. In 1123 duke Richard confirmed to the consuls that he would not change Gaeta's copper coinage, thereby recognising the importance of commercial activities to the city's leaders.[2] In 1127 he conceded to them the building of the *curia* in Gaeta.[3]

Gaeta's history in the early twelfth century adds a valuable new perspective to the study of the development of communes and consulates in the North of Italy, and should temper our perception of communal government as one which could only flourish as an independence movement. And, while it is true that some of the city's more original activities in the fields of politics and piracy were suppressed by the creation of the Norman kingdom, its success as a trading city under Norman rule is an important counter argument to the more common picture of small, enterprising cities of the South, notably Amalfi, being stifled by Norman influence.[4] It can be argued that the creation of a unified kingdom opened up new markets to individual cities, the essential difference being that those cities' exchanges were now focused within the kingdom. Gaeta took advantage of this, but still seems to have been able to maintain intermittent contact with Genoa. Amalfi, whose most spectacular trading successes had always been outside Italy, lost ground in these markets to the northern cities, with whom it does not seem to have been able to reach agreement, and was unable to compensate with the type of internal trade that Gaeta came to specialise in.

It should be added that many cities of the North, including Genoa, Pisa and Rome, feature men surnamed Caetani in their charter collections. It is unlikely that these were men of Gaeta; rather, they may have had Gaetan ancestors from whom they took their distinctive surname. Toubert has raised the problem of trying

[2] *CDC* 301. [3] *CDC* 311.

[4] For example, G. Day, *Genoa's Response to Byzantium, 1155–1204* (Urbana, Ill., 1988), p. 22, characterises the Norman conquest as a time of disruption in the commercial links between the southern cities and Byzantium. The issue of whether the Normans stifled the commercial life of the southern cities is a contentious one, and recent work by Abulafia, *Commerce and Conquest*, essay I and Delogu, 'The crisis of Amalfitan trade', paper read to the Medieval Society, University of Birmingham, November 1990, revises the rather gloomy picture of the fate of their trading activities.

to identify ethnic origin by personal names; his warning is equally applicable to surnames deriving from cities.[5] This certainly seems to be true in the cases of the 'Sirrentini' in Naples and Amalfi (derived from Sorrento), and the 'Capuani' in the latter city.

The problem of surnames such as these and their meaning has not received much attention from historians. Here again, a future line of inquiry across traditional North/South boundaries, mapping such surnames and perhaps deriving a better idea of how far individuals travelled or how common the surnames were, could produce striking results. Only when studies devoted to individual cities are compared, or less circumscribed studies undertaken, will the potential for such discoveries be fulfilled. Until then, the example of Gaeta, a tiny duchy under Norman rule, serves as a reminder that the division between North and South in Italian historiography is a tool for the convenience of historians rather than a reflection of political and economic reality.

The type of family history which has dominated this study can again give a more accurate picture of the impact of the Norman conquest. Power could be gained by intermarriage at a local level, as the pre-Norman history of the area demonstrates. Such a means of spreading their influence seems to have been used by the Crescentii family of Rome in their dealings with the dukes of Fondi and Terracina. The Gattulas of Gaeta may well have obscured the identities of less powerful families in that city by their marital tactics. The most successful example of a kin group dominating an area is that of the Docibilans at Gaeta, but their achievements rested as much on the number of children they were able to produce in each generation as upon the political unions that they made.

There is evidence to suggest that the Normans were well aware of the benefits of such unions, as Robert Guiscard's second marriage to Sikelgaita of Salerno illustrates. What is less clear is the level of success such an approach had. We know that most of the previous petty rulers in the South were replaced by Norman local rulers or administrators. However, the pattern of local, family power in each of the individual states that were taken over seems to have remained relatively constant until at least 1130. To judge by the private documents issued between the late eleventh and mid-twelfth centuries, the Normans had little effect on daily life. This is not surprising – there were not all that many Normans. Politically,

[5] *Structures*, I, p. 693.

they merely superimposed a layer of power above the local elites, most of whom were not displaced. Only very gradually do we become aware that Normans are present at all, in the odd reference to disruption when a city is besieged, or a Norman name appearing among the landowners of a particular area.

The use of intermarriage to extend political influence was not limited to Italy in the early Middle Ages. In an age when state boundaries throughout Europe were still subject to fluctuation, the kin group could provide cohesion and a focus for loyalty. The Normans themselves had initially expanded their power in northern France by astute use of marital bonds.[6] Historians have long been aware of the Normans' very strong sense of family identity, which has been ably exploited in studies of Norman England.[7] Southern Italy can provide valuable material for comparative study, much of which remains underused.[8]

The patterns established in the analysis of individual families in the Tyrrhenian documents may also be applicable elsewhere in Europe. The success of the use of German lead-name methods on the southern Italian documents suggests that some patterns were common to European families as a whole. By refining the ways in which relatives can be identified when no surnames are available, further work on political and kin groupings (often the same thing, in an early medieval context) may be possible. Strong and recurrent themes in the evidence surveyed in this study are the use of the lead-name in alternate generations, which consolidated the family vertically, and the naming of nephews after their uncles, which did so laterally.

The importance of this kind of work in early medieval studies is self-evident. It is often very difficult to establish hierarchies in societies where political structures were informal and based not so much on a legally defined right to rule as on the level of support for a particular ruler. Returning to the area studied in this book, Tom Brown has argued that the rulers of the smaller states of the Tyrrhenian, Amalfi and Gaeta, were late in assuming the consular

[6] On this, see, E. Searle, *Predatory Kinship and the Rise of Norman Power* (Berkeley, 1988).

[7] Close study of the families in power in Norman England in the early twelfth century can reveal impressive amounts of information, as J. Green, *The Government of England under Henry I* (Cambridge, 1986) illustrates.

[8] Loud, 'How Norman?', and Matthew, *Norman Kingdom*, have pioneered the use of northern evidence to explain and make comparison with the southern experience, and point the way to future work.

title because they still recognised the right of the duke of Naples, their erstwhile ruler, to hold that title; in doing so, he argues, they held on to some memory of the late Roman *cursus honorum* and were aware of their subordinate position.[9]

This view has much to recommend it, and can be augmented from the subsequent histories of both states. For, when their rulers did assume the ducal title, they had little legal reason or justification for doing so. Consequently, both rulers used more informal ways to secure their power, including (in the case of Gaeta) the establishment of members of their extended families in key positions in the new duchies, and (in both cities) the association of their sons in power with themselves to ensure the continuation of their families' dominance. Both then set about building up support, using the landed resources of their limited territories to win over other noble families in their duchies. The difference between the two dukes was in their level of success: at Gaeta the Docibilans were able to become firmly entrenched, but in Amalfi there were several false starts before one family was able to enjoy an extended period in power.

Thus studies of the informal networks of power, via land transactions, marriages, the expansion of individual families and their own sense of self-identity, can often be as revealing, if not more so, than the occasional contemporary chronicle of a particular area's rulers. One effect of this type of research has been a reassessment of the apparently powerless members of medieval states. This has been most apparent in the field of medieval women's history. Few medieval women were accorded a formal role in the public life and administration of their towns or states. Thus historians working from legal and public or prescriptive material tended to ignore the women living in these places. The emphasis on the private relationships of medieval rulers and their major subjects, however, has revealed a much greater level of female influence than had previously been thought possible. Future research in the southern Italian archives may produce similar results.

For the moment, it is necessary to adjust the focus of study away from the fragments of evidence for public institutions in southern Italy. The lack of use to which the southern Italian documents of the tenth and eleventh centuries have been put may reflect our own

[9] 'Gentlemen and officers', p. 56.

'filter' of what we expect a medieval state to be. The surviving charter evidence has perhaps been ignored in favour of the more accessible chronicles from the South; but with its emphasis on the day-to-day transactions and negotiations of private individuals, it may give a more accurate picture of the nature of political power.

Appendix 1

GREEK SIGNATURES IN NEAPOLITAN DOCUMENTS

*Capasso's comments

Document	*Date*	*Signature*
RN 1	912	ΙΟΑΝΝΕC ΦΙΛΙΟΥΣ ΔΝ MARINI
RN 2	914	ΘΕΟΔΟΡΟΥC Φ ΔΝ ΟΥΡCΙ $\overline{\text{ΤΡΒ}}$
RN 5	917	ΜΕΚΧΡΙΟΥΣ Φ $\overline{\text{δν}}$ ΙΟΧΑΝΝΙ
RN 6	920	ΜΑΡΙΝΟΥΣ ΦΙΛΙΟΥΣ $\overline{\text{ΔΝ}}$ ΠΕΤΡΙ, ΙΟΑΝΝES ΦΙΛΙΟΥΣ $\overline{\text{ΔΝ}}$ ΘΕΟΔORI
RN 7	921	εγω ιοαννεσ φιλιουσ $\overline{\text{δν}}$ πετρι
RN 9	921	μακαριο ηγουμενουσ $\overline{\text{σου}}$
RN 11	924	ΣΤΕΦΑΝΟC Φ ΔΝ CΕΡΓΙ $\overline{\text{ΜΟΝ}}$, ιω φ δν γρεγορυ
RN 15	928	ΘΕΟΔΟΡΟΥC ΦΙΛΙΟΥΣ ΔΝ ΒΙΤΑΛΙ $\overline{\text{ΚΟΜ}}$
RN 18	931	ΣΕΡΓΙΟΥΣ ΦΙΛΙΟΥΣ $\overline{\text{ΔΝ}}$ ΛΕΟΝΙ
RN 21	932	ΓΡΕΓΟΡΙΥC $\overline{\text{CΥΒ}}$, ΙΟΑΝΝΕC ΦΙΛΙΟΥΣ $\overline{\text{ΔΝ}}$ ΘΕΟΔΟΡΙ, ΙΟΑΝΝΕC ΦΙΛΙΟΥΣ $\overline{\text{ΔΝ}}$ ΑΠΠΙ, ΣΤΕΦΑΝΟΥC ΦΙΛΙΟΥΣ $\overline{\text{ΔΝ}}$ ΑΝΔΡΕ
RN 22	932	ΘΕΟΔΟΡΟΥΣ ΦΙΛΙΟΥΣ $\overline{\text{ΔΝ}}$ ΒΙΤΑΛΙ
RN 24	934	ΙΟΑΝΝΕC ΦΙΛΙΟΥΣ ΔΝ ΣΤΕΦΑΝΙ, ΙΟΑΝΝΕC ΦΙΛΙΥC ΔΝ ΑΠΠΙ, ΜΑΡΙΝΟΥΣ ΦΙΛΙΥC ΔΝ ΠΕΤΡΙ
RN 25	934	ΜΑΡΙΝΥC ΦΙΛΙΥC $\overline{\text{ΔΝ}}$ ΠΕΤΡΙ, ΙΟΑΝΝΕC ΦΙΛΙΥC $\overline{\text{ΔΝ}}$ ΣΤΕΦΑΝΙ, CΕΡΓΙΥC ΦΙΛΙΥC $\overline{\text{ΔΝ}}$ ΙΟΑΝΝΙ
RN 34	936	ΒΕΝΕΔΙΚΤΟΥC $\overline{\text{ΗΜΕΝ}}$ΟΥΣ, CΤΕΦΑΝΟΥC $\overline{\text{ΠΡΒ}}$ ΕΘ Μ° $\overline{\text{CΟΥΒ}}$
RN 37	937	CΤΕΦΑΝΟΥC ΦΙΛΙΟΥΣ $\overline{\text{ΔΝ}}$ ΕΟΥΣΤΡΑΤΙΙ
RN 38	937	ΓΡΕΓΟΡΙΟΥC Φ $\overline{\text{ΔΝ}}$ ΑΤΑCΛΑΡΥΚΥ, CΕΡΓΙΟΥC Φ ΔΝ ΙΟΑΝΝΙ
RN 43	941	ΓΡΕΓΟΡΙΟΥC Φ $\overline{\text{ΔΝ}}$ ΚΟΝCΤΑΝΤΙΝΙ
RN 44	941	*'et testes subscripti sunt omnes caractere greco'
RN 46	942	ΓΡΕΓΟΡΙΟC Φ $\overline{\text{ΔΝ}}$ CΤΕΦΑΝΙ
RN 49	942	αασιλιουσ $\overline{\text{δν}}$ ιοαννι, ΜΑCΑCΠΙΟΥC Φ $\overline{\text{ΔΝ}}$ ΙΟΑΝΝΙ $\overline{\text{ΜΟΝ}}$
RN 50	943	ΙΟΑΝΝΕC Φ $\overline{\text{ΔΝ}}$ ΑΠΠΙ, CΕΡΓΙΟΥC Φ $\overline{\text{ΔΝ}}$ ΒΑCΙΛΙΙ
RN 56	946	ΒΕΝΕΔΙΚΤΟΥC ΗΓΟΜΜΕΝΟΥC, $\overline{\text{ΙΩ}}$ $\overline{\text{ΠΡΒ}}$ ΕΘ $\overline{\text{Μ}}$, CΤΕΦΑΝΟC $\overline{\text{ΠΡΒ}}$, ΙΟΑΝΝΕC ΦΙΛΙΟΥC $\overline{\text{ΔΝ}}$ ΣΤΕΦΑΝΙ, ΘΕΟΔΟΡΟΥΣ ΦΙΛΙΟΥC $\overline{\text{ΔΝ}}$ ΠΕΤΡΙ

RN 57	946	ΒΕΝΕΔΙΚΤΟΥΣ ΗΓΟΜΕΝΟΥϹ, ΙΟΑΝΝΕ Φ ΔΝ ϹΤΕΦΑΝΙ, ΘΕΟΔΟΡΟΥϹ Φ ΔΝ ΠΕΤΡΙ
RN 62	947	ϹΕΡΓΙΟΥϹ Φ ΔΝ ΛΕΟΝΙ
RN 65	948	ΑΝΔΡΕΑ Φ ΔΝ ΙΩ ΚΟΜ
RN 67	949	ΒΕΝΕΔΙΚΤΟΥϹ ΗΓΟΥΜΕΝΟΥϹ, ΙΩ ΠΡΕϹΒΥΤΕΡ, ιω πρε ετ μο, ϹΤΕΦΑΝΟΥϹ Φ ΔΝ ΓΡΕΓΟΡΙΙ
RN 68	949	ΑΝΔΡΕΑϹ Φ ΔΝ ΙΩ ΚΟΜ
DCDN 3	949	ΙΟΑΝΝΕϹ ΚΟΝϹΟΥΛ ΕΘ ΔΟΥΞ, ΓΡΕΓΟΡΙΟΥϹ ΛΟΙϹΙϹ Φ ΔΝΙ ΙΩ
RN 70	950	ΙΟΑΝΝΕ Φ ΔΝ ϹΤΕΦΑΝΙ, ϹΕΡΓΙΟΥϹ ΔΝ ΔΟΜΕΤΙ, ΙΩ Φ ΔΝ ΚΕϹΑΡΙΙ
RN 72	951	ϹΕΡΓΙΟΥϹ Φ ΔΝ ΙΟΑΝΝΙ, ΜΑΡΙΝΟΥϹ Φ ΔΝ ϹΕΡΓΙΙ
RN 73	951	ΙΩ ΑΡΧΙΠΡ
RN 75	951	ΙΟΑΝΝΕϹ Φ ΔΝ ΕΥϹΤΡΑΤΙΙ, ΓΡΕΓΟΡΙΟΥϹ Φ ΚΕϹΑΡΙΙ, ΙΟΑΝΝΕ ΚΟΝϹΟΥΛ ΕΘ ΔΟΥΞ
RN 76	952	ΓΡΕΓΟΡΙΟΥϹ Φ, ΓΡΕΓΟΡΙΥϹ Φ ΔΝ ΑΛΙΓΕΡΝΙ, ΓΡΕΓΟΡΙΟΥϹ Φ ΔΝ ΠΕΤΡΙ
RN 77	952	ΓΡΕΓΟΡΙΟΥϹ, ΓΡΕΓΟΡΙΟΥϹ
RN 79	952	ΙΟ Φ ΔΝ ΠΕΤΡΙ
RN 85	955	ΙΩ Φ ΑΝΑΚΛΙ Φ
RN 86	955	ΠΕΤΡΟΥϹ Φ ΔΝ ΑΝΑϹΤΑϹΙΙ, ΓΡΕΓΟΡΙΟΥϹ, ϹΕΡΓΙΟΥϹ Φ ΔΝ ΝΙΚΕΤΑ ΠΡΦ, ΓΡΕΓΟΡΙΟΥϹ Φ ΔΝ ΒΑϹΙΛΙ
RN 87	955	*'et testes sunt graeco caractere subscripti'
RN 89	956	ΓΡΕΓΟΡΙΟΥϹ Φ ΔΝ ΚΕϹΑΡΙΙ, ΓΡΕΓΟΡΙΟΥϹ Φ ΔΝ ΠΕΤΡΙ
RN 90	956	ΠΕΤΡΟΥϹ Φ ΔΝ ΙΩ, ΠΕΤΡΟΥϹ Φ ΔΝ ΑΝΑϹΤΑϹΙΙ, ΜΑΡΙΝΟΥϹ Φ ΛΕΟΝΙ
RN 92	956	ΑΝΑϹΤΑϹΙΟΥϹ Φ ΔΝ ΚΡΙϹΤΟΦΟΡΙ, ΘΕΟΡΥϹ Φ ΔΝ ΛΕΟΝΙ, ΙΩ Φ ΔΝ ΛΕΟΝΙ
RN 100	957	ϹΤΕΦΑΝΟΥϹ, ΙΟΑΝΝΕϹ
RN 105	959	σεργηουσ φιουσ δν τεοφιλακτη, ϹΕΡΓΙΟΥϹ Φ ΔΝ ϹΤΕΦΑΝΙ
RN 106	959	ΑΝΑϹΤΑϹΙΟΥϹ Φ ΔΝ ΚΡΙϹΤΟΦΟΡΙ, ΓΡΕΓΟΡΙΟΥϹ Φ ΔΝ ΓΡΕΓΟΡΙ
RN 109	959	ΜΑΡΙΝΥϹ Φ ΔΝ ΠΕΤΡΙ
RN 111	960	ΓΡΕΓΟΡΙΟΥϹ Φ ΔΝ ΜΑΥΡΟΝΙ ΚΟΜ, ΙΩ Φ ΔΝ ΠΕΤΡΙ
RN 112	960	ΠΕΤΡΟΥϹ Φ ΔΝ ΑΝΑϹΤΑϹΙΙ, ΠΕΤΡΟΥϹ Φ ΔΝ ΙΩ, ΙΩ Φ ΔΝ ϹΕΡ
RN 114	960	ΜΑΡΙΝΟΥϹ Φ ΔΝ ΘΕΟΦΙΛΑΚΤΙΙ, ΓΡΕΓΟΡΙΟΥϹ Φ ΔΝ ΠΕΤΡΙ, ΓΡΕΓΟΡΙΟΥϹ Φ ΔΝ ΚΕϹΑΡΙΙ
RN 116	960	ΙΩ Φ ϹΕΡΓΙΙ
RN 117	961	ΑΛΙΓΕΡΝΟΥϹ Φ ΔΝ ΒΟΝΙ
RN 119	961	ΓΡΕΓΟΡΙΟΥϹ Φ ΔΝ ΠΕΤΡΙ, ΓΡΕΓΟΡΙΟΥϹ Φ ΔΝ ΕΥϹΕΒΙ, ΙΩ Φ ΔΝ ΙΩ

RN 121	962	ΓΡΕΓΟΡΙΟΥC Φ ΔΝ ΑΛΙΓΕΡΝΙ
RN 123	962	CΕΡΓΙΟΥC Φ ΔΝ ΓΡΕΓΟΡΙΙ
RN 126	963	ΙΩ Φ ΔΝ CΕΡΓΙΙ, ΠΕΤΡΟΥC Φ ΔΝ ΑΝΑCΤΑCΙΙ, ΠΕΤΡΟΥC Φ ΔΝ ΙΩ
RN 129	963	ΘΕΟΔΟΡΟΥC Φ ΔΝ ΓΡΕΓΟΡΙΙ
RN 136	964	ΑΝΑΣΤΑΣΙΟΥΣ Φ ΔΝ ΠΕΤΡΙ, ΚΕΣΑΡΙΟΥΣ Φ ΔΝ ΙΩ, ΘΕΟΔΟΡΟΥΣ Φ ΔΝ ΙΩ
RN 138	964	CΕΡΓΗΟΥC ΗΓΟΥΜΕΝΟΥC, ΙΩ ΠΒR, CΕΡΓΗΟΥC ΠΒΡ, γρεγοριουσ πρε, *ΙΩ* Φ ΔΝ CΕΡΓΙΙ
RN 146	965	ΙΩ Φ ΔΝ CΕΡΓΗ, ΚΕCΑΡΙΟΥC Φ ΔΝ ΙΩ, CΤΕΦΑΝΟΥC ΑΝΑΚΛΙ
RN 147	965	ΙΩ Φ ΔΝ ΠΕΤΡΙ, ΑΛΙΓΕΡΝΟΥC Φ ΔΝ ΙΩ
RN 148	965	ΑΝΑCΤΑCΙΟΥC Φ ΛΝ ΠΕΤΡΙ, ΙΩ Φ ΔΝ CΕΡΓΙΙ
RN 150	965	ΜΑΡΙΝΟΥC Φ ΔΝ ΠΕΤΡΙ
RN 152	966	*'et testes subscripti sunt caractere greco'
RN 154	966	CΤΕΦΑΝΟΥC ΔΝ ΙΩ
RN 156	966	CΕΡΓΗΟΥC ΗΓΟΥΜΕΝΟΥC, ΙΩ ΠΡΕCΒ, ΓΡΕΓΟΡΙΟΥC ΠΡΕΒ, ΙΩ ΠΡ
RN 157	966	ΙΟΑΝΝΕC Φ ΔΝ ΓΡΕΓΟΡΙΙ
RN 160	967	ΘΕΟΔΡΟΥC Φ ΔΝ ΙΩ
RN 164	968	*'et testes sunt greco caractere'
RN 165	968	ΙΩ ΗΓΟΥΜΕΝΟΥC, γρεγοριουσ μοναχος, ΙΟΑΝΝΕC ΜΟΝ, CΕΡΓΙΟΥC ΠΡΕ
RN 168	968	CΤΕΦΑΝΟΥC Φ ΔΝ ΙΩ, ΙΩ Φ ΔΝ ΓΡΕΓΟΡΙ
RN 169	969	CΕΡΓΙΟΥC Φ ΔΝ ΙΩ, ΙΩ Φ ΔΝ ΛΕΟ, ΙΩ Φ ΔΝ ΛΕΟ
RN 174	970	ΙΩ Φ ΔΝ ΠΕΤΡΙ
RN 175	970	ΑΝΑCΤΑCΙΟΥC Φ ΔΝ ΙΩ, ΠΕΤΡΟΥC Φ ΔΝ ΑΝΑCΤΑCΙΙ, CΕΡΓΙ Φ ΔΝ ΠΕΤΡΙ
RN 177	970	ΓΡΕΓΟΡΙΟΥC Φ ΔΝ ΓΡΕΓΟΡΙΙ
RN 178	970	ΙΩ ΗΓΟΥΜΕΝΟΥC
RN 179	970	ΙΩ ΗΓΟΥΜΕΝΟΥC, ΙΩ ΜΟΝ, ΙΩ ΠΡ ΜΟΝ
RN 184	970	ΓΡΕΓΟΡΙΟΥC Φ ΔΝ ΓΡΕΓ, ΙΩ Φ ΔΝ ΠΕΤΡΙ
RN 185	970	ΘΕΟΔΟΡΟΥΥC Φ ΔΝ ΓΡΕΓΟΡΙΙ
RN 188	971	ΙΩ Φ ΔΝ ΠΕΤΡΙ
RN 189	971	ΙΩ Φ ΔΝ ΑΝΔΡΕΕ
RN 191	972	*'et testes subscribuntur caractere greco'
RN 192	972	*'et testes subscribuntur in idiomate greco'
RN 202	974	ΙΩ Φ ΔΝ ΛΕΟΝΙ, ΙΩ Φ ΔΝ ΚΕCΑΡΙΙ
RN 203	974	ΙΩ Φ ΔΝ CΕΡΓΙΙ
RN 205	975	*'et testes caractere greco'
RN 207	975	ΑΝΑCΤΑCΙΟΥC Φ ΔΝ ΙΩ
RN 212	977	ΠΕΤΡΟΥC Φ ΔΝ CΕΡΓΙΙ
RN 216	978	CΤΕΦΑΝΟΥC Φ ΔΝ ΙΩ
RN 218	978	ΘΕΟΔΟΡΟΥC Φ ΔΝ . . .
RN 220	979	CΤΕΦΑΝΟΥC Φ ΔΝ ΙΩ, ΜΑΡΙΝΟΥC Φ ΔΝ ΙΩ
RN 222	979	ΙΩ Φ ΔΝ CΕΡΓΙΙ

RN 229	981	CTEΦANOYC
RN 230	981	μαρινους διστορ, ΘΕΟΔΟΡΟΥC Φ ΔΝ ΓΡΕΓΟΡΙ
RN 234	982	ΙΩ Φ ΔΝ ΠΕΤΡΙ
RN 241	983	ΘΕΟΔΟΡΟΥC Φ ΔΝ ΓΡΕΓΟΡΙΙ, ΙΩ Φ ΔΝ ΓΡΕΓΟΡΙΙ
RN 243	984	*'et testes subscripti sunt caractere greco'
RN 244	985	ΙΩ Φ ΔΝ ΠΕΤΡΙ
RN 246	985	ΘΕΟΔΟΡΟΥC Φ ΔΝ ΛΕΟΝΙ, λεο φ δν σεργι, ΑΛΙΓΕΡΝΟΥC Φ ΔΝ CΠΑΡΑΝΙ
RN 251	987	CΕΡΓΙΟΥC Φ ΔΝ CΕΡΓΙΙ ΜΟΝ, ΑΝΑCΤΑCΙΟΥC Φ ΔΝ ΠΕΤΡΙ, ΘΕΟΔΟΡΟΥC Φ ΔΝ ΙΩ
RN 257	988	CΕΡΓΙΟΥC ΑΡΧΙΠΒΡ, ΙΩ Φ ΔΝ ΠΕΤΡΙ, ΠΕΤΡΟΥC Φ ΔΝ ΓΡΕΓ, ΓΡΕΓΟΡΙΟΥC Φ ΔΝ ΠΕΤΡΙ, ΚΕCΑΡΙΟΥC Φ ΔΝ ΑΝΑCΤΑCΙΙ, ΑΝΑCΤΑCΙΟΥC Φ ΔΝ ΙΩ
RN 259	989	ΙΩ Φ ΔΝ CΕΡΓΙΙ
RN 263	990	*'et testes subscripti sunt caractere greco'
RN 267	990	ΙΩ Φ ΔΝ ΓΡΕΓΟΡΙΙ, CΤΕΦΑΝΟΥC Φ ΔΝ ΙΩ
RN 268	990	φιλιπποσ αμαρτολοσ και αναξιοσ ηγουμενοσ, ΛΕΟ ΜΟΝ ΠΡCΒ, νειλοσ αμαρτωλοσ και αναξιοσ πρεσυιτεροσ, ΙΩ ΔΗΑΚΟΝΟC ΕΘ ΜΟΚΟC
RN 270	991	φιλιπποσ αμαρτολοσ και αναξιοσ ηγομενοσ, ΛΕΟ ΠΡΒ ΕΘ ΜΟΝ, νειλοσ μο και αναΞιοσ πρεσβυτεροσ, ιω αμαρτολοσ μο
RN 274	992	ΑΛΙΓΕΡΝΟΥC Φ ΔΝ ΙΩ
RN 275	992	ΓΡΕΓΟΡΙΟΥC Φ ΔΝ ΙΩ
RN 276	992	ΑΛΙΓΕΡΝΟΥC Φ ΔΝ ΙΩ
RN 278	993	ΑΛΙΓΕΡΝΟΥC Φ ΔΝ ΠΕΤΡΙ
RN 279	993	μαρινους διστριυουτορ, ΓΡΕΓΟΡΙΟΥC Φ ΔΝ ΙΩ
RN 292	996	ΙΩ Φ ΔΝ CΕΡΓΙΙ
RN 295	997	φιλιπποσ αμαρτωλοσ και αναξιοσ ηγουμενοσ, πανκρατιοσ μοναχοσ και ιερευσ, ΙΩ ΔΙΑΚΟΝΟC ΕΘ ΜΧ, νικολ μοναχοσ και ιερ
RN 319	1003	ΙΩ Φ ANDREAE
RN 324	1005	CΕΡΓΙΟΥC Φ ΔΝ ΑΛΙΓΕΡΝΙ
RN 334	1009	ΑΝΑCΤΑCΙΟΥC
RN 343	1012	ΚΕCΑΡΙΟΥC Φ ΔΝ ΑΛΙΓΕΡΝΙ
RN 347	1012	ΑΛΙΓΕΡΝΟΥC Φ ΔΝ CΠΑΡΑΝΙ
RN 352	1014	ΑΛΙΓΕΡΝΟΥC Φ ΔΝ CΠΑΡΑΝΙ
RN 359	1016	πανκρατιος ιγουμενος, λαυρεντιος αμαρτωλος πρεσυιτερ, πετρος πρεσυιτηρ μοναχος, ιω αμαρτωλος κριρικος
RN 362	1016	ΠΕΤΡΟΥC Φ ΔΝ ΛΕΟΝΙ
RN 363	1016	ΠΕΤΡΟΥC Φ ΔΝ ΛΕΟΝΙ
RN 373	1017	ΠΕΤΡΟΥC Φ ΔΝ ΛΕΟΝΙ
RN 379	1019	ΠΕΤΡΟΥC Φ ΔΝ ΛΕΟΝΙ
RN 381	1019	ΠΕΤΡΟΥC Φ ΔΝ ΛΕΟΝΙ
RN 383	1019	ΑΛΙΓΕΡΝΟC Φ ΔΝ CΠΑΡΑΝΙ
RN 385	1020	ΠΕΤΡΟΥC Φ ΔΝ ΛΕΟΝΙ

RN 387	1020	πανκρατιος υγουμενος, λαυρεντιος πρεσυιτερ και μοναχος πετρος αμαρτυλος πρεσυιτερ, ΙΩ ΠΡ ΜΟ, κεσαρειυς φειλεω δω ιοανεις
RN 388	1021	ΠΕΤΡΟΥC Φ ΔΝ ΛΕΟΝΙ
RN 398	1023	κεσαρειυς φ δν ιοαννει
RN 401	1025	ΠΕΤΡΟΥC Φ ΔΝ ΛΕΟΝΙ
RN 406	1026	ω αμαρτωλος μοχ και πρ, CΤΕΦΑΝΟΥC ΜΟΝ, ιω μοχ και αμαρτολος, λεο αμαρτολος πρ και μοχ
RN 411	1027	ιω
RN 414	.027	ιω αμαρτωλος αββα πρ, κοσμας μο πρ, ΕΓΩ ΔΕΟΝ ΑΒΒΑ ΠΡ, CΤΕΦΑΝΟΥC ΜΟΝ
RN 419	1028	ΠΕΤΡΟΥC Φ ΔΝ ΛΕΟΝΙ
RN 420	1028	ΠΕΤΡΟΥC Φ ΔΝ ΛΕΟΝΙ
RN 421	1029	*'et 2 testes caractere greco'
RN 423	1030	CΕΡΓΙΟΥC Φ ΔΝ CΠΑΡΑΝΙ
RN 428	1031	ΠΕΤΡΟΥC Φ ΔΝ ΛΕΟΝΙ
RN 430	1031	ΠΕΤΡΟΥC Φ ΔΝ CΤΕΦΑΝΙ
RN 432	1031	ΚΕCΑΡΙΟΥC Φ ΔΝ ΑΛΙΓΕΡΝΙ
RN 435	1032	κεσαρειυς φ δν ιοαννει
RN 437	1032	λαυρεντιος πρεσβυ μοναχ και ρεκτορ, ιω πρ και μοχ, κοσμασ κληρικος και μοχ, βηταληος κληρικος και μοχ
RN 441	1033	ΛΑΝΔΟΛΦΟΥC Φ ΔΝ CΤΕΦΑΝΙ
RN 443	1033	*'et testes subscripti caractere greco et langobardo'
RN 456	1036	ΛΑΝΔΟΛΦΟΥC Φ ΔΝ CΤΕΦΑΝΙ
RN 468	1038	*'testes subscribunt . . . caractere greco et langobardo'
RN 489	1058	ΓΡΕΓΟΡΙΟΥC ΔΙCΤΡΙΒ
RN 519	1074	μαρεινους φ σεργειει
RN 556	1093	γεοργηος κληρηκοσ σουβκρηψηϑ, νηκολαος σουβδηακονο
RN 568	1095	ηακουος ηερευς και μοναχος, υιταλιος μοναχος, υαρϑολομεος ιερευς και μοναχος
RN 608	1113	ηγουμενος καησβος ταπινος, πακουνιος μοναχος, γειρασιμος μοναχος, μαρκος μοναχος
RN 631	1126	ΝΗΚωΔΙΜωC ΗΓουΜΕΝΟσ, Ιο ΙΕΡΕυς, στεφανος μοναχος, σεργηους μοναχος

BIBLIOGRAPHY

PRIMARY SOURCES: UNPUBLISHED

Montecassino, Archivio:
  Aula II, Caps. LIII, fasc. 1, nos.1,2,3.
  Aula III, Caps. VII, no.13.
Montecassino, Biblioteca:
  Codex Diplomaticus Pontiscurvi ab anno 953 ad anno 1612.
Naples, Archivio di Stato:
  Sezione Politico-Diplomatica, *Inventari delle pergamene* 99.
  Monasteri Soppressi 3437.
Rome, Biblioteca Apostolica Vaticana:
  Cod.Vat.Barb.Lat. 3216, ff.196–218 (notebook of C. Caietano, 1601–2).
  Cod.Vat.Lat. 12634 (inventory of Terracina documents, 1782).

PRIMARY SOURCES IN PRINT

Ahimaaz ben Paltiel, *The Chronicle of Ahimaaz*, trans. M.Salzmann (New York, 1924, repr. 1966).
Amatus, *Storia de'Normanni di Amato*, ed. V. de Bartholomeis (Rome, 1935).
Le Carte che si Conservano nello Archivio del Capitolo Metropolitano della Città di Trani, ed. A. Prologo (Barletta, 1877).
Chronica Monasterii Casinensis, ed. H. Hoffmann (*MGH*, SS, 34, Hanover, 1980).
Chronica Sancti Benedicti Casinensis, ed. G. Waitz (*MGH*, SS series 3, 1, Hanover, 1878).
Chronicon Salernitanum, ed. U. Westerbergh (Stockholm, 1956).
Chronicon Salernitanum, Italian translation, A. Carucci (Salerno, 1988).
Codex Diplomaticus Cajetanus, I (Montecassino, 1887), II (Montecassino, 1891), III (Montecassino, 1967).
Codex Diplomaticus Cavensis, I–VIII, ed. M. Morcaldi et al. (Milan, Naples, Pisa, 1873–93), IX–X, ed. S. Leone and G. Vitolo (Badia di Cava, 1984, 1991).
Codice Diplomatico Amalfitano, ed. R. Filangieri di Candida, I (Naples, 1917), II (Trani, 1951).
Codice Diplomatico Barese:
  III: *Le Pergamene della Cattedrale di Terlizzi, 971–1300*, ed. F. Caraballese (Bari, 1899).
  VIII: *Le Pergamene di Barletta, Archivio Capitolare, 897–1285*, ed. F. Nitti di Vito (Bari, 1914).
  IX: *I Documenti Storici di Corato, 1046–1327*, ed. G. Beltrani (Bari, 1923).

Codice Diplomatico del Monastero Benedettino di S. Maria di Tremiti (1005–1237), 3 vols., ed. A. Petrucci (Rome, 1960).

Codice Diplomatico Pugliese:

xx: *Le Pergamene di Conversano, 901–1265*, ed. G. Coniglio, (Bari, 1975).

xxi: *Les Chartes de Troia, 1024–1266*, ed. J.-M. Martin, (Bari, 1976).

Codice Perris: Cartulario Amalfitano, i, ed. J. Mazzoleni and R. Orefice (Amalfi, 1985).

Deusdedit, *Collectio Canonum*, ed. P. Martinucci (Venice, 1869).

Geoffrey Malaterra, *De Rebus Gestis Rogerii Calabriae et Siciliae Comitis*, ed. E. Pontieri (Bologna, 1927).

Giorgi, I., 'Documenti Terracinesi', *BISI*, 16 (1896).

Honorantie Civitatis Papie, ed. C.-R. Brühl and C. Violante (Köln-Wien, 1983).

Italia Pontificia, ed. P. F. Kehr, i (Berlin, 1906), ii (Berlin, 1907), VIII (Berlin, 1935), ix (Gottingen, 1962).

Leccisotti, T., *Abbazia di Montecassino: I Regesti dell'Archivio*, i (Rome, 1964), ii (Rome, 1965), viii (Rome, 1973), x (Rome, 1976).

Liber Censuum, ed. P. Fabre and L. Duchesne, i (Paris, 1905).

Liber Pontificalis, ed. L. Duchesne, i (Paris, 1886).

Liutprand of Cremona, *Works*, trans. F. A. Wright (London, 1930); reprinted with new Introduction by J. J. Norwich, (London 1993).

Bernardo Maragone, *Annales Pisani*, ed. M.L. Gentile, (Rerum Italicarum Scriptores, iv, ii, Bologna, 1930).

Monumenta ad Neapolitani Ducatus Historiam Pertinentia, ed. B. Capasso, i (Naples, 1881), iii (Naples, 1885), iiii (Naples, 1892).

Monumenta Germaniae Historica:

Constitutiones et Acta Publica Imperatorem et Regum, i, ed. L. Weiland (Hanover, 1893).

Epistolae, vii, eds. E. Caspar et al. (Munich, 1978).

Pergamene degli Archivi Vescovili di Amalfi e Ravello, i, ed. J. Mazzoleni (Naples, 1972), ii, ed. C. Salvati (Naples, 1974), iii, ed. B. Mazzoleni (Naples, 1975).

Le Pergamene del Monastero di S. Gregorio Armeno di Napoli, ed. J. Mazzoleni (Naples, 1973).

Pergamene di Capua, i, ed. J. Mazzoleni (Naples, 1957).

Regesta Chartarum, i, ed. G. Caetani (Perugia, 1925).

Regesto di Farfa, eds. I. Giorgi and U. Balzani, i (Rome, 1914), ii (Rome, 1879), iii (Rome, 1883).

Regesto Sublacense, eds. L. Allodi and G. Levi (Rome, 1885).

Regii Neapolitani Archivii Monumenta, ii, iii, iv, eds. M. Baffi et al. (Naples, 1845–54).

Registrum Johannis VIII Papae, ed. E. Caspar (*MGH*, *Epp*. viii, Munich, 1978).

S. Jean-Théristes (1054–1264), ed. A. Guillou (Vatican City, 1980).

Ughelli, F., *Italia Sacra*, i–x (2nd edn., Venice, 1717–22).

Die Urkunden der Normannische-Sizilienischen Könige, ed. K. A. Kehr (Innsbruck, 1902).

Bibliography

SECONDARY WORKS

Abulafia, D., *Commerce and Conquest in the Mediterranean, 1100–1500* (London, 1993).

The Two Italies (Cambridge, 1977).

Amante, B. and Bianchi, R., *Memorie Storiche e Statutarie del Ducato di Fondi* (Rome, 1903).

Arthur, P., 'Naples: a case of urban survival in the early middle ages?', *MEFRM*, 103 (1991/2).

Balzani, U., *Le Cronache Italiane nel Medio Evo* (Milan, 1884).

Bartoloni, V., 'Indagine preliminare del sito di Asprano', *BISALM*, 12 (1987).

Berza, M., 'Amalfi preducale (596–957)', *Ephemeris Dacoromana*, 8 (1938).

Blanchère, M.-R. de la, *Terracine: Essai d'Histoire Locale* (Paris, 1884).

Bloch, H., *Montecassino in the Middle Ages* (Cambridge, Mass., 1986).

'The schism of Anacletus II and the Glanfeuil forgeries of Peter the Deacon', *Traditio*, 8 (1952).

Bloch, M., *Land and Work in Medieval Europe*, trans. J. E. Anderson (London, 1967).

Bordone, R., 'Le "elites" cittadine nell'Italia communale (XI-XII secolo)', *MEFRM*, 100 (1988).

La Società Cittadina del Regno d'Italia (Turin, 1987).

Bordone, R. and Jarnut, J., eds., *L'Evoluzione delle Città Italiane nell'XI Secolo* (Bologna, 1988).

Borsari, S., 'Monasteri bizantine nell'Italia meridionale longobarda (sec. X e XI)', *ASPN*, n.s. 32 (1950–51).

Boyd, C. E., *Tithes and Parishes in Medieval Italy* (New York, 1952).

Boyle. L., *A Survey of the Vatican Archive and its Medieval Holdings* (Toronto, 1972).

Brand, P., *The Origins of the English Legal Profession* (Oxford, 1992).

Brown, T. S., *Gentlemen and Officers: Imperial Administration and Aristocratic Power in Byzantine Italy, 554–800* (Rome, 1984).

Buckler, G., 'Women in Byzantine law about 1100 A.D.', *Byzantion*, 11 (1936).

Cahen, C., *Le Régime Féodal de l'Italie Normande* (Paris, 1940).

Capasso, B., 'Pianta della città di Napoli', *ASPN*, 16 (1891), 17 (1892), 18 (1893).

Cassandro, G., 'Il ducato Bizantino', in *Storia di Napoli*, II,i (Naples, 1967).

'La Liburia e i suoi tertiatores', *ASPN*, n.s. 65 (1940).

Castrichino, R., *Gli Antichi Episcopati di Minturno e Traetto* (Minturno, 1975).

Chalandon, F., *Histoire de la Domination Normande en Italie et en Sicile*, 2 vols. (Paris, 1907).

Cherubini, P., 'Nuovi documenti dei principi di Salerno in parafrasi', *ASPN*, 3rd series 19 (1980).

Chiappa Mauri, L., 'I mulini ad acqua nel milanese (secoli X–XV)', *Nuova Rivista Storica*, 67 (1983).

Cilento, N., *Le Origini della Signoria Capuana nella Langobardia Minore* (Rome, 1966).

'I Saraceni nell'Italia meridionale nei secoli IX e X', *ASPN*, 77 (1959).

Citarella, A., 'Il declino del commercio marittimo di Amalfi', *ASPN*, 3rd series 13 (1975).
'Patterns in medieval trade: the commerce of Amalfi before the crusades', *Journal of Economic History*, 28 (1968).
'Scambi commerciali fra l'Egitto e Amalfi in un documento inedito dalla Geniza di Cairo', *ASPN*, 3rd series 9 (1971).
Condorelli, B., 'La molitura ad acqua nella valle del torrente Farfa', in *Atti del 9° Congresso Internazionale di Studi sull'Alto Medioevo*, II (Spoleto, 1983).
Contatore, D. A., *De Historia Terracinensi Libri Quinque* (Rome, 1706).
Conte-Colino, G., *Storia di Fondi* (Naples, 1901).
Cowdrey, H. E. J., *The Age of Abbot Desiderius* (Oxford, 1983).
Craven, K. R., *Excursions in the Abruzzi and the Northern Provinces of Naples* (London, 1838).
Davies, W. and Fouracre, P., eds., *The Settlement of Disputes in Early Medieval Europe* (Cambridge, 1986).
Decarreaux, J., *Normands, Papes et Moines en Italie Méridionale et en Sicile, XI-XII Siècles* (Paris, 1974).
Delogu, P., 'Il ducato di Gaeta dal IX all'XI secolo: istituzioni e società', in *Storia del Mezzogiorno*, eds. G. Galasso and R. Romeo, II,i (forthcoming).
Drew, K. F., *The Lombard Laws* (Philadelphia, 1973).
'The immunity in Carolingian Italy', *Speculum*, 37 (1962).
Duby, G., *The Early Growth of the European Economy* (London, 1974).
Hommes et Structures du Moyen Age (Paris, 1973).
Duby G. and Le Goff, J., eds., *Famille et Parenté dans l'Occident Médiéval* (Rome, 1977).
Dussaix, C., 'Les moulins à Reggio d'Emilie aux XIIe et XIIIe siècles', *MEFRM*, 91 (1979).
Engels, O., 'Papst Gelasius II (Johannes von Gaeta) als Hagiograph', *QFIAB*, 5 (1955).
Fabiani, L., *La Terra di S. Benedetto*, I (2nd edn., Montecassino, 1968).
'Il placito di Castro Argento', *BISALM*, 4 (1966).
Falco, G., 'L'amministrazione papale nella Campagna e nella Marittima', *ASRSP*, 38 (1915).
Falkenhausen, V. von, 'Il ducato di Gaeta', in *Storia d'Italia*, III, ed. G. Galasso (Turin, 1983).
'Reseaux routiers et ports dans l'Italie méridionale bizantine (VIe-XIe siècles)', in *I Kathimerini Zoi sto Byzantio* (Athens, 1989).
Untersuchungen über die byzantinische Herrschaft in Süditalien vom 9. bis ins 11. Jahrhundert (Wiesbaden, 1967).
Fedele, P., 'La battaglia del Garigliano dell'anno 915 ed i monumenti che la ricordano', *ASRSP*, 22 (1899) .
'Il ducato di Gaeta all'inizio della conquista normanna', *ASPN*, 29 (1904).
'La famiglia di Gelasio II', in *Scritti Storici*, pp. 434–40.
Scritti Storici sul Ducato di Gaeta (Gaeta, 1988).
Ferraro, S., *Le Monete di Gaeta* (Naples, 1915).
Memorie Religiose e Civili della Città di Gaeta (Naples, 1903).
Fiengo, G., *Gaeta: Monumenti e Storia Urbanistica* (Naples, 1971).

Figliuolo, B., 'Gli Amalfitani a Cetara', *Annali, Istituto Italiano per gli Studi Storici*, 6 (1979–80).

Gaetani d'Aragona, O., *Memorie Storiche della Città di Gaeta* (Caserta, 1885).

Galasso, G., 'Le città campane nell'alto medioevo', *ASPN*, n.s. 38 (1959), 39 (1960).

Gargano, G., *La Città davanti al Mare* (Amalfi, 1992).

Gattola, E., *Ad Historiam Abbatiae Casinensis Accessiones* (Venice, 1734).

Historia Abbatiae Casinensis (Venice, 1733).

Gay, J., *L'Italie Méridionale et l'Empire Byzantin* (New York, 1904).

Gerstenberg, O., 'Studien zur Geschichte des Römischen Adels am Ausgang des 10. Jahrhunderts', *Historische Vierteljahrschrifte*, 31 (1937/9).

Giuliani, C., 'Fondi', *Quaderni dell'Istituto di Topographia Antica dell'Università di Roma* 2, 1966.

Guillou, A., 'Inscriptions du duché de Rome', *MEFRM*, 83 (1971).

Studies on Byzantine Italy (London, 1970).

Guiraud, J.-F., 'Le reseau de peuplement dans le duché de Gaeta du Xe au XIIIe siècle', *MEFRM*, 94 (1982).

Herlihy, D., 'The agrarian revolution in southern France and Italy', *Speculum*, 33 (1958) .

The Social History of Italy and Western Europe, 700–1500 (London, 1978).

Hodges, R., ed., *San Vincenzo al Volturno 1* (British School at Rome, 1993).

Hoffmann, H., 'Chronik und Urkunde in Montecassino', *QFIAB*, 51 (1972).

Holt, R. A., *The Mills of Medieval England* (Oxford, 1988).

Hughes, D. O., 'Urban growth and family structure in medieval Genoa', *Past and Present*, 66 (1975).

Hyde, J. K., *Society and Politics in Medieval Italy* (London, 1973).

Jones, P. J., 'An Italian estate, 900–1200', *Economic History Review*, 2nd series, 7 (1954).

Keller, H., 'Gli inizi del commune in Lombardia: limiti della documentazione e metodi di ricerca', in *L'Evoluzione delle Città Italiane nell'XI Secolo* (Bologna, 1988).

Kreutz, B., *Before the Normans: Southern Italy in the Ninth and Tenth Centuries* (Philadelphia, 1991).

Leccese, A., *Le Origini del Ducato di Gaeta e le sue Relazioni coi Ducati di Napoli e di Roma* (Gubbio, 1941).

Leyser, K., 'The German aristocracy from the ninth to the early twelfth century', *Past and Present*, 41 (1968).

Lizier, A., *L'Economia Rurale dell'Età Prenormanna nell'Italia Meridionale* (Palermo, 1907).

Lopez, R. S., 'The silk industry in the Byzantine Empire', *Speculum*, 20 (1945).

Lopez, R. S. and Raymond, I. W., eds., *Medieval Trade in the Mediterranean World* (London, 1955).

Loud, G. A., 'A Calendar of the diplomas of the Norman princes of Capua', *PBSR*, 49 (1981).

Church and Society in the Norman Principality of Capua, 1058–1197 (Oxford, 1985).

'Churches and churchmen in an age of conquest: southern Italy, 1030–1130',

The Haskins Society Journal, 4 (1992) .

'How "Norman" was the Norman conquest of southern Italy?', *Nottingham Medieval Studies*, 25 (1981).

Luzzati Lagana, F., 'Le firme greche nei documenti del ducato di Napoli', *Studi Medievali*, 3rd series 23:2 (1982).

Luzzatto, G., *An Economic History of Italy* (London, 1961).

McKitterick, R., *The Carolingians and the Written Word* (Cambridge, 1989).

McKitterick, R., ed., *The Uses of Literacy in Early Medieval Europe* (Cambridge, 1990).

Mancone, A., 'Il Registrum Petri Diaconi', *Bullettino dell'Archivio Paleografico Italiano*, 2–3 (1956–7).

Matthew, D., *The Norman Kingdom of Sicily* (Cambridge, 1992).

Mazzoleni, J., *Le Fonti Documentarie e Bibliografiche dal Secolo X al Secolo XX conservate presso l'Archivio di Stato di Napoli* (Naples, 1978).

Merkel, G., 'Sopra un documento dell'anno 994 risguardante la città di Fondi', *Il Saggiatore* (1846).

Merores, M., *Gaeta im frühen Mittelalter (8. bis 12. Jahrhundert)* (Gotha, 1911).

Metz, W., 'Reichsadel und Krongutverwaltung in karolingische Zeit', *Blätter für deutsche Landesgeschichte*, 94 (1968).

Monetti, D., *Cenni Storici dell'Antica Città di Gaeta* (Gaeta, 1872).

Muendel, J., 'The distribution of mills in the Florentine countryside during the late middle ages', in *Pathways to Medieval Peasants*, ed. J. A. Raftis (Toronto, 1981).

Nicosia, A., 'La valle della Quesa e il monastero greco di S. Pietro', *Benedictina*, 24 (1977).

Osheim, D., 'Conversion, *conversi* and the Christian life in late medieval Tuscany', *Speculum*, 58 (1983).

Poupardin, R., *Les Institutions Politiques et Administratives des Principautés Lombardes de l'Italie Méridionale* (Paris, 1909).

Reuter, T., ed., *The Medieval Nobility* (Oxford, 1979).

Rossetti, G., *Forme di Potere e Strutture Sociale in Italia nel Medioevo* (Bologna, 1977).

Ruggiero, B., *Principi, Nobiltà e Chiesa nel Mezzogiorno Longobardo: L'Esempio di S. Massimo di Salerno* (Naples, 1973).

Sambon, G., *Il Tari Amalfitano* (Milan, 1891).

Santis, A. de, 'La toponomastica del commune di Minturno', *BISALM*, 3 (1965).

'Centri del basso Garigliano abitati nel medioevo e abbandonati nei secoli XVI e XVII', *BISI*, 75 (1963).

Scandone, F., 'Il gastaldato di Aquino dalla metà del secolo IX alla fine del X', *ASPN*, 33 (1908), 34 (1909).

Schipa, M., 'Storia del principato langobardo di Salerno', *ASPN*, 12 (1887).

Schwarz, U., *Amalfi im frühen Mittelalter (9.-11. Jahrhundert)* (Tübingen, 1978).

Amalfi nell'Alto Medioevo, trans. G. Vitolo (Amalfi, 1985).

Serafini, A., *L'Abbazia di Fossanova e le Origini dell'Architectura Gotica nel Lazio* (Rome, 1924).

Skinner, P. E., *The Mobility of Landowners between the Tyrrhenian City-States of Italy, c.850–1050A.D.* (unpubl. M.Phil. thesis, University of Birmingham,

1988).
'Noble families in the duchy of Gaeta in the tenth century', *PBSR*, 60 (1992).
'Urban communities in Naples, 900–1050', *PBSR*, 62 (1994, in press).
'Women, literacy and invisibility in medieval southern Italy', paper presented to the conference *Women and the Book*, St Hilda's College, Oxford, August 1993.
'Women, wills and wealth in medieval southern Italy', *Early Medieval Europe*, 2 (1993).
Sterpos, D., *Communicazioni Stradali attraverso i Tempi: Roma-Capua* (Rome, 1966).
Storia d'Italia, III: Il Mezzogiorno dai Bizantini a Federico II, ed. G. Galasso (Turin, 1983).
Structures Féodales et Féodalisme dans l'Occident Méditerranean (XI-XIIIe Siècles) (Collection de l'Ecole Française de Rome 44, Rome, 1980).
Stutz, U., 'The proprietary church as an element of medieval Germanic ecclesiastical law', in *Medieval Germany 911–1250*, ed. G. Barraclough, II (Oxford, 1938).
Tabacco, G., L'origine della dominazione territoriale del Papato, *Rivista Storica Italiana*, 101 (1989).
The Struggle for Power in Medieval Italy (Cambridge, 1989).
Takayama, H., *The Administration of the Norman Kingdom of Sicily* (Leiden, 1993).
Taviani-Carozzi, H., *La Principauté Lombarde de Salerne, IXe-XIe Siècle*, 2 vols. (Rome, 1991).
Toubert, P., *Histoire du Moyen Age et de l'Italie Médiévale* (London, 1987).
Les Structures du Latium Médiéval (Rome, 1973).
Touring Club Italiano, *Guida d'Italia: Campania* (Milan, 1963); *Lazio* (Milan, 1964).
Travaini, L., *La Monetazione nell'Italia Normanna* (Rome, Istituto Storico per il Medioevo, forthcoming).
'I tari di Salerno e Amalfi', *Rassegna del Centro di Cultura e Storia Amalfitana*, 19–20 (1990).
Treppo, M. del, 'La vita economica e sociale in una grande abbazia del Mezzogiorno: S. Vincenzo al Volturno nell'alto medioevo', *ASPN*, 74 (1955).
Treppo, M. del and Leone, A., *Amalfi Medioevale* (Naples, 1977).
Tucciarone, R., *I Saraceni nel Ducato di Gaeta e nell'Italia Centromeridionale (secoli IX e X)* (Gaeta, 1991).
Vehse, O., 'Das Bundnis gegen die Sarazenen vom Jahre 915', *QFIAB*, 19 (1927).
Waley, D., *The Italian City-Republics* (3rd edn., London, 1988).
Wickham, C. J., *Early Medieval Italy* (London, 1981).
The Mountains and the City (Oxford, 1988).
Il Problema dell'Incastellamento nell'Italia Centrale: l'Esempio di S. Vincenzo al Volturno (Florence 1985).
Willard, H., and Citarella, A., *The Ninth-Century Treasure of Montecassino in the Context of Political and Economic Developments in Southern Italy* (Montecassino, 1983).

INDEX

Cambridge Studies in Medieval Life and Thought
Fourth Series

Titles in the series

1 The Beaumont Twins: The Roots and Branches of Power in the Twelfth Century
D. B. CROUCH
2 The Thought of Gregory the Great*
G. R. EVANS
3 The Government of England under Henry I*
JUDITH A. GREEN
4 Charity and Community in Medieval Cambridge
MIRI RUBIN
5 Autonomy and Community: The Royal Manor of Havering, 1200–1500
MARJORIE KENISTON MCINTOSH
6 The Political Thought of Baldus de Ubaldis
JOSEPH CANNING
7 Land and Power in Late Medieval Ferrara: The Rule of the Este, 1350–1450
TREVOR DEAN
8 William of Tyre: Historian of the Latin East*
PETER W. EDBURY AND JOHN GORDON ROWE
9 The Royal Saints of Anglo-Saxon England: A Study of West Saxon and East Anglian Cults
SUSAN J. RIDYARD
10 John of Wales: A Study of the Works and Ideas of a Thirteenth-Century Friar
JENNY SWANSON
11 Richard III: A Study of Service*
ROSEMARY HORROX
12 A Marginal Economy? East Anglian Breckland in the Later Middle Ages
MARK BAILEY
13 Clement VI: The Pontificate and Ideas of an Avignon Pope
DIANA WOOD
14 Hagiography and the Cult of Saints: The Diocese of Orléans, 800–1200
THOMAS HEAD
15 Kings and Lords in Conquest England
ROBIN FLEMING
16 Council and Hierarchy: The Political Thought of William Durant the Younger
CONSTANTIN FASOLT
17 Warfare in the Latin East, 1192–1291*
CHRISTOPHER MARSHALL
18 Province and Empire: Brittany and the Carolingians
JULIA M. H. SMITH
19 A Gentry Community: Leicestershire in the Fifteenth Century, *c.* 1422–*c.* 1485
ERIC ACHESON

20 Baptism and Change in the Early Middle Ages, *c.* 200–1150
PETER CRAMER

21 Itinerant Kingship and Royal Monasteries in Early Medieval Germany, *c.* 936–1075
JOHN W. BERNHARDT

22 Caesarius of Arles: The Making of a Christian Community in Late Antique Gaul
WILLIAM E. KLINGSHIRN

23 Bishop and Chapter in Twelfth-Century England: A Study of the *Mensa Episcopalis*
EVERETT U. CROSBY

24 Trade and Traders in Muslim Spain: The Commercial Realignment of the Iberian Penninsula, 900–1500
OLIVIA REMIE CONSTABLE

25 Lithuania Ascending: A Pagan Empire within East-Central Europe, 1295–1345
S. C. ROWELL

26 Barcelona and its Rulers, 1100–1291
STEPHEN P. BENSCH

27 Conquest, Anarchy and Lordship: Yorkshire, 1066–1154
PAUL DALTON

28 Preaching the Crusades: Mendicant Friars and the Cross in the Thirteenth Century
CHRISTOPH T. MAIER

29 Family Power in Southern Italy: The Duchy of Gaeta and its Neighbours, 850–1139
PATRICIA SKINNER

*Also published as paperback